THE CULT OF ART IN NAZI GERMANY

Cultural Memory
in
the
Present

Mieke Bal and Hent de Vries, Editors

THE CULT OF ART
IN NAZI GERMANY

Eric Michaud

Translated by Janet Lloyd

STANFORD UNIVERSITY PRESS

STANFORD, CALIFORNIA

2004

Stanford University Press
Stanford, California

The Cult of Art in Nazi Germany was originally published in French in 1996 under the title *Un Art de L'Éternité: L'image et le temps du national-socialisme*, © 1996, Éditions Gallimard.

Publication of this book has been aided by a grant from the Millard Meiss Publication Fund of the College Art Association.

MM

This work, published as part of a program of aid for publication, received support from the French Ministry of Foreign Affairs and the Cultural Services of the French Embassy in the United States.

Library of Congress Cataloging-in-Publication Data

Michaud, Eric.
   [Art de l'éternié. English]
   The cult of art in Nazi Germany / Eric Michaud ; translated by Janet Lloyd.
      p.   cm.
   Includes bibliographical references and index.
   ISBN 0-8047-4326-6 (cloth : alk. paper)—
ISBN 0-8047-4327-4 (pbk. : alk. paper)
      1. National socialism and art.   2. Art, German—20th century.
3. Hitler, Adolf, 1889–1945—Influence.   I. Title.
N6868.5.N37M5313   2004
700'.943'09043—dc22   2004003613

Original Printing 2004
Last figure below indicates year of this printing:
13   12   11   10   09   08   07   06   05   04

Typeset by James P. Brommer in 11/15 Garamond

For Sophie

Contents

x *Contents*

Positions

The present work does not retrace the history of Nazism. It also is not a history of the art produced under the Third Reich. Readers therefore will find in it neither an account of the succession of events that marked the cultural life of National Socialist Germany nor a balanced selection of images reflecting the works produced in the various branches of the fine arts by the artists who supported or tolerated the regime. They also will not find examples of the works of artists who opposed or resisted Hitler.

Instead, this book endeavors to enter and work through the Nazi myth, tracing its metaphors and seeking to reveal a structure. In the process, it analyzes the points of contact where the myth communicates with history as well as with its contemporary non-German reality, intending to show the ever-present necessity to "de-Germanize" Nazism, which has never ceased to be presented as a specifically German phenomenon capable of securing the German people's own identity. During the winter of 1945–46, Karl Jaspers devoted a course of lectures to the spiritual situation of Germany following its military defeat and the collapse of the Nazi regime and was already making the following undeniable point: "It was in Germany that the explosion of all that had been developing in the Western World happened. It took the form of a spiritual crisis, a crisis of faith." That point in no way diminished the culpability of the Germans, for "it was here in Germany, not elsewhere" that the explosion took place. However, he added, "it does save us from total isolation. It provides a lesson for others, for it is a matter that concerns everybody."[1] Lionel Richard has a different way of making the same point: "Nazism does not belong solely to the Germans."[2]

This is why I have not judged it necessary to insist on the German origins of Nazism and its art and thereby to add to the already impressive list of works showing why it was "in Germany, not elsewhere" that Nazism made its appearance. By emphasizing the Nazi phenomenon's "continuity" with the German past, or by drawing attention to the *Sonderweg* (singular path) followed by Germany throughout the history of the European nations, the theses that these works present, though seldom erroneous, nevertheless support all the assertions of the ideology they claim to be attacking.

From the moment of the emergence of the ideas of Nazism, and of Hitler's ideas in particular, attention has repeatedly been drawn to their lack of originality. A considerable proportion of the works devoted to these ideas has been committed to showing that many of their theoretical sources are, on the contrary, rooted in a common European past. Significantly, however, there has been a general disinclination to conclude on the basis of that lack of originality that Nazism reached a blind spot in the cultural and political thought of Europe as a whole. As a result, behind the interest that National Socialism continues to attract, there remains a taboo at the heart of our "democratic" system that complacently regards Nazism and its leader as the incarnation of an evil now fortunately vanquished. Part of that taboo seems to stem from the links that continue to bind us, willy-nilly, to what lay at the heart of the National Socialist myth: namely, the assimilation of work into artistic activity, the two being confused in the concept of "creative work," from which Nazism expected the very best of "performances" (*Leistungen*)—an expression that seems strangely familiar today (see the glossary of Nazi terms beginning on p. 255).

To understand the coherence and homogeneity of Nazism's self-referential system and its powers of attraction, it is necessary to sketch an analytical account of Nazism's myth, which took perfectly seriously its own constant reference to two major models: art and Christianity. The question of whether or not the Nazis believed in their own myth is of secondary importance; what matters first and foremost is that they were convinced of the myth's efficacy and acted in accordance with that belief in the performativity of the myth.

Idee und Gestalt was the generic expression included in the title or subtitle of countless brochures and books produced by the Nazi ideologues. What National Socialism sought to highlight in both of its models, art and Christianity, was a process that was able to lead from *idea* to *form*. It was this process, placed under the direction of a führer who presented himself as both the German Christ and the artist of Germany, that was designated by the expression "creative work."

This work, under the direction of an artist, was also inspired by the classical concept of art: the Nazi Idea had to be realized in a form, and the purity of its intention had to be preserved right up to the stage of its final realization. The Idea itself was incorporated into that realization as a dream or vision of happiness—and that is why the process of its realization constituted a guarantee of future happiness. Creative work, as a process of the production or realization of the Idea, was to constitute the joyful onward march of the "community of work" bent on finding itself.

Under the direction of the German Christ, at the head of the mystical community of a people at work, the realization of the Idea, or the Idea given form, constituted the process through which the spirit of the people would form its own body and become incarnate there in all its purity. Nazism fused its two models, art and Christianity, so as to exploit their exemplary performativity.

However, as is well known, the Nazi myth was of an "Aryan" race that was supposed to be naturally superior to the rest of the human race; but this myth of a people elected by nature or Providence that had been weakened by racial interbreeding needed to be given body. This is why Hitler declared that "one cannot deduce capacity from race, but one can deduce race from capacity."[3] Thus it was creative work and its *Leistungen* (performances, realizations) that bestowed consistency on the myth, sketching in the outline of the German race and detaching it from its background of parasites so that it at last appeared purged of its adulteration.

The more the successes of the myth seemed to testify to its truth, the greater was the faith placed in the myth and in its power. But that faith could be shored up only by a double manipulation of historical time: by recalling past successes and anticipating successes yet to come. The object of this "art of eternity" was to fuse the three dimensions of time in a religion of success and Aryan performance.

OCTOBER 1994

Acknowledgments

I would like to thank all those whose help, friendly listening, and valuable comments have encouraged me in the writing of the present work. My gratitude goes in particular to Pierre Ayçoberry, Fritz Breithaupt, Werner Hamacher, François Hartog, Pierre Hauger, Jean-Claude Lebensztejn, Michel Monheit, Jean-Louis Schefer, Zeev Sternhell, Jérôme Thélot, and Armand Zaloszyc.

THE CULT OF ART IN NAZI GERMANY

ARTIST AND DICTATOR

Life can only be rendered good, beautiful, and happy at the level of art.
—Keyserling, *Life Is an Art*

The history of the metaphor of the artist-prince has yet to be written. It would no doubt be a history of the slow progress that leads to the concrete realization of the metaphor, to its embodiment in the only figure possible: the artist-dictator. I shall attempt no more than to sketch in that figure in order to establish the assumption that lay behind the twentieth-century discourse that turned the figure into a norm: namely that the legitimation of power through a divine right was replaced by legitimation through artistic genius.

"A statesman is also an artist. For him, the people is merely what stone is for a sculptor. The Führer with the masses poses no more of a problem than does a painter with color." These words are spoken by Michael, the hero of a novel written by Joseph Goebbels in the 1920s. Michael is presented as an idealist in whose eyes "geniuses consume men," not for themselves but solely to accomplish their task.[1] This literary example of the metaphor was certainly only one in a long genealogy of more or less similar formulas. In 1931, Goebbels' *The Fight for Berlin* reformulated the metaphor more concisely: "For us the masses are simply a shapeless material. Only under the hand of an artist can a people be shaped from the masses, and a nation from the people."[2] It was not, however, until after these artists working on the people won political power that the metaphor became truly active and its effects were felt by the people, regarded as the masses.

Authority Founded on Art

It was apparently left to the twentieth century not merely to *produce* artist-dictators but above all to give a normative justification for their existence by identifying political activity with artistic activity as a matter of principle. Hellmut Lehmann-Haupt has rightly pointed out that the role played by art in the dictatorships of the twentieth century would have been fundamentally the same even without Hitler's particular passion for it.[3] As early as 1934, Paul Valéry justified this role when, in the preface to a work on Portuguese dictator Antonio Salazar, he observed, "Politics always tends to treat people as things," and went on to declare, "There is something of the artist in every dictator, and an aesthetic element in all his ideas. He has to fashion his human material and work on it, and make it suited to his designs."[4]

In 1848, political philosopher Pierre Joseph Proudhon issued a warning against "a revolution provoked by lawyers, accomplished by artists, and led by novelists and poets," reminding his readers that "once, early on, Nero was an artist, a lyric and dramatic artist, a passionate lover of the ideal, a worshipper of the antique. . . . That was why he was Nero."[5] Proudhon's warning was based precisely on the exceptional character of that Roman emperor and his historical crimes. In the first half of the twentieth century, on the contrary, the identification of a statesman with an artist took on a normative value. Despite his hostility, as a matter of principle, toward all authoritarian regimes, German biographer Emil Ludwig, recording his *Conversations with Mussolini*, sought not only to provide a certain insight into the personality of the Italian dictator, but over and above this to make "a general contribution to a better understanding of men of action and to reveal, yet again, the links of kinship that exist between a poet and a statesman."[6] As for Mussolini himself, while opening an exhibition by the Novecento group in 1922, he declared that he was "speaking as an artist among artists, for a politician works above all with the hardest and most difficult of all materials, man."[7] Fascist rhetoric had long ago dubbed him "the sculptor of the Italian nation" when he told Ludwig of his ambivalent feelings as an artist about the material on which he worked:

When the masses are like wax in my hands . . . or when I mingle with them and am almost crushed by them, I feel myself to be part of them. All the same, there persists in me a certain feeling of aversion, like that which the modeller feels for the clay he is modelling. Does not the sculptor sometimes smash his block of marble into fragments because he cannot shape it to represent the vision he has conceived? Now and then this crude matter rebels against the creator. . . . Everything turns upon one's ability to control the masses like an artist.[8]

Hannah Arendt once remarked that in Plato's *Republic* (IV, 420), the philosopher-king "makes" his city as a sculptor "makes" his statue, and she stressed that

violence, without which no fabrication could ever come to pass, has always played an important role in political schemes and thinking based upon an interpretation of action in terms of making. . . . Only the modern age's conviction that man can know only what he makes, . . . brought forth the much older implications of violence inherent in all interpretations of the realm of human affairs as a sphere of making.[9]

It is also quite true that the violence of fabrication has never been understood in an unequivocal fashion but has sometimes been justified by identifying it with the violence of a creative God, sometimes been condemned in the name of the violence of divine justice.

When Robespierre, at the height of the Terror in France, invoked the transcendent idea of the Supreme Being—an idea that he insisted was "social and republican" and meant to operate as "a constant recall to justice"—he did so in a last attempt to legitimate but also to limit a sovereignty that could no longer be founded on any divine right. It is with this idea in mind that we should understand the opposition he drew between the sphere of art, which was necessarily dominated by passion, and the sphere of "public morality," which on the contrary should be unaffected by passion. "To be skilled in the arts, one must follow only one's passions, whereas to defend one's rights and respect those of others, one must overcome them."[10] By the same token, however, he found himself obliged to return to the discourse of monarchical power. He was well aware that the legitimacy of monarchical power could be founded not on its humanity but only on the divine nature of its function, which alone was untouched by passion. Louis XIV reminded the Dauphin (his eldest son) of the task of a sovereign as follows: "We, who exercise a purely divine function in this world, must appear to be incapable of the agitations that might lower it." The monarch went on to say that even if one's heart were unable to belie the weakness of its human nature, reason at least should conceal those "vulgar emotions . . . as soon as they begin to harm the public good, for the sake of which we are born."[11]

In total contrast, Mussolini, soon to be emulated in this respect by Hitler, liked to emphasize the violent passion inspired in him by the masses he saw as his "material." In his view, this passion, which likened him to an artist and which he now confused utterly with the exercise of power, was an essential feature of his political genius and he prided himself on it. Yet it was also necessary for the masses to become an object for him—an object that he could confront, being himself no longer "a piece" of it and constantly in danger of being crushed by it. Like an artist, who begins by identifying with his subject but must detach himself in order to master it and work on it, Mussolini too needed to overcome his sense of belonging to the masses so that the masses could at last belong to him.

In the case of Hitler, two images nineteen years apart quite successfully reflect these two moments of initially belonging to the crowd and then later mastering it as though it were material. A famous and remarkable photograph (Figure 1) taken by Heinrich Hoffmann, Hitler's future official photographer, quite by chance showed Hitler in the midst of the crowd that poured into Munich's Odeonplatz on August 2, 1914, enthusiastically celebrating the declaration of war. Under the Third Reich this photograph was never published without a white circle isolating from the crowd the man who had since become its Führer. Only in an enlargement was it possible to recognize the euphoric face of the artist who at the time the photograph was taken was making a living from his painting. It was only by detaching him from the chorus that the photographer transformed him into a hero. Later, in the year that Hitler came to power, O. Garvens, a satirical illustrator for *Kladderadatsch* magazine, depicted him as the "Sculptor of Germany" (Figure 2). After violently smashing his fist into the work of a Jewish sculptor that represented a mass of men fighting among themselves, Hitler, wearing an artist's smock over his corporal's uniform, refashions the clay into the splendid figure of a colossus standing alone. Now that he was its master, Hitler restored to the masses the unanimity and dignity of the people that had been lost in 1918.

Even better than the Mussolini metaphor, these drawings illustrate exactly what Goebbels had recently declared in a famous open letter addressed to conductor Wilhelm Furtwängler: "We who are giving form to modern German politics feel ourselves to be artists entrusted with the lofty responsibility to form from the raw masses a full and solid image of the people."[12] But first and foremost, even more than simply illustrating a pronouncement already lifted to the rank of an official doctrine, and more than encapsulating in an image the principle of unity promoted by the new regime (*Ein Reich, ein Volk, ein Führer*), these drawings affirmed that the violence of the artist had become a virtue for the statesman.

Nevertheless, at this fictional level, the violence of the artist-Führer was not deployed against the Jewish sculptor in person but against his work: a crowd of men fighting among themselves and symbolizing the chaos of parliamentarianism, which as the Nazis saw it would characterize a Weimar Republic dominated by Jews. The battle for art fought by National Socialism thus here seems to touch only the image of the people, or the people's representation, leaving the people itself unscathed. (In the third drawing of the series, however, both the destroyed work of art and its author disappeared from the scene, thereby anticipating the fate that the Nazis had in store for the Jews and their works of art.) The essential point was perfectly clear: Hitler had managed to transpose to the political sphere his artist's conviction that "art is a sublime mission that demands fanaticism."[13]

Valéry seemed to recognize that certain characteristics of the artist are also possessed by the dictator: namely the tendency to do violence to one's human material so as to make it conform to one's plans. It was more difficult for Valéry to see, however, that the artist also possesses characteristics of the dictator. For even though Valéry lived at a time when "the exchange of dreams for reality [had been] furiously accelerated,"[14] he clung to his belief that the sphere of art was autonomous and that intellectual activities were addressed purely to the intellect. Yet the violence exerted by the artist both upon his material and against the established rules of his art—that violence traditionally regarded as the undeniable sign of his "genius"—was increasingly transgressing the limits of art because art itself was tending to be confused with the transgression of all limitations. Ever since the eighteenth century, European thought had in general identified artistic genius with the genius of liberty,[15] so each new violence done by the artist was soon seen as a new conquest of liberty. In France, the liberal Romantics turned the liberty of art into "the necessary complement of individual liberty" and "declared war on rules."[16] "Poets are free. . . . That is the law," Victor Hugo wrote in 1829 in the preface to his *Orientales*, after Adolphe Thiers proclaimed that art must be free, "and free in the most limitless fashion."[17] Later in the century, one of the fathers of naturalism declared that "far from setting a limit," this movement did away with barriers: "It does not violate the painter's temperament but liberates it. It does not bind the painter's personality but gives it wings. It tells the artist, 'Be free!'"[18] This paradoxical exhortation urging the artist to seize limitless liberty had in truth constituted, as it were, the secret model of liberal individualism ever since the "death of God." "Be free!" was the implacable double bind on which that liberalist and individualist order was founded. As we shall see, Nazism would sort out this paradox in its own way by installing an artist-führer, who alone would assume this problematic liberty, thereby delivering the artistic community of the people from what Hitler himself called "the burden of liberty." This is also something that the drawings in *Kladderadatsch* conveyed.

It was, however, within the modern movement—which Nazism would subsequently set out to reduce to silence—that the insistence on liberty was first firmly linked to the "dictator" element in the artist. Here as elsewhere, the Great War, speeding up a process that had long been gestating, constituted the decisive turning point that was to lead to the incarnation of the metaphor of the artist–head of state.

On the eve of the First World War, the ardent promoters of Cubism, Albert Gleizes and Jean Metzinger, were glorifying their new art on the grounds that it finally replaced the "partial liberties" won by their great predecessors, Gustave Courbet, Edouard Manet, and Paul Cézanne, with "an infinite liberty." In opposition to the crowd, which always clung to conventions, they set the genius of the painter, who considers "all objective knowledge . . . to be a fantasy." For painters they recognized "no laws other than those that rule over colored forms," and because they knew that the ultimate aim of painting was "to touch the crowd," they brutally concluded, "There is only one truth, ours, when we impose it upon everyone."[19]

In tones that were more Nietzschean, the Futurists prided themselves on setting forms and colors free, just as their master Filippo Tommaso Marinetti had procured "absolute liberty" for words. But they did so in order to dominate better a public to which they denied all "freedom of comprehension" and which, they insisted, should "completely forget its intellectual culture in order not to take possession of the work of art, but to surrender to it utterly."[20] What was essentially at stake here was played out in the most commonplace of terms, which are also those that tend to provoke dissension. The new formal language that was spreading throughout Europe was resuscitating the old Romantic opposition between the artist and the bourgeois. The "crowd," at once an enemy to be fought and a public to be won, or better still to be created, was hated all the more by the artist because the artist stemmed from it and continued to depend on it. A public to be won over or a crowd to be resisted: the outcome depended on whether the public was disposed "to surrender blindly" to a work of art or, on the contrary, to reject its incomprehensible language: "Painting should address the crowd not in the crowd's language but in its own, so as to move, dominate, and lead it, not so as to be understood by it. The same goes for religions."[21] Thus, what the critics since the previous century had been calling "chapels," small *ecclesiae*, came to be formed, each of these mystical bodies headed by an artist. As Hugo wrote, "Cathedrals are slipping through the hands of the priests and into the power of the artists."[22] Ever since the death of God, the religion of the art of the Romantics, the new priests and seers, had entrusted to the community of artists the heritage no longer assumed by the Christian Church: namely the task of winning people over by rejecting the life of this world and offering in exchange an image of a better world to come, an image able to lead people toward physical and moral perfection. This was exactly what Valéry called an exchange of reality for dreams and of dreams for reality.

Over and above all their differences, the Futurists, Cubists, and Expressionists were united in their condemnation of the visible world, which they identified with the established order, and in the struggle, generally considered to be one of the spirit, against materialism and the regime that went with it, namely parliamentary democracy. Wassily Kandinsky thus contrasted the piercing vision of the few elect perched at the summit of a "spiritual triangle" with the blindness of the lower parts of the triangle. That was where the masses of those who, as atheists and socialists, stagnated, convincing themselves that "the 'heavens' were empty" and that "God was dead": "Politically speaking, they are partisans of the representation of the people, or republicans."[23] In Italy, Marinetti, with all his customary violence and reactionary irony, declared himself to be against parliamentarianism. He claimed to be "happy to abandon it to the vengeful claws of women," whose access to the vote would bring in its wake "a total animalization of politics."[24] In France there were many, even "atheists," who felt nothing but distrust toward parliamentary democracy. In a *Montjoie* review that claimed to "give a lead to the elite," Fernand Léger did not hesitate to condemn the taste of the "vast majorities."[25] Toward the end of the Great War, Guillaume Apollinaire (who at that time, along with André Gide, Marcel Proust, and Auguste Rodin, professed admiration for the extremely Catholic, nationalistic, anti-Semitic, and antidemocratic *Action Française*, produced by the royalist Charles Maurras)[26] ironically and somewhat deprecatingly declared, "O time of democratic tyranny,/A fine time when we all ought to love one another/And be loved by no one at all/Leave nothing behind us/And prepare for the pleasure of one and all/In a fashion neither too sublime nor too minimal."[27]

Europe was still at war, physically ravaged and morally desolated, but it was already preparing for reconstruction. In Germany, as virtually everywhere, there were many artists who had ardently wanted this war, hoping that it would bring the old bourgeois world with all its false values to an end. They now forcefully announced their desire to take part in the tasks of reconstruction, convinced that at last their time had come. All the divergent currents of Expressionism could recognize themselves in the snappy formulation in which, as early as the spring of 1918, poet and essayist Kasimir Edschmid articulated the deeply held conviction, "No-one doubts that what appears to be external reality cannot be authentic. External reality needs to be created by ourselves. . . . "[28] A true artist was thus necessarily revolutionary: the very exercise of his liberty as an artist implied a kind of negation of the real world that was reflected in his works. Of equal necessity, however, he was conservative by reason of his traditional function as a guardian of the values and power of the spirit, confronting the repeated assaults of a reality perceived as deceptive. On that strictly functional level, it mattered little whether that spirit was primarily the spirit of the artist himself—as most of the Expressionists, bent on affirming their own ego, believed—or conceived to be the spirit of the people or nation, as it was formulated not only by the nationalists but also by public opinion as a whole. For the historians of art had long been classifying artistic "schools" according to their national origins in such a way that the particular genius of each individual artist naturally took its place within a school dominated by a national spirit or genius. The function of art, in all cases, was thus to ensure the continuity of whatever its subject happened to be, that is to say, to fabricate and guarantee its particular identity. So, among many artists the desire to participate in political power was simply a desire to extend that function of art on a state scale, the better to guarantee the survival of the spirit that was threatened by the values of materialism and bourgeois mercantilism. It was Thomas Mann who, as the war ended, best summed up the ambivalences: even if patriotic art could not be considered a superior form of art, "supreme art" nevertheless remained "deeply related to national life," albeit in a manner that was hard to define. On that account, previous experiences of the spiritual evolution of a people constituted its "treasury," and "the state, the supra-individual community, [was] unquestionably the guardian of that treasury." In this sense, the function of conservation that fell to the state corresponded exactly with the function of art as defined by Mann: "Art is a conservative power, the strongest of all; it preserves spiritual possibilities that, without it, perhaps would die out."[29] Whatever the nature of this writer's subsequent, and for a long time ambivalent, opposition to Nazism, he was at this point quite exactly describing the frame of mind to which Hitler and his ideologues were to tack on the notion that the "national treasure" was determined by the idea of the German race. Both Mann and Hitler admired the thought of Richard Wagner, for whom art, which was conservative as long as it existed in the public consciousness of the Greeks, became revolutionary once it existed only in the consciousness of separate individuals, where it found itself "opposed to the public consciousness." When, however, each individual became an artist, Wagner went on to say, art would again be conservative. So it was not a matter of restoring Hellenism and, along with it, the narrow limits of a national spirit: "If a Greek work of art contained the spirit of a fine nation, the artwork of the future would surely contain the spirit of a human race free from all limitations of a national nature." At least that was what Wagner thought in 1849 when he wrote *Art and Revolution.*[30] Less than twenty years later, however, his *Mastersingers of Nuremberg* combined a most violent attack on the existing world with a resurrection of German tradition that was considered vital. In this way, Wagner gave a contemporary twist to the two moments of art—that of revolution and that of conservation.

Revolutionary and *conservative*: in Germany, these two terms together characterized the ideological laboratory of Nazism, represented under the Weimar Republic by the movement known as the Conservative Revolution.[31] In truth, however, they also characterized all the European Fascist movements that were aiming to get a national idea to triumph by force. In this context, this dual determination could, without much difficulty, be superimposed on the double nature, at once human and divine, that the Christian West had attributed to both the sovereign[32] and the artist. For were not both of these figures capable, if necessary, of proving themselves "revolutionary" and of doing violence to their contemporaries, the better to fulfill their function, which was to ensure the temporal continuity of the transcendent Idea they nurtured?

Ernst Kantorowicz has shown how the idea of "equivalence" between poet and prince, first expressed by Dante, was subsequently, in 1341, realized by the crowning of Petrarch as poet laureate on the Capitol in Rome. Symbolically clad for the occasion in the purple robes of royalty lent to him by Robert of Naples, Petrarch reckoned that the crown of laurel leaves was the due of "both warfare and ingenium," deserved by prince and poet alike. Ever since Frederick II von Hohenstaufen, in the thirteenth century, had invested himself, following the model provided by Roman law, the sovereignty of kings and emperors had been recognized by reason of the divine inspiration attached to their functions. By promoting painting, sculpture, and architecture to the ranks of the liberal arts, the Renaissance had soon recognized all artists as possessing the same sovereignty, thanks to the same divine inspiration to which their *ingenium* testified. It was thus after a long and difficult struggle that artists, rising to the same rank as poets, became in their turn—by right, at least—the equals of princes. And if princes had up until then modeled themselves on the pope, whose status as the "vicar of God" they appropriated, they could now also take as their models artists, their equals, laying claim not so much to their *ingenium* as to a similar creative talent inspired by God.[33]

Meanwhile, comparison of the artist to God the Creator had already become commonplace by the sixteenth century, even before God was in turn set up as the Great Architect. Even more than the artist's work, it was his very person that was now held in high esteem, even to the point of becoming the object of a veritable cult, as Michelangelo did. For the authority of the artist lay not in his imitation of the products of creation but in the act of production itself. As Lord Shaftesbury put it, that was how the "genius" of the artist was akin to the "genius of the world." However, for the authority of the artist, rather than that of God, to provide the basis of the sovereignty of the prince, at least two conditions had to be satisfied: the divine will had to be legally identified with the will of the people, and the sovereignty that the people had been recognized to possess had to be withdrawn. The thinking of the Enlightenment fulfilled the first condition; the Romantics' return to Christianity fulfilled the second. Stripped of its sovereignty, the people became an indeterminate abstraction, subjectivity without individuality. "The people without its monarch [. . .] is a shapeless mass." wrote Hegel,[34] in reply to Friedrich Schelling, for whom the state had to be a work of art. Meanwhile, in poet Novalis's works, the person of the artist-sovereign was already presented as an ideal figure, the head of the organic community of the people, but a people who had, as a whole, become artists and for whom everything could become art.

To put it another way, if in the course of the first half of the twentieth century the artist was deemed worthy to exercise the power of a head of state, it was because progressively and over a long period he had been invested with the role of guardian and guarantor of a national memory that the nineteenth century had elevated to the rank of a sovereign and divine power. Once the artist was in power, to the authority conferred upon him as guardian of the memory that had been identified with the spirit of the people he added the limitless liberty that he inherited by artistic right.

What imparted a paradoxical air to the behavior of the artist-dictator, and to the behavior of Hitler in particular, was that although he founded his authority on the *spirit* of the people, it was somehow on the *body* of that people that he exercised his limitless liberty. For it was certainly there, on what Goebbels called "the raw masses," that Hitler worked as a veritable artist while making sure that the traditional fine arts—painting, sculpture, and architecture—on the contrary preserved their conservative (or as Hitler preferred to say, "eternal") character, which underpinned his authority and legitimated his power. French statesman and historian François Guizot once observed that the primary feature of political legitimacy is always "to reject force as a source of power and cleave to some moral idea."[35] Hitler conformed to that rule by seeking his legitimacy in classical and German art. But art and force have never been mutually exclusive.

Perhaps Garvens, the *Kladderadatsch* illustrator, was being prudent rather than critical of the Führer when he associated brute force with art. Perhaps he simply adopted the Führer's own view of the situation. After all, Garvens's drawings may be interpreted in two possible but opposed ways. The first way would be to understand them as stemming from propaganda, as setting out to deceive, to conceal the truth, because Hitler, far from building up a strong, healthy people, had on the contrary mutilated, disfigured, and deformed it, to the point of rendering it unrecognizable. That interpretation would conform to the role that is generally attributed to propaganda by the vast majority of the historiographers of Nazism. The other interpretation—without a doubt the more accurate of the two—would be that Garvens was so sensitive to Hitler's thinking that he expressed the realization of Hitler's dream. Molded by the hands of the artist-Führer, the people had finally taken the only form that could legitimate Hitler's power, a form that roughly approximated the Greek classicism whose sole heir he believed the spirit of the German people to be. Hitler, like an authentic artist, found himself justified by and through his oeuvre. His very violence was retrospectively legitimated, because its sole purpose had been to restore and preserve the values of the spirit—and that aim had been achieved in this people that had become a work of art in accordance with that spirit.

In *Mein Kampf,* Hitler distinguished three bases for authority: popularity, power, and tradition. Although popularity was the first and necessary basis, it could not on its own guarantee that the authority was secure. That is why the second basis consisted of power and force. A combination of popularity and force that lasted long enough could engender a new kind of authority that rested on an even more solid base: "If at last popularity, force, and tradition are united, the authority that stems from this may be considered to be unshakeable." In Hitler's view, it was the 1918 revolution that had undermined the authority of tradition, tearing it apart not only by doing away with the old form of state, but also by destroying "the former sovereign emblems and symbols of the Reich."[36] We should remember that in *Mein Kampf* Hitler indissolubly linked the "political collapse" with the "cultural collapse" that preceded and prefigured it, and he perceived an equally close association between National Socialism's "years of struggle" and the rebirth of an authentically German art. This is why there can be no doubt that to his mind the authority of tradition was vested in the forms of the art of the past. He therefore believed that he could realize the program that he had laid out for himself in *Mein Kampf* by working to reactivate those forms of authority, using all the means now available to him through power and force. In this enterprise, Wagner remained his best guide, now that the destiny of Germany seemed to depend not on Germany itself but on the nations that had been victorious in the Great War:

> Beware! We are threatened by hard blows!
> The German people and empire are about to disintegrate;
> With so many sovereigns,
> Soon no prince will understand his own people.
> They will implant their foreign
> Mists and nonsense here, in German soil.
> No one would remember what is true and German
> Were it not that it lives on in the honor of the German masters.
> That is why, I tell you,
> You must honor your German masters.
> In that way, you will still have spirits to protect you!
> If you support their action,
> Even if the Holy Roman Empire crumbles into dust,
> What will always remain will be
> The art that is noble and healthy—German art![37]

A painting by Fritz Erler confirms both the central function of art in the new regime and the constant identification of artists with the desires of Hitler. Erler's "Portrait of the Führer" (Figure 3), painted in about 1939, shows Hitler booted, in uniform, and facing the spectator. He stands erect, on the top of some building, in front of a gigantic statue brandishing the eagle and the sword that protect the Reich, its dark silhouette looming over the city. Below Hitler can be seen two vast public buildings: the one on the right is Munich's Maximilianeum; the other, in a severe neoclassical style, is a building commissioned by the new regime and completed two years earlier, the House of German Art. "Our buildings are rising in order to increase our authority," Hitler declared in 1937, in line with his belief expressed in the earliest days of the regime that German art constituted "the proudest defense of the German people." The instruments lying at his feet, designed for chiseling stone, are reminders of his function as the builder of the Third Reich, but also as the sculptor of the German people. Erler's painting shows that in 1939

Hitler's authority was still claimed to be based on symbols of the body of the people that he himself had built up with art, drawing on forms from the past. This image certainly realized the Führer's dream: in it he saw himself as the man who had restored not only the signs of the Reich's sovereignty but also its authority, rendering it unshakeable by founding it on the supreme authority of artistic tradition.

Clearly, then, for National Socialism, the art of the past—considered to be the only true art—possessed a truly religious function, if the word *religion* is given the sense that it had in Cicero's Rome, as Hannah Arendt has reminded us: "Here religion meant literally *re-ligare*: to be tied back, obligated to the enormous, almost superhuman and hence always legendary effort to lay the foundations, to build the cornerstone, to found for eternity."[38]

One of the Reich's foremost sculptors went so far as to fabricate what one can only call the two bodies of the Führer. Designed to flank the principal entrance of the court of honor of the new chancellery of the Reich, built by Albert Speer, the two monumental bronze sculptures by Arno Breker were officially entitled *The Party* (Figure 4a) and *The Army* (Figure 4b), but the sculptor also called them "Spiritual Man" and "Defender of the Reich."[39] The twofold nature of the power, both spiritual and temporal, of the master of the chancellery was expressed by symbols that were the only differences between the two nude figures, which had identical gleaming muscles and furrowed brows. The torch that one of them grasped kept alive the flame of the national spirit by which the party was animated, while the sword of the other defended the frontiers of the empire. As soon as he crossed the threshold of the chancellery, a visitor thus knew that the man who reigned here combined within his person these two bodies: the spiritual sovereign and the temporal sovereign.

The use that Hitler made of such concepts forged during the Middle Ages[40] was altogether deliberate. During the early years of the regime, he liked to distinguish between the Führer's perishable body and the body of the eternal Führer, which ensured the continuity of the spirit and mystical body of the German nation. In September 1935, in Nuremberg, he declared, "Today I myself, as Führer of the Reich and Nation, can continue to give it my aid and my counsel, but the principles of action must find a way forward to what is eternal in the individual. Führers will come and go, but Germany must live on! And affirmation of that continuity alone can lead Germany to that life."[41] It was not without reason that Hitler very early on proclaimed himself to be a "pope-Führer,"[42] thereby imitating the famous example of Emperor Frederick II, whose reincarnation some claimed Hitler to be.

Hitler himself, however, judged that if he could lay claim to a spiritual sovereignty, it was by reason of his quality as an artist inspired by the *Volksgeist*.[43] He was thus fulfilling the desire expressed forty years earlier by Julius Langbehn, the *völkisch* writer who called for a Savior who was not a pope-emperor but "at once a Caesar and an artist"—what he called "an emperor of the spirit" [Geisteskaiser]."[44]

For Hitler, the German *Volksgeist* was the spirit of art itself, for it was the creative spirit by which Aryans were animated that distinguished them from all other races and made them the sole creators of a culture (*Kulturbegründer*). Of all the obligations incumbent upon an artist-Führer with regard to his artist-people, the first was never to force the gifts of the latter. Hitler once exclaimed to Hermann Rauschning, "Don't you know how an artist works? Well, a statesman, like an artist, must allow not only his own thoughts to ripen but, even more, the creative forces of the nation. . . . He cannot create life when under duress. . . . That creative tension which always makes a true artist hold his breath must be kept alert and alive. That is the one thing that must never be allowed to fade away."[45]

Thus Hitler considered the links of interdependence between the Führer and his people to be analogous to those between a master and his disciples. A photograph taken by Heinrich Hoffmann and published in 1932 in a widely circulated collection showed Hitler "the Architect" taking the SA (*Sturm Abteilung*) members of Thuringe around the ancient monastery of Paulinzella (Figure 5). The caption read, "The home of the SA of Thuringe is Paulinzella." Hitler's gesture as he pointed to a feature high atop the edifice indicates clearly that he, with his legendary simplicity, was quite capable of turning himself into a modest tourist guide and sharing his knowledge with the elite of his people. At the same time, that very gesture also showed that he was truly the "guide" (*Führer*) and educator (*Erzieher*) capable of leading his disciples to discover their own spiritual and artistic sources, of which they were not yet aware. In short, he was the Führer who could awaken within them the "creative tension" of the German race. Later, the function allotted to the motorways of the Reich—the Adolf Hitler routes—similarly initiated the German people into the German landscape, returning that people to the now-visible essence of its being. In this fashion, the Führer and his people were able to work together in the great artist's studio that was the Reich.

The task that awaited them in this studio, however, was not confined to the creation of the Reich as a splendid work of art, with its roads and bridges, its radiant countryside, and its purged and pacified cities. Nor was it simply a matter of completing the program set out by a state that was a work of art. For according to the *völkisch* (see Glossary of Nazi Terms, p. 255) concept of the state, the state's task was rather "to clear the way for the forces in power"—in other words, for the race. For Hitler, the state was simply "a means to an end," and that end lay "in the preservation and advancement of a community of physically and psychically homogeneous creatures of the same species [Art]"[46] (see Glossary of Nazi Terms, p. 255). In similar fashion, in 1934 he told the workers gathered at the Nuremberg congress that what gave the party's program "its deepest sense" was "the formation [*Bildung*] of a true community of the people with faith in itself."[47] The true subject for the art of the statesman could only be his people. This instrumental concept of the state, however, was by no means incompatible with the idea that the state itself was a work of art. For the work of art had assuredly long been conceived by the artists themselves as a means, the end of which was man. Hitler thus claimed to be constructing his *völkisch* state just as an artist creates a tool for himself—a tool with which to impart to his material the form most suitable for the idea by which he is possessed.

The Art of Life

In the thirties, the concept of the state as a work of art was sometimes applied to the state in the strictest sense of the word and sometimes to the people living in that state, and it was, in its very ambivalence, essential to a growing number of thinkers only tangentially connected with racist circles. One of these thinkers was Count Herman Keyserling, who in 1920 founded the School of Wisdom in Darmstadt. Keyserling aspired to bring about the spiritual rebirth of Europe by, as he said, synthesizing western rationalism and eastern wisdom. He was a philosopher of life and the author of forty or so neo-idealist essays that had been translated into all the principal European languages and enjoyed a huge success. Born in 1880 into a noble German family of the Baltic region, Keyserling never lost a sense of his own superiority. With the benefit of a cosmopolitan education (in Geneva, Heidelberg, and Vienna), he was capable of expressing himself fluently in several languages and was proud of it. As he himself acknowledged, in his youth he had been an intimate friend of Houston Stewart Chamberlain, the principal popularizer of Joseph Gobineau in Germany and author of the extremely popular *Grundlagen des 19. Jahrhunderts* ("Foundations of the Nineteenth Century").

Keyserling was only twenty-five years old when Chamberlain dedicated his book on Kant to him.[48] However, as he did not share the racist ideas of his first "master," Keyserling eventually broke with him after Chamberlain became the son-in-law of Richard Wagner and took it upon himself to be a vehement propagandist of the composer's racist theories. Keyserling was an indefatigable traveler and often visited Paris, where he continued for a long time to frequent the salon of Doctor Gustave Le Bon, despite the fact that the latter was as fiercely racist as Chamberlain. Other frequenters of the salon included not only Henri Bergson, Paul Valéry, Marie Bonaparte, and the Princess Marthe Bibesco, but also Raymond Poincaré and Theodore Roosevelt.[49] Keyserling, beguiled by Bergson's vitalist philosophy of becoming, became particularly friendly with him and kept up a correspondence, as he also did with Bertrand Russell, Benedetto Croce, Walter Rathenau, Max and Alfred Weber, and Le Bon. Keyserling was a conservative, ideologically close to Thomas Mann in the aftermath of the Great War, and like Mann he wanted to "depoliticize" Germany, but in order to create a veritable *Volksstaat* ("People's State") in which it would be "culture [that] presided over the destinies of economic and political activities."[50] Ten years later, after tackling the psychology of peoples in one of his most famous essays,[51] he published several articles criticizing National Socialist racism: "In Germany, anyone who places the accent mark on blood rather than spirit is in the deepest sense of the word a racial alien [*Artfremd*], and not the person in whose veins no Nordic blood flows."[52] In April 1932, in a review of Alfred Rosenberg's *The Myth of the Twentieth Century*, Keyserling described the book as absolute nonsense that reheated and served up the old ideas of Chamberlain. He wrote, "Rosenberg's book has finally made it clear to me that National Socialism, in its present form, is fundamentally an enemy of the spirit." Furtwängler, deploring this condemnation of Nazism, tried to make Keyserling see that "the new movement" deserved greater sympathy: in the last analysis, its idea of a human group with superior racial qualities was simply a substitution for the old idea of nobility. Keyserling retorted that however acceptable this explanation might be for the faith the Nazis placed in race, anyone who believed in the superiority of the spirit had to oppose any excessive importance ascribed to blood.[53]

When Nazism came to power, Keyserling was subjected to a number of humiliations, ranging from obstacles raised to his traveling in Spain, where he was supposed to be giving some lectures, to the retraction of his German citizenship and that of his two sons—a retraction made legally valid in the case of Germans who had obtained it through naturalization. At this point Keyserling decided to regard the "German revolution" as alluding specifically to "the present world revolution, the first action of which was a revolt on the part of age-old forces long repressed." In the murderous brutality of its leaders and troops he could now see only a passing phase that was necessary for the true spiritual rebirth of Germany, and in their very frenzy he saw only the promise of a new elite in the realms of both thought and action. Having recovered his German nationality, thanks to the intervention of the minister of internal affairs in Prussia, he wrote, in French in the last months of 1933, a book entitled *La Révolution mondiale et la responsabilité de l'Esprit*. Prefaced by Paul Valéry, this work claimed to present "the first explanation for the world crisis, and in particular for the Fascist and Hitlerian phenomena, and the first vision of the path that led from revolt in the deepest depths to the spiritual revolution." Keyserling declared that National Socialism was "pacific" and constituted "the first nonimperialist movement in modern history."[54] What is more, he now believed that history had misled him: neither "absolute truth" nor literature affected real life as he had believed they did. "To act on life, you have to address yourself *ad hominem.*" That is what Gobineau did in his *Essay on the Inequality of Races,* which admittedly was "certainly no literary masterpiece," and what Le Bon had done in his *Psychology of Crowds,* which was read "by all those who have contributed or are contributing to the world revolution." Keyserling had also been mistaken when he "smiled upon hearing Chamberlain, as early as 1922, pick out Adolf Hitler as the prophet and leader of the Germany of the future. The fact is that from a historical point of view it is not the truth of ideas that counts" any more than it is "literary perfection [that] situates a thought at any level other than that of real life or life as it is lived." What did matter was "the belief that race, as such, is a value." It mattered little whether that belief was true or false, for what seemed certain to him was that from now on it was necessary "to take account of the belief in race, as one of the factors of the history of tomorrow."[55] The same renunciation of his convictions, in the name of the force of the "fait accompli" that had become a "historical truth," was repeated in 1935, in "Life Is an Art," one of the texts he wrote in French and included in a volume entitled *On the Art of Life,* which he published the following year.

Consistently enough, in this work he tried to reconcile the "historical truth" of life not with literature, which cannot touch "real life," but with the visual arts, which are addressed "ad hominem." It was thus painting and sculpture that provided him with the metaphors he needed to establish that "life can only be rendered good, beautiful, and happy at the level of art." For him, herein lay the truth of artistic fiction.

Keyserling explained that the imperative of the *amor fati* of the ancients could not give man the spiritual happiness to which he always aspired because "obedience to that imperative contains no motive for the *superation* [surmounting] of Destiny." But that superation did become possible once the immediate factors of life were considered "raw material, in the same sense as marble is a raw material for a sculptor." It was thus only through "a creative or artist's attitude" that the full liberty and sovereignty of man could be manifested. The art of life was thus the only way possible to confer harmony on the contradictory forces at work within man, which were attributing to the spirit, man's vital center, things that did not belong to it. The best illustration of the fact that "only art can perfect human life" was provided by the state and by its personification in the great statesman who dominated it. But it was important to distinguish between the statesman and the politician, for the two were as different from each other as a "painter is different from a chemist or a retailer of paints." As if recalling the distinction that Hitler introduced in *Mein Kampf* between a theoretician (*programmatiker*) and a politician, two beings who sometimes coincided in an exceptional statesman of genius,[56] Keyserling assigned to the latter the task of "using every existing means to achieve his ends":

A great statesman must thus also know how to kill at the right moment, or how to constrain, do violence, imprison, confiscate, exile, ruin, deceive, and lie. If he observes solely the postulates and needs of culture and liberty, he will never govern for the good of the people.

"[T]he art of the statesman," however, "is the most difficult of all." If his task is to transform the state into a work of art by subordinating natural elements to the spirit, the form of the state-as-a-work-of-art could not be judged *in abstracto* but only in relation to "the raw material that had been mastered" and the "style" that was appropriate for that material. It was not possible to express exactly "the same thing in marble as in bronze, nor to embody the same values in the style of Rembrandt as in the style of Rubens."

Keyserling went on to explain that if the "materialistic state" of the nineteenth century had failed, it was because joy and true happiness were only "attributes of the spirit" and so were always subjective:

Only a state inspired by the spirit, which above all embodies a spirit and relates everything to spiritual values, can make its subjects happy. Hence the enthusiasm that reigns to such a degree in Italy, in National Socialist Germany, and even in Bolshevik Russia, but is never encountered, so far as the state is concerned, in any of the liberal countries.

Faithful to his own vitalist philosophy and alluding to Nietzsche, for whom "art is the greatest stimulant of life," he finally added, "the work of art that a state, in itself, constitutes exalts the strengths of its citizens." That was why "deep inside him, every individual who has a sense of community prefers even a tyrant, provided that he is an artist, to an idealist who is not one."

Keyserling could hardly have made a more explicit offer of his support to the regime that had reigned in Germany for the past two years and that, having now entered into the struggle against the Jews promised in its manifesto and forced everyone to "fall into step," had assassinated Chief Ernst Röhm and other leaders of the SA and was now preparing the Nuremberg racial laws. Admittedly, an immediate precedent for his justification of murder in the name of the great art of the state was provided by the words with which Reich President Paul von Hindenburg had recently evoked the June 30, 1934 liquidation of the leaders of the SA: "Whoever wishes to make history must also be prepared to shed blood."[57] The historical interest of Keyserling's pronouncements, however, lies primarily in the mode of legitimation—one he shared with the Nazi ideologues—that he applied to the tyranny of the artist-statesman: the wholly spiritual desire for happiness manifested by a people could only ever be satisfied at the level of art, and this satisfaction involved making a necessary selection and sacrificing everything harmful to the unity of that work of art.

Whereas the Nazi language set the amorphous masses in opposition to a people molded into shape, Keyserling contrasted the people, which could "never be representative of the spirit," with the nation, which could be. In this respect he still seemed quite close to the ideas of British Prime Minister Benjamin Disraeli, who in the preceding century had rejected the notion of the people as nonpolitical: "It is an expression taken from natural history. A people is a species; a civilized community constitutes a nation. In our own times a nation is a work of art and of time."[58] Keyserling added that the condition for a people to turn into a nation was that it should be capable of attaining "a personal spiritual style," that is to say, the "perfected form," on which its existence depended. And "any form implies limits; it implies the deliberate exclusion of whatever does not fit in or whatever it cannot succeed in subordinating to itself." Keyserling thus ended up contradicting himself. What he had previously called the politician's contribution to the great statesman, that obscure part that must not "take into account the postulates of culture and liberty"—in other words, that must be capable of violence and murder, imprisonment and exile—he now recognized to be the very foundation of the statesman's art.

Joseph Goebbels had forestalled Keyserling when, two years earlier, he had identified politics with art and specified their common task: "The mission of art and of the artist is not simply to produce unity: it goes much further. It is their duty to create, to impart form, to eliminate that which is sick and open up the way for that which is healthy."[59] As for Hitler, as early as 1923 he had transposed his "experience as an artist" to the political sphere: "There are two things capable of uniting men: common ideals and common crimes."[60]

Ultimately, Keyserling, like Thomas Carlyle and Charles Baudelaire before him, amalgamated the figures of the saint, the hero, and the artist. Having done so, he could complete his work of theoretically unifying the people under the aegis of art, understood as the "realm of the spirit." Because states and nations had "their place at the level of art," they were able to spiritualize the raw material represented by the people. Dostoevsky had to be right: for each individual, the nation was the road that led to God, which was why all gods were initially national gods. In conclusion, Keyserling declared, "If the nation and culture belong to the level of art, and if the same goes for the heroic life and the holy life, then technically speaking religion too is an art, . . . the art of coordinating human life and divine life."

In the name of art and the spirit, Keyserling had come around to justifying the entire Nationalist Socialist enterprise while at the same time maintaining, in a last derisory gesture of fidelity to himself, that "it is not the race in itself that embodies a value, but the race as a vehicle for a certain kind of spirit."[61] Was what the Nazis were saying really any different?

There were no doubt many who ended up believing in the fiction of the German race to the point of making it efficient at the legal, political, economic, and artistic levels, and of killing in its name. It was, however, primarily in the name of the "spirit" and the "soul," in paradoxical fidelity to Friedrich von Schiller ("it is the soul that constructs the body"[62]) and above all to Paul de Lagarde ("German character is not in the blood but in the mind"[63]), that Alfred Rosenberg defined the race as "the outward image of a definite soul," the visible basis and vehicle of an inner god.[64] This concept of a body determined by its soul or spirit could be called neo-Platonic but is here extended to an imagined collective body—a concept that, as we shall see, was central to the Nazi theory of art; nevertheless, it coexisted with another concept, that there are links between the visible and the invisible. The author of a school textbook (*Das ABC der Rasse*) explained, "Of course we should not confuse race with appearance pure and simple. What race means is soul, and some people externally present real signs of their belonging to the Nordic race but are nevertheless Jews in their souls."[65] Similarly, an ideologue of "political biology" warned the *Volksgemeinschaft*, "As long as we have not annihilated the Jew within ourselves, and our survival remains in question, the Jewish problem cannot possibly be resolved."[66]

To be sure, the spirit always created and determined the body; but as long as that spirit had not become wholly visible, any body could be suspected of harboring a hostile spirit. "Primus in orbe Deos fecit timor"[67]: National Socialism was also an amplified echo of man's primeval anguish in the face of the opacity of bodies, so it is not altogether out of place to regard its activities as a huge propitiatory endeavor. Nazism understood politics to be the art of winning over souls or spirits and transfiguring bodies so as to render them *heimlich*, familiar. In this sense, art and propaganda constituted one aspect of Nazi politics: they were designed to render visible the protector god who would make it possible for the body of the German race to live eternally. Its other aspect was that of extermination. It had to reduce to silence and death all bodies that harbored the invisible, resistant part of the spirit that resides solely in language. Whatever the physical criteria for their elimination may have been, Jews, Gypsies, "degenerates," and homosexuals were shut away and exterminated for the same reasons as were the strictly political opponents of Nazism: because of what all these "Jews in spirit" might say that was *unheimlich* (unfamiliar and disturbing) to Nazism. The Nazi vision of the world (*Weltanschauung*) (see Glossary of Nazi Terms, p. 255) was clearly not a contemplative philosophy. It was an active "vision," that aimed continually to transfigure the whole world in order to render it familiar and to eliminate whatever remained alien to it. As Wagner, one of the few precursors whom Hitler was happy to acknowledge, wrote, the people "has only, by the force of necessity, to render nonexistent whatever it does not want and to destroy what needs to be destroyed for something in the guessed-at future to present itself of its own accord."[68]

In February 1934, Hitler—on whose lips any criticism became a promise of annihilation—repeated Wagner's assertion in his own words: "The direction of the creation of the future stems from [our] criticism of our opponents."[69] The new power thus not only found in art the authority of the past that legitimated it, but also discovered from its creative process how to conjure up the form of the future by eliminating and weeding out certain kinds of matter.

2

THE ARTIST-FÜHRER: A SAVIOR

A true prince is the artist of all artists, that is to say the one who leads artists.
Every man should be an artist. Everything can become a fine art.
    —Novalis, *Faith and Love*

Exactly two days after Hitler came to power, Dietrich Bonhoeffer, a young Protestant theologian, denounced the rivalry between National Socialism and Christianity in a radio broadcast:

The moment the *Volksgeist* is considered to be a divine metaphysical entity, the Führer who embodies that *Geist* assumes a religious function, in the literal sense of that expression. He is the messiah, and with his appearance the ultimate hope of every individual begins to come true, and the kingdom that he necessarily brings with him is close to the eternal kingdom.[1]

That statement condensed in a most remarkable fashion the essentials of the religious structure of the Nazi myth. In contrast to all those who would never wish to regard National Socialism as anything but an ersatz religion, Bonhoeffer was anxious to leave no doubt about the *literal* nature of the religious function assumed by Hitler in the Nazi myth. The reason he stigmatized the identification of the *realization* of the thousand-year Reich with the moment of the apparition of the Führer was that he understood that Nazism opposed Christianity only in order to take its institutional place and to reduce its principle of universalism to the dimensions of a national religion. It was quite clear that the essentials of the dogma of the incarnation—the very foundation of Christianity—remained structurally intact, that the National Socialist religion likewise rested on a belief in salvation through the visible incarnation of the deity, and that it could therefore afford to declare, exactly as Saint Augustine had, that the thousand-year Reich was no longer a dream but had begun with the appearance of the messiah.

Hitler himself, moreover, explicitly identified the moment of the political and religious rebirth of the German people with the moment of its artistic rebirth. "At some future date, people will be astonished to find that at the very time when National Socialism and its leaders were fighting to a finish a heroic struggle for existence—a life-and-death struggle—the first impulses were given toward a revival and resurrection of German art."[2] The Nazi myth was principally founded on a shared belief that if the spirit of the German people—the *Volksgeist*, which a lost war, through a criminal treaty, prevented from manifesting itself openly—could once again affirm itself freely, then the Third Reich—the predicted reign of the Spirit, which would take over from the kingdom of the Father and the Son—would begin. It was indeed in order to liberate the "German soul," which had been stifled by the *diktat* of Versailles (the nationalistic perception of the treaty) in 1919, that Alfred Rosenberg, in his *Myth of the Twentieth Century*, recalled the words of Paul de Lagarde: because "nations are thoughts of God . . . every nation needs a national religion."[3]

Thus, only a national god could cure a people stricken in both body and soul by the countless deaths and the humiliation of a defeat that broke it and deprived it of its *Kultur* (see Glossary of Nazi Terms, p. 255), burdening it with a material debt that would be impossible to discharge and ascribing to it total responsibility for the most bloodthirsty war in history.[4]

That is how it was that the links of love that bound together Hitler and the people subsisted for as long as the Führer was able to restore to the Germans reasons for loving themselves. This was truly the moment of the Third Reich, the time of the "eternal Reich": a time purged of all debt and all culpability.

If this Reich did not remain the exclusive realm of the spirit and the imagination, the reason should no doubt be sought in the very depth of the narcissistic wound, the only cure for which lay in shaping a fantasy of refound, unadulterated success. Hitler perceived that the task of restoring to the German people a sense of their own existence was bound up with the need to produce a visible and tangible token of that people's imaginary representations, which he called the *Volksgeist* and identified, as did most of his contemporaries, with the world of culture.

In the striking exercise of self-analysis constituted by Thomas Mann's *Reflections of a Nonpolitical Man*, written during the Great War, the author's "cultural pessimism" led him to declare that "when Germany condescends to Western democracy, she has lost the war spiritually." But Mann—whose view that all *Kultur* dissolves into "civilization" was close to that of philosopher Oswald Spengler—at the same time maintained that "it can never be and never will be Germany's mission and task, her 'destiny,' to realize ideas politically."[5] Conversely, despite sharing the same pessimistic school of thought, Arthur Moeller van den Bruck in 1923 concluded his book *Das dritte Reich* (*The Third Reich*) with an appeal to the spiritual Third Reich to become politically embodied: "I am thinking of Germany down the ages, the Germany with a past that stretches back over two thousand years, the Germany that is eternally present, which lives on the spiritual plane but wishes to ensure its safety in positive reality and can do so only politically."[6] The compulsion that drove Hitler and those close to him to realize what Hitler called the "ideal Reich" (*ideales Reich*) in a city—in other words, in a tangible political fashion—was precisely what won the assent of a growing number of Germans.

Ever since the nineteenth century, the time and space of German *Kultur* and *Art* had often been identified with the time and space of a new Germany of the future, in which the entire people would be artists and would be guided by an artist-führer. The most powerful symptom of this trend, still detectable in Herman Keyserling's claim that "life can only be rendered good, beautiful, and happy at the level of art," was the book published by Julius Langbehn in 1891, *Rembrandt als Erzieher* ("Rembrandt as an Educator").[7] When Stendhal said, "Beauty is a promise of happiness," his utterance did not in itself constitute a sign of any political or ideological affiliation. But a declared aim to turn German art into a promise of German happiness, as expressed by Richard Wagner in the libretto of *The Mastersingers*, became a rallying cry for all the nationalists of both the Second and the Third Reich. Hitler could not fail to win their support when he wrote as follows in *Mein Kampf*: "How many people are aware of the infinite number of separate memories of the greatness of our natural fatherland in all the fields of cultural and artistic life?"[8] This was why Thomas Mann grew so incensed by the Nazi use of the idea of the Third Reich when, having broken with the ideology of the conservative revolution, he addressed the Socialist workers of Vienna: "Art always was and always will be the perfect Third Reich, of which so many great humanist spirits have dreamed and the name of which is so wrongly used today."[9] It was also precisely why Hitler presented himself not only as a "man of the people" and a soldier with frontline experience (*Fronterlebnis*), but also and above all as a man whose artistic experience constituted the best guarantee of his ability to mediate the *Volksgeist* and turn it into the "perfect Third Reich."

A Government of Artists

If *Kultur* in general and art in particular occupied from the start a central position in the discursive strategy of the Nazi leaders, it was thus certainly not for tactical or purely propagandist reasons. It was primarily, and far more radically and simply, because a number of those leaders themselves harbored pretensions to the status of artist. The legendary and omnipresent figure of Hitler, the failed painter or architect, gradually blocked out the "artistic" nature of the figures by whom he was surrounded. Yet very early on, many opponents underlined the importance of the bohemian character, first, of the National Socialist party and, later, of the leadership apparatus that became established around Hitler. So it was not simply propaganda when the writer Hans Friedrich Blunck, president of the Chamber of Literature of the Reich, emphasized that the government of the new Germany was "composed of members half of whom are men who originally intended to devote themselves to some kind of creative work." He went on to say that these men held a "religious conviction" about the "importance of artists," for they were "the true mediators of the people." "This government, rooted in opposition to rationalism, is well aware of the nameless longing of the Volk that it governs, of their dreams that stay between heaven and earth, which can be explained and expressed only by the artist."[10]

Gottfried Benn, the expressionist poet who at first rallied to Nazism but later went into what he called his "internal exile," was thus not alone in recognizing that the leaders of the new Germany possessed "natures productive in art." Had not the Führer himself been presented to the electorate in 1932 as "the candidate of the German artists"?[11]

It was no accident that Hitler, whom Heinrich Mann as early as 1933 described with bitter irony as "the most artistic of the whole bunch,"[12] surrounded himself with men such as Dietrich Eckart, Joseph Geobbels, Baldur von Schirach, Alfred Rosenberg, Walther Funk, Julius Streicher, and Albert Speer. These men were united primarily by a shared faith in the cultural and artistic mission of the German people, and by an equal conviction that this mission was bound to take the form of a struggle. Each of them prided himself on playing an active part in the struggle to restore a "German art" which Hitler claimed in 1933 would be "the proudest defense of the German people."

In Munich, Dietrich Eckart, the son of an adviser to the king of Bavaria, had been "Hitler's best friend, and may be considered as his spiritual father."[13] He was primarily a poet and a playwright. His translation of *Peer Gynt*, completed in 1914, had brought him the greatest success, both critical and financial, in the theater world. During the war, this was the play most often performed, no doubt because under Eckart's pen Ibsen's drama had been transformed into a quest for the German identity. In March 1920, this member of the Thulé Society and director of a racist (*völkisch*) newspaper, *Auf gut Deutsch*, flew off to Berlin with Hitler, hoping to take part in the Kapp Putsch. On November 9, 1923, accompanied by members of the Munich putsch and under the admiring gaze of Frau Winifred Wagner, Richard Wagner's daughter-in-law, Eckart and Hitler sang together *"Deutschland erwache!"* ("Germany, Awake!"). This song composed by Eckart was sung all over Germany right up until 1945. One month after the failed Munich putsch, Eckart, an alcoholic and morphine addict, died. He was buried in the village of Berchtesgaden, to which he had introduced Hitler. Two years later, Hitler concluded the second volume of *Mein Kampf* with a passage in memory of "this man who dedicated his life to reawakening his people through his poetry and thought and eventually also through his actions."[14] In the middle of the Second World War he was still describing Eckart as his "polar star."[15]

Alfred Rosenberg moved from Estonia to Munich, where Eckart introduced him to Hitler. Rosenberg was an architect who held diplomas from Riga, Latvia, and Moscow. The second of the three parts of his *Myth of the Twentieth Century*, published in 1930, was devoted entirely to "the essence of German art." He succeeded Eckart as editor-in-chief of the *Völkischer Beobachter* and then of the *Nationalsozialistische Monatshefte* (Monthly National-Socialist Journal), the political and cultural organ of the Nationalsozialistische Deutsche Arbeiterpartei (NSDAP). Then, in 1941, he was appointed minister for the Eastern Territories, where he could at last implement the racial policies he had always advocated.

Baldur von Schirach shared with Hitler an absolute passion for Wagnerian opera. Through his father, manager of the Weimar Court Theatre, he met Hitler at the age of sixteen and joined the Nazi party two years later, in 1925. He was the brother of a well-known singer and, like Hitler, an assiduous visitor to Bayreuth. They also met at the Wahnfried Villa, home of their common friend Winifred Wagner, who had provided the necessary paper for Hitler to write *Mein Kampf* while he was in prison. Schirach, who was a poet, composed songs later roared out by eight million young Hitlerians, marching in uniform, and brandishing flags and standards in a Germany that had been transformed into a gigantic set for a military opera. In 1933 he wrote the most famous of his songs for the film *Quex: The Young Hitlerian* (*Der Hitlerjunge Quex*). For twelve years the streets and countryside rang with its sound.

Joseph Goebbels, the Reich's head of propaganda and Rosenberg's greatest rival where cultural hegemony was concerned, obtained a doctorate in literature and philosophy at the University of Heidelberg in 1921. It was in the climate of the last days of Expressionism that he wrote his autobiographical novel, *Michael:*

The Diary of a German Destiny. It was rejected by a number of publishers, including Ullstein & Mosse, and did not appear until 1929, when it was published by Franz Eher, the Nazi party's publisher in Munich. Goebbels, who was by then a deputy at the Reichstag, dedicated the book to his friend Richard Flisges, who had been responsible for Goebbels's discovery of Dostoevsky, but also of Marx, Engels, and Walter Rathenau. After writing his book and before it was published, Goebbels unsuccessfully applied to work, in a literary capacity, on a number of newspapers, and wrote various verse-plays that were never published. In the mid-1920s, a theater producer in the Rhineland was visited in his office by a small man with a limp and "flashing eyes" who declared that he "ardently wished to become a theater director or at least to work on the production of a play." "My name is Goebbels," he said, "and I have no experience whatever of work in the theatre."[16] As is well known, as Minister of the Reich for the Education of the People and for Propaganda, Goebbels became one of the principal ideologues of the political activity he regarded as "the most elevated and vast art that exists."

Then there was Walther Funk, chosen by Hitler to be minister of finance and president of the Reichsbank but seen in the company of artists more often than among businessmen and bankers. Funk was prone to declare that his greatest ambition had been to be a musician but his destiny as an artist had been "foiled by his vocation as an economist,"[17] very much as Hitler liked to say that "had it not been for the war, he would certainly have become an architect, possibly—indeed probably—one of the greatest, if not the greatest architect in Germany."[18]

This Bohemia also included Julius Streicher, the astounding pornographer whose brutality alarmed even his collaborators on the *Stürmer,* the violently anti-Semitic newspaper he founded in Nuremberg. What he had in common with Hitler, whose rival he was before he eventually allied with him at the time of the 1923 putsch, was a certain talent as a watercolorist, of which he was manifestly proud. Another associate was Rudolph Hess, a student at the University of Munich who was also a member of the Thulé Society, where he met Eckart before moving on to commit himself wholly to Hitler. Hess wrote Romantic poems, which he managed to get published after 1933. Yet another associate was Joachim von Ribbentrop, who became the Reich's minister for foreign affairs. During the 1920s, well before he joined the party in 1932, Ribbentrop wrote a play entitled *On the path of the Führer*. And another associate was former vigilante Ernst Röhm, leader of the SA, who was assassinated, as ordered by Hitler, on June 30, 1934. Like Eckart and Schirach, Röhm composed hexameters, which he sent to the Führer, who repaid him, however, with scant gratitude.

Finally, there was also Albert Speer, scion of a family of architects, who graduated from the Technical Academy of Berlin in 1927 and joined the party in 1931. It was not long before Goebbels appointed Speer as overall artistic director of the festivals and assemblies organized by the National Socialists, even before Hitler chose him as the Reich's principal architect. Speer soon became one of the Führer's most intimate confidants and in 1942 was promoted to the post of armaments minister, in which capacity he organized the planning of the war economy. It was with the cooperation of Speer, who was promoted from his role as the Reich's architect-in-chief to the role of director of production of the Reich's armaments, that the fight for German art became fully identified with the war.

The idea that this Bohemia might never have resorted to arms if it had enjoyed any artistic success has been around for a long time. In 1933, Heinrich Mann wrote of Hitler as follows: "An artist among other artists, he was not content to be a housepainter. He painted pictures and submitted them to juries that rejected them—a fact that some members of those juries bitterly regret now that he has become successful at a different level. Whether he became a dictator or remained a simple failure had hinged upon their decision."[19] Similarly, publisher Rudolf Ullstein one day remarked jokingly that he had been wrong to turn down Goebbels's manuscript *Michael*. "Had he not done so, he might have diverted Goebbels into activities other than politics."[20] Pleasantries such as these, still in circulation today, are certainly founded on Freud's now generally accepted hypothesis of sublimation and *Kulturversagung*: the narcissistic, erotic, and aggressive components of an individual can be satisfied and *limited* by the production of works of art, which alongside work and over and above all kinds of religion is one of the surest guarantees for the development of culture.

In making jokes of this kind, however, we tend to forget that the Aristotelian notion of the cathartic value of works of art, in which the passions of artist and public alike are exhausted, was opposed in advance by the Platonic declaration that such a work of art may be dangerous by reason of its contagious power. Parallel to the tradition of catharsis is another tradition that runs through the history of Europe. According to this tradition, art, whether condemned (Plato) or glorified (Nietzsche), does not provide an outlet for the passions, but rather constitutes the best means of passing them on as "a great 'stimulant' to life."[21] This alternative tradition, instead of recognizing the possibility of an artist finding "release from himself" through his work, draws attention, according to Nietzsche, to his "will for power." The catharsis of the spectator is set in opposition to the glory to which the artist accedes by "momentarily exercising [his] own divinity."[22] This was clearly the tradition with which National Socialism identified, and it is why all speculation about how the world would have looked had Hitler only been admitted to the Vienna Academy fails to appreciate both the modern aims of art and those of National Socialism.

Joachim Fest, rightly considered to be Hitler's best biographer, nevertheless observed that in the watercolors and oil paintings Hitler produced in Munich (Figures 6 and 7), where the Expressionist movement was developing, "he remained [as in Vienna] the modest postcard copier who had his visions, his nightmares, and his anxieties, but did not know how to translate them into art."[23] This may seem a somewhat surprising remark given that Hitler never dreamed of assigning art the function of expressing the artist's "nightmares and anxieties."

According to Hitler, the artist should, on the contrary, master his anxieties, which stem from subjectivity and contingency, in order to depict only "a beautiful eternal form." In this respect, he certainly did remain on the side of classicism and so was secretly on the same wavelength as the academy that had rejected him. Besides, it seems all the more difficult to criticize Hitler's inability to transpose his anxieties in his paintings given that he in fact did transpose them, but at the level of the "art of the State," where he purged his "human material" with the most violent of passions.

While the exceptional place that the new regime granted to art and culture right from the start evoked general surprise, there were many who thought they could account for the phenomenon simply by resorting to the term *propaganda*: Nazism was making art serve its political ends. This assessment, however, failed to see that the very text of *Mein Kampf* constituted an astonishing development of the Coué method (autosuggestion), which Hitler applied not only to himself but also to his people:

Particularly our German people, which today lies broken and defenseless, exposed to the kicks of the world, needs that suggestive force that lies in self-confidence.[24]

In his opening address to the Nuremberg Congress that followed his accession to power, Hitler repeatedly referred to the basic need for "faith in one's own self" and "fanatical faith in the victory of the movement" in order to effect a "cure for the people."[25] In his closing speech at the same congress, he stressed "the effects of that which is visible and perceptible" in order to convince his people of "his own enduring self-affirmation."[26] To present the broken *Volk* with an image of its "eternal *Geist*" and to hold up to it a mirror capable of restoring to it the strength to love itself was the first task that Hitler, also known as "the doctor of the German people," set for himself.

It was for this reason that the *Geist*, the internal or spiritual Reich, was immediately phenomenalized by art, politics, and propaganda, all of which were intimately linked in the process of autosuggestion. Just as Nietzsche thought that "art is the great stimulant to life," Hitler was convinced that German art contained the power that, because it was narcissistic, could save the sick Germans. In answer to party militants who queried the need to "sacrifice so much to art, when all around us there is so much poverty, misery, distress, and lamentation," he retorted confidently that what had to be achieved was no less than the "strengthening of the protective moral armor of the nation":

Never is it more necessary to lead a people to this unending force of its eternal inner character and being than when political or economic cares might only too easily weaken its faith in its higher values and thus in its mission. When the weak, human spirit, pursued by suffering and anxiety, fails in its faith in the greatness and future of its people, then is the moment to raise it up anew by pointing to those evidences of the inner, imperishable, and highest value of a people, which no political or economic distress can destroy. And the more the natural claims of a nation's life are misunderstood or suppressed—even denied—the more important it is to give to these natural claims the character of a higher right through the visible demonstration of a people's higher values. . . . [27]

Hitler clarified his idea of the autosuggestive nature of art when he declared his belief that artistic activity is the process by which a people produces itself as a people. He claimed to be convinced that "art, since it forms the most uncorrupted, the most immediate reflection of the life of the people's soul, exercises unconsciously by far the greatest direct influence on the masses of the people."[28] He therefore, reasonably enough, saw autosuggestion as the power of autoformation, a natural and organic process the model for which was provided by Romanticism. Novalis wrote, "Art belongs to nature. . . . it is as it were nature observing itself, imitating itself, forming itself."[29]

On April 24, 1936, the *Völkischer Beobachter* published on the front page of its Munich edition an article entitled "Art as the Basis of Creative Political Power: The Führer's Watercolors":

The philosopher Nietzsche says that there is nothing more fantastic than chance. Today we know that it was not by chance that Adolf Hitler did not at the time become one of the many students studying painting at the Academy of Vienna. He was destined for a greater task than simply becoming a good painter or perhaps a great architect.

His gift for painting is nevertheless not an aspect of his personality that is simply due to chance, but is a fundamental characteristic that touches the very kernel of his being. There is an internal and indissoluble link between the artistic works of the Führer and his great political undertaking.

Art is also at the root of his development as a politician and a statesman. In the case of this man, his artistic activity is not simply an occupation of his youth, due to pure chance. It is not a deviation from his political genius, but is the primary condition of his creative idea of the totality.

If we regard history as the creative fashioning of spiritual forces, we are bound to see that the phenomenon of a statesman such as Hitler could only be engendered by artistic bases the essential elements of which are constructiveness and an imaginative vision that gives form.

National Socialism is not an intellectually constructed principle, nor a rational program like Marxism, but a spiritual movement born of the innate formative powers of the soul of the people, a *Weltanschauung* born from a total spiritual conception.

All the same, the author added, distinctions must be drawn. On the one hand, there is politics as understood by Marxism and the state as ruled by Marxists, known, appropriately enough, as "the politics of lawyers" (*Advokatenpolitik*). On the other hand, there is another kind of politics: "The Führer has given the concept of politics a constructive content [*einen aufbauenden Inhalt*], and he was able to do so only because his political ideas developed from his understanding of an autocreative artistic activity [*einer künstlerisch selbstschöpferischen Tätigkeit*]."[30]

In a remarkable fashion, this text combines the three fundamental motifs of the self-image presented by National Socialism. Through the person of Hitler, it asserted itself to stem from the people, from the spirit, and from art. It was therefore basically opposed to parliamentary democracy, and to criticism and debate (of the *Advokatenpolitik* type). Finally, it was politically determined by the autoformative or autocreative nature of the constructive artistic activity that constituted its very essence. Later, when addressing the members of his general headquarters, Hitler produced a more concise reformulation of this theory of autoproduction,[31] which he naturally applied in the first instance to himself: "If our school teachers cannot as a general rule recognize a future genius but, on the contrary, reckon him to be without value—you have only to think of Bismarck, Wagner, or Feuerbach, who, having been rejected by the Academy of Vienna, was ten years later feted and lauded by it—it is because *only a genius can turn himself into a genius.*"[32] When taken out of its trivial context, this formula might surprise anyone ignorant of the congruence of Nazism and of the part of Romantic thought that fully embraced the notion of the autoformation of a genius. But what Nazism lacked was the other half of this line of thought, namely *irony.* With this concept that Hegel was to describe as "the point of view of a *self* who sets everything up and then destroys it all,"[33] the German Romantics identified what deterred them from seeking to realize their dreams in any but a fragmentary fashion. It was certainly in reaction to the Romantic rejection of any kind of totalization that Hans Friedrich Blunck, president of the Reich's Chamber of Literature, appealed for "a new creative will to take the place of irony and eternal negation."[34] And Goebbels unwittingly recognized the inflexibility of National Socialism when he described it as a "Romanticism of steel [*stahlernde Romantik*]."[35] It was thus in all seriousness and completely wholeheartedly that Hitler, "the artists' candidate," at the head of a government of artists, set out to realize the dream previously formulated by Novalis for the young King Frederick-William III, who in 1797 had just acceded to the throne of Prussia:

A true prince is the artist of artists; that is, he is the director of artists. Every person should be an artist. Everything can become a fine art. Artists are the prince's material; his will is his chisel: he educates, places, and instructs artists, because only he can oversee the picture as a whole from the right standpoint, because only to him [is] the great idea, which is to be represented and executed through combined forces and ideas, . . . perfectly present. The regent presents an infinitely diverse spectacle, where stage and parterre, actor and spectator, are one, and he himself is at once poet, director, and hero of the play.[36]

When, in one of his speeches, Hitler later proclaimed "the dictatorship of genius," he did so without a hint of irony.[37]

Suggestion and Incorporation

"The party is Hitler, but Hitler is also Germany, just as Germany is Hitler," Rudolf Hess exclaimed in Nuremberg in 1934.[38] Ernst Kantorowicz produced a masterly study of the history of the inverted formula that presupposed a mutual incorporation and identification of the body of the prince and the body politic.[39] Its source was the Gospel of Saint John, 14:10—"I am in the Father and the Father is in me"—and its model was Christ's relationship to the Church, his mystical body, which the European monarchies were to identify with the body politic. As is well known, the national messianism that characterized Europe throughout the nineteenth century preserved and developed that organic analogy.[40] Presuming to follow from that political-historical naturalism, Nazism pushed this organic logic to its extreme consequences: the expected and desired power of the national body could certainly come only from itself, but only if a head could give that body faith in itself and in its own ability to grow.

Just as in *Mein Kampf* Hitler appealed to the people to obtain self-confidence through autosuggestion, so too he advocated the use of "mass-suggestion" to increase the mass's power and to swell its volume. The determining factor in a mass meeting, he declared, was not the content of a speech but its "visible success," for when it was successful, "the will, the longing, and also the power of thousands are accumulated in every individual."[41] Hitler explained this principle even more clearly in 1926, in a speech to the Nationalklub of Hamburg:

Above all one must get rid of the idea that ideological concepts can satisfy the crowd. For the masses, knowledge is an unstable basis. What is stable is feeling, hatred. . . . What the masses need to feel is triumph in their own vigor [*Stärke*].

In such conditions, he explained, an isolated individual could sense "the vigor and uprightness of the movement" and thus add his own faith to that of the crowd:

He sees two hundred thousand people, all of whom fight for an ideal that he himself cannot even understand, that he does not necessarily have to understand. He has a faith, and this faith is daily reinforced by its visible power.[42]

Thus mass-suggestion and autosuggestion were combined to increase the power of the faith by a visible demonstration of itself, thus boosting faith and confidence in the visibility of the power that was to come. The regime of auto-production set off a quasi-automatism that, in an organicist logic deployed to produce a perfect circularity of cause and effect, was akin to autoeroticism.

That is how the stage management of each of the public appearances of this Führer who *was* his people depended on both suggestion and autosuggestion. Many people have noted the "orgiastic atmosphere" that prevailed at these great National-Socialist rallies and have described "the exhausted state of Hitler by the end of these great public séances in unequivocally sexual terms."[43] Hitler himself said he lost weight at each of these gatherings, during which his skin absorbed the blue dye of his undervest. But the films and photographs of these huge crowds and all the eyewitness reports confirm that the state of the participants could be described in the very same terms. Without a doubt, the "great stimulant to life" that those spectacles represented, led as they were by an orator whose ecstatic style often came close to Expressionism, constituted the narcissistic experience that both the Führer and "his" people wanted: an experience of the "authentic," of the here and now, and of the recovered unity of the *Volksgeist* and its *Volkskörper* (see Glossary of Nazi Terms, p. 255). It was an experience that turned the people into a single subject, excluding any diversity and activating the autoeroticism of the relationships involved, making everybody present feel the same way. A passage in *Mein Kampf* runs as follows:

[The orator] will always let himself be borne by the great masses in such a way that instinctively the very words come to his lips that he needs to speak to the hearts of his audience. And if he errs even in the slightest, he has the living correction before him. As I have said, he can read from the facial expression of his audience. . . . If he suspects that they do not seem convinced of the soundness of his argument, he will repeat it over and over in constantly new examples. He himself will utter their objections, which he senses though unspoken, and go on confuting them and exploding them until at length even the last group of an opposition, by its very bearing and facial expression, enables him to recognize its capitulation to his arguments.[44]

It was thus during an amorous trance, while the erect figure of Hitler brought the "feminine"[45] crowd to its climax, that the body of the people came to be one with its spirit, thereby embodying with its partner that ideal Reich known as the *Volksgemeinschaft*.

This is why these great ceremonies were never simply means to an external end. On the contrary, their end was realized in the *Erlebnis* (see Glossary of Nazi Terms, p. 255), the "lived experience" of a community closed in upon itself. On these occasions, every person present could believe that Hitler was Germany and Germany was Hitler, a reciprocity of which he himself was well aware: "I know you owe to me all that you are, and for my part, I owe all that I am solely to you."[46] The reciprocal shaping of the masses and their leader, to which Hitler so often referred, did in truth appear to be the autoformation of a single political-religious body.

The success of these great narcissistic regressions, however, depended on the disappearance of anything that was likely to obstruct the formation of a monad. The lovers' relationship was established through a series of questions and answers in an exchange that welded the loving partners ever closer together. The crowd's yeses and nos[47] constituted an index of what should and should not be included or excluded for the "authentic experience" to continue; thus the appearance of Hitler always entailed, as its corollary, the progressive disappearance of all enemies who were rejected by the *Volksgemeinschaft*. During the shaping of an ideal self, all those to whom Hitler referred as *kritikaster*—"criticizers" who would not profess faith in the community of love that had now become visible and tangible—were rejected and expelled from the common field of vision represented by the shared Nazi *Weltanschauung*.

In this way, a situation of pure immanence was elaborated, in which the pleasure of seeing and being seen no longer implied any externality, and in which the assembled people gave birth to its now-visible soul while the Führer beheld the formation, before his very eyes, of the people he had brought into the light of day in accordance with his vision. The words with which Rudolf Hess affirmed that Germany and the Führer were one and the same perfectly expressed that pure, now-visible immanence in which "all, including Hitler himself, fully believe[d] in the image . . . they [had] created."[48] The reason Alfred Rosenberg could exclaim at the same congress that "*[t]he world of the eye*, which Goethe once described as the original source of his life, now reigns again in Germany"[49] was that autosuggestion and mass-suggestion now converged with what Goebbels called "creative propaganda." The unity and recovered health of the people could now be seen by the whole of Germany, and the price of that unity was the lopping off of the parts of the body that were judged to be "sick." What had thus been realized first in the world of the eye was "that desire of Germans" that Rosenberg, in his *Myth of the Twentieth Century*, believed he could detect in the expression formulated by Meister Eckhart—namely the desire "to be at one with oneself."[50] But the sense of those words had been fearsomely twisted: what had initially been a mystical union of each individual with an invisible God had been turned into the mystical union of the community with its visible Führer.

Propaganda and Anticipation

All analyses of National Socialism stumble when attempting to determine the moment when, after Hitler acceded to power, "the myth and the reality [became] one."[51] Even quite recently, Ian Kershaw declared that "where Nazism was ambitious—and extraordinarily so—was in attempting a transformation in subjective consciousness rather than in objective reality."[52] Martin Broszat had already said something similar: "National Socialism was an extreme attempt to change the world by means of a transformation of subjective consciousness (rather than overturning objective relations)."[53] The naivety of statements such as these made by eminent historians of Nazism is both surprising and disturbing: could a "transformation of subjective consciousness" have been possible without at the same time "overturning objective relationships"? Did Nazism really leave "objective reality" intact? Did the emancipation of certain categories of the population, the terror that accompanied this, the acceleration of production, and in the end all the extermination exist only in the "subjective consciousness"? Even if it was merely a matter of affirming the maintenance of preexisting relations of production, such formulations would, to put it mildly, be inadequate. Even more sinister is the resurgence today of the idea that a "double life" was imposed on the Germans under the Third Reich. Even as he declared that "the contradictions between the propaganda and the reality were not very deep," Christian von Krockow described, in a work that is nevertheless remarkable, the "split personality" of the Germans of that time—at once dozing in the apolitical normality of worthy citizens *and* marching along in step, drunk with a will for power. According to Krockow, "the division of existence into two distinct domains" that was tolerated and encouraged was reflected in the production of films by the Third Reich that paid no attention to anything having to do with the regime: its insignia, its uniforms, its salutes, and its pomp and ceremony.[54] Yet, like other seemingly neutral distractions, these films were an integral part of the myth. To sustain the efforts that Robert Ley demanded from his "soldiers of work," certain recreational zones were made available—zones capable of maintaining and sustaining the productive forces of the *Volksgemeinschaft*. The misunderstanding arises from the fact that it was not only possible but essential to tolerate anything that was likely to encourage the people's feeling of happiness without spoiling the fabrication of the myth, the "realization of the Idea." After all, the regime needed such distractions for the same reasons it needed "a positive Christianity" (point 24 in the 1920 party's manifesto). As one partisan of moderation said (opposing the excesses of Rosenberg, which he judged to be unnecessary), "the Third Reich needed Christianity and the Churches, because it had nothing to put in the place of the Christian religion and morality."[55] Because this was almost invariably the dominant political line, provided it did no harm to the myth, nothing was suppressed; as a result, the myth was never isolated from the reality. On the contrary, it impregnated reality in exactly the same way that, as Goebbels said, the Idea was spreading among the masses—"just as gas penetrates more solid objects."[56]

In his course of lectures devoted to the question of German culpability, during the winter of 1945–46, Karl Jaspers was more penetrating on the subject of this double life: "*Life lived beneath a mask*—which was unavoidable for anyone who wished to survive—involved a moral culpability. . . . Disguise constituted one of the fundamental characteristics of our life. It weighs upon our moral conscience."[57] We shall return later to the exonerating function this "disguise" was supposed to serve. But first we should remember that Nazi propaganda, which was founded on suggestion, did distinguish between one's internal disposition (*Stimmung*) and one's visible behavior (*Haltung*). It was by imposing the wearing of a "mask," a particular type of *Haltung*, that such propaganda sought to obtain a favorable *Stimmung* in those who remained internally recalcitrant. This propaganda no doubt reckoned that life lived beneath the mask would eventually conform to the mask. In the last analysis, however, orthodoxy was less important than *orthopraxy*, to borrow the felicitous expression that Jacques Ellul has used to characterize modern propaganda.[58] So the disparity that might exist between an individual's play-acting and his inner convictions was of secondary importance. What was crucial was the quality of the play-acting, the efficacy that the actor brought to his task—his performance (*Leistung*). What really mattered was the measurable "talent" of each individual at the place and in the role assigned to him in the spectacle. For Goebbels, this was the true criterion, right to the end, as can be seen in the words of encouragement he addressed to his collaborators in the last days of the regime: "Gentlemen, in a hundred years' time a fine Technicolor film will be made of the terrible days through which we are living. Do you not wish to play a role in that film? Stand fast now, so that the spectators . . . do not boo and hiss when you appear upon the screen."[59] In similar fashion, during the weeks leading up to the collapse, Hitler several times expressed his fear of being "an exhibit in the Moscow zoo" or obliged to appear in "a show trial staged by the Jews."[60] For although he was the first to believe that, as Keyserling said, life could "only be rendered good, beautiful, and happy at the level of art," he could not imagine himself not being, as Novalis stated, "at once the poet, director, and hero of the play."

For many years it was believed that photographs of Hitler the orator using his postexpressionist gestures belonged to the Führer's secret archives or to those of his photographer-friend Heinrich Hoffmann, and that they were taken simply to help the orator work on his gestures in his studio. We now know that that was not the case at all, because they were published several times over as early as the beginning of 1928 in the *Illustrierter Beobachter*, and six of them were then sold and mass-produced as a series of postcards (Figure 8). That they were still widely available in the late 1930s (Chaplin used them when working on his role in *The Dictator*) shows clearly that, far from being work tools reserved for Hitler's private use, they were in fact aimed in a most calculated fashion at the widest possible general public. Rudolf Herz, who made this discovery, notes that these gestures are nevertheless not repeated in the filmed documentation of Hitler's public speeches. What the photographs depicted were manifestly "just postcard poses, authentic documents testifying to Hitler's own exalted scene-setting."[61] A journalist of the 1930s had already compared them to photograms, each with its own lighting.

The huge success of these postcards makes it easier to understand what the masses expected of Hitler in their meetings, what kind of play-acting tricks would take them out of themselves, transport them for the duration of the spectacle to a world where the shadows and light were more clearly defined and choices seemed more simple. The reason that Hitler, for his part, decided to publish the photographs and diffuse them as captioned postcards was without a doubt in order to arouse expectations from which he would benefit at the rallies. The code of gestures seems deliberately old-fashioned, closer to the images one might find in a nineteenth-century textbook for orators than to the more recent Expressionist style. Hitler himself remarked, "If propaganda renounces primitiveness of expression, it does not find its way to the feeling of the broad masses."[62] This collection of gesticulations with touches at once popular and solemn was intended to intrigue those who had not yet attended one of the rallies and to give others an unaccustomed sense of at once proximity and distance.

Amid the mutual expectations of the Führer and the masses, a common image took shape, one that would take material form at their meetings. Success clearly depended not on the sincerity of the partners but on their belief in that common image, which was both the condition and the object of the spectacle.

In 1934, when analyzing the religious and magical features that become attached to money in "primitive cultures," French sociologist and anthropologist Marcel Mauss stressed "the importance of the notion of expectation, of counting on something in the future, which is precisely one of the forms of collective thinking." He went on to point out, "In society we are among ourselves, all expecting some result or other; that is the essential form taken by a community." Mauss, who was remarkably sensitive to the troubles of his age, then described one of the turning points in his research:

In the past we may have used expressions such as constraint, force, authority, and they do have their value; but this notion of collective expectation is, in my opinion, one of the fundamental notions on which we should work. I know of no other notion that generates both rights and economics. "I expect . . . " is the definition of every action of a collective nature. It is at the origin of theology: God will hear—I say not grant but hear—my prayer.[63]

At the very point when Mauss was formulating these remarks, however, Fascism and Nazism already knew how to ensure that the prayer that was heard also appeared to be granted. Goebbels's words on "knowledge and propaganda," pronounced on January 9, 1928, were in this respect exemplary:

Ideas, we say, are in the air, and when someone arrives who expresses in words what we all feel in our hearts, then each of us feels: yes, that is what I have always wanted and hoped for. This is what happens when one hears one of Hitler's great speeches. I have met men who, for the first time in their lives, have attended one of Hitler's meetings. At the end of his speech they were saying, "All that I have been seeking for years, this man has expressed in words. Now, for the very first time, someone has come along and shaped what I have been wanting.[64]

That "shaping" resulted in expectations being satisfied, thanks to which the orator increased his prestige. As we know, today that is exactly what marketing does. Its techniques for the investigation of collective expectations create nothing: their object is to summon up the image of a momentarily shared desire and give it body. It is fair to say that Hitler could not have achieved success "without the Depression" that reigned in Germany and "without the external conditions which exposed the electoral 'market' to the Nazi political alternative."[65] A description such as this, however, does not help us to understand the immanence of the process. For if Hitler embodied an early resolution to the crisis, the essential point was that that anticipation was instantly comprehended, in the *Erlebnis* of the mass rally, as actually resolving the crisis.

In their own way, these postcards constituted not only an appeal, but at the same time a preparation for the meetings, for the postcards also anticipated the resolution of the crisis. The caption printed beneath the first of them was particularly clear: "Are you fulfilling your highest duty to your people? If so, you are our brother! If not, you are our mortal enemy." That kind of binary resolution, subsequently repeated in the yeses and noes of the meetings, cast all mortal enemies into the shadows, the better to display in the full light an image of the salvation of the *Volksgemeinschaft* of the future and the community of happy brothers. Hitler's promise of salvation to his people was presented in the spectacular process of *the division drawn* between the damned and the elect. Many members of the "elite" were won over by this, anticipating total triumph and jubilation. There was a repetition of what Hannah Arendt has called "the more than embarrassing fact that men of unquestionable stature—including Tertullian and even Saint Thomas Aquinas—can have believed that the joys of paradise would consist of the privilege of contemplating the spectacle of the unspeakable torments of Hell."[66] Jurist Carl Schmitt, for instance, who aspired to be to Hitler what Eusebius had been to Emperor Constantine, by legally founding the concentration of temporal and spiritual powers in a single person, made the "friend/enemy grouping" the very "criterion of politics."[67] However, for Schmitt the term *politics* "does not describe its own substance, but only the intensity of an association or dissociation of human beings whose motives can be religious, national (in the ethnic or cultural sense), economic, or of another kind."[68] The "revelation" of that polarity or dissociation, real or virtual, which provided "a principle of identification," was what was meant by the *Entscheidung* (see Glossary of Nazi Terms, p. 255), the sovereign decision of the dictator, to whom it fell to resolve "an exceptional situation," that is to say, a chaos in which the norms of ordinary law could not be applied.[69] Using the artist's vocabulary to which he was accustomed, Hitler spelled out this principle of the *Entscheidung* rather less elegantly: "My pedagogy is hard. Whatever is weak and mildewed [*das Schwache*] must be struck away with the hammer."[70] What remained essential, however, was that sovereign gesture that separated light from darkness.

Not many artists risked attempting a tangible image of that gesture. In 1937, Hermann Hoyer exhibited a painting entitled *In the Beginning was the Word* (Figure 9). It showed Hitler in a pose more or less resembling one of the postcards, on a platform, haranguing the public during the "period of the struggle [Kampfzeit]." The countenance and hand of the Führer shed a little of their light on the fighters of those early days, who are certainly attentive but appear somewhat bored. To be fair, though, it is almost possible to detect Hitler's preference for meetings held in the evening when he said, "in the artificially made yet mysterious twilight in Catholic Churches" it was easier "to encroach [upon] man's freedom of will." But in this painting there is no hint of the atmosphere of the earliest meetings, which Hitler described as "a clash between two opposed forces";[71] here there is no sign of any enemy for Hitler, through the power of his words alone, to cast back into the shadows from which it came.

Later, hoping to confer upon the word of Hitler the authority of a German philosophical tradition, Arthur Kampf—a fateful name—painted a large fresco in the hall of the University of Berlin (Figure 10). In the middle of a rather sparse and inattentive crowd that nevertheless was supposed to represent the wide diversity of the German people, the philosopher Johann Fichte was seen in one of Hitler's favorite poses delivering one of Fichte's speeches to the German nation. The fresco clearly could not convey that the philosopher was addressing *the people* par excellence, nor that he was telling *"all-mann"* (everyman) that it was primarily their language that differentiated them from the other peoples who, led by Napoleon, were then invading their country. In truth, in this bleak clearing, the gesticulations of Fichte, perched on a curious plinth that turned him prematurely into a statue, conveyed very little at all.

Far more remarkable was the mastery with which photographer Heinrich Hoffman gathered together forty or so young SA members from all over Germany in the Brown House, headquarters of the NSDAP in Munich (Figure 11). In serried ranks, with their joyful faces filling the whole protective alcove, they are gazing at Hitler. The caption reads, "How their eyes shine when the Führer is close to them!" The gazes from all those faces, some of them positively pop-eyed with love, converge to meet the magnetic look of the Führer. He, far from gesticulating, is sitting quietly, his clasped hands resting on a sturdy table covered by a modest waxed cloth. A few cups lie scattered on the table, left over from a light meal recently consumed in private. Drawn there by the presence of the Führer, the youthful crowd forms a compact mass that at first glance seems overwhelming. But the impact of this photograph stems precisely from the way it makes all those eyes gazing down at him testify to Hitler's powerful hold over the masses. No definite shadows are to be seen in the image, just a chapel-like glow gently and uniformly illuminating this fraternal gathering of which Hitler is indeed a part and yet remains its leader. This seems an authentic *corpus mysticum* (mystical body), in which the people and its savior are united by a sweet bond of love. The sight of this photograph might itself have won over beholders who responded to the appeal of the divine eye in the center of the image, represented by the swastika on one youth's armband.

No enemies appear in these images. Nazi imagery never, or hardly ever, presented both the racially pure body of the people and that of the enemy at once. Indeed, if the *völkisch* Idea was to appear in all its purity, it was essential that no "weak and mildewed" part of the people be there to defile the image. By excluding all enemy figures, the propagandists of the new faith demonstrated above all that the *decision* of the Führer had replaced their own decisions as artists. Even before they put his image together, each of them anticipated the *Weltanschauung* of the Führer and the gesture with which he separated the good grain from the chaff.

In 1935, Bernhard Rust, Nazi minister of education, published a decree stipulating that all teachers should "respond to the desire of the Führer" by convincing all their pupils "of the importance and need for pure blood."[72]

A little earlier, one Nazi dignitary had already declared that everyone in the Third Reich had "a duty to try to work towards the Führer along the lines that he would wish."[73] As the educators of the German people, for whom and in whose name they worked, the people's artists were, even more than many others, bound by duty "to work towards the Führer" and "to respond to his desires." This meant renouncing the choice and freedom that had conferred the artist's status upon him ever since the Renaissance, when Leon Battista Alberti compared the painter to "another god." With Romanticism, furthermore, transgression of the common professional and moral norms had become inseparable from the limitless liberty that artists enjoyed in their own domain. Now, by anticipating the decision of the Führer, these workers of the eternal Reich on the contrary never overstepped the professional and moral limits that defined the *Volksgemeinschaft*. They recognized Hitler as the foremost artist of the empire and made themselves his humble executives, thereby coming themselves to embody the dream of Novalis. They too made themselves matter for the Führer to work on with the chisel that made his decision. Hitler educated, placed, and instructed these artists. He alone could see every aspect of a work, and from the right vantage point, for there was present in him alone the great Idea that must now be executed by a harmonious and convergent body of representative forces and thoughts. As early as 1934, an anonymous article in the *Völkischer Beobachter* had declared in the name of "German artists":

Everyone knows it: it is to the company of true artists, among all the millions of Germans, that the Führer constantly claims to belong. German artists are grateful to the Führer for his great and warm interest. Now and forever the authority of the Führer and that of the artists are as one. In the Reich of Adolf Hitler there is not a single German artist who does not respond affirmatively, out of his deepest convictions, to the Führer's plan and spirit in both politics and art.[74]

By a kind of tacit contract, they transferred their liberty and strength to the person of the artist-Führer and in exchange received his protection: buyers for their works, exhibitions, allocated studios, decorations, and dispensation from frontline fighting in the war. Under the Third Reich, those who worked in the art of propaganda, like other members of the community but perhaps even more so, played their part in the construction of the Leviathan by increasing the strength of the Führer. If they were required to produce an image of the enemy, they likewise acted as his agents and were careful only to present the enemy in a space quite separate from that occupied by the luminous body of the *Volksgemeinschaft*. On posters—the paper of which was not designed to last for all eternity as were the canvas, stone, and bronze that embodied the racially pure people—the enemy did sometimes appear, disfigured by caricature and sometimes with the "degenerate" appearance of the art that Hitler condemned. Borrowing from that art or from the caricaturist's style, the images of the enemy that were produced not only demonstrated in advance the fate reserved for the "weak and mildewed" part of the community; it also provoked and justified that fate by depicting the signs of a difference that otherwise remained invisible.

The mobilization of all these makers of images thus created the appearance of an intense and constant anonymous activity: "*Es war immer was los*' (there was always something going on) is the phrase on the lips of people who, in Germany today, try to convey the atmosphere of the Third Reich to those who did not experience it."[75] What was going on was the heroic transformation of a divided people into a community of soldier-artists working toward the realization of the National Socialist Idea, to make it visible. This was creative activity that portrayed the Idea as *Gestalt*, that is to say, by detaching its parasitical background, the better to emphasize "the law of the outline" in all its purity of form—the law that the poet Gottfried Benn called "the law for heroes only."[76] This was also what was conveyed by the word *los*, making it a part of the *Entscheidung*—something detached and unbound, unleashed and at the same time liberated. The ambivalence of the word echoes the active ambivalence of the continuous creation of a collective autonomy at once cultural and racial, economic and political, religious and military, which could be produced only by a narcissistic withdrawal that was inseparable from aggression directed against all attempts at control from outside. The plebiscite of November 12, 1933, which approved Germany's withdrawal from the League of Nations, and that of August 19, 1934, which gave full powers to Hitler, constituted repeats, on the scale of the entire country, of the acceptance of the decision that was supposed to hasten the moment of redemption.

To prolong, both spatially and temporally, the pleasure shared in the mass rallies, and to maintain the amorous tension through which the *Volksgemeinschaft* existed as such—therein consisted the sum of the political life of the Third Reich, which was founded on the delimitation of the zones in which hatred and violence were to be exercised. The erection of the figure of Hitler before the crowds corresponded not only to the stiff, nude figures of the stone colossi that symbolized the people and were sculpted by Arno Breker, Josef Thorak, Karl Albiker, and Willy Meller, but also to the monumental constructions that were supposed to embody the community of the people and that Hitler claimed to be erected "in order to increase our authority." These works of art constituted the boundary stones marking out the public space that were supposed to keep open the space of salvation of the "community of feeling." In similar fashion, the visible German salute *Heil Hitler!* which seemed to make the Führer's promises suddenly a reality opened up a vista of redemption. Those raised arms certainly signified the salute of the Germans *to* Hitler, but also their salvation *through* Hitler, the healer of the German people, the Savior whose vision or Idea of the eternal Reich was embodied at the moment of the salute.

It was through art and in art—understood in the widest sense, that is to say, incorporating the whole perceptible environment and even the behavior (*Haltung*) of each individual—that the links holding the community together could and had to be maintained. Goebbels made no bones about it when he declared, "The German art of the next few decades . . . will create both obligations and bonds, or else will not exist at all."[77] In 1934, Hitler imagined his Germans to be as solidly bound together as the stones in the vast buildings he was constantly sketching. "The German way of life is precisely fixed for the next millennium," he announced in Nuremberg.[78]

Wagnerian Rehearsals

Hitler was fond of saying, "Whoever wishes to understand National Socialist Germany must know Wagner." He claimed to have himself penetrated the entire thought of the man he placed among "the great reformers," alongside Luther and Frederick the Great. "At the various stages in my life, I have always returned to him," he confided to Hermann Rauschning.[79] August Kubizek, a companion of his Viennese years, has told of the hours and whole nights that Hitler spent sketching vast sets for operas he dreamed of one day producing. Much later, when Robert Ley tried to persuade him to change the introductory music played at all his party congresses, Hitler explained that his choice of the overture to Wagner's *Rienzi* was based on the libretto as much as on the music. "This son of a humble innkeeper, at the age of twenty, persuaded the people of Rome to eject its corrupt senate. He did so by evoking the prestigious past of the Roman Empire. I myself, as a very young man, while listening to this great music in the theater of Linz, had a vision of a German Reich whose greatness and unity I would engineer."[80] Even when the Chancellery of the Reich was his, Hitler still sometimes designed sets for Wagnerian operas (Figure 12), including both *Tristan and*

Isolde and the entire *Niebelungen* cycle, claiming to have spent three weeks working by night on his models.

As Hitler saw it, the greatness and unity of the Reich demanded that the greatest care be taken with the staging of the new Germany. He never left anything to chance in the planning of the timing of either ceremonies or campaigns, always calculating the propitious hour for the spectacular arrival of the plane carrying the Savior he was, the right moment for him to begin to speak, and the best speed for the delivery of his speeches. In exactly the same way he also checked every last visual detail of all the ceremonies in which he was the author, the spectator, or the hero, or even, as frequently happened, all three at once. As Joachim Fest reports, he specified "every detail relating to every entrance on stage and to the march-past of each group, just as he did for the flower arrangements, the disposal of flags, and even the precise spot where guests of honor should be seated." Now that he was in power, he could satisfy all the ambitions of his youth. In 1934, after the Nazi press professed to be scandalized by the production of *Parsifal* at Bayreuth, Hitler immediately issued a state decree that all stage sets and costumes for the Bayreuth festival should in the future be submitted to him for his approval.[81] But his creative energy was even more inexhaustible when it came to setting the whole people on stage. The passion he devoted to designing or redesigning the various costumes of his Hitler Youth (*Hitler Jugend*) groups, the mess kit of his *Schutz Staffel* (SS) officers, tank guns, and the "constructions of the Führer" was summed up neatly enough by Himmler in one of his secret speeches: "The Führer is always right, whether it be a matter of evening gear, a bunker, or one of the Reich's motor roads."[82]

It was therefore, naturally enough, in Wagnerian mode that he organized the realization of Novalis's project: to model the spectacle of the prince on the Passion of Christ. "I have built up my religion out of *Parsifal*. Divine worship (*Gottesdienst*) in solemn form . . . without pretenses of humility. . . . One can serve God only in the garb of a hero."[83] If he regarded Wagner as his only true predecessor, it was because he too believed that the unificatory and formative power of art should take over from both Christianity and politics:

Better than any *aging religion, repudiated by the public spirit,* and in a more striking manner that *state wisdom that has long since lost confidence in itself,* Art, forever young, which
can constantly find a source of new freshness in itself and in the noblest aspects of the
spirit of the age—Art can provide the onward flow of social passions, which can so easily be diverted by wild reefs or in shallows, with a goal that is fine and lofty, the goal of
a noble humanity.[84]

Only in the creation of the great collective work of art, what Wagner called
"the common artwork of the future" could the entire people find redemption.
Hitler's anti-Christianity was modeled exactly on his intellectual guide. For Wagner, Christianity was a "veritable Utopia," a "truly inaccessible ideal" that led to
"a brutal contrast between the Idea and its realization" because "it transgressed
against the truth, the healthy nature of man." In opposition to the impossibility
of that Utopia, Wagner appealed "to nature, which alone has a visible existence
that can be seized upon."[85] Thus the Idea, which was based on the visible existence of concrete nature, could be realized satisfactorily only within the visible
order of a great work of art:

Unless it communicates with the eye, all art remains unsatisfying and therefore unsatis-
fied and unfree. So long . . . as it is not fully communicated to the eye, it remains an art
that can do no more than *wish* and that as yet lacks full *power*; but art must possess power,
for in our language it is precisely from *power* [*Können*] that art [*Kunst*] derives its name.[86]

There can be no doubt that in formulations such as these Hitler found the
essential bases for his own ideology. It was certainly not on the basis of the traditions of the jurists that he declared that "success justifies the right of the individual" or that every great political period "demonstrates the justification for its
existence . . . through its cultural realizations," let alone that those realizations
testify to "the moral right to existence" of the peoples that created them.[87] The
fact that National Socialism was simultaneously a religion of art, nature, and
work was due to it being first and foremost a religion of success through the realization of a culture designed as an extension to nature and understood as an effective force. The fact that creative will could be thought of as the will of either
a god or a natural force was of secondary importance. All that mattered was the

"visible success" of its creations, which justified its agent's "right to existence"—whether that agent was an individual, a revolutionary moment, a people, or a race—and testified to the superiority of both the Idea that inspired the agent and the agent himself.

It is true that Martin Bormann, Hitler's private secretary, whom historian Joseph Wulf has called "Hitler's shadow," maintained that the ideas of National Socialism and those of Christianity were "incompatible," given that the former was founded on science and the latter on dogma "established two thousand years ago," that took "no account of realities." We should not be misled by the word *incompatibility*, for what it turned out to mean was simply "rivalry," once what was at stake became the power of the party, which Bormann set in opposition to the power of the Church. In the same text in which he declared that incompatibility, he unwittingly set the limits of the anti-Christianity he shared with Alfred Rosenberg:

Our National Socialist *Weltanschauung* is far superior to the ideas of Christianity, which essentially were borrowed from Judaism. That is an added reason why we have no need of Christianity. *The one known as the good God does not at all, himself, convey to the youth of today a sense of his existence.* So if our youth one day learn no more about that Christianity, the precepts of which are so inferior to ours, Christianity will simply disappear of its own accord.[88]

Just as Wagner condemned *aged religion* to fade away before the eternal youth of the work of art of the future, Bormann announced its imminent disappearance to the advantage of a realized Nazi *Weltanschauung*. The superiority of the latter over Christianity stemmed from its totally un-utopian but perfectly realizable nature: its cultural realizations, which were both visible and tangible, gave it rightful justification. So it would soon supplant a religion that was fated to disappear because it was founded on a god who was invisible. It is thus not hard to understand that the reason Nazism was incompatible with Christianity was primarily because of the Jewish legacy of a god who was invisible—and whose invisibility appeared to be inseparable from universality. As for the rest—that is to say, the *ecclesia* (the organization of the party and the community), on the one hand, and the structure of the Incarnation, with all its salvationary powers, on the other—Nazism certainly revealed itself to be Christianity's rival, for it constituted a strict imitation of it: the *Volksgeist* god, embodied in the person of the Führer at the head of a government of artists and what would soon be a people of artists, offered salvation through art and culture. This was a salvation far more tangible than that offered by the good God whose religion was disappearing of its own accord because, despite the Christ he provided for the very purpose, he did "not at all, himself, convey a sense of his existence."

The *Gottesdienst* (Protestant service) that Wagner set on stage in Bayreuth in *Parsifal* thus became a *Führerdienst* (service of the Führer) on the general stage of Germany. In its very widest sense the "Führer's service" could mean performing all the tasks that were directed "towards the Führer"; but the expression was particularly used to designate the kind of "biological marriages" that were designed to purify the race through the coupling of its very best specimens.[89] The whole *Volksgemeinschaft* was thus, in the last analysis, gathered to serve the Führer, which meant the same as serving the blood. National Socialist Germany thus presented a continuous performance of *Pasifal* in which Hitler was supposed to be the hero. Wagner's *Parsifal* might perhaps, as Igor Stravinsky claimed, be seen as an "unconscious aping of the sacred rite," for the ceremony of the Grail in which Christ's blood was collected and in which bread and wine were distributed was indeed a replica of the Eucharistic Mass and sacrifice. But National Socialism presented itself unequivocally as a religion revealed by blood. As jurist Carl Schmitt said, it was the "real presence" of the Führer-Christ and his essential *Artgleichheit* (similarity of race or species) with his people that conferred upon the community the links, both spiritual and physical, that bound it together and that seemed to point the way to salvation.[90]

Nazi ideology and its ceremonies were very soon understood to be what they truly were and were analyzed accordingly: as replicas of Christianity and its rites. As early as 1930, Ernst Bloch wrote, "The master of the blood replaces Jesus. The warrior state stands in for the community of the faithful."[91] In the wake of Dietrich Bonhoeffer, cited earlier in this chapter, Cardinal Michael von Faulhaber in his turn condemned this rivalry: "*It was not German blood that redeemed us*, but the precious blood of our Lord on the cross." He was, however, of the opinion that "there is nothing objectionable about an honest study of race nor about a policy that aims to safeguard a race."[92] (In November 1936, following a three-hour interview with the Führer, Faulhaber noted in a confidential report that he had been much impressed by and convinced of the deep religiosity of Hitler's personality: "The Reich Chancellor undoubtedly lives in belief in God. He recognizes Christianity as the builder of Western Culture."[93]) In 1933, too, Eric Voegelin stressed the continuity of Nazism with Christianity: the same concept of the Church as the mystical body of Christ that had been perpetuated in the dynastic concept of the European monarchies had now reappeared in the National Socialist Idea, which was embodied in a führer-Christ and his mystical body, the *Volksgemeinschaft*.[94] In 1938, the very year when Edmond Vermeil, in France, was passionately stigmatizing the "theological simplification" to which Nazism was leading,[95] Voegelin was developing his own argument to prove, on the contrary, "from a scholarly point of view," the full complexity of Nazism and how it differed from the Fascism of Italy. He cited the following explanation produced by "a German theorist" which certainly had the merit of clarity: "The Führer is penetrated by the Idea; it works through him. But it is also he who has the ability to give a living form to that Idea. In him the spirit of the people is realized and the will of the people is formed. It is in him that the people . . . acquires its visible form. He is the representative of the people." Therefore, Voegelin's commentary went on to say, "the Führer is the point where the *Volksgeist* breaks through into historical reality. The God within the world speaks to the Führer just as the God above the world spoke to Abraham, and the Führer changes the divine words into orders to his partisans and the people." Recalling the similarity between this notion and that of Thomas Hobbes's *Leviathan*, in which the person of the sovereign was already called the "representative" of the commonwealth, Voegelin underlined what it was that differentiated Fascism and Nazism, those two avatars of the *Leviathan*, from each other. "The Italian *Volksgeist* is understood in a more spiritual fashion, whereas in German symbolism the spirit is linked with the blood and the Führer becomes the spokesman of the *Volksgeist* and the representative of the people, thanks to his racial unity with that people."[96] It is certainly true that the distinctive feature of the Nazi doctrine was the solemnity with which it developed the Christian metaphor of the *Corpus mysticum*, even to the point of its extreme materialization in the physical body of each member of its church, the *Volksgemeinschaft*. For Nazism, there had to be no break in the continuity between the "spiritual community" and the "physical community," the *Volksgeist* and the *Volkskörper*, any more than between the Idea and its realization. In the last analysis, however, this was simply a repetition of Hobbes's organicist interpretation of the Scriptures: "The word *spirit* . . . signifieth . . . either properly a real substance or, metaphorically, some extraordinary ability or affection of the mind or of the body."[97] This is certainly the sense in which Rosenberg, whatever his hostility to Christianity, was to be understood when he wrote that "race is the outward image of a definite soul."[98]

During the first year of the regime in particular, the whole of the Wagnerian mythology was resuscitated in order to set on stage the "real presence" of the *Volksgeist* in the *Volkskörper* and its representative. One popular image (Figure 13) thus had no qualms about transfiguring Hitler into a Wagnerian Siegfried clad in an animal skin, with his bare hands forging upon Mime's anvil the sword that was to kill the dragon, Fafner (*Siegfried*, I, 3). After all, Hitler had concluded the first volume of *Mein Kampf* with the following description of the first great rally of the NSDAP: "A fire was kindled from whose flame one day the sword must come which would regain freedom for the German Siegfried and life for the German nation."[99] Hitler, the new Siegfried, was preparing to avenge a betrayed Germany: three generations of Germans had become accustomed, thanks to Wagner's *Ring*, to believing that no German hero could be vanquished except by a stab in the back, such as the blow that the sinister Hagen dealt Siegfried.[100]

But soon Wagner was summoned to the public space. On October 15, 1933, the Day of German Art was celebrated, the high point of which was certainly Hitler laying the first stone of the House of German Art in Munich. On this occasion, Hans Schemm, the Bavarian Minister of Culture, published an article that made the front page of the *Völkischer Beobachter*. It was forthrightly entitled "Hail to the German Artist!" In it he wrote as follows: "In both art and politics, the Führer is no less than the people's thought become flesh and blood." The German creative genius, anchored in "the thought of the organic rally," stood in opposition to its eternal adversary: namely, "all that is destructive, all that has a disintegrating effect, all that divides and annihilates." And it was thanks to the Wagnerian dramas that those two spirits locked in their eternal battle could be named:

In *Siegfried, Parsifal, Stolzing, Lohengrin, we recognize the eternally German principle of life.* This principle can be found in the young German who, with the straightforward assurance of a sleepwalker that characterizes the original naive man, radiant and happy, fighting and conquering, and always searching, once again arouses an impotent world in chains and propels it forward. Advancing against him comes the dark and negative power of egoistic man, who is separate from the community: Alberich, Beckmesser, Hagen. It sows discord and disintegration, and casts the world into impotence and decline.[101]

The *Nationalsozialistische Monatshefte*, under the direction of Rosenberg, dedicated its July issue to Richard Wagner. It celebrated the Bayreuth genius for having anticipated the reconciliation of art with politics and for his "discovery of artist-man, which would bear fruit in the process of the healing of the German people."[102] Wagner had indeed thought very early on that "all future social behavior" should be "of a purely artistic nature," and that, as he sketched out in *Art and Revolution*, art and its institutions should "become the precursors and models for all future communal institutions." On that account he wished to "raise the altar of the future, both in life and in living art, to the two most sublime initiators of humanity: Jesus, who suffered for humanity, and Apollo, who raised it to its joyful dignity."[103] It is no exaggeration to say that Hitler, in the Wagnerian dream he tried to embody, almost simultaneously took on the roles of both Jesus and Apollo. He was at once both Christ suffering for the redemption of his people and Apollo the conqueror, whom Wagner called "the sovereign god, the national god of the Hellenic races." Hitler probably harbored a secret preference for Apollo, "the fine, strong, and free man" who was "the killer of the Python, the dragon of chaos." Wagner regarded Apollo as the most satisfactory expression of the "Greek spirit, as manifested at its noblest in the state and in art," because Apollo "executed the will of Zeus in the land of Greece; he *was* the Greek people,"[104] just as Hitler was Germany.

In truth, however, Hitler was prepared to take on all roles, either one by one or simultaneously: Hans Sachs and Lohengrin, Parsifal and Siegfried, Jesus and Apollo. But his dragon was neither Python nor Fafner; it was the dark, god-killing Jew, the spirit that "disintegrates everything." To vanquish that spirit it was necessary for him to occupy every stage, those of the theater as well as those of the Church, in private space and public space alike. One of Hoffmann's photographs (Figure 14) shows Hitler emerging from the church of Wilhelmshaven, his head surmounted by a cross, the better to confound accusations of heresy (*Ketzer*) and to provide tangible proof of his "sacred mission." In another photo, Hitler's image is positioned in a place of pride on the private altar of a German family (Figure 15), flanked by two generations, the grandparents on one side, the grandchildren on the other. Above the Führer hang the words "*Und Ihr habt doch gesiegt*" (you have conquered after all), while at his feet the work *Gebt mir vier Jahre Zeit* (give me four years) constitutes a reminder that the promises made on February 11, 1933 at the Berlin Sports Palace have been kept. The grandfather rejoices at "having lived to see all this," while the granddaughter, alongside her brother, who is giving the Hitlerian salute, impatiently demands, "When can I see the Führer?" Remarkably enough, Hitler occupied the position of the generation missing from the image: he was at once Son and Father, the very Image (in the sense of *Ebenbild*, image of God) in which all times met.

The rivalry with Christianity was even greater when the SS took to organizing the "naming ceremony," which replaced baptism (Figure 16). The image of the Führer was set on the altar (Figure 17), and in civil marriages young couples were presented with a copy of *Mein Kampf*, the new German bible. National Socialism did not hesitate to fabricate heroes for itself, so veritable cults could be addressed to them (Figure 18). Sometimes the Christian space would be totally taken over by Nazi symbols. For example, a service in honor of Peter Voss, the

Standartenführer, was organized in the Lutheran church of the Berlin garrison (Figure 19). On either side of the altar stood swastika standards, which had the effect of identifying the *Gottesdienst* with the *Führerdienst*. Likewise, large businesses built "chapels whose main aisle led to a Hitler bust beneath the symbol of the Labor Front, flanked by heroic-sized worker figures; in effect, little temples to the National Socialist god of work."[105] In smaller businesses, a space known as the "flag corner" (*der Fahnenecke*) was set aside to house the Führer's bust, flanked by the flags of the Nazi party and the Labor Front (Figure 20).

Every one of these photographs illustrates the process of the identification of Hitler and Christ that had long been promoted via the use of words. Goebbels, who recounted his "conversion" to the Führer in his novel *Michael*, was as early as 1926 speaking of Hitler as a being capable of "accomplishing a miracle of light and faith in a skeptical and despairing world." Within the party, Gregor Strasser declared Hitler to be "the hero of the new fighters for liberty," and Rudolf Hess considered him to be "a great founder of religion who undoubtedly communicates an apodictic faith to his listeners."[106] Although the French wife of Count Reventlow was in the habit of introducing Hitler as "the future Messiah" at the meetings she organized in the early 1920s, Hitler, for his part, still regarded himself as "just a little Saint John." Joachim Fest compared the spirit of the first party members to that which animated the early Christian communities: "The masses seemed to understand even before he did that he was the miracle-man they had been waiting for and, as one commentator remarked at the time, they flocked to him 'as to a Saviour'."[107] But by September 5, 1923, at the second congress of the NSDAP in Nuremberg, Hitler exclaimed, "It is from our movement that redemption will come—that today is the feeling of millions. That has become almost a new religious faith!"[108] Ten years later, a Munich schoolteacher dictated the following text in a local school:

Just as Jesus liberated man from sin and hell, Hitler has saved the German people from perdition. Jesus and Hitler were both persecuted but, whereas Jesus was crucified, Hitler was appointed chancellor. Whereas the disciples of Jesus denied their master and abandoned him, the sixteen comrades[109] died for their Führer. It was the apostles who brought the work of their Lord to fulfillment. We hope that Hitler himself will be able to accomplish his own work. Jesus built for heaven. Hitler [builds] for the land of Germany.[110]

This exemplary and often-cited parallel between Hitler and Jesus sets out the reasons for Hitler's manifest superiority over Christ, leading up to the most essential reason of all: the construction in the here and now of the city of God on the *civitas terrena* (earthly city) of Germany. Moreover, the schoolteacher's dictation stemmed partly from Hitler himself, for a few years earlier, during a Christmas celebration held by a Munich section of the party, Hitler had declared that National Socialism "would realize the ideals of Christ. The task that Christ had undertaken but not been able to fulfill, he, Hitler, would carry to completion."[111]

But comparison was on the whole less frequent than identification pure and simple. One member of a consistory in Thuringe declared, "Christ has come to us through the person of Adolf Hitler."[112] Meanwhile, the bishop of the Mecklenburg Rendtorf publicly proclaimed himself in favor of "the Führer Adolf Hitler, whom God has sent us."[113] Such statements reflected perfectly what was evolving in the new Germany: an idolatrous cult that was simultaneously a radical auto-idolatrous movement. By June 1936, such was the gravity of the situation that the provisional Head Office of the Churches of the Reich addressed a letter directly to Hitler "to inform him of the concern of pastors at the frequent habit adopted by some of the faithful, who had taken to addressing to the Führer 'devotions in a form due to God alone'."[114]

The most famous example of this fusion of the new National Socialist drama with the religious liturgy was *The German Passion* 1933, produced by Richard Euringer, who assembled choirs of more than a thousand men, women, and girls for the performance. Hildegard Brenner has correctly pointed out that this spectacle recounting the death, sufferings, and resurrection of the German people was perfectly in tune with the expectations of the ideologues of the new Nationalist Socialist theater. They specifically recommended "the incarnation of the Christian spirit in the Teutonic-German body" and represented "the sacrifice of the Savior" as "the first and last model of the sacrifice of the Hero."[115] In *The German Passion* 1933, Hitler-Christ, the new Parsifal, was designated the "unknown soldier" who came back to life from among those who had died in the Great War and, after a long struggle (the Passion, in the strict sense of the expression) against the dark forces of the wicked spirit that dominated Germany, brought with him the "new Reich." As Klaus Vondung, a disciple of Voegelin, observed, the hero triumphed over death just as Christ did, and the immortality of the Führer was confirmed as that of an eternal survivor.[116]

This spectacle, frequently staged in the open air and synchronizing powerful scenic means with impressive crowd movements on stage, violent rhythm changes, and swathes of flags and emblems carried by uniformed cohorts, was one of the first put on by the *Thing* theatre. The word *Thing*, which designated a circular amphitheater, the open-air "ring" of the ancient Teutons also evoked the Wagnerian cult: "At the time of the ancient Teutons, the ancestors of our people, had a 'Ring' or 'Thing' where they would gather around their Führer."[117]

By 1935, twenty Thing theaters had been constructed and almost four hundred were planned throughout Germany (Figure 21). According to one ideologue, these amphitheaters, situated in spots "consecrated by history" and in many cases designed to accommodate more than ten thousand spectators, would make it possible, through the dramatic parable, for the people to internalize their recently rediscovered community. Another ideologue rejoiced that spectators and actors were "yoked together by the idea of the blood-fraternity that had created the community of the people." Yet another admired the way in which the *Erlebnis* of an artistic act could do away with individualism and solder together thousands of compatriots to form a single will. The declared function of the choral form of this kind of theater was "to educate the German people, with a view to mass rallies" and to "prepare the way for what would be the only possible form of a popular theater . . . and the battalions of *discipline, order, and obedience* from which henceforth poets would be recruited as well as actors and spectators."[118]

As Hildegard Brenner noted, the decline of Thing theater from 1935 on coincided with when it became virtually impossible to distinguish between such theater and the mass ceremonies and demonstrations organized by the regime in the streets and the stadiums. Today, however, it is hard to make out which representations served as models for which. The mission of Thing theater, just like the mission of the party ceremonies, was to succeed in creating "an absolute and invariable bond between the people as spectators and the people as actors."[119] For the common aim of all these spectacles was an integral part of them: an *Erlebnis* of the community that would wipe out all the class and generational conflicts that had divided it in the past:

> *August.*—Believe it or not, Papa, but that is the way it is. The young no longer pay any attention to those old slogans. . . . They are disappearing. . . . The class struggle is disappearing. . . .
> *Schneider.*—Oh, right. . . . And what are you living, then?
> *August.*—The *Volksgemeinschaft!*
> *Schneider.*—And is that not a slogan?
> *August.*—No, it's an *Erlebnis!*[120]

What was experienced was a myth that was lived because it was realized (or in the process of realization). Euringer, who wrote *The German Passion* 1933, formulated his own theses on Thing theater. The spectacle had to include as elements "fire, water, air, and earth, stone, the starry sky and the orbit of the sun." It was a matter not of "making legend live" but of "making everyday life itself a legend"; not of "taking mythology as a theme," but of "turning everyday life into myth." Anonymity for the actors had to be the rule, for this was theater about the people and its sacrifice. "The subject of Thing theater is the cult of the dead. The country's dead are rising up and the spirit's cry wells up from the stones. The subject of Thing theater is not 'art' but religion."[121]

November 9: The *Erlebnis* in Painting

In 1935, Hitler himself organized the takeover of this theatrical cult of the dead with the first staging, in Munich, of the new ceremony for the commemoration of the dead of November 9, 1923. In the preceding summer, after attending the Bayreuth festival, Hitler had gone to Neuschwanstein for a ceremony in honor of Richard Wagner, where Hitler declared that it was now up to him to take on the task of executing the plans of Louis II of Bavaria.[122] But he saw himself not so much as a patron but as the artist of artists, the prince described by Novalis, a sovereign organizing a spectacle "in which he himself is at once the poet, director, and hero of the play."

Although the blood of the Führer had not itself been shed for Germany, that of the sixteen members of the NSDAP who had fallen on November 9, 1923, at the time of the grotesque failed putsch in Munich, came to symbolize the sacrifice made to obtain the redemption of the *Volksgemeinschaft*. This blood progressively eclipsed that of those who had fallen in the Great War. Through its "sixteen bleeding martyrs" (*Blutzeugen*), victorious National Socialism retrospectively gave its own meaning to the war victims. In this way Hitler appropriated the millions of dead, to whom he seemed to be saying, "*Und Ihr habt doch gesiegt* [You did win after all]!"

Of all the National Socialist festivals that punctuated the time of the new Germany, the one on November 9 was most vehemently declared to be sacred. By honoring the dead on the very spot of their sacrifice (Munich's Feldherrnhalle, where Hitler had a large bronze plaque bearing the names of the dead erected in 1933), Hitler commemorated no less than the founding of the *Volksgemeinschaft*. He dedicated the first volume of *Mein Kampf* to these "martyrs of the movement," and the early editions of his book carried reproductions of the martyrs' portraits. It was their "sacrifice" that prompted his resolve to obtain power by legal means. The commemoration of his access to power on January 30, 1933, could thus be only a celebration of the resurrection of Germany, as was indeed proclaimed by all the speeches and songs of the time. The period between the Reichs—the *Zwischenreich*, the term the Nazis used to designate the Weimar period—was the time of the Passion and of struggle (*Kampfzeit*) against the spirit of evil. But the ceremony of November 9 commemorated both death and resurrection. Hans Jochen Gamm has justifiably compared it to a Passion play[123] in which the parade of Christian ritual was replaced by a solemn march by the movement's "veterans" all the way from the Bürgerbräukeller to the Feldherrnhalle. Later, Klaus Vondung revealed the full complexity of the ritual and showed how the Resurrection had been added to the Passion.[124]

In his dedication of *Mein Kampf* to the dead, Hitler declared that they had fallen "in a faithful belief in the resurrection of their people."[125] The ceremony of November 9 was designed to signify that resurrection, to testify that the "faithful belief" of the fallen had not been in vain and that the dream had now become reality. The ritual that Hitler inaugurated in 1935 and that remained unchanged until the war was made possible thanks to the completion of the Temples of the Heroes (*Ehrentempel*) on the Königsplatz. These were buildings that Hitler himself had conceived along with architect Ludwig Troost. Each of the two temples built in honor of the sixteen martyrs was designed to receive the bronze sarcophagi of eight heroes (Figure 22). Thus restructured, the Königsplatz could be transformed into a gigantic stage for the thousands of actors who symbolized the now resuscitated and redeemed people. In his speech given at the Bürgerbräukeller, as in all his speeches addressed to the "veterans," Hitler recalled the heroic history of the party, which had become a legend, but one that they had lived together. The sixteen martyrs were now to become a part of "German immortality"; because they had only sensed the advent of the Reich but had not been able to see it, the Reich now had to see them. Hitler, who in *Mein Kampf* had expressed his indignation that the National Government had refused those heroes a communal burial, now had their bodies exhumed and exhibited in the Feldherrnhalle on November 8. Late at night he went there in an open car, passing slowly through the "victory gateway," through the torches, flags, and assembled crowd. Alone he climbed the red-carpeted steps that separated the crowd from the sacred precinct. He meditated for a long time before each of the coffins lined up against a background of brown draperies. The urns blazing above the sixteen catafalques, along with the torches of the SA and SS units and the smoke spiraling up from them, added to the manifest solemnity of the moment and the place. Two of the most productive authors in the service of Goebbels had been detailed to impart the right meaning to the liturgy. Both likened the rising steps of the Feldherrnhalle to a sacred altar that, through the blood of the dead, opened the way to eternity. The glory radiating from this altar shed its light on the assembled people. Herbert Böhme had written a piece for the occasion entitled *Cantata for November 9*:

The earth, through your death, was dying.
With your glory our life begins . . .
Führer, now step out of the hall of glory,
Let the shadows of the night fall away from you,
There where you held the torch, at the steps of death.
Carry faith before us in the full light,
So that the very stones tremble at the power of your tread.[126]

Hitler, who as early as 1923 had compared defeated Germany to Christ dying on the cross, now emerged transfigured. He was restoring the glory of the martyrs and, as a providential survivor from the kingdom of the dead, carried with him the salvation of the eternal Reich. "He stands before us like a statue, already beyond all earthly measurement," commented the *Völkischer Beobachter* the following day: "A new man has emerged from the depths of the people. He has established a new doctrine, set up new tablets, created a new people, which he has raised up from those same depths, the depths from which arise great poems—poems from mothers, blood, and the soil."[127] Sixty thousand party members filed past the dead in Hitler's wake. As Moses descended from Sinai to bring God's commandments to his people, and as Christ rose from the dead to keep faith with his promise, Hitler brought back from the realm of the dead commandments written in blood for his people to obey and thereby acquire form and eternity. But the great innovation of 1935 was that this first resurrection was followed by a second, in which the eternity of the Reich was consigned to stone.

The next day, November 9, the traditional procession of the veterans, clad in their 1923 uniforms (a special office had been set up to produce exact replicas of them) passed from the historic beer hall to the Feldherrnhalle, along the very route taken in 1923, until it reached the spot where the victims had fallen. There shots from sixteen cannons rang out and, after a preliminary roll call of names, Hitler placed a wreath at the foot of a large memorial plaque. Bearing the coffins along with it, the procession proceeded toward the Temples of the Heroes. Hitler marched at its head with a small group of the faithful (Figure 23), preceded by the "flag of blood" (*Blut fahne*) which had been gathered up on that day in 1923. (Ever since the second party congress in 1926 this relic had been said to possess the power to transmit new strength purely by contact. But it was shown publicly only on these two annual occasions.) Next came the "order of the blood," which comprised all the survivors from the failed putsch, followed by the great mass of party members. The route was marked by 240 tall pylons draped in red, on which stood urns in which the eternal flame of memory burned. The names of the movement's dead and wounded were recited as the slow procession moved forward, and loudspeakers diffused party songs and the national anthem. When it reached the Königsplatz, the procession deposited the coffins in front of the two temples. Goebbels then proceeded to make a last roll call (borrowed from the Fascist ritual of the Italians): one after another the names of each of the sixteen martyrs were called, and each was followed by a cry of "Present!" from a chorus of Hitler Youth members. The coffins were then lowered into the temples' depths but remained exposed to the open air as Hitler had decreed (Figure 24). "For us," he declared, "they are not dead. These temples are not tombs but represent an eternal watch (*eine Ewige Wache*). They are here for Germany and [they] watch (*wachen*) over our people. They lie here as the true martyrs of our movement." His decision to make this day forever a "festival of the German nation" rested on the fact that it had fallen to these men who had died for their true faith "once more to raise up the German people."[128] The temples kept watch over the movement's martyrs, but those martyrs *were not dead.*

The two Temples of the Heroes were part of a vast set of edifices known as the "Constructions of the Führer," buildings commissioned by Hitler, the fabrication of which he even supervised personally. An official publication described them as "an autopresentation of the most arch-original powers of the *Kultur* of a reawakened people conscious of its race, the incarnation of a faith transformed into stone."[129] The National Socialist system of thought proceeded by way of a series of identifications and takeovers: the dead of the Great War lived on in the movement's "martyrs," those martyrs lived on in Hitler. All were perpetuated in these stone temples and, through them, perpetuated forever in the German people. The same blood flowed in the veins of men as in the veins of the stone quarried from German soil. The same soul fortified the same bodies in their eternal struggle to survive beyond their own selves (Figure 25). Georges Bataille sensed this when he wrote in 1929, "In the morphological process, human beings seem to represent simply a stage between monkeys and great buildings. Forms have become increasingly static and dominant. So the human order has from the start been a part of the architectural order, which is simply a development from it."[130] Official discourse, however, described the reverse of such a development, with the architectural order determining the human order:

In these buildings the Führer shapes the most noble characteristics of the German community. In them, the art of building educates a new people. The artistic genius of the creator of the German *Weltanschauung* has given them the style of heroism that leads to victory the struggle of decisiveness against disintegration and collapse. The spiritual greatness eternalized in stone will continue, even in the most distant future, to spread the heroic spirit of its creator throughout the entire people.[131]

In 1938, Werner Rittich again stressed the function of exemplarity, which had the power to trace the future of the community; but the body of the martyr, identified with a body of stone, almost explicitly called on the people, in its turn, to become embodied in stone:

The sixteen martyrs who have found a common tomb and who now, *in the midst of life*, mount "an eternal watch" are, through their willing availability and their sacrifice, a permanent example for the entire people, a permanent exhortation to fulfill one's duty and one's own commitments and to make one's own sacrifice.[132]

This statement confirms the perfect circularity of this formational movement, conceived as the autoformation (*die Selbstgestaltung*) of the German people through its perpetual resurrection in stone, thanks to the sacrifice made by each individual for the salvation of all. The life of the present community came from stone and would return to stone so that the community of the future would live. Within this circle, the figure of the Führer played a role that was symmetrical to the role of architecture: he, the eternal survivor, had emerged as Savior from the "shadows of the night," to teach his people to save itself. He was at once the mediator and the end, as was forthrightly proclaimed in the last line of one of the songs sung by the members of the Hitler Youth organization: "You alone, my Führer, are both the way and the goal!"[133] Never far away was *Parsifal,* with the words that Wagner gave the chorus to bring the opera to its conclusion: *"Höchsten Heiles Wunder! Erlösung dem Erlöser!"* ("Miracle of supreme salvation! Redemption for the Redeemer!").

Lest anyone escape the *Erlebnis* of the sacred moment, the ceremony of November 9 was broadcast from every public radio station in Germany. Yet this *Erlebnis*—surely one of the regime's key words—then had to be prolonged in both time and space, to extend its sway over all: newsreels and newspaper photographs played their role here while the songs and poems of the ceremony were diffused by countless brochures, to be eventually reproduced in school textbooks.

Once the diffusion of filmed images was over, however, all that remained were the photographs, whose news value, so essential to the *Erlebnis,* soon faded. As Roland Barthes has observed, "Every photograph is a certificate of presence, but *it is without future,*" for in the end it "produces death while trying to preserve life."[134] In the Nazi apparatus for the production of images, the role of preserving life fell instead to painting. While the value of the photographic image remained linked with the fleeting moment of the *Erlebnis,* affording it only a weak temporal extension, the job of a painting, by contrast, was to reactualize the *Erlebnis* in perpetuity, conferring upon it the eternal value that was immanent in it.

In 1942, Paul Herrmann painted two works for the Great Exhibition of German Art in Munich. They were titled *Und Ihr habt doch geseigt* (You Did Win After All) (Figure 26) and *Die Fahne* (The Flag) (Figure 27), and each was a copy of a famous photograph of the November 9 ceremony taken by Heinrich Hoffmann, Hitler's photographer and friend. Together with Hoffmann, Hitler had selected the works to be shown in the first Great Exhibition of 1937, but thereafter Hoffmann alone was responsible for the selection. He enjoyed the absolute confidence of the Führer, for he was at once Hitler's eye and his mirror and was totally wedded to Hitler's *Weltanschauung.* The photograph that inspired *Die Fahne* was all the more securely lodged in people's memories because it had been used as the cover for the November 11, 1937, issue of *Illustrierter Beobachter* (Figure 28).

In the painting, only a few of the photograph's details had been changed. In the upper part, a banner and the overhead tram wires had been eliminated. The tram rails were not blanked out but were repositioned to present a more imposing axial perspective and lead straight into the advancing Führer's group. The raison d'être of this painting was clearly to change the status of the image from mechanical to artistic—that is, to charge it with the *Weltanschauung* and the creative values of the community. Clearly it was not the personal genius of the artist that gave the painting its value. As with the Temples of the Heroes built by Troost, the value could stem only from "the artistic genius of the creator of the German *Weltanschauung*"—in other words, the Führer. This is precisely why these two works by Herrmann, which consecrated November 9, were hung one on each side of a portrait of the Führer in battledress painted by Hans Schachinger. The resulting triptych greeted the visitor to the 1942 Great Exhibition as he entered, as if addressing him with a solemn injunction.[135] The commentary provided by art theorist Robert Scholz was, in the very banality of its vaguely Kantian tone, altogether unequivocal. It reminded the reader of the Futurist painters' insistence that the public should "completely forget its intellectual culture, in order not to *take possession* of the work of art, but to *surrender* to it utterly":[136]

The right way to accede to art is immediately to take in what the artist is expressing, without allowing the intellect to intervene. The authentic work of art addresses the forces of the heart [*Gemüt*], not those of the intellect. It is not what the intellect seizes upon when faced by a work of art, but solely whatever the heart feels that, rising above fleeting impressions, becomes the *Erlebnis* that fashions the spectator. It is upon this relationship that concentrates upon the Erlebnis that a true rapport between art and the people can be founded. . . .

The intention of National Socialist artistic practice with regard to the arts, and likewise the aim of the Great Exhibitions of German art in Munich, is to lead the people immediately to the *Erlebnis* of this work that has emerged from the creativeness of this age, a work in which the *Erlebnis* of the age, given form by art, is mirrored and reflected by the spectator [*Betrachter*], thereby enabling him to participate in the superior will of the community, which has been given a visible form in works of art. . . . By giving the determination of an image to the indeterminate will [of the people], the artist creates the values of the *Erlebnis* and the contents of the representations that shape the people into a community of visions [*Gemeinschaft der Anschauungen*], because these are created out of the strengths and wishes of the people.[137]

It was all the more pressing that this "community of visions" engendered by the shared *Erlebnis* should be refounded through the dignity of art because in that year, 1942, the war was more than ever demanding sacrifice from every individual, for love of the Führer and the survival of the community. Furthermore, given that the war was inevitably hampering the organization of festivals and ceremonies, the "cultural work" of artists was becoming ever more important for supporting and strengthening the community of visions.

In what respect could painting be more successful than photography at ensuring the immediacy of the *Erlebnis* that was supposed to lead the spectator "to take part in the superior will of the community"—in other words, to make sacrifices? What painting added to the black and white of the mechanical images reproduced in the press and pamphlets—over and above the personal touch that signaled the visible presence of the artist's soul—was color. In the general consciousness as much as in the tradition of European aesthetics, from the writings of the Church Fathers down to those of Diderot, Hegel, and Matisse, color was always perceived and presented by theorists as an affirmation of sensuality, the special medium for conveying a sense of life. In other words, while photography targeted recollections and the memory, painting, through color, targeted the present. To look at a painting was not only to see history in the present, but also to feel it and repeat it within oneself; it was to make one's own behavior, one's *Haltung*, conform to the demands of the destiny of the community. Werner Rittich wrote:

In many of the works [in this exhibition] we see the incarnation of behavior (*Haltung*) that is liberated from individual actions and destinies, yet that extends the latter and incorporates them into its importance. . . . The representation of the march of November 9 here grows into an image that echoes and unifies celebration and honor duly rendered, one's consciously accepted responsibility for one's own destiny and one's desire to live life to the full, the past and the present, the high deed and the people's participation [*Teilnahme*] in it.[138]

If the stone of the temples sheltering the heroes was designed to propagate faith, what the regime demanded of images was that they should become integrated into the liturgy of a now-legendary everyday life in order to encourage, through the *Erlebnis*, the participation that was so necessary for the end product of "a faith transformed into stone."

3

EXHIBITING THE GENIUS

> He [the Aryan] is the Prometheus of mankind from whose bright forehead the divine spark of genius has sprung at all times, forever kindling anew that fire of knowledge which illumined the night of silent mysteries and thus caused man to climb the path to mastery over the other beings of this earth.
>
> —A. Hitler, *Mein Kampf*

National Socialism's faith in itself rested in its belief in the creative genius of the Aryan race. These creative faculties might have been latent in certain periods of history but, according to Hitler, they needed to "be aroused to practical realization by certain outward conditions."[1] To make the genius of the race visible to that race was to restore its faith in itself by making it conscious of its historic mission. Conversely, that restored self-confidence made it possible to see clearly once more: "It is faith in our people that . . . has restored our sight and united us all."[2] All the rhetoric of *Mein Kampf*, the later speeches of Hitler, and much of the general Nazi discourse was ruled by the opposition between the visible and the invisible, the seer and the blind man, appearance and disappearance. It was a system of oppositions that borrowed in particular from the Christian tradition but also from a long tradition of literature on the subject of art. Two fundamental sources of authority were thus interlocked in a conventional fashion: God, to whom man submits as his creature, and creative man, who by his very nature is a law unto himself. These two sources were together used to legitimate anti-Semitism as a fight necessary for the survival of all culture.

The Visibility of the Aryan Genius:
A National Christianity

Elaborating his own myth, Hitler first synchronized the break in his own life with the break in history. The painter he was initially made himself into a politician precisely at the moment of the German defeat. He appeared as he truly was just as Germany was disappearing. His conversion took the violent form of a blinding followed by illumination. His eyesight was affected by gas in October 1918, and it was just as he was hearing of the capitulation that "suddenly, everything went black before [his] eyes" and he feared he was "going blind forever." Revelation came to him through "the voice of [his] conscience," which was the conscience of his country: "Only now did I see how all personal suffering vanishes in comparison with the misfortune of the Fatherland." This remark made in 1924, in which he linked his vision of collective suffering with the disappearance of his own suffering, echoed the major principle set out as early as 1920 in the party manifesto: "The general interest overrides individual interests [*Gemeinnutz geht vor Eigennutz*]." Immediately he saw what the cause of all the suffering was: "In these nights hatred grew in me—hatred for those responsible for this deed [of capitulation]. . . . There is no making pacts with Jews; there can be only the hard either-or. I, for my part, decided to go into politics."[3]

The distress of his country had changed Hitler's outlook. His view was no longer that of a self-centered artist with a limited visual horizon. It now embraced the destiny of the whole world and was thus transmuted into a veritable world vision. This *Weltanschauung* suddenly gave him new and sharper perceptions. He no longer stopped short at the surface of things but plunged into darkness, now perceiving a reality that had remained concealed from the painter: the war between nations had concealed the Jews' war against *Kultur*, not in Germany alone but throughout the whole of Europe.

This biographical myth is what gave *Mein Kampf* its structure and served as a matrix for Hitler: light against darkness, health against sickness, the visible against the invisible, form against formlessness, culture against decadence, Aryan against Jew.

The value of the various races could be measured by their ability or inability to emerge from historical obscurity and by their capacity or incapacity to produce a *Kultur* that is visible: "If we were to divide mankind into three groups— the founders of culture [*Kulturbegründer*], the bearers of culture [*Kulturträger*], [and] the destroyers of culture [*Kulturzerstörer*]—only the Aryan could be considered the representative of the first group." The instinct to preserve, although subjectively the same for every race, differed in each case through "the form of its practical realization."[4] The value of a race could thus be measured by its *Kultur*, understood as "the realized form in which a race preserved itself." At several points, Hitler's text establishes the central opposition between the Aryan and the Jew as the Aryan being a producer and a the Jew being a destroyer of what is visible. The other races were merely *Kulturträger*, "lower peoples [that] became the first technical instrument in the service of a developing [Aryan] *Kultur*."[5]

Hitler set up a primary opposition between *idealism* and *egoism*. For an Aryan, the instinct for preservation took the form of sacrifice in the name of the community: "Not in his intellectual gifts lies the source of the Aryan's capacity for creating and building *Kultur*," but in his "self-sacrificing will" to give his personal labor and, if necessary, his life for others. "The basic attitude from which such activity arises, we call—to distinguish it from egoism and selfishness—*idealism*."

Idealism "alone formed from pure spirit the creative force which, by a unique pairing of the brutal fist and the intellectual genius, created the monuments of human *Kultur*." Idealism, which meant, quite simply, "the subordination of the interests and life of an individual to the community," thus corresponded to "the ultimate will of Nature": it made men into "a dust particle of that order which shapes and forms the whole universe."

It was in this respect that the Jew was radically opposed to the Aryan: his instinct for preservation was more powerful but "his will to sacrifice" went no further than "a simple instinct of self-preservation."[6] The reason that the Jew stood in "the strongest possible contrast" to the Aryan was that he lacked the very thing that makes a *Kulturvolk* (people of culture): namely, an "idealistic way of thinking." Everything about this egoistical people was a matter of appearances.

Its sense of sacrifice was merely *apparent*: it was no more than "a very primitive gregarious instinct" that vanished as soon as the danger had passed. Its intellectual faculties were no more than *apparent*, and it had no more than an *appearance* of culture (*Scheinkultur*). The Jew had nothing of his own. As for his state, that was *invisible* because "territorially, it was *frontierless*." The limitless (*unbegrenzt*) nature of his state had the effect of rendering him invisible unless he was masked. As Hitler one day confided to Hermann Rauschning, "Israel hides behind England, behind France, and behind the United States. Even when we have ejected the Jew from Germany, still he will always remain our world enemy."[7]

At a later stage, Hitlerian discourse set up a more specific opposition between Aryan-Christian visibility and the invisible Jew. Thus, *"One of the most obvious manifestations of decay* in the old Reich was the slow decline of the level of the *Kultur*," which was opposed by *Zivilisation*, which is "hostile to a truly high standard of thinking and living." Toward the end of the nineteenth century, "an element began to intrude into our art, [an element that was] foreign," and amid this degeneration of art one could already detect "the political collapse which later became *more visible*."[8] It was the same sickness that affected the art of the German people, its physical body, and its body politic. But caring for "the outward form of a sickness, its symptom which *strikes the eye* [and is] easier to see and discover than the inner cause" was not enough.[9] It was also important to *perceive*, through the detectable symptoms, that the *"less visible* causes" for the cultural and political debacle lay in the impurity of the blood.

For *völkisch* Hitler, by 1922 the struggle against the Jew was already clearly identified with the *Kulturkampf* of Bismarck's Reich. The "fight for art" (*Kampf um die Kunst*) of the Nazis was a continuation of the struggle against *Zivilisation* and the "ideas of 1789": "It is a struggle which began nearly 120 years ago, at the moment when the Jew was granted civic rights in the European States. The political emancipation of the Jews was the beginning of an attack of delirium." The attack was led

by a people of robbers. [The Jew] has never founded any *Kultur*, though he has destroyed cultures by the hundreds. He possesses nothing of his own creation to which he can point. Everything that he has is stolen. Foreign peoples, foreign workmen build him his temples. . . . He has no art of his own: bit by bit he has stolen it all from the other peoples or has watched them at work and then made his copy. He does not even know how merely to preserve the precious things which others have created: as he turns the treasures over in his hand they are transformed into dirt and dung.[10]

Two years later, *Mein Kampf* resumed and further developed this theme of the anti-artist Jew. "We must always bear in mind . . . that there has never been a Jewish art and accordingly there is none today either." The Jew only "takes over foreign culture, imitating it or rather ruining it. . . . The best proof of this is that he is mostly found in the art that seems to require the least original invention, the art of acting." Even here, however, he was no more than "an imitative ape," a "pitiful comedian." His corrosive action on all cultures was like that of parasitic plants: "Wherever he appears, the host people dies out after a shorter or longer period."[11]

Of course this rhetoric that opposed the Aryan creator to the Jew who had neither art nor culture was not new, nor was it of German let alone Nazi origin. Suffice it to remind the reader at this point that in France this rhetoric permeated the writings of Hippolyte Taine, Ernest Renan, Georges Vacher de Lapouge, Gustave Le Bon, and Charles Maurras. "The Semite has no creative faculty; in contrast, the Aryan is inventive," wrote Edouard Drumont forty years before *Mein Kampf* in *La France juive* (*Jewish France*), which ran into as many as 114 editions in the year of its publication.[12] For Hitler and many others, the absence of an art of its own was proof that this Jewish people with no "visible ideal" threatened to return the Earth to its original darkness.

In contrast, it was the Aryan's idealism, his ability to give visible form to the common ideal of his race, that made him "the Prometheus of mankind." One wonders whether Hitler, who was constantly invoking providence, knew that the name Prometheus meant "the foreseeing one." Whether he did or not, in *Mein Kampf* Prometheus became the sacrificial figure who symbolized the great principle of the Nazi party: "The general interest overrides personal interest." And just as Hitler's best friend Dietrich Eckart called the Aryan a *Lichtmensch* or "man

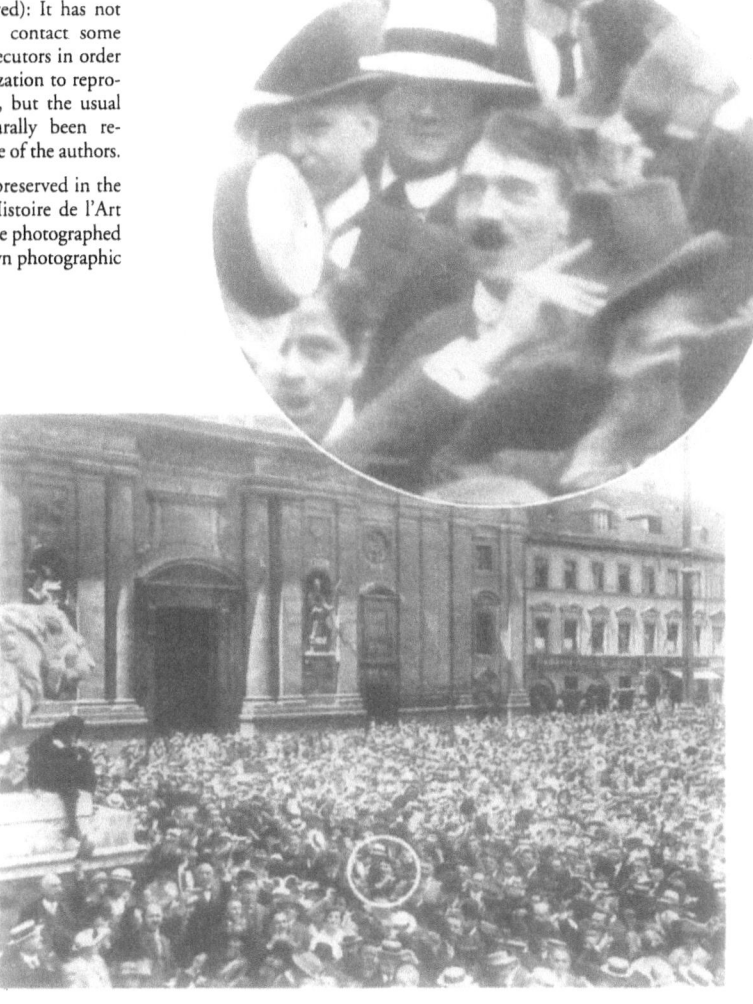

1. Hitler in the crowd assembled in front of the Fedlherrnhalle in Munich at the time of the declaration of war, August 2, 1914. Photo by Heinrich Hoffmann. Published in Hoffmann (ed.), *Hitler wie ihn keiner kennt: 100 Bilddokumente aus dem Leben des Führers*, Introduction by Baldur von Schirach (Berlin: Zeitgeschichte-Verlag, 1940; originally published 1932), no pagination. Document preserved in the Bibliothèque de l'Institut d'Histoire de l'Art de Strasbourg.

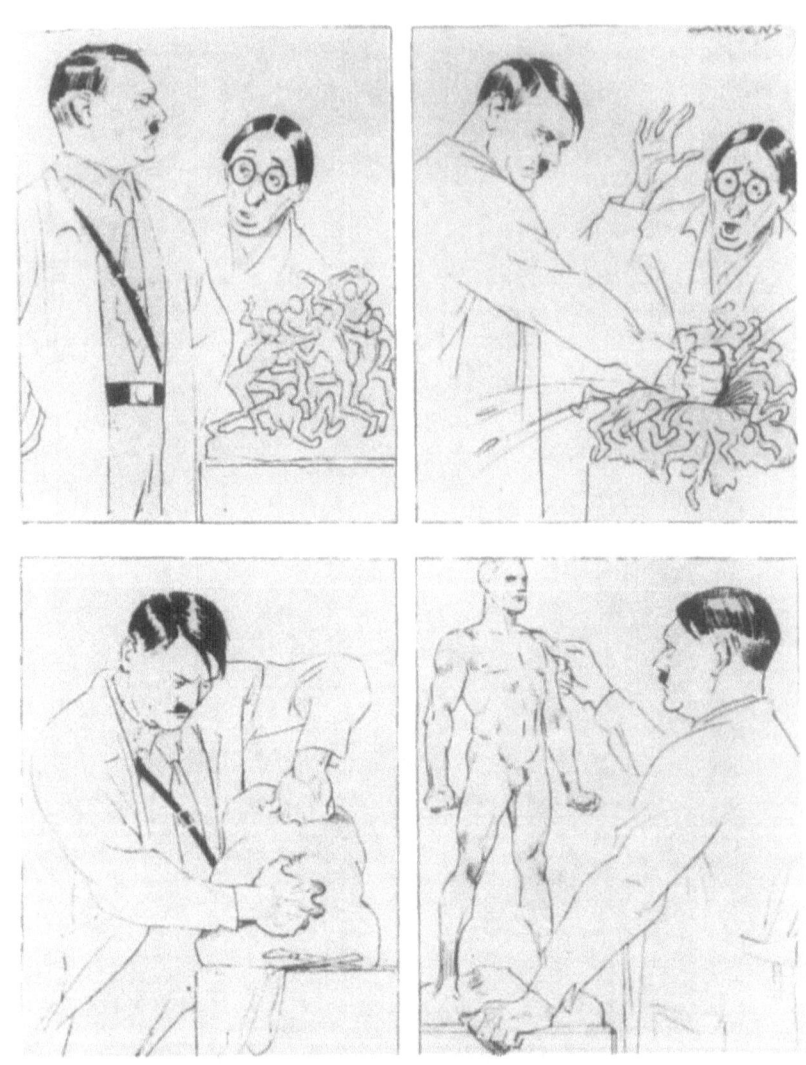

2.   O. Garvens, "The Sculptor of Germany,"
Kladderadatsch, 1933, vol. 46, no. 49, p. 7. RR.

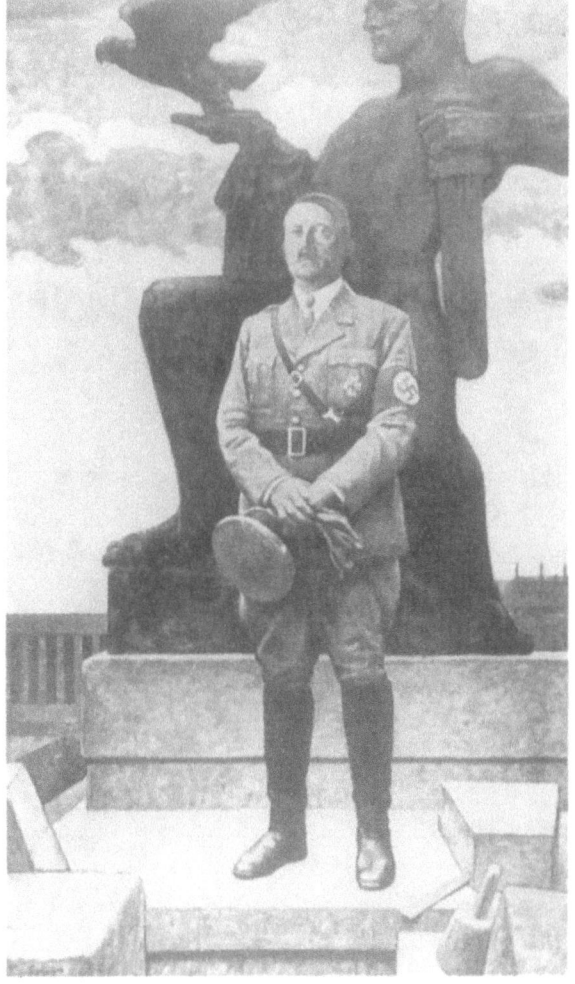

3. Fritz Erler, *Portrait of the Führer*, circa 1939. Exhibited in the Great Exhibition of German Art, 1939. Photo by Zentralinstitut für Kunstgeschichte, Munich.

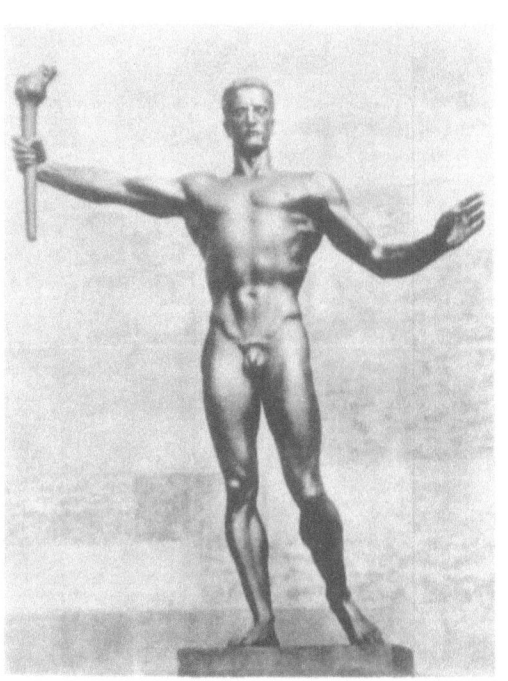 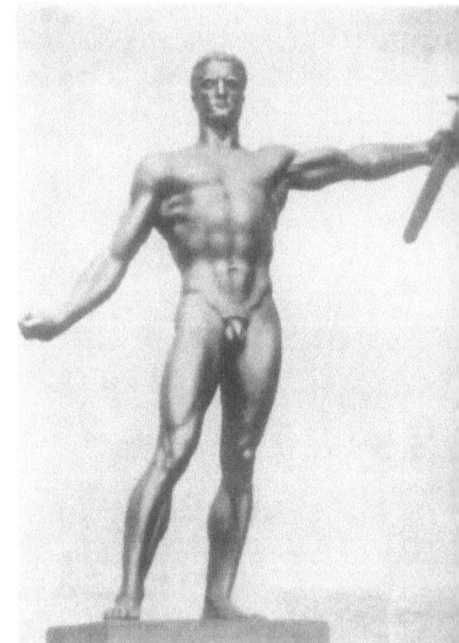

4ab. Arno Breker, *The Party* and *The Army* (bronzes).
Court of Honor of the Chancellery of the Reich,
Berlin, 1938. Photos by AKG Paris.

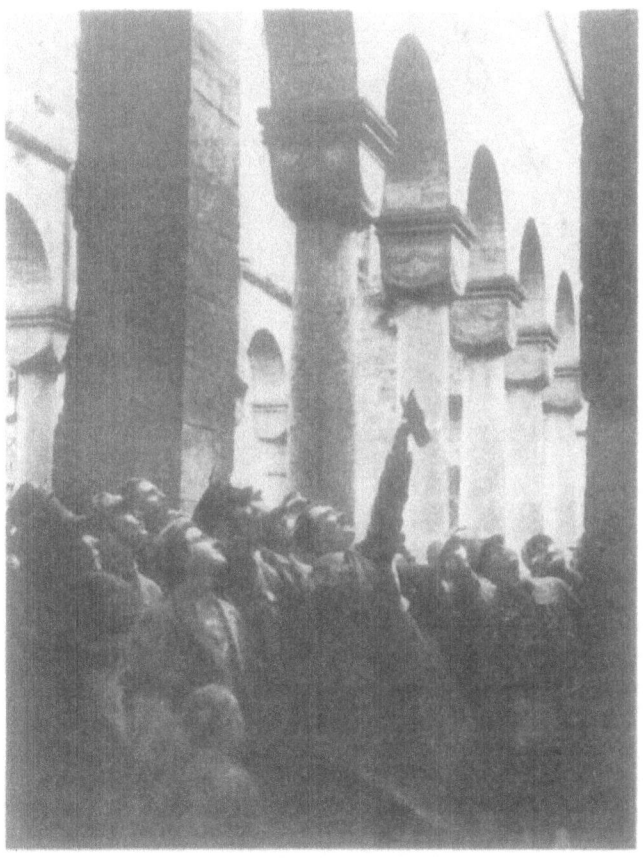

5. "Hitler, the Architect, showing the SA around an ancient cloister at Paulinzella in Thuringe." Photo by Heinrich Hoffmann. Published in Hoffmann (ed.), *Hitler wie ihn keiner kennt.* Document preserved in the Bibliothèque de l'Institut d'Histoire de l'Art de Strasbourg.

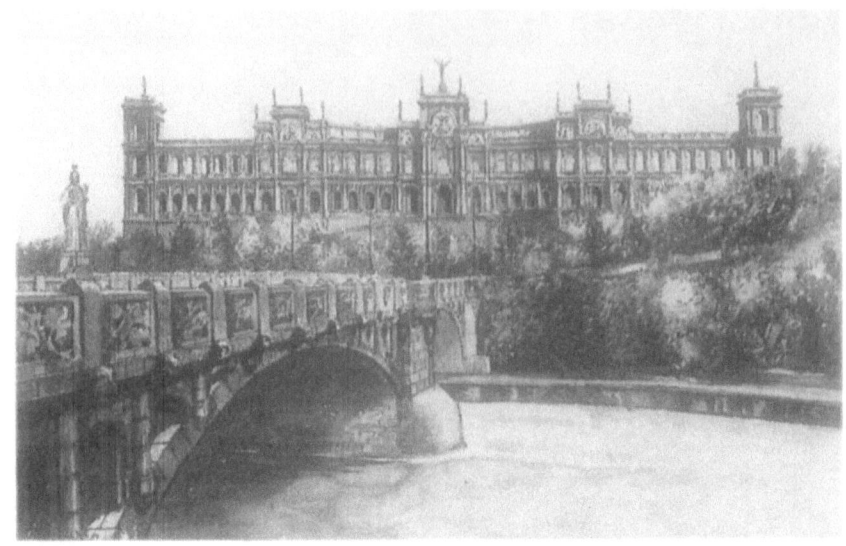

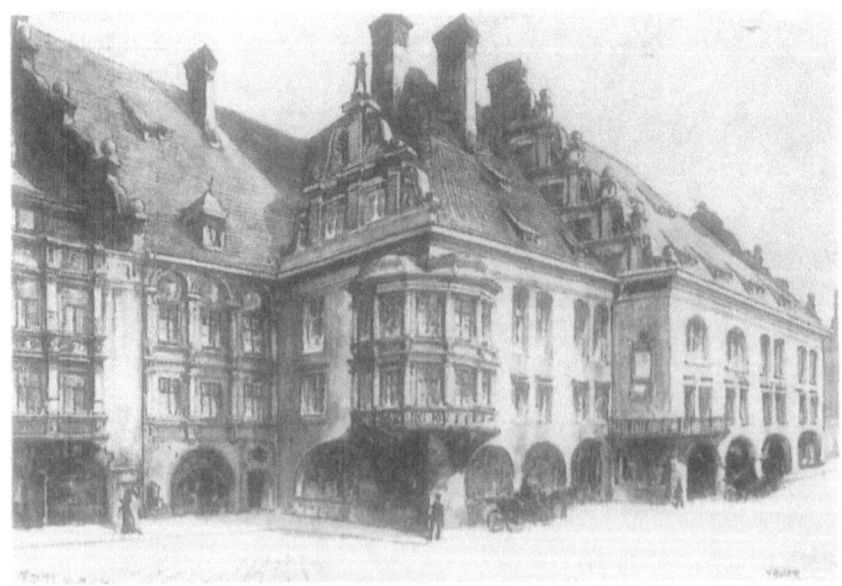

6. *(top)* Adolf Hitler, *The Maximilianeum and the Maximilian Bridge in Munich, 1913–1914* (watercolor). Photo by August Priesack, Munich.

7. *(bottom)* Adolf Hitler, *The Hofbraühaus, Munich, 1913–1914* (watercolor). Photo by August Priesack, Munich.

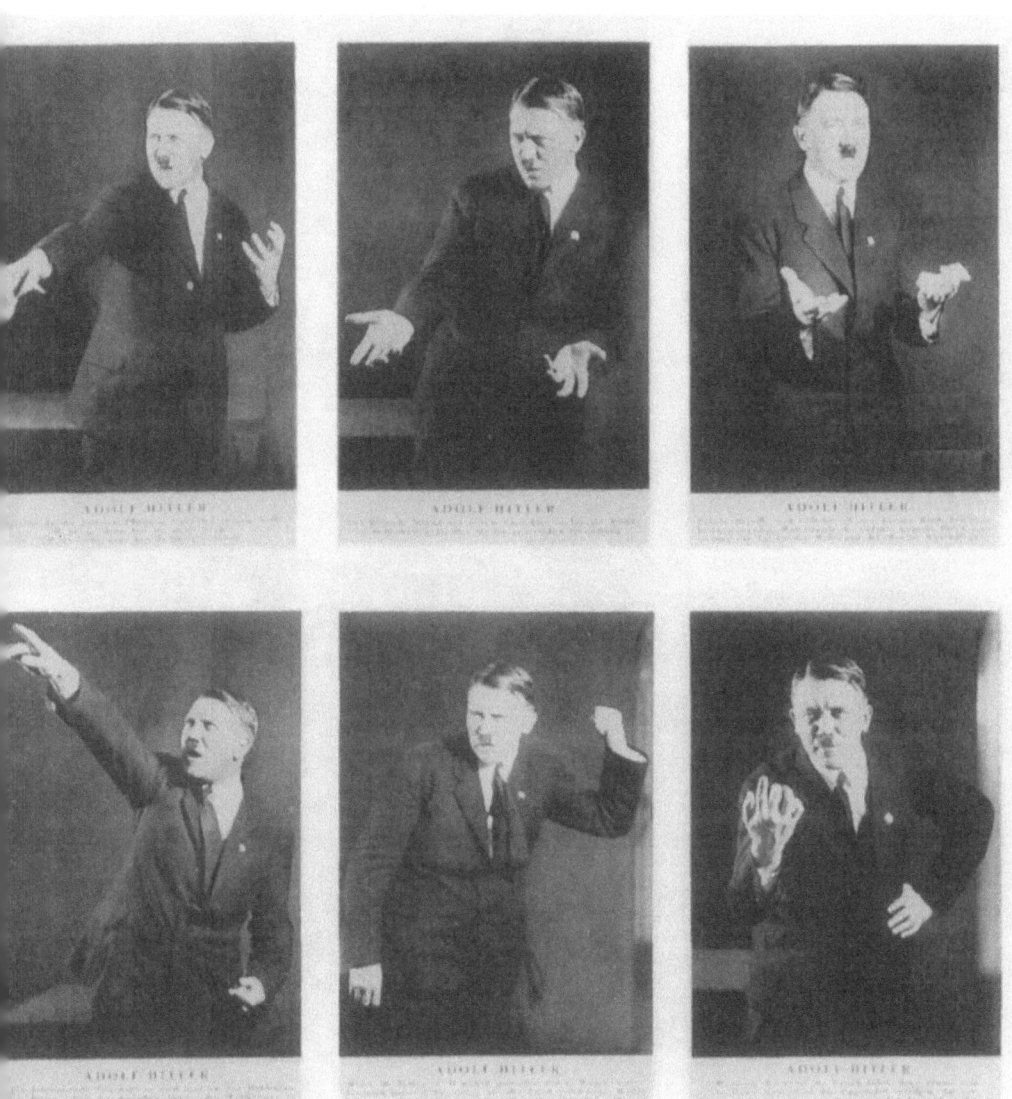

8. Adolf Hitler, before August 1927: Series of six postcards. Photos by Heinrich Hoffmann. Photo by Rudolf Herz, Munich.

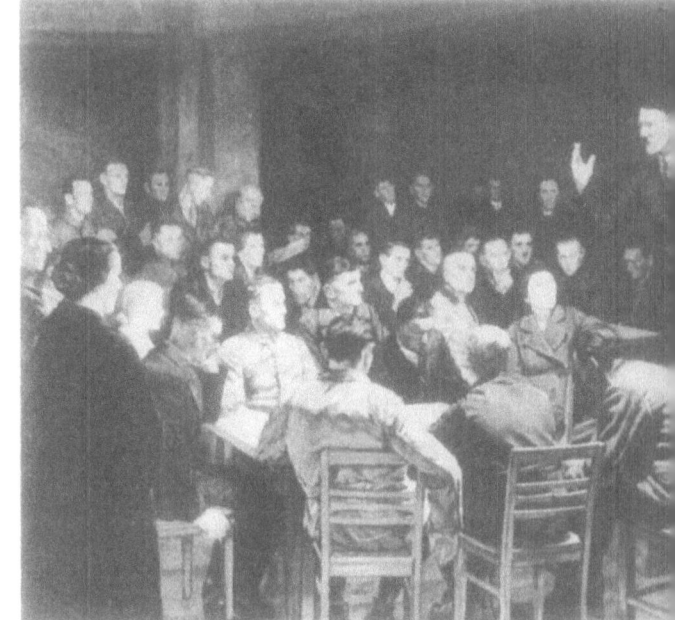

9. *(right)* Hermann Hoyer, *In the Beginning Was the Word* (oil on canvas), circa 1937. Exhibited in the Great Exhibition of German Art, 1937. Photo by Zentralinstitut für Kunstgeschichte, Munich.

10. *(below)* Arthur Kampf, *Fichte's Speech to the German Nation* (fresco), circa 1942, Hall of the University of Berlin. Published in *Die Kunst im Deutschen Reich* (Art in the German empire), 1943, no. 2, pp. 36–37. Document preserved in the Bibliothèque de l'Institut d'Histoire de l'Art de Strasbourg.

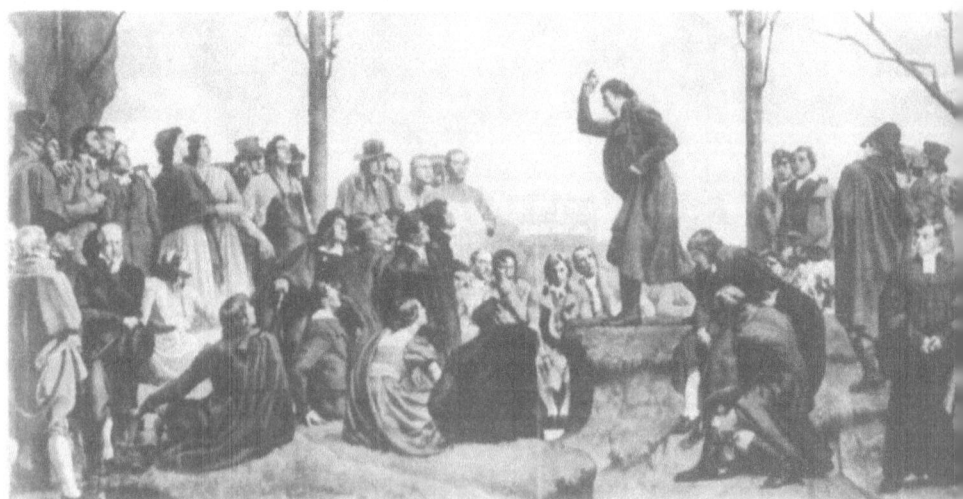

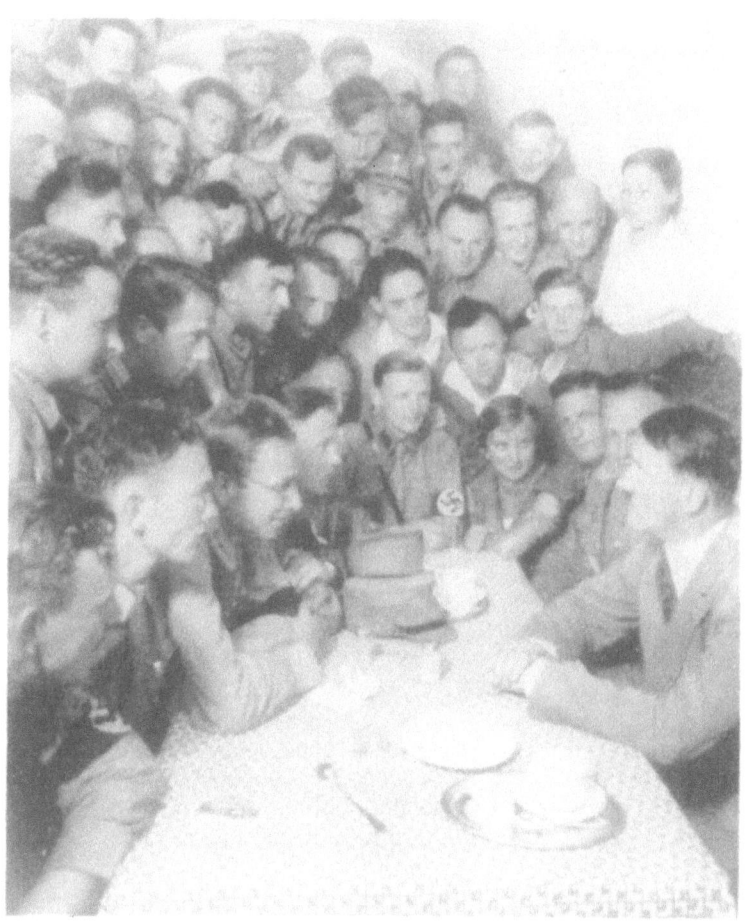

11. In the Munich Brown House: "How their eyes shine when the Führer is close to them!" circa 1932. Photo by Heinrich Hoffmann. Published in Hoffmann (ed.), *Hitler wie ihn keiner kennt.* Document preserved in the Bibliothèque de l'Institut d'Histoire de l'Art de Strasbourg.

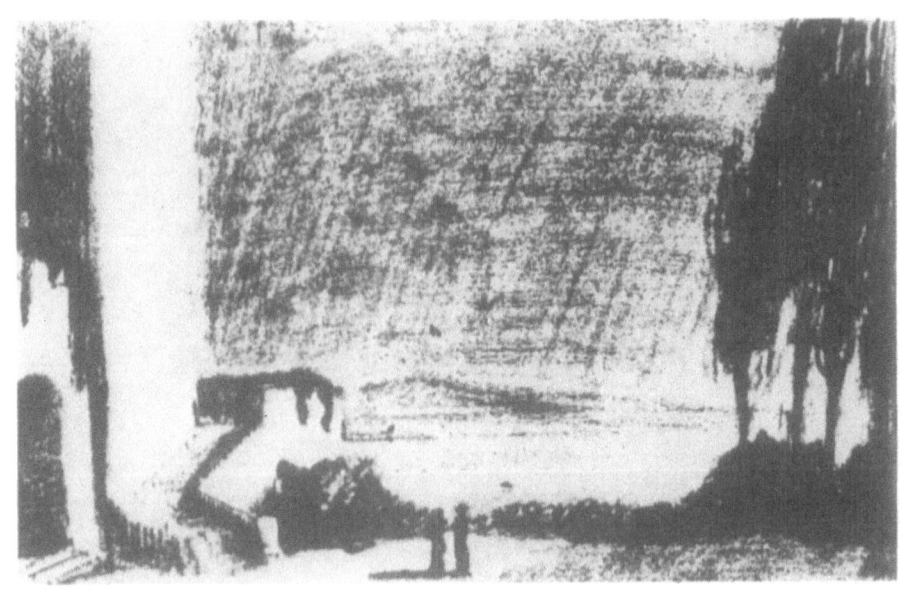

12. Adolf Hitler, *Sketch for Wagner's Tristan and Isolde*, act 2, circa 1925–26. Sketch presented to Albert Speer by Hitler. RR.

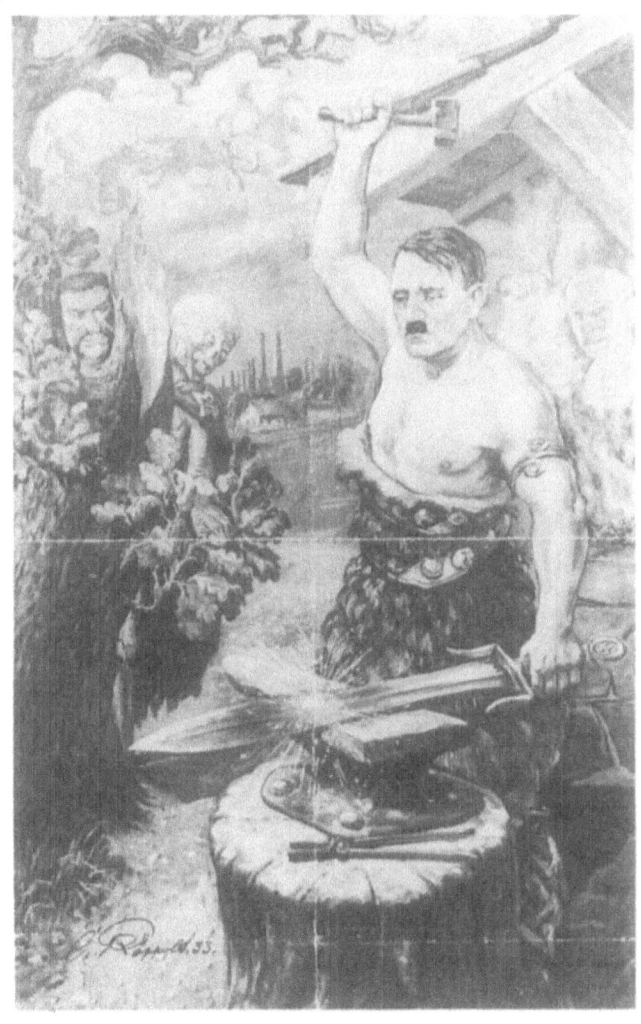

13. L. Röppold, popular
poster, 1933. Photo by
Württembergisches
Landesmuseum, Stuttgart.

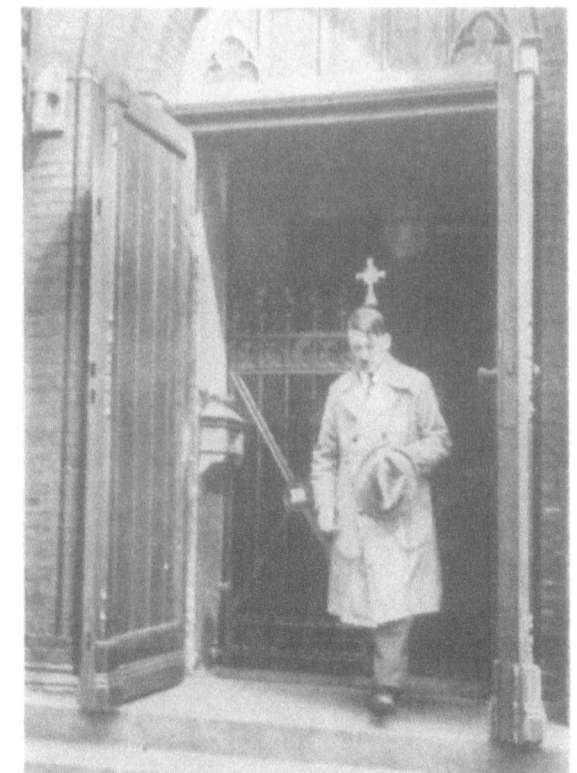

14. *(right)* "A chance becomes a symbol: Adolf Hitler, said to be a 'heretic,' emerging from the church of Wilhelmshaven," circa 1932. Photo by Heinrich Hoffmann. Published in Hoffmann, *Hitler wie ihn keiner kennt.* Photo by Bayerische Staatsbibliothek, Munich.

15. *(below)* A "private altar," circa 1937. Photo by Bundesarchiv, Coblenz (Image no. 146/69/55/50).

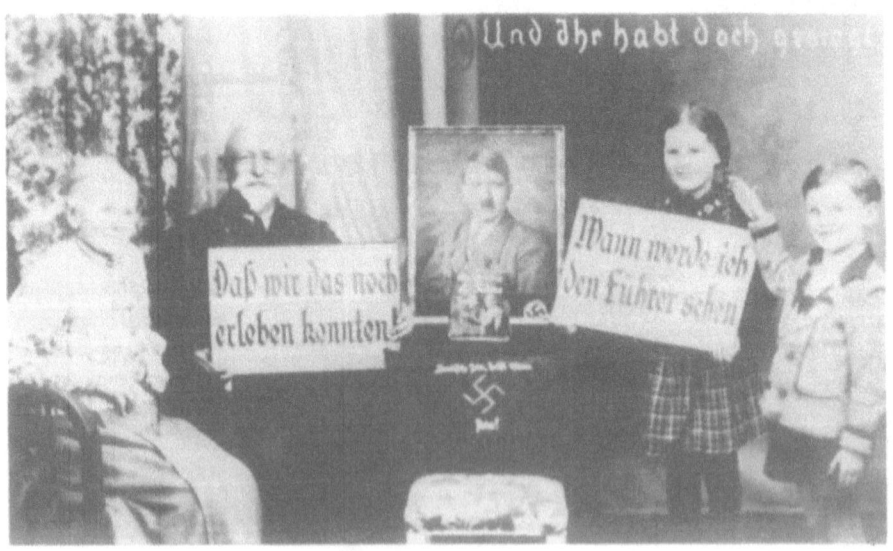

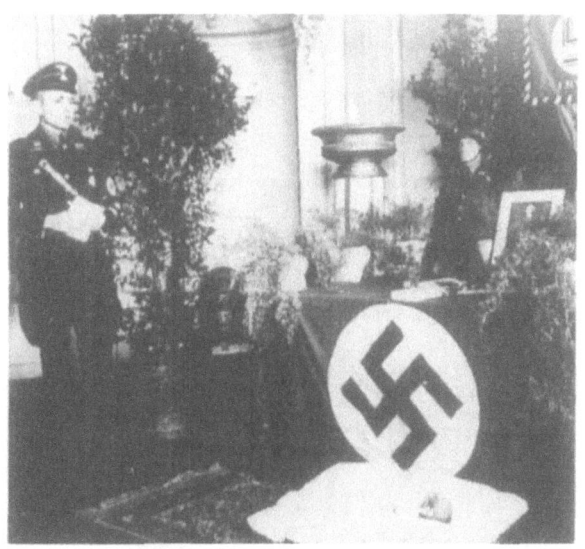

16. The "naming ceremony" replaces baptism. Photo by Bundesarchiv, Coblenz (Image no. 146/69 62 A/64).

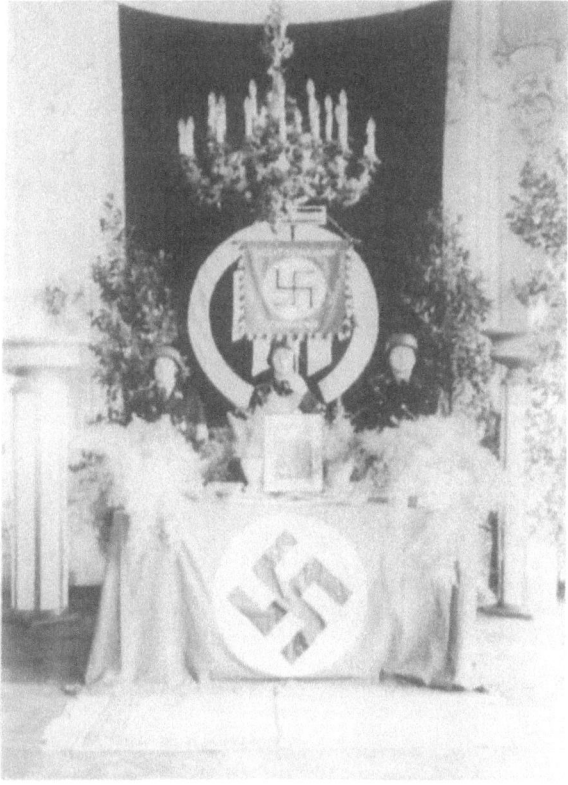

17. SS altar. Photo by Bundes-archiv, Coblenz (Image no. 146/69 62 A/62).

18. The cult of a Nazi "hero," circa 1934–1935: "The Schlageter cross on Golzheim Moor." Published in Hans Schemm, *Deutsches Volk, Deutsches Heimat* (Munich: Deutscher Volksverlag, 1940; originally published 1935), p. 213. Author's collection. Photo preserved in the Bibliothèque de l'Institut d'Histoire de l'Art, Strasbourg.

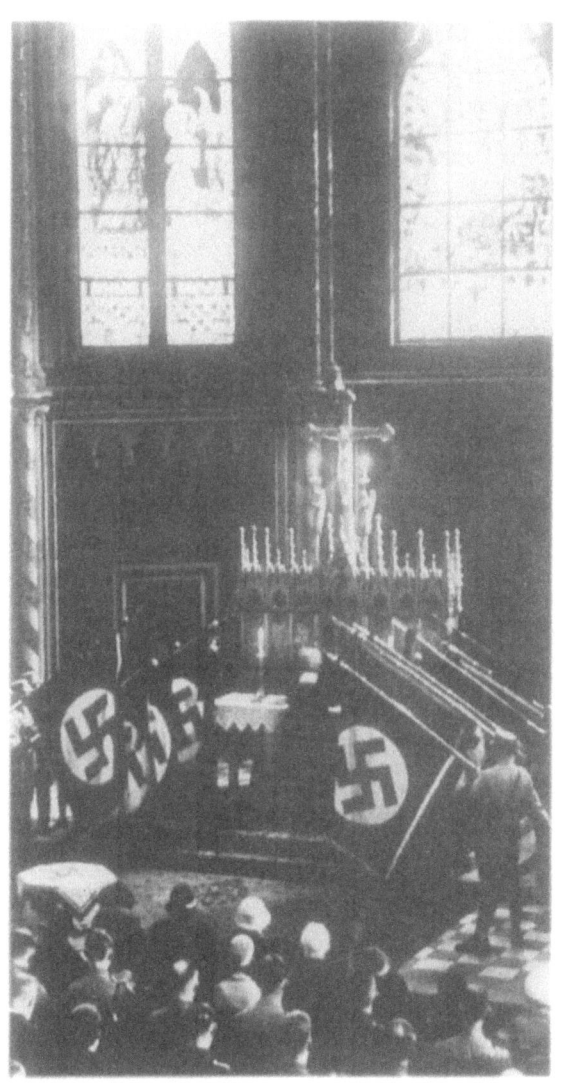

19. Religious service in the Lutheran church of the Berlin garrison, in honor of Standartenführer Peter Voss. RR.

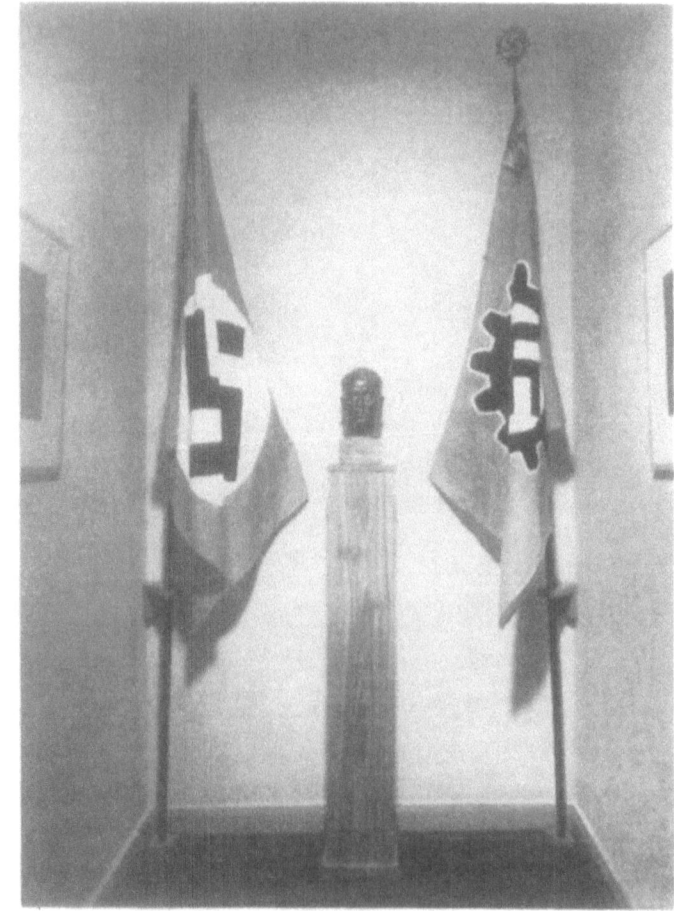

20. A small business's "flag corner" with a bust of Hitler. Published in Anatol von Hübbenet, *Das Taschenbuch Schönheit der Arbeit* (Berlin: Verlag der deutschen Arbeitsfront, 1938), p. 135. Author's collection. Photo preserved in the Bibliothèque de l'Institut d'Histoire de l'art de Strasbourg.

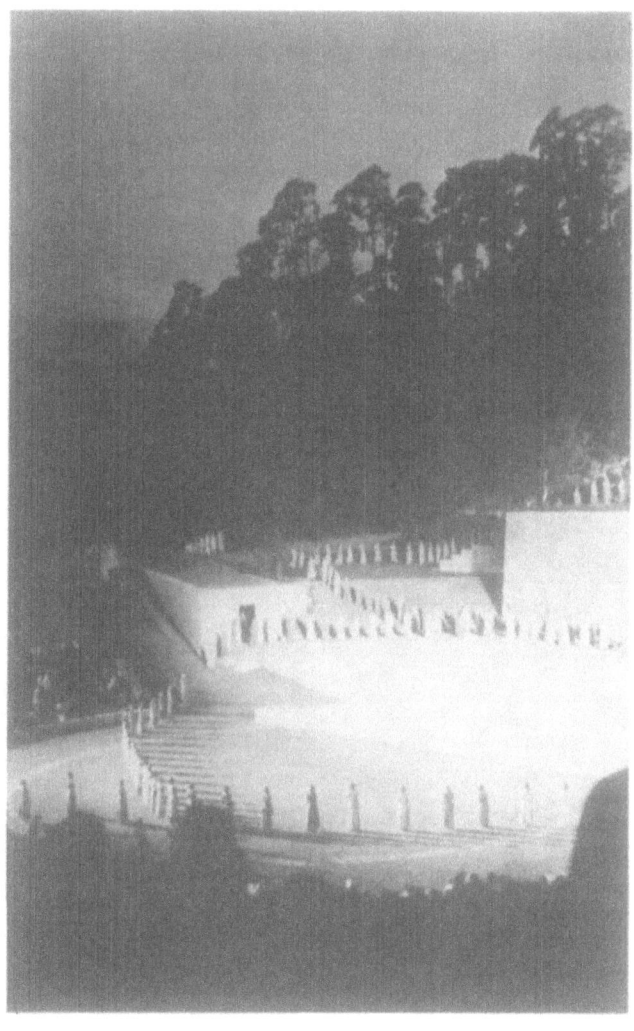

21. The Dietrich Eckart *Thing* theater, Berlin-Grünewald. Published in *A Nation Builds: Contemporary German Architecture* (New York: German Library of Information, 1940), p. 54. Document preserved in the Bibliothèque de l'Institut d'Histoire de l'Art de Strasbourg.

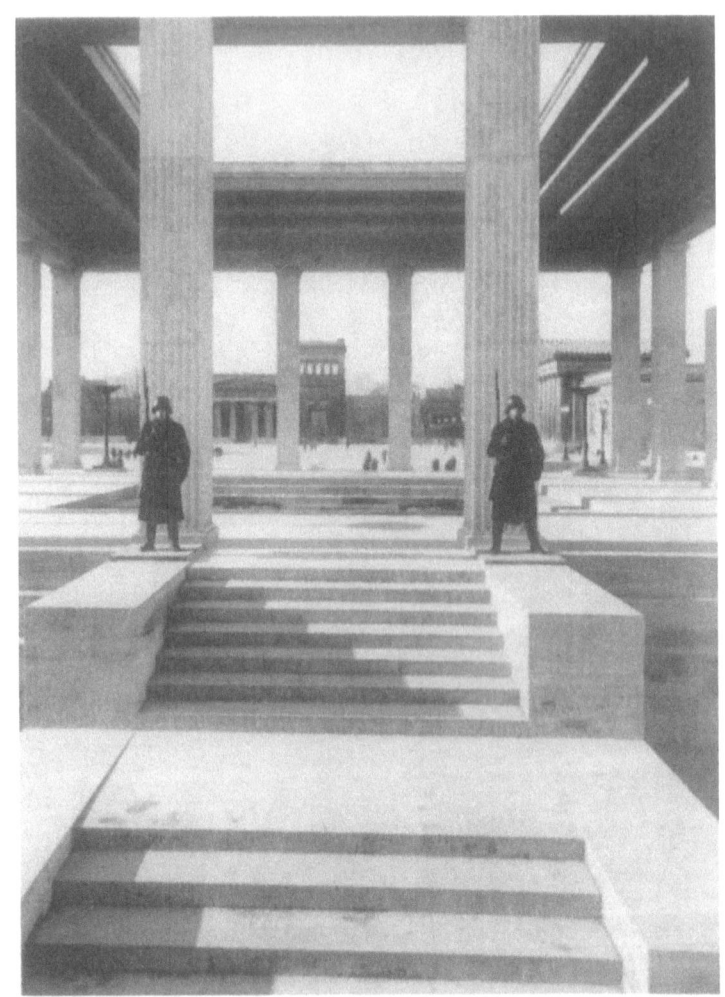

22. Paul Ludwig
Troost, *The Temples of
the Heroes* (*Ehrentempel*),
Munich, 1935. Photo by
Bayerische Staatsbiblio-
thek, Munich.

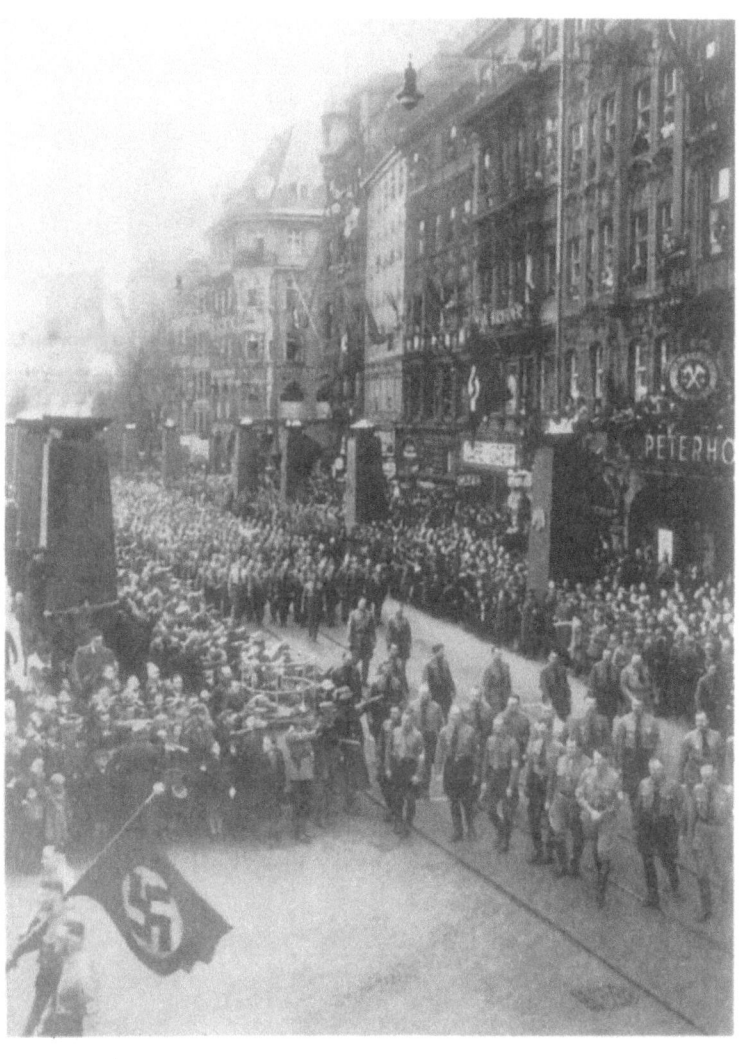

23. The "traditional procession" in the Marienplatz, Munich, 1935. Photo by Heinrich Hoffmann. Bayerisches Hauptstaatsarchiv, Abteilung V, Munich.

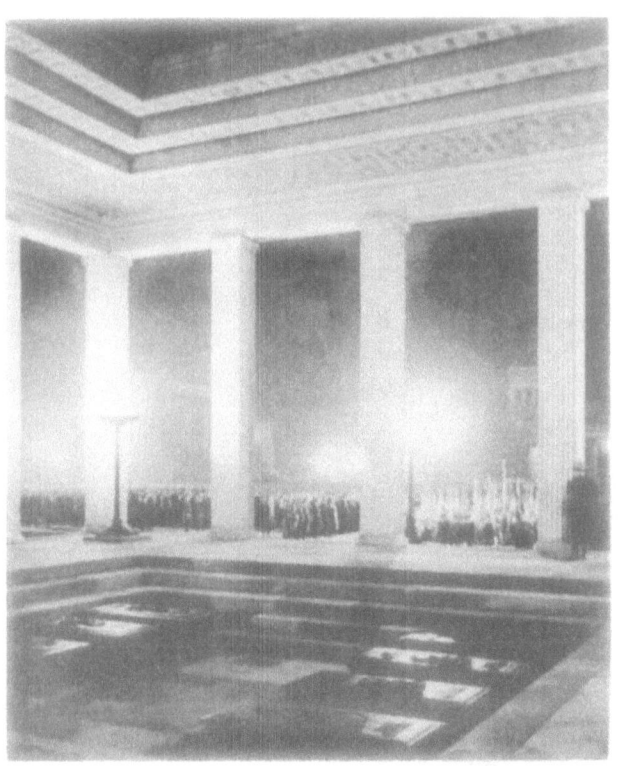

24. Paul Ludwig Troost, "In the temples of the Nordic heroes of the eternal Guard," Munich, 1935. Published in Hans Schemm, *Deutsches Volk, Deutsche Heimat* (Munich: Deutscher Volksverlag, 1940; originally published 1935), p. 216. Author's collection. Photo preserved in the Bibliothèque de l'Institut d'Histoire de l'Art de Strasbourg.

25. Paul Ludwig Troost, The Eternal Guard (*Die Ewige Wache*), Munich, 1935. Published in Gerdy Troost (ed.), *Das Bauen im neuen Reich* (Bayreuth: Gauverlag Bayerische Ostmark, 1939), p. 46. Document preserved in the Bibliothèque de l'Institut d'Histoire de l'Art de Strasbourg.

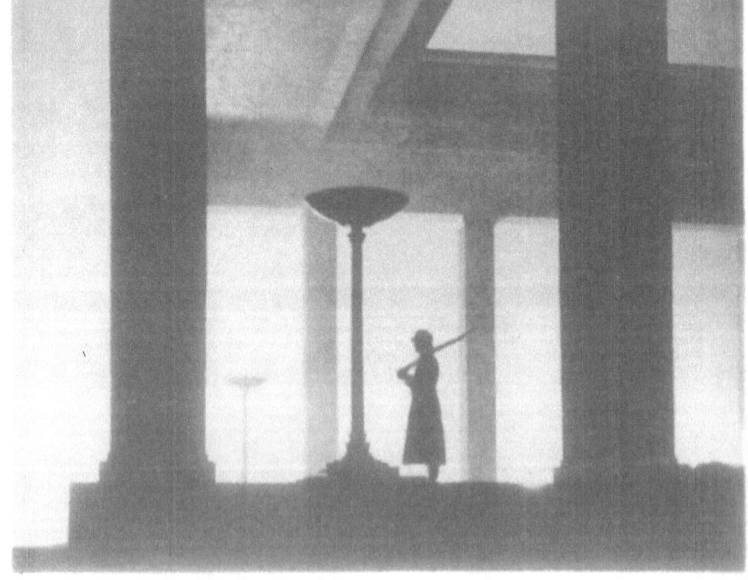

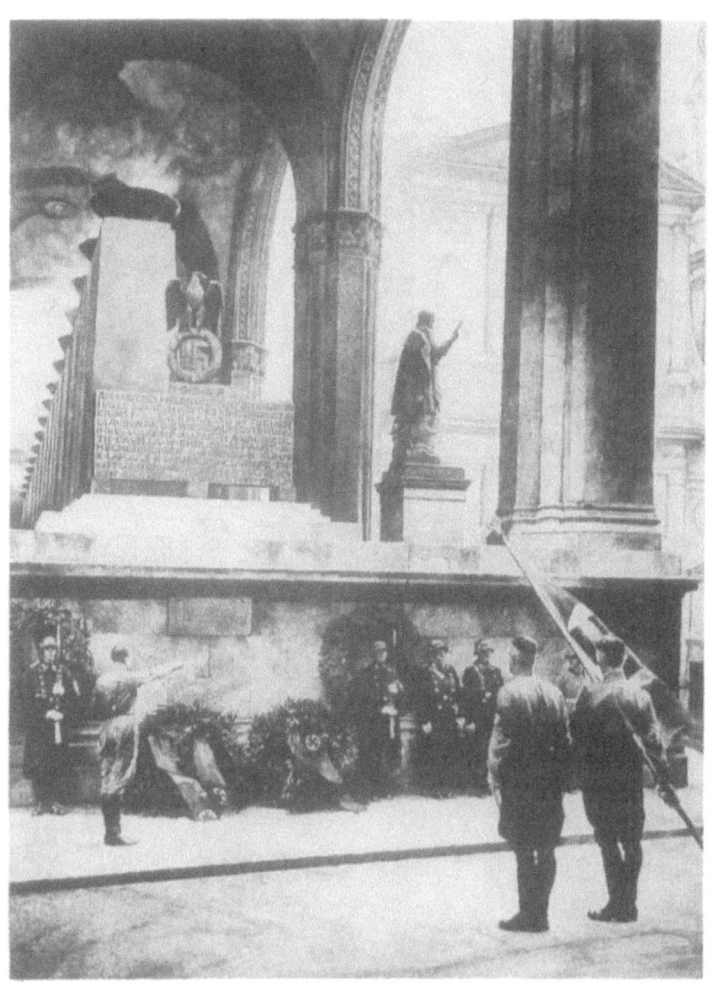

26. Paul Herrmann,
You Did Win After All
(*Und Ihr habt doch gesiegt*)
(oil on canvas), 1942.
Photo by AKG, Paris.

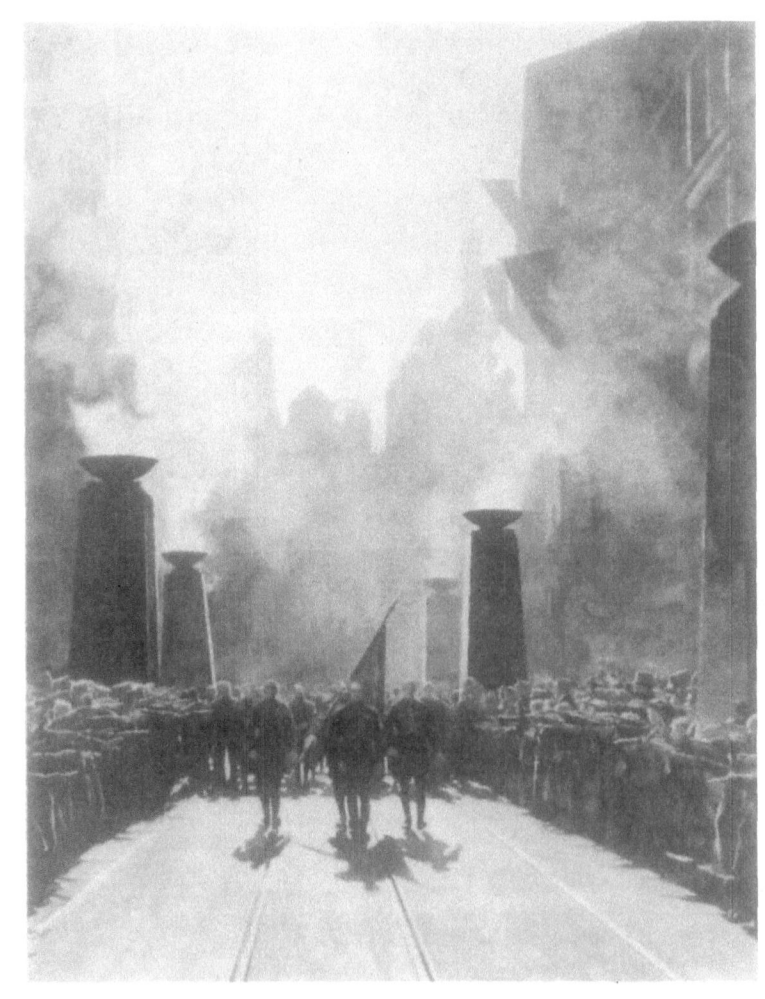

27. Paul Hermann,
The Flag (oil on can-
vas), 1942. Photo by
AKG, Paris.

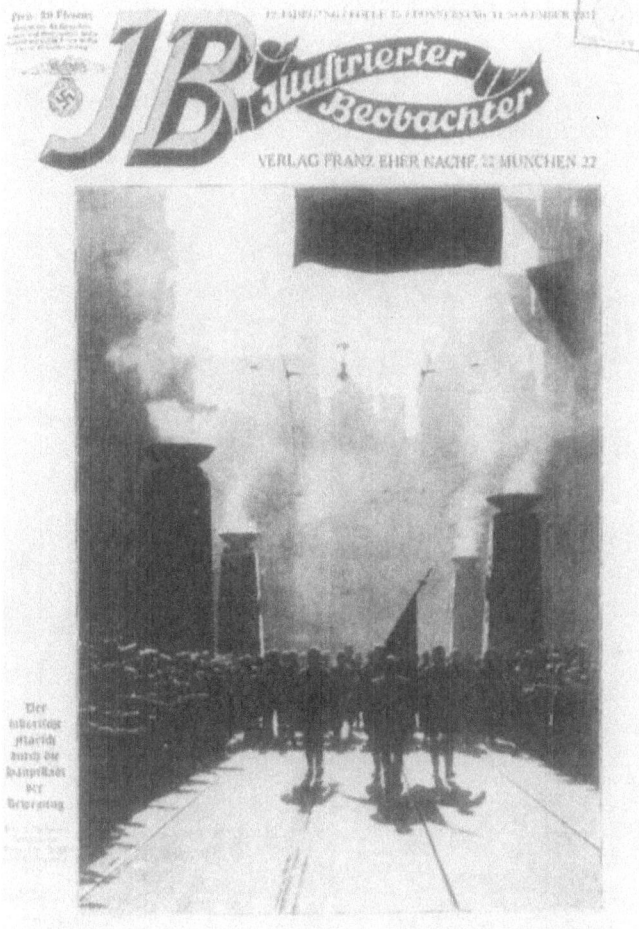

28. November 9, 1937, Munich. Photo by Heinrich Hoffmann. *Illustrierter Baobachter*, no. 45, 11 November 1937, front page. RR.

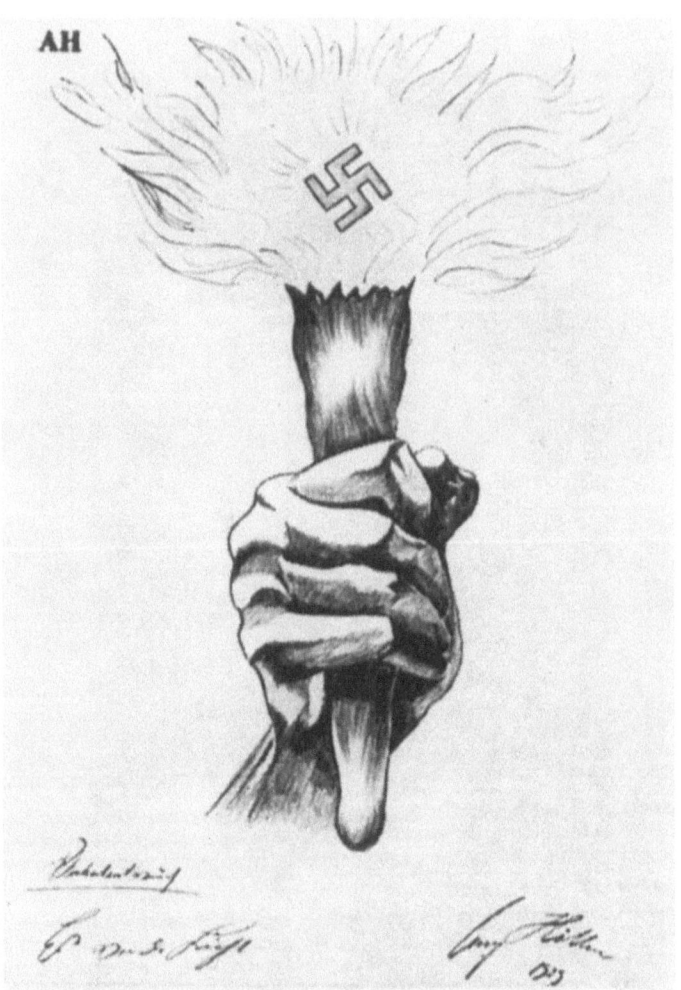

29. Adolf Hitler, "Let There be Light!" Design for a poster, 1929. Photo by August Priesack, Munich.

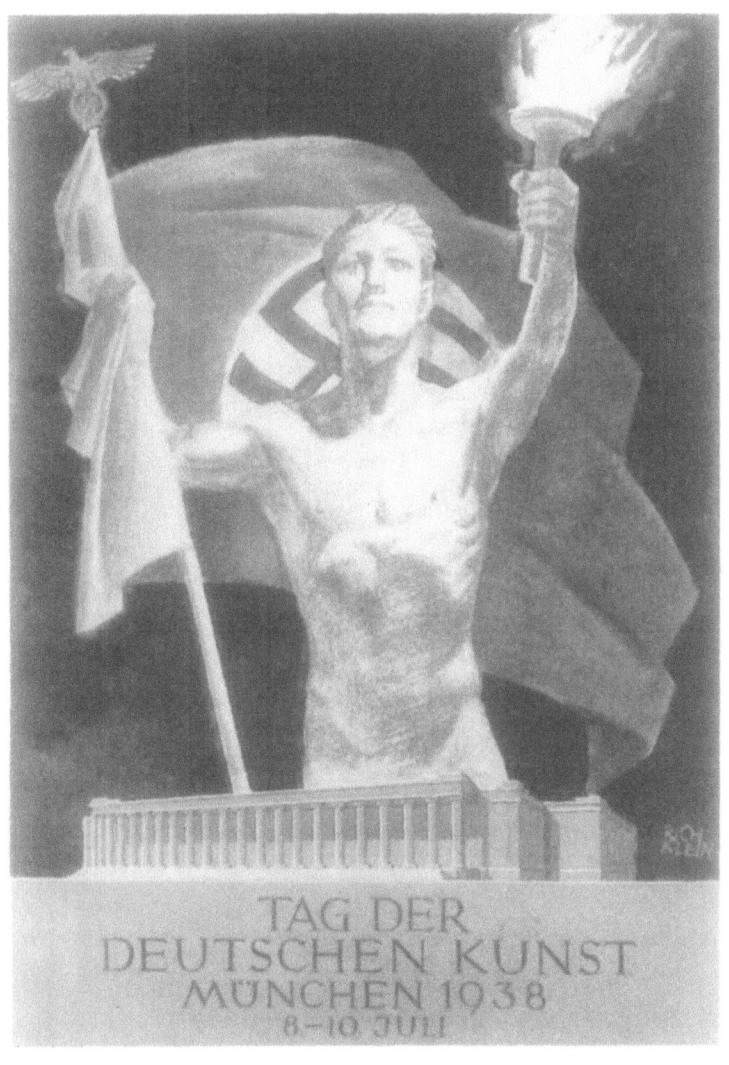

30.   Richard Klein,
Poster for the Day of
German Art, 1938. RR.

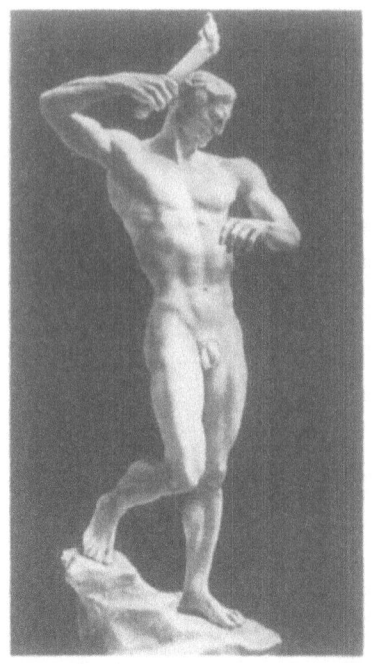

31. *(right)* Arno Breker, *Prometheus*, circa 1938. Photo by Charlotte Rohrbach. Published in *Arno Breker*, ed. E. König, Introduction by W. Rittich (Paris: Verlag der Deutschen Arbeitsfront, n.d. [1942]), plate 11. Author's collection. Photo preserved in the Bibliothèque de Institut d'Histoire de l'Art de Strasbourg.

32. *(below)* Willy Meller, *Torch Bearer*, 1936, Ordensburg Vogelsang. Published in Bruno E. Werner, *Die deutsche Plastik der Gegenwart* (Berlin: Rembrandt Verlag, 1940), p. 149. Document preserved in the Bibliothèque de l'Institut d'Histoire de l'Art de Strasbourg.

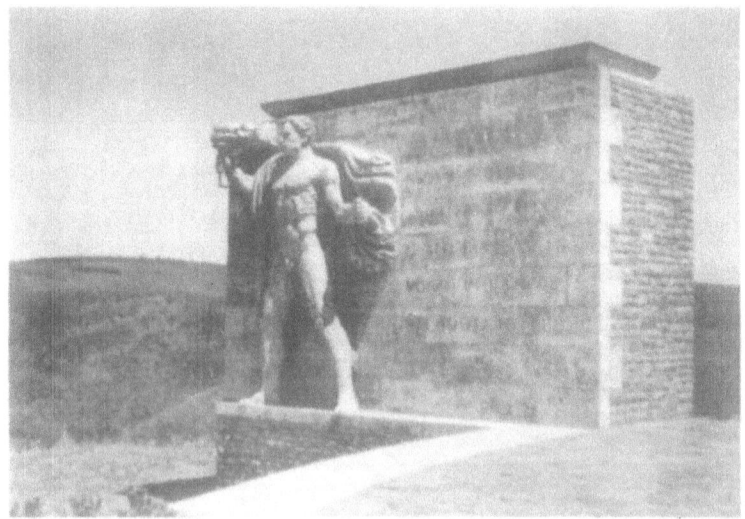

of light,"[13] so too did Alfred Rosenberg remind the Aryan people of its solar origin: "Ahura Mazda, the eternal god of light, is the divine protector of Aryanity"; his "enemy is the dark Angro Mainyu" (also known as Ahriman), "against whom he battles for world domination."[14] As for Hitler, he did not hesitate to declare that if this Prometheus with his "luminous brow" was made to disappear, "a deep darkness would descend upon the Earth; within a few decades, human *Kultur* would fade away and the world would become a desert." "Let there be light!" ran the caption beneath his design for a poster for the 1929 campaign (Figure 29); and a poster by Richard Klein (Figure 30) for the 1938 Day of German Art looked like an illustration for *Mein Kampf*: rising above the House of German Art, Klein's *Prometheus* lit up the night with the very same torch and, like the Prometheus of Arno Breker or Willy Meller (Figures 31 and 32), showered the world with the light of the National Socialist Idea.

"As soon as egoism becomes the ruler of a people, the bonds of order are loosened and in the chase after their own happiness men fall from heaven into a real hell."[15] Five times in *Mein Kampf*, the threat of the disappearance of the Aryan, and with him the world, is repeated. Perhaps Hitler was remembering the warning that Johann Fichte gave the "all-man": "If there is truth in what has been expounded in these addresses, then you of all modern people are the one in whom the seed of human perfection most unmistakably lies, and to whom the lead in its development is committed. If you perish in this your essential nature, then there perishes together with you every hope of the whole human race for salvation from the depths of its miseries."[16]

The discourse of *Mein Kampf*, however, identified that salvationary perfection with visible beauty and linked that German responsibility indissolubly with racial purity. If "our planet, . . . as it did thousands of years ago, move[s] through the ether devoid of men"; if the Aryans "succumb" and if "whatever makes the Earth beautiful descends with them into the tomb"; if the disappearance of the Aryan causes "the dark veils of an age without culture [to] again descend on this globe"; and if, finally, "the destruction of the last representatives of the superior race" definitively "turn[s] the Earth into a desert"[17]—then the blame will not fall primarily on the "all-man," the *Volk* par excellence, but on the Jews. The anti-people or antirace (*Gegenvolk, Gegenrasse*), devoid of art and a form of its own, contaminated the creative genius of the Aryan with its blood (and its dream, added Rosenberg and his friends); it would prevent the ideal of the latter from ever taking shape, in exactly the same way that for two thousand years it had been opposing "the Lord's image" and his "aesthetics."

These remarks were no mere "theological conceits," as was sometimes hastily assumed.[18] They really did constitute a major link between National Socialism and anti-Semitism. Barely taking it out of context, Hitler was here recycling the argument produced by the Church, initially in Byzantium, in which it had turned the cult of holy images into an act rewarded by salvation. According to the patristic definition, Christ was "the first icon of the invisible god" (John of Damascus), and his visible presence in the image conferred upon it Christ's own redemptory powers. Just as the Word had become flesh in order to redeem human beings, the image renewed the Incarnation and its work of salvation. It was this Christian heritage of salvation through the image that Hitler was presuming to take over. At once the Christ and artist, he was the incarnation of the *Volksgeist* and the image of its divinity, bringing salvation to his people through his example and his art. Christianity had introduced a split into the one God of the Jews, dividing him into, on the one hand, an object of fear and, on the other, an object of love, and setting apart from his invisible critical authority an intercessor Christ who visibly satisfied human desires, that is to say, performed miracles. It was on the basis of this division that Hitler made conscience a "Judaic invention,"[19] and Nazism assimilated all criticism of "German art" into the destructive power of the Jewish spirit. Goebbel's 1936 ban on art criticism replaced it with art "reviews,"[20] which were justified as necessary for the survival of the Idea incarnate, the German God given form (*Gestalt*), whereas criticism undermined the German people's self-confidence and threatened the redemptive love it felt for its own miraculous image, reflected by its Führer and its art. This division of the one God took on unequivocal meaning in the following appeal to Hitler Youth members published in a picture book:

Den deutschen Führer lieben sie,
Den Gott im Himmel fürchten sie,
Die Juden, die verachten sie.
Die sind nicht ihresgleichen;
Drum müssen sie auch weichen!

They love the German Führer.
They fear the God in heaven.
They despise the Jews.
The Jews do not resemble them;
So they must knuckle under and give in![21]

This poem contrasted love for the Führer, the German Christ, with the persistent fear of the universal and invisible God of the Jews, which the Third Reich never managed to dispel. A link was thus created between the invisible but universal Jewish conspiracy against Germany[22] and the Führer, who was the incarnation of the German idea of God and who protected his people from the antipeople, which was utterly other and which aspired solely to repeat its action of deicide by making Germany disappear. For "*Gott ist sichtbar mit ihm*" (With him [Hitler], God is visible)."[23]

As early as April 20, 1923—Hitler's birthday—in a speech entitled *Why We Are Anti-Semitic*, Hitler stigmatized the threat of the invisible. The Jews, he declared, sought constantly "to spread *their invisible state* as a supreme tyranny over all the other states in the world. . . . He who wishes *to see* that *can see* it, and he who *refuses to see it* no one can help." What National Socialism wanted, Hitler added, was "to prevent our Germany from suffering, as another did, the death upon the cross."[24] The following year he wrote, "*By defending myself against the Jew, I am fighting for the work of the Lord*."[25] This battle was, in the last analysis, simply a battle between the visible and the invisible; it referred to the art of making visible the eternal German *Volksgeist*, which was under constant threat from the Jew, the "destroyer of *Kultur*." Hitler used a striking expression to declare that the "whole existence [of the Jew] is an embodied protest against the aesthetics of the Lord's image" (*Ihr ganzes Dasein ist der fleischgewordene Protest gegen die Aesthetik des Ebenbildes des Herrn*).[26] It was because only the Aryan opposed this threat that menaced "the image of the Lord" that the very visibility of the world depended on him: "If he dies out or declines, the dark veils of an age without culture will again descend on this globe, . . . possibly within no more than a few centuries. Human culture would fade away and the world would become a desert."[27] As if carried along by the Christian logic of the image—that is to say, by the theology of the redemptive Incarnation—Hitler rediscovered one of the major arguments used in the Byzantine world to combat iconoclasm: "It is not just Christ but the whole universe that disappears if there is neither outline nor icon."[28]

Such was the legitimation of the struggle launched against the invisible Jewish universality in order to restore and maintain the visibility of the German-Aryan world. It was also a struggle fully identified with "the struggle for art" (*der Kampf um die Kunst*) led by Nazism. Founding the German people's "moral right to life"[29] on culture and art (its most visible achievements), Hitler entered with his people into a process of compulsive realization of the Idea, with an *outline* and a *form*, in the face of the hostile and destructive forces of critical conscience. Hitler was confronted by the Jew, seen as the *Verführer* of the German people, its "evil genius" or "seducer," a seductive and corrupting führer, to some extent its antiführer,[30] who stood in opposition to the figurative expression of the "eternal soul" of the people. The Jew represented the *Gegenvolk* and the *Gegenreich*, the antipeople and the anti-Reich: "His life is only of this world and his spirit is inwardly as alien to true Christianity as his nature two thousand years previous was to the great founder of the new doctrine."[31] So "no one need be surprised if among our people the personification of the devil as the symbol of all evil assumes the living shape [*Gestalt*] of the Jew."[32]

The same national Christianity was the inspiration for Rosenberg's *The Myth of the Twentieth Century*, despite his theoretical anti-Christian sentiments. But whereas *Mein Kampf* designated the Jew as the "evil demon" of the German people, Rosenberg isolated "the evil demon of the Jew" within the very heart of the Jewish people. He cited as evidence the testimony of "half-Jew" Oskar Schmitz in order to stigmatize the damned part of the Jew, the part that prevented him from ever being a founder of culture (*Kulturbegründer*):

The evil demon of the Jew is . . . Pharisaism. It is certainly the bearer of the hope of the Messiah, but simultaneously is the guardian that prevents any messiah from arriving. . . . That is the specific, most dangerous form of the Jewish denial of the world. . . . The Pharisee actively denies the world. He ensures that, where possible, nothing takes shape [*Gestalt*].

His is "the spirit which, behind the ecstatic proclamation of a Utopian being who can never come to be, always conceals and denies the advent of the Messiah."[33] Needless to say, what Oskar Schmitz stigmatized in a collection of papers devoted to anti-Semitism—a collection that included among its contributors Arnold Zweig, Alfons Paquet, Léon Blum, George Bernard Shaw, Heinrich Mann, and Martin Buber[34]—was the basis on which Christian anti-Semitism rested—precisely what Rosenberg was now taking over, appropriating it entirely to Nazism: the Jew had denied the salvation that the Incarnation had nevertheless realized; in the name of an unrealizable Utopia, the Jew was the negator of a redemption that had already taken place and that was already visible. The eternal Jew (*der ewige Jude*) was "always the same," one who broke every idol and opposed the redemptive image with the text of his law. The synagogue was forever blind: no more than they could see the Messiah in Jesus could the Jews, or "Jews in spirit," see the Savior in Hitler or seek their redemption in German art.

The anti-Semitism and extermination practiced by the Nazis are intelligible only from this historical perspective of the sublation (*Aufhebung*) of an invisible God by an incarnate God—a sublation that turned into a contrast between redemption and the critical authority that had to be abolished. The anti-Semitism and extermination made sense only on the basis of a postulated identity between that redemptive power and an art understood to be a production of oneself. This is why the Third Reich integrated artistic activity into the general work process, always presented as the German people's fight for its identity. Art was assuredly the "noblest part" in this struggle, for it constituted both a production of that identity and a fight against "the Jew" and those who were "Jewish in spirit"—a fight against their "critical conscience," which prevented the German people from being "at one with itself."[35] As we shall see, all work conversely had to be raised to the level of artistic activity, which in the National

Socialist vocabulary was called "creative work." The reason Hitler declared that "the idea of creative work has always been and will always be anti-Semitic"[36] was that he was convinced that only the *Leistung* (performance) of production and its accomplishment in the final product, whatever it might be, could put an end to the Jew's unsustainable absence of an identity of his own.[37]

Awakening into the Myth

Therefore, what needed to be restored to the German people—workers and artists alike—was the desire "to be at one with itself." This meant it had to re-discover its original "creative genius," which now was submerged beneath the mixture of bloods and was disappearing into the mediocrity of everyday life.

The Nazi doctrine on the genius was composed of a multiplicity of elements derived as much from Neoplatonism as from the Roman notion of *genius*, and as much from Romanticism as from vitalist psychology. Based on the idea of an original inequality between the human races and of the hereditary nature of "true genius" (the "gift" conferred upon the Aryan race by nature or by God), Hitler's *Weltanschauung* took the form of a twofold secularization: the theology of the Fall became a theory of degeneration, and the history of salvation became a process of regeneration.

In the beginning, he wrote, the small Aryan peoples subjugated inferior peoples and founded a *Kultur* that was appropriate for their superior nature. Soon, however, these conquerors, betraying the principle of the preservation of the purity of their blood, entered into unions with indigenous people and thereby brought their own reign to an end. "The original sin committed in paradise has always been followed by the expulsion of those who were guilty." One millennium later, that ancient people of masters nevertheless, has left a "visible trace" of itself in the "fairer complexion" of the now-fallen people and its petrified *Kultur*. So the memory of the master race—the visible memory of its genius, which was inscribed both in flesh and in stone—lived on.[38] In perfect agreement with the psychology of his time, which in this respect was heir to the organicism of the eighteenth century, Hitler conceived of the evolution of peoples or races as analogous to the evolution of an individual. The "mixing of blood," which generated colorless human beings, thus corresponded to the individual's "monotonous daily life." Hidden beneath this undifferentiated surface, however, seeds of the primitive genius were still alive. "Just as in everyday life what is called genius needs a definite motive—in many cases a veritable impulsion—to accede to the light, so too it happens in the life of peoples, for the race with genius." That is why what is almost always needed is "a shock that gets the genius to enter the lists," both in the life of an individual and in that of his race. War, better than anything, was able, "by breaking through the coating [*Hülle*] of daily life, to reveal to the eyes of an astonished world the kernel [*kern*] that until then had remained hidden." So it was only through its acts that the genius of a people could ever make itself known: "The rest of the world, incapable of recognizing genius as such, could see only its visible expressions in the form of inventions, discoveries, buildings, images, and so on." The creative power of genius, "always present and available," needed only "to be reawakened in accordance with external conditions in order to manifest itself practically." This was the mission that National Socialism had set for itself. It was a task that stemmed as much from Socratic maieutics and Platonic reminiscence as from the biological purging of the racial "kernel." The language in which the nation's reawakening was equated to the arousal of German awareness of its "Germanity" (*Deutschtum*) was presented as the instrument for the reconstruction of "Paradise," or the eternal Reich; but it was also an end in itself, for it was in the speech act that revealed its original form or image and in the plastic act that gave it concrete being that the "ideal Reich" found realization.

"*Deutschland erwache!*" (Germany, awake!) was the most pervasive of the slogans of National Socialism. It was copied by members of the SPD (*Sozialdemokratische Partei Deutschlands* or Social Democratic Party) in "*Volk, erwache!*" (People, awake!), to which Goebbels of course responded, "Yes! We, the people, are awake!" During the war this slogan expanded into "Europe, awake!" and also appeared in a number of vernacular variants such as "France, awake!" which was tried out in 1941 by Ludovic Zoretti, the former SFIO (French Socialist Party) member who rallied to the Vichy regime's National Revolution.[39]

In Germany, the slogan was at first linked with the medieval myth about the emperor who, like Barbarossa in the twelfth century or Frederick II von Hohenstaufen, was supposed to awaken soon in his mountain tomb and emerge to liberate his people. (As Ernst Bloch remarked, "the old Sbylline oracle, "*vivit, non vivit*," is constantly resuscitated in folklore."[40]) Poet Stefan George turned the myth into a poem entitled *Geheimes Deutschland* (Secret Germany): "Only what is still slumbering / There where nobody feels it, / Only what is sheltered most deeply / And sleeps in the sacred earth, / Today an incomprehensible miracle, / Can be the destiny of tomorrow."[41] The slogan also chimed in "*Wach auf, du deutsches Land!*" (Awake, you German land!) sung by sixteenth-century poet Johannes Walther[42] and roared out every January 30, the day the Nazis assumed power. Perhaps it also called to mind the Protestant movement of Awakening (*Erweckungsbewegung*), which at the end of the eighteenth century exhorted souls despairing of this material world to turn in themselves toward the "heavenly fatherland." But it was even more reminiscent of the "*Wach auf! es nahet gen den Tag*" (Awaken, the day is nigh) of the chorus of Wagner's *The Mastersinger*, which reduced Goebbels to tears on August 2, 1932,[43] and later became a national anthem with the power to enflame the masses. This injunction to Germany, which urged it to awaken, was thus primarily an injunction to remember its past and to construct its future on the ideal model of that past.

When Dietrich Eckart composed the *Sturmlied*, in which the slogan appeared for the first time, Hitler drew an ink sketch of him, to which he added the caption, "Dietrich Eckart, editor-in-chief of the *Völkischer Beobachter* and creator of the battle slogan '*Deutschland erwache!*' age fifty-four, in 1922."[44] The same year he had these two words imprinted on the party standard, which he himself had designed. Once produced, this standard was seen everywhere in Germany, right up to the end of the Third Reich, as though it were an involuntary confession that, in truth, Germany had still not awakened to its myth. The words composed by Eckart, "the German poet who will never be forgotten by his people," were better known through the title "*Sturm, Sturm, Sturm,*" which was reproduced in every school reading book: "Attack! Attack! Attack! / . . . Let the bells ring out from every tower! . . . Judas appears to conquer the Reich!/ . . . Let the earth shake beneath the thunder of redemptive vengeance! Woe to the people still dreaming today! Germany, awake, awake!"[45]

An artist of the *Kampfzeit* (the period from 1919 to 1933) first associated the slogan with the tocsin (alarm) that was to awaken a country in flames (Figure 33). But after the Nazi takeover of power, on the eve of the Reichstag elections (March 5, 1933), when the "day of the awakening nation" was proclaimed,[46] the slogan soon appeared on every kind of everyday object, emphasizing the symbolic function of those items associated with communication—pencils, radio sets, matchboxes (Figures 34 and 35). Every single German had to be snatched from the slumber of everyday life, judged to be so monotonous, and restored to the creative genius that was the source of the heroism of the racial community.

This lexicon of awakening also included slumber, along with its dreams and visions. Even before Rosenberg provided the theory of the German people's dream, a certain Bruno Schestak, on the occasion of a speech by Hitler in Plauen in 1925, composed a song that in effect constituted "an anthology of Nazi slogans and symbols,"[47] putting them together to form a clear message:

Deutschland erwache aus deinem bösen Traum
Gib fremden Juden in deinem Reich nicht Raum.
Wir wollen kämpfen für dein Auferstehen,
Arisches Blut darf nicht untergehen.

Wir sind die Kämpfer der N. S. D. A. P.
Kerndeutsch im Herzen, im Kampf fest und zäh.
Dem Hakenkreuz ergeben sind wir,
Heil unserm Führer, Heil Hitler, Dir.

Germany, awake from your bad dream.
Leave no room in your Reich for the alien Jew.
We are fighting for your resurrection,
Aryan blood must not disappear.

We are the fighters of the NSDAP,
Very German in our hearts, firm and strong in battle.
We are committed to the swastika,
Hail to our Führer, Hail to thee, Hitler.

This song, commonly known as *Heil Hitler, Dir,* invoked a Reich that, although still spiritual, was already a spatial entity. This Reich was clearly an inner realm, because this was where the "bad dream" of Germany unfolded; but it was also geographical—a space from which the Jew had to be expelled. But was this Reich a German dream that was "bad" because it contained the Jew, or was it invaded by a "bad dream" dreamed by the Jew? In any event, clearly the ejection of the Jew coincided with the awakening from the bad dream and the awakening coincided with the resurrection of Germany, and together the expulsion, awakening, and resurrection were identified with the very struggle of the NSDAP, the struggle of Aryan blood for its own preservation. This song thus presented a truly mythical structure in which succession was abolished in favor of simultaneity, and all relations became coincidence: the cause fused with its effect, what was internal was also external, and space was the measure of time. The song was myth in the making, so the ideal Reich was already being achieved. As Germany sang, it was awakening within its "own" myth.

It was necessary, however, that something of that myth be visible at the moment of awakening. Just as the process of mass suggestion at work in the rallies required the presence of some kind of real prop (generally the presence of the Führer), so the awakening into the myth required the presence of signs capable of showing that the myth was indeed coming true in reality. The surface of the everyday world had to be struck off to allow the mythical-racial kernel to emerge and finally to be revealed so it could testify to the presence of the eternal soul of the race, which had been buried beneath all the strata piled on it by history.

In this sense, the awakening of Germany stemmed from archaeology, and as a scientific discipline, archaeology de facto became one of the motors of the awakening of Germany.[48] Among the results, sometimes cosmetically enhanced, of countless excavations undertaken both in Germany and elsewhere in Europe, a privileged place was reserved for exhumed swastikas. Like the specialist journals, Rosenberg's *Nationalsozialistische Monatshefte* was always prepared to reproduce photographs of swastikas, whether they came from Middle Eastern mosaics, from Scandinavian goldwork, or from the potteries or architecture of

Christian Germany (Figure 36). In each case, what was immediately visible was "the heritage from the ancestors" (*Ahnenerbe*).[49] So a visible link legitimated the Nazi swastika as it tied it to the soil and culture of the ancestors. This cross, which Rosenberg called "the symbol of the awakening" or "the sign of ascendant life,"[50] seemed at last to link the present life of the community with its most authentic source. The visualization of roots fused the soil of the ancient Teutons with the redemptive heaven of the Nazis. This symbol of the sun and cosmic energy belonged so intimately to the Teutonic people that it was even eaten each year in the form of cakes baked by the peasants of central Germany at Christmas time (Figure 37). So it was that the people was reborn as itself through this communion with the Earth, by absorbing the bodies of its chthonic gods ("What a lot of gods are ripening here!" Frederick II von Hohenstaufen, exclaimed at the sight of a field of wheat, alluding to the Eucharist).[51]

The persistent and "visible traces" left in the *Kultur* by the Aryan genius were necessary for the awakening, but they did not suffice. The world had to be renamed, or rather all the objects of the *Kultur* did, in order to make their Aryan or Germanic-Nordic origin quite clear, in the same way as it would later be necessary to rename the world conflict in accordance with the Nazi *Weltanschauung*: "This is not the Second World War; it is the Great Racial War."[52] Waldemar Hartmann, brilliant pupil of Georg Dehio and Josef Strzygowski, devoted his energies to manifesting "the unity of German art" by renaming architectural styles: "The name of Romanesque art given to the religious art of the eleventh and twelfth centuries is incomprehensible because all of the constructions of that period stem from the military architecture of the Teutons, the essential feature of which is the square-based tower." The Romanesque style should therefore be called "the style of the semicircular arch of the eastern Teutons," to differentiate it from the Gothic style, which became "the style of the broken arch of the northwestern Teutons," while the pointed arch stemmed from the gables of the ancient Teutons' primitive wooden buildings.[53] As early as the winter of 1939–40, art historian Pierre Francastel quite correctly pointed out that the history of French art served as a model for the German historians, especially the work of Louis Courajod, a reactionary and nationalist whose opinions he summarized as follows: "God alone creates the races; France is the instrument of the Nordic, barbarian, Germanic genius who gave new life to the dead traditions of the ancient world. . . . The genius of the Middle Ages is, par excellence, a religious genius; it was faith that gave us our art. . . . At any rate, it was [in Courajod] that Strzygowski found the concept of Christianity identified with the northeastern genius."[54] Even when they turned against France, it was certainly these French theories dating from 1890 to 1900 that led away from the internationalist view that prevailed in the mid-nineteenth century and toward the racist nationalism of the Nazi doctrines.

In truth, the visual arts have frequently been not merely the instruments of power but essential for the auto-affirmation of that power as a spatial and trans-historical unity. Underlining how essential the formation of a *lingua visiva* (visible language) had been to Italian unity in the sixteenth century in order to overcome the *campanilismo* (regional focus) or *municipalismo* that had preceded it, Charles Dempsey has drawn attention to the way Mussolini attempted to refound the power of Fascism on the territorial and historical continuity of art. "The Duce" had even judged it necessary to appoint one of his comrades from the March on Rome to the position of director of historical research, with a mission to unearth from the documents of the past the sources of an authentic *stile fascista.*[55]

Historical research has been all too prone to make the object (albeit unconfessed) of its inquiries what National Socialism wanted above all but failed to establish—namely the German people's identity. As early as 1946, David Rousset issued a warning: "To set out to discover [in Nazism] the atavisms of a race is precisely to echo the SS mentality."[56] It is equally necessary to guard against the specter of a "German soul" forging itself in the course of history. To exhume from the "German" past traces on which to base the determination of the *Sonderweg*, the "singular path" by which Germany, unlike other European nations, is supposed to have arrived at Nazism, is also to fall into the identity trap. It is to restore—this time apparently with all the guarantees of "true" science—Himmler's *Ahnenerbe*, a fantasy "heritage from the ancestors." To seek in German history "guides to the discovery of an identity" is, as both Jürgen Habermas and Martin Broszat have stressed, to make historical consciousness a substitute for religion, and national history a substitute for a national religion.[57] This is why the task of "de-Germanizing" Nazism does not mean trivializing it but rather entails a most elementary rejection of the fantasy of autonomy. By the end of the war, this was already the response with which a number of people opposed the impulse to seek identity—an impulse that is always imperialistic and at once criminal and suicidal.

Rosenberg, on the contrary, expressed his firm conviction that a people was "lost as a people" if it failed to establish union between its history and its "will to the future." History was not about the development "from nothing to something." In "the first popular-racial (*rassisch-völkisch*) awakening," manifested by heroes, gods, and poets, a summit had been attained for always. "One form of Odin is dead," but "Odin as the eternal mirrored image of the primal spiritual powers of the soul of Nordic man lives on today as it did five thousand years ago."[58] As it renamed reality and left its stamp on all physical entities, Nazism proclaimed a world at last restored to its original *Deutschtum*. In the mirror of the laws of the Aryan *Kultur* and genius, Nazism brought into view a world at last stripped of the lies of "civilization." The *völkisch* leanings were therefore, for example, to debaptize the Christian festivals and consecrate them instead to the gods of the Teutons, who constituted the *Volksgeist*, the "heritage from the ancestors" or the genius of the race. The claim was that it was simply a matter of restoring the purity that Christianity had perverted.

All the same, while Hitler thought the genius of the race could be expressed only through the genius of the great man, the "great reformer" and visionary *Programmatiker* who "works for posterity,"[59] Albert Rosenberg, for his part, would invoke the genius of the race only in reference to its "great dreamers." He also did not divide the human race into "founders," "transmitters," and "destroyers" of *Kultur*, as Hitler did. He preferred to distinguish men according to their ability to dream and the nature of their dreams. First, there were races whose prophetic dreams brought about "a fruitful reality" by force. Then there were those that, having no dreams, allowed the reality produced by the dreams of the superior race to disappear. Finally, there were races with dreams that truly brought about destruction, such as the dream of gold, of hatred, of lies, and of world domination, which the Jews had been carrying around the world for three thousand years. Until 1933 that destructive dream of the Jews had dominated Germany because, Rosenberg claimed, "we had ceased to realize *our* dream and were clumsily trying to live the dream of the Jew, and this brought about the collapse of Germany." But now people should rejoice at a great happening: "A mythical awakening. . . . We have begun, once again, to dream our own primal dream."[60]

"*Deutschland erwache!*" thus meant that Germany, as Schestak's song summoned, had to awaken from the bad dream imposed by the Jews and at last live the dream produced by its own genius. This "mythical awakening" was envisaged as an awakening *into* the myth, that is to say, the awakening of the race to its dream. In the early days of the regime, a certain kind of popular *völkisch* art represented this awakening of the people in a kind of "real allegory" (Figure 38): a meeting between an SA member and a peasant, beneath the twofold light streaming from the rising sun and the swastika, both of which were shedding their beams on the fertile German earth. The caption beneath the picture reminded the peasant of the role that fell to him as eternal guardian of the values of the race: "At last the time has come/When our people is awaking/But that does not apply to the German peasant./He, for a long time already, has been alert." It was by turning once more to the men of the soil that the people could again become "at one with itself."

This *völkisch* version of the awakening may have been of a kind to seduce the peasant world, which Richard Walther Darré's agricultural policy was pampering, but a painting produced four years later by Richard Klein was of a different nature. Director of the Munich School of Applied Arts, one of Hitler's favorite painters, and designer of countless commemorative medals, postage stamps, and trophies, Klein in 1937 addressed the cultivated or semicultivated public of the First Exhibition of German Art in Munich. He had designed the exhibition's poster, *The Awakening* (Figure 39), which was also used as the cover for the new glossy review *The Art of the Third Reich*. It showed in close proximity a profile of Pallas Athena, Goddess of war, wisdom, and the arts; the Reich eagle; a Promethean torch; and the swastika. It was deemed not to need a caption or a swastika, the "uncontested symbol of organic Germanic truth," in order to lead the German back to the organic truth of his own myth, which was understood to be his own dream.[61]

Reappropriating the space that the language of neoclassicism and Romanticism, like ancient religious painting, had assigned to supernatural apparitions, Klein created an elaborate composite work, a strange amalgamation of Ingres and Leni Riefenstahl, of *The Dream of Ossian* and *The Blue Lamp*. As in Ingres's painting, it was the color of the flesh and the light in which the bodies in the vision were bathed that distinguished them, floating in space, from the body of the hero. But instead of a sleeping Ossian, here was a hero awaking, naked, in his dream, at the top of a mountain. In this painting, the first rays of a sun as yet invisible are dissipating the shadows of the night and striking the bodies in a Valhalla reduced to six figures, possibly those of Odin, the Norse god of war and the arts, surrounded by five Valkyries. Or is the hero himself perhaps foreseeing in his dream his future stay in Valhalla? For the Valkyries were reputed to appear only to the happy warrior chosen by Odin to die in battle and be buried in Valhalla. While one Valkyrie holds a sand timer, the shining crystal ball held at arm's length by another evokes not so much Odin's magic ring as the blue light radiating from Monte Cristallo in Riefenstahl's film. A number of mythologies definitely intersect here. But how is one to tell whether these feminine beings with unveiled bodies are there to guide the hero to the day's battle or to offer themselves to him? For these naked bodies are not separated from the hero by the distance that was required for a vision in earlier paintings. On the contrary, they are so close that one of them even seems to be lightly touching his foot. Klein seems to have wished to rival Adolf Ziegler, president of the Chamber of Plastic Arts and nicknamed "the master of pubic hair." The realism of the anatomy that is so characteristic of the figures of this master venerated by Hitler also played a role in the awakening of creative genius. The poet Johann Hamann remarked, "My own crude imagination has always prevented me from representing a creative genius without *genitalia*." For even if *The Awakening* was an awakening into the myth of the creative genius, its purpose was, as we shall see, to incite the spectator to love as well as battle, and to reproduce the genius race as much as to defend it.

The continuity of the race's past with its present was expressed by a similar division of space in a mural painted by Ferdinand Spiegel, a landscape and portrait painter known for his renderings of the faces of soldiers and members of the SS. *Tank* (Figure 40), reproduced in a magazine as early as March 1939, showed a column of fighting tanks. Their advance toward the spectator seemed all the more threatening because these heavy war machines were painted from below just as they were about to plunge down a slight slope, leaving the imagination to conjure up an entire army behind them. Exploding shells projected their black smoke, which did not, however, rise as far as the sky. Up there, in the clouds, which in classical paintings customarily accommodated more peaceful figures, another struggle was taking place. The battle in the sky accompanied the one taking place on Earth, uniting the fighters past and present into a single community founded in a destiny. The Prussian cavalry was falling on the enemy in the same right-to-left movement as that of the tanks, in such a way that a mythical history was guiding and already supporting the battles of the present and the future. Under National Socialism, the awakening into the myth was primarily an awakening to war. The painter was mindful of the lesson of *Mein Kampf*, according to which the uniqueness of the Aryan genius lay in its "idealism," that is to say, in its capacity for sacrifice to ensure the survival of the *Kultur* of the community. This is why, whereas the cinema had long been using the technique of superimposed images to signify the eruption of the imaginary into the hero's present, the painter of this picture preferred to preserve two distinct but parallel spaces. What he had to signify were not the imaginary representations of a single individual but the mythical continuity of the history of an entire people, a repetition of its "first popular-racial awakening."[62]

All of this imagery, however, constituted a merely derisory attempt to illustrate a process of far greater scope. No doubt *The Awakening* and *Tank* did manage, albeit clumsily, to set on stage the sacrifice that the Führer expected from every member of the community. But awakening into the myth was primarily a matter for the *Erlebnis* (lived experience) of a world that was continually being transformed in accordance with the vision of the Führer. Because Nazism invested art itself with the power to awaken, there was no need for art to depict the actual awakening. All it had to do was present the vision of the Führer—the myth itself—in order to produce an awakening at the heart of that salutatory vision.

The first consequence of the role of awakener conferred upon art affected its relation to reality. In the autumn of 1941, while opening an exhibition of Viennese art in Düsseldorf, Baldur von Schirach, then Gauleiter (governor) of Vienna, made a speech about "art and reality" that neatly summed up the position of Nazi aesthetics. "Art serves not reality but the truth," he said. If German art were to continue to measure itself solely against "the truth of reality," it would inevitably decline immediately. Color photography corresponded to such a dogma and thus constituted the ultimate artistic achievement. Just as painting two eyes on the profile of a face was typical of degenerate art, it was also degenerate to paint a man, an object, or a landscape in accordance with the dogma of "the truth of reality." To limit oneself to that dogma, von Schirach went on to say, would be to condemn the ballads of Friedrich Schiller, in which the characters express themselves in verse rather than in prose. The apples in Dutch still-life paintings were "as unreal as those of Courbet or Vincent van Gogh," but they were "all true." "The apples of Dutch and French painting," as such, have "their own reality." The fact was that even if "art and nature have truth in common, their reality differs." Similarly, the reality of the material of art was not that of human material: just as the reality of a living soldier served as the model for a sculpture, the reality of the stone or bronze made its own demands. "However, consolation is at hand," von Schirach added. "Thanks to the *ingenium* of that great master-builder, our Führer," a new order was about to emerge and would do justice to the essence of each of the arts. For architecture had a leading and educative mission: it was "not only the art of space, but also the space of art. In other words, in architecture all arts find their homeland." Launching out from that last remark, Schirach concluded his speech with an evocation of the eternal dimension that ought to be the goal of all art:

Any artist who believes that he should paint for his own time and follow the taste of that time has not understood the Führer at all. Nor has our people created its Reich just for its own time. Not one soldier fights and falls purely for his own time. Any commitment on the part of the nation covers the whole of eternity. The meaning of all human action is to create timelessness out of its own time. The same applies to art, which is a struggle for immortality on the part of mortals. Therein lies the piety of the artist. The Führer's warning applies to him, too: "Woe betide whoever lacks faith!" Even if, among the countless artistic creators, that sacred goal of highly human and artistic life is but rarely achieved, any work that has pretensions to be art must absolutely manifest a thirst and pressing desire for eternity. The perfect artists Michelangelo and Rembrandt, and Beethoven and Goethe, do not represent an appeal to return to the past, but show us the future that is ours and to which we belong.[63]

The most distressing aspect of this speech was clearly the banality of the aesthetic positions it defended. Apart from the obligatory praise of the Führer, it conveyed a measured modernity that, after all, adequately reflected the tendencies of the widest of publics, and also of most artists. The description of the key function of architecture added to a long and generally accepted tradition and its definition of the space and homeland of all the arts might even have won the approval of the exiled masters of the Bauhaus. As for photographic realism and avant-garde art stemming from Cubism and Expressionism, both were sent packing, as being degenerate. Baldur von Schirach rejected them in the name of a truth that was distinct from reality but defined only by a work's reaching for a future temporality identified with eternity. All in all, there was absolutely nothing out of the ordinary about these remarks. They conformed to the beliefs defended by most artists, historians, and art theorists not only before the Great War but even during the 1930s.

Although history has essentially noted only the avant-garde artistic production of this period, at the time such work was limited to a minority of artists, and continued to meet with solid resistance. Furthermore, the period was marked by a "return to order," which manifested all over Europe as a return to both classical and realist values. At the Venice colloquia on "Art and Reality" and "Art and the State" held in 1934 under the auspices of the League of Nations, the greatest confusion reigned over terms. There were many art historians, such as

Austrian Hans Tietze and Frenchman Henri Focillon, who settled for thinking that "all art is both reality and a rejection of reality." Along with others, they stressed "the uncertainty of the vocabulary." Only Englishman Herbert Read pointed out that "our conception of what should be understood by 'reality' has completely changed." More numerous were those who, like French critic Waldemar George, thought "the problem of art" was not so much aesthetic as psychological and social: the modern and abstract tendencies of art were "attribute[s] of a period that is prey to the worst kind of materialism," and the gulf that had separated the artist from the public ever since the nineteenth century could be closed only if art lost its aspect of "luxury" and reverted to being "a part of national life": "I think that art is once again filling the place that belongs to it in society when the whole of life is orchestrated, paced, and organized as a fine work of art."[64] Any attempt to define reality was thus again relegated to a place of secondary importance, and meanwhile the value of art was assessed in relation to its ability to project a future and effect a reconciliation with the people.

In France, artists committed to the PCF (*Parti communiste français*) also thought, as did Louis Aragon and Paul Nizan, that bourgeois realism, bitterly critical of reality, constituted an impasse. Socialist realism, conversely, stood apart thanks to its "ability to have some perspectives"; it had to "move toward the future of that reality" and embrace "a certain exaltation of the future." Similarly, Jean Lurçat regarded the painter not simply as a "recording apparatus" but "above all as a transformer of energy whose task is to act upon the external world . . . and whose duty is to transform it."[65] While everyone agreed that art had by then broken with the tradition of *mimesis*, understood as pure imitation of visible reality, everyone also regarded art as the matrix from which the future would be born.

Over and above all their differences and even their oppositions, the supporters of surrealism and of abstraction were united by the same faith: future reality would be immanent in art if art were able to appropriate present reality. André Breton called on the works of his friends "to call out imperiously to something in external reality that responds to them." Meanwhile, Piet Mondrian called on geometrical abstraction to unveil "pure relations," hidden until then in "natural reality," and went on to declare that the new painting "is preparing the super-reality of the future; it is 'real' in that it expresses that reality."[66]

Fundamentally, over and above all formal and ideological differences, what all these artists were asserting was that future reality should correspond to present images. It is therefore at once true and false to suggest, as did filmmaker Hans Jürgen Syberberg, that "none of the traditional arts—literature, painting, sculpture, or architecture—was able to realize the representation of the Hitlerian dream of a Greater Germany," that such a dream could be embodied only in the state itself, "considered as a total work of art that included propaganda, the machinery of extermination, and war."[67] It is true because Hitler's vision or dream was indeed that described by Waldemar George: a life entirely orchestrated, paced, and organized as a fine work of art, founded on the exclusion of the "weak and mildewed" part of the community. In this sense, no "specialized" art could lay claim on its own to represent that dream. But to say, as did Syberberg, that "the intrinsic art of the Third Reich was not to be found in the traditional disciplines" is false, for the task of each work of art was not to represent but, in a fragmentary way, to prepare for the realization of the ideal Reich.

In its very simplicity, the statement made by Baldur von Schirach blended perfectly with the concept of art that dominated modern times: the truth of the work of art was no longer conceived to lie in the image's conformity with the superior reality of an idea, nor in the reality of visible nature, but rather in the future reality's conformity with the image. Because the truth of art was linked to the future, it became confused with the promise held out by Nazi rhetoric—invariably, the promise of eternity. Whether or not the image representing the future had a model mattered little in regard to the power to transform present reality, with which it was invested. It was not that the nature of the model was a matter of indifference—on the contrary, the model was the very myth that had to be reproduced—but the image itself was primarily regarded as the model, vehicle, and vector of the establishment of a better world. Therein lay its reawakening power, which was conceived to be the power of the truth immanent in the image.

This awakening into the myth, however, far from being simply a sign of modernity, was rather the delayed result of an essentially Christian orientation of art: to reawaken, through the sight of an image, the memory of exemplary actions of the past, in order to encourage their imitation in the future. Jean-Claude Schmitt has pointed out that in the medieval West, where, as in Byzantium, an image "made invisible powers visibly present," it represented an "intermediary mediation to be seized upon," because what was at stake theologically and politically was "the government of the world; and this depended on mastery of the hinge joining the two faces of the world, its visible and invisible faces, by means of symbolic objects that guaranteed their connection."[68] When the Christian religion collapsed, sweeping away the monarchical system that was linked to it, Romanticism tried to replace it with a religion of art; then Wagner, with his political and theological ambitions, laid claim to this heritage, insisting that art must always communicate "fully to sight" in order not to limit itself to *willing* but to accede to "total *power*."[69] Time and again the image was invested with the power to awaken into the myth, that is to say, to make an invisible power visibly present so as to ensure that it was mimetically obeyed. As a result, the power of the image was identified with the binding power of the truth itself.

The Church Fathers used a fine Neoplatonic formula to justify the cult of images: *per visibilia invisibilia*, "it is by means of visible things that one accedes to invisible things." Just as Christ (whom John of Damascus called "the first icon of the invisible God") said, "Whoever sees me has seen the Father," an image offered access to the invisible prototype it contained. In the nineteenth century, with the announcement of "the death of God" and the growing impact of immanentism, the earlier formula seemed to have changed to *per visibilia visibilia* —it is through visible things that visible things are produced. Wagner's thought was symptomatic when, in forming his images, he rejected the invisible ideal of Christianity, preferring to entrust himself to "nature, which alone has a visible and tangible existence." The way that Robert Scholz, a Nazi art theorist, put it differed hardly at all: "The desire to create of the German people is always born from two roots: a strong sensitive inclination toward nature and a deep metaphysical aspiration. The ability of Germans to render divinity visible within nature and to illuminate the perceptions of the senses by spiritual values satisfies Wagner's demand that art should become religion."[70]

Rosenberg, who cited these words of Wagner's in his *Myth of the Twentieth Century*, added that "only in Europe had art become the medium of a veritable victory over the world, a religion in itself."[71]

For a long time the invisible had already been stripped of its power unless it had become visible. The *transitus* was no longer the path that linked the image with divine intelligibility, as it had been for the Church Fathers. Instead, it was the path that, always proceeding from the visible to the visible, linked the present image with a future one. The past no longer belonged to the category of the invisible: the fledgling archaeology, which was unearthing and collecting the still-visible evidence of the past in order to reconstitute and reproduce the history, was followed by the invention of photography, which prevented the present from sinking into the invisibility of history and retained it, ever available, at the surface of time. Nazism quite deliberately made itself the heir of that double movement of a general absorption of the invisible into the visible and of history into the present. One of the regime's ideologues perfectly summed up the way in which myth could become identified with a present that, having absorbed an invisible past, then laid claim to mastery over the future, which was conceived as an immediate extension of it:

We certainly live in a historic century, that is to say, one that fashions history; not a century of historical reflection but rather one in which the center of gravity lies in the present, in the constant availability and vigilant expectation of immediate action, in a word: in action itself. . . . National Socialism—and herein lies its *daimon*, its great power, and its historical efficacy—. . . is nearing its goal, that is to say, the profound revolution that will deliver us from historical subjection and bind us to the present. . . . Historical thinking, which is thinking that plans, fixes upon objectives, and prepares ways forward, has launched itself into the future. In Germany today, nothing comes about that has not been set in motion by that planning thinking. Whereas in the nineteenth century the present sank deeper and deeper into concern for the past, to the point where it was technicians who achieved the greatest efficacy, . . . today we proceed deliberately, hour by hour, toward the projected future.[72]

The awakening into the myth was thus generally conceived as an awakening to the present, in the presence of an image that was a recapitulation of a past directed toward the future. As von Schirach declared, "The perfect artists Michelangelo and Rembrandt, and Beethoven and Goethe, do not represent an appeal to return to the past, but show us the future that is ours and to which we belong." By making himself visible, the genius revealed to his race both its origin and its end.

Producing the Genius

One of the first measures that Hitler took after he came to power was to entrust the construction of the House of German Art to Ludwig Troost, whom he met in Munich in the autumn of 1930. One art historian wrote, "For this project, the project manager and the architect have collaborated closely, with a love and deep understanding never shown by any Führer of the people since King Louis I of Bavaria."[73] In resolving to create this museum devoted exclusively to the "purely German art" of his time, Hitler decided to provide the creative genius of the race with a place of its own. The idea was not to fill it with great works from the national patrimony, which would have testified to the permanence of that genius throughout German history. Rather, by gathering together there each year, in a vast exhibition, works selected for their authentic "Germanity," Hitler summoned the genius of the race to manifest its eternity in the present day through concrete productions that would provide the most convincing demonstration of it. His purpose, however, was also to draw the German people there so that, by coming face to face with the most noble part of itself, it would at last awaken to its eternal creative essence.

October 15, 1933, the day when Hitler solemnly laid the first stone of what he called the Temple of German Art, was the occasion of a great festival in the town of Munich. After a procession of several thousand SA and Hitler Youth members to the site of the future building, Hitler was welcomed by the body of masons, clad in medieval costume, to the strains of the overture to Wagner's *The Mastersinger*. In memory of Louis I, who in the early nineteenth century had endeavored to turn Munich into a new Athens ("Athens on the Isar"), the Führer delivered a speech in which he promoted Munich to the status of "the capital of German Art." In the absence of the projected museum, a gigantic demonstration to mark "two thousand years of German art" was proposed, in order to reconcile art and the people immediately, there in the street.

The Processions

In the four weeks leading up to this celebration, the Bavarian press daily reported on the intense preparations designed to restore Munich to its former glory through the sumptuous decoration of its streets and squares. Sculptor Josef Wackerle had been put in charge of the artistic direction of the "solemn procession" (*Festzug*) that would pass through the town on the occasion of this First Festival of German Art. At last the great day arrived. It was later described by the prestigious magazine *Die Kunst*, in an article that is worth citing at length:

The procession was led by the kettledrummers, dressed in grey, red, and silver. They were followed by a powerful eagle (fashioned by the sculptor Göbl), symbolizing the political movement. With a fanfare of twelve trumpets, twelve heralds clad in red announced the appearance of the arts: symbolizing architecture, an Ionic capital (by the sculptor Buchner) advanced [on a float]. It was followed by the emblems of painting—ancient wall-paintings (reproduced by Richard Klein)—and sculpture—a copy of a Greek torso of Heracles and a gilded statue of Pallas Athena (the work of the sculptor Allmann). Then came thirty girls in green, with garlands of flowers, and Amazons clad in red silk. In striking contrast to them, two horsemen in black armor, embodying the spirit of heroism, and sixty pages surrounded the Gothic float [Figure 41], which carried a very charming construction, a Gothic fountain composed of two shells arranged one on top of the other. In front was a feminine figure with a lyre, embodying the *Minnesang*, the poetry of the troubadours. At the foot of this group were small copies of the world-famous Marusca dancers from Munich's old Town Hall. The blue and white of the region dominated the group of Bavarian Rococo [Figure 42], with its charming putti representing hunting, fishing, agriculture, and valor, surmounted by a genie blowing a trumpet (by Andreas Lang, Franz Mikorey, J. Seidler, and H. Panzer). All the periods of the past arrived and passed by, all the high spots of the German *Kultur*. . . . A central and magnificent moment was that of the group representing the House of German Art [Figure 43]. The large-scale model, based on the sketches of Professor P. L. Troost, was carried by eighteen costumed men. Six boys on horseback rode before them, accompanied by musicians playing fanfares and flanked by youths in green and gold carrying garlands and wreaths. Following these came representatives of the corporations, in their ancient artisan costumes, bearing emblems of their respective trades. The boilermakers carried a figure representing Bavaria (in chased copper, by Ragaller), freely copied from the crowned figure of the temple of the Hofgarten. Next came the German Art Group [Figure 44]. The famous Bamberg horseman (by Klein and Allmann) stood on a float drawn by six horses; behind the float marched sixteen boys carrying golden shields bearing the names of the most famous German artists. These were followed by the figure of Fortuna (Lommel); then the float of German fairy tales (Märchen), drawn by a white horse [Figure 45]; the mystical unicorn (by the sculptor Heinlein) represented legend and was covered by a gracefully decorated awning; a crown of multicolored flowers encircled the plinth, symbolically representing the art of poetry, which finds its source in such tales. Girls carrying flowers accentuated the poetic character of this group. The next to pass was the German legend float, with Saint George slaying the dragon (produced under the direction of K. Killer). Four chargers drew the poetry float, bearing a rearing Pegasus of shining silver (by the sculptor A. Hiller); on the front of the float were silver tragic masks (by E. A. Rauch) and crossed thyrsoi, followed by boys and girls clad in ancient costumes. The parade was completed by floats bearing the Mastersingers (Julius Dietz) and Corporations (by Schwarzer), around which thronged a joyful, youthful crowd carrying emblems and flags. . . .

And was all this purely for the pleasure of the parade and the cavalcade? Simply to intoxicate the crowd? Certainly not! It was in order to show clearly the new state's commitment to art, and to make public the truly "fated" vocation and mission of the artistic metropolis of southern Germany.[74]

The astonishing mismatch between the declared ambitions of this Day of German Art and the unbelievable kitsch of the Munich parade did not prevent it from being a truly popular success—on the contrary. The myth within which the people were supposed to be awakened was suddenly deployed, live, before their eyes. All at once, in the very streets, a whole legendary Germany was resuscitated, a blessed Germany that knew nothing of the warfare, crises, and nightmares of the Weimar *Zwischenreich*. Thanks to the new state, the people was now reconciled with the whole of its art, all of it stamped with the seal of the same German genius that had survived through the ages and through all the styles now paraded on horseback. By including the classical Greek legacy, to which the German-Aryan notion of *Kultur* insistently laid claim, along with most of the artistic styles of the past, as well as the traditional trades and their emblems, the parade aimed to suggest that all European manifestations of "creative work" could be incorporated into the concept of a "German art," the unity of which stemmed solely from the race.

In *The Myth of the Twentieth Century*, Rosenberg had already written as follows: "While we value the Gothic, the Baroque, and the Romantic, and with good reason, they do not matter much; the fact remains that ultimately what is important is not the form of the expression of Northern blood but above all that that blood still survives, the old will of the blood lives on."[75] Art, whatever its form, first and foremost constituted tangible proof of the permanence of a will to live that had never changed. The Aryan "will of the blood" (*Blutswille*) was identified with its "will for form" (*Formwillen*), so it was not history that made art, but race or blood.

The concrete composition of the procession, however, conflicted with the desire to appropriate more or less the whole of European culture, as becomes quite clear from the report just quoted. The precise mention of each of the local artists who had contributed to the great Day of German Art was an indication of the strong provincialism of part of the artistic activity that would characterize the regime. Just as each of the international styles that had marked Europe (Gothic, Renaissance, Baroque, and so on) were reduced to the proportions of a German national art, so too was that national art almost always reduced to its most limited regional form.

On that day, October 15, 1933, the minister of culture, Hans Schemm, was not content simply to salute Hitler, the "German artist" who was the incarnation of "the totality of the artistic and political genius." He also recalled "the long periods of terrible poverty, autodissolution, and bitter distress" after which, unfailingly, "a German reawakens to consciousness of his dignity [because he wishes] to have a German art as well as a German state." Schemm went on to say, "What the people demands of artistic genius is not distraction or pastimes, but sublimity itself." Invoking Kant, he added that "sublime German art," which corresponded to the people's sensitivity, "did not need to hide away in museums or in private aesthetic circles. . . . Public life and art had to condition each other mutually. . . . The German people could not under any circumstances live without art, on pain of losing its soul."[76] That condemnation of the very principle of museums, coming on the precise day when the Führer laid the first stone of the House of German Art, certainly seemed paradoxical. However, from the moment of its conception, the House of German Art was destined to transcend itself. Displayed in the form of a giant model carried on a triumphal float, it was linked in a very special relationship with the parade, the very heart of which it constituted. Was this the procession of a resuscitated history, soon to be fixed in stone? Or did it represent the contents of a museum that in advance was destined to overflow from stone into life? Was it an end in itself or the promise of a rebirth?

Three and a half years later, the ceremony was repeated at the inauguration of the museum, on the occasion of the first Great Exhibition of German Art, which opened on July 18, 1937. This was the Second Day of German Art, significantly given the same name as the first: "Two Thousand Years of German *Kultur*."[77] The three-kilometer procession, even more gigantic than that of 1933, comprised thirty floats, five hundred horsemen, and 2,000 men and 2,500 women in historical costumes. The organizers of the show, Hermann Kaspar and Richard Knecht, who were members of the Munich Academy of Fine Arts, decided to repeat but amplify the parade of 1933. Once again, amid a huge sea of flags and banners, the various ages marched past, each one represented by several floats bearing sculptures and models of buildings, each one in the same style. The Teutonic Age (Figure 46) was symbolized by Ägit and Rau, the god and goddess of the sea, beneath the spread wings of the eagle Hreswelda. This was followed by the Roman, Gothic (Figure 47), Renaissance, Baroque, Classical, and Romantic Ages, and finally by the New Age, which was symbolized by figures representing faith and loyalty (Figure 48). These floats presented a bold synthesis of historical styles: neoclassical figures were drawn along by horses covered in swastikas, and the horses were led by men clad in Teutonic costumes. A monumental head of Pallas Athena (Figure 49) was carried along like a Virgin Mary. There could be no doubt, however, that the costumes of those surrounding the idol expressed the eternal Teutonic "will for life," forever unchanging even in its perpetual metamorphosis.

The immense procession that passed on that day in front of the new House of German Art had something of the character of a circus parade, inviting the massive crowds to enter into the temple precinct; it also smacked somewhat of a lesson in the history of art, preparing the same crowd for the rediscovery of the unity of the German genius. But the historical nature of the forms displayed was eclipsed by their actualization, so the history of art turned into a live presentation of the myth. The very form of the procession in truth constituted a negation of the past and a celebration of the live simultaneity of the myth in all its parts. This procession, a veritable living "guide" (Führer) to the exhibition, constituted an emanation of this temple that was already overflowing into life, revealing in advance in the public space what was contained within the stone walls. As one university teacher in Munich put it the previous year, "Art is the guide [Führer]; it is what guides and accompanies our life. It shows us, in the form of a myth, where we come from and where we are going. It is a symbol of ourselves and presents an image of the goal of our will. With its melodies, it accompanies us all the way to the grave."[78] Goebbels likewise attributed this extended temporal dimension to German art. It was to "express the immortal soul of the people, by drawing it from the past and the present, in a poetic and artistic form, and to bestow upon its ever-active creative ability strength for the future."[79]

The official program of this Second Day of German Art clearly set out the purpose of the ceremony: "Through forms drawn from the distant and recent past of German culture, we ourselves, as an entire people, become part of the solemn parade of German power [*des Deutschen Könnens*] and of German history." The intention definitely was to empower the people by recapitulating the historical forms of its art. The equation that Wagner formulated had become official doctrine: German art should not be content simply to aspire but must realize its German essence, as reflected in the German language; it must accede to and provide access to power (*Können*). Thus German art not only produced German history as a single visible totality, but was the very means that made it possible for that history to start up again and be reborn. The most striking formulation of this lofty function assigned to art can be found in the lectures of 1935–36 given by Martin Heidegger called *Origin of the Work of Art*:

Any beginning [*Anfang*] already, in reserve, contains the end. . . . Each time art comes to be, that is to say, there is a beginning, a thrust of history takes place; history begins or starts again. History here does not mean the unfolding of facts in time—facts that, despite the importance they may hold, always remain mere incidents. History means the awakening of a people into its appointed task as entrance into that people's endowment. . . . Art is history in the essential sense that it grounds history. . . . The origin of a people's historical existence is art. This is so because art is by nature an origin, nothing more—a distinctive way in which truth comes into being, that is, becomes historical.[80]

French historian Pierre Ayçoberry has noted that as early as 1943 an English socialist asked "an embarrassing question," which Ayçoberry summarized as follows: "Is not that country simply a caricature of our own countries?"[81] In Heidegger's exhortation to the Germans to awaken themselves through art—that is to say, to bring their future into conformity with the art that unveiled the truth of its Greek origins—his words were as close to Nazi thinking as they were to the conservative and nationalistic thinking of the rest of Europe. National Socialist Germany had set out not along a *Sonderweg* (particular path) of its own, but rather on the path of national particularism, to which it became more deeply committed than did the other European nations—possibly to the point of caricature. That a people preserved its genius in its art and should draw from the latter the strength necessary for its national rebirth was an idea that Louis Aragon, for example, defended in France against Fascism. Wishing "to exalt the set of realities that we call a nation," he declared "the defense of culture to be identical to the defense of the nation." The conclusion to the speech he delivered on July 16, 1937 to a congress of writers should not be forgotten:

Plunge into national reality, to be reborn streaming with the most real humanity. In the bubbling springs of your nation, seek for the deep inspiration that will express you by expressing it. . . . Faced with phony nationalisms, set up the national reality, set up the nation composed of men and women who work, love one another, and give birth to laughing children, for whom you prepare a pacific future in which the bread will be white for everyone and in which nationalists in the Franco mode will not shower swastika-covered bombs upon innocence, work, and love. . . . You will become excellent engineers of souls if you collaborate in the creation of a culture that will be truly human because *it will be national in form and socialist in content.*[82]

One year later, the dual *national* and *socialist* character of art was said by Aragon to be the fruit of history: "So believe me, the whole movement of art, throughout its history of a thousand reversals, is proceeding toward the triumph of the national reality."[83]

As for the conviction that "truth" (as an "unveiling" that generates the history and reality of the future) was immanent in art—a conviction initially held by all the philanthropic reformers of the nineteenth century—it was then, as we have seen, shared equally by most revolutionaries, whether they conceived of revolution as conservative or as progressive. It seemed clear that the only people able to escape from immanentism were those who regarded art not as the presentation of how things ought to be but as criticism of how things are.

Under the Third German Reich, as elsewhere—but more so than elsewhere—the task of historians of national art, who seemed suddenly to take over from the history of national churches of the past, was often to collect a series of images of historical forms, which they then presented in a book, as if in a parade. Invariably the historians showed successive metamorphoses of a national god who had to be revealed in the full light of day in order to illuminate the future, as one professor at the University of Bonn explained in the preface to his *History of German Art*:

This book aims to contribute to the understanding of the German path taken by the spirit, which remains visible in the works of art of every age. This should become apparent as in a *Bildungsroman* [educative novel] which, starting with the blood and soil determinations peculiar to the birth of the hero, then describing the formative experiences that are productive for him, leads on to the works in which he fulfils himself. The breadth and depth of the spiritual Reich of the Germans need to be drawn again in order to make visible the heritage that is preserved within us and that requires us to show where we come from and who we are, and thereby contribute to the orientation of the future.[84]

Over and above the differences between this statement and those of Heidegger and the program of the Day of German Art, the professor's theme is identical in its structure: because art projects the past into the future it determines, it has a "fateful" value. It acquires all its power to awaken and to be formative once it is remembered, that is to say, once it is presented as its own repetition and visible recapitulation.

The Temple

If the parade of German art appeared to be a live emanation of the new museum, the museum itself was presented as a temple that radiated outward the truth immanent in its works of art. When, in September 1937, Mussolini accompanied his host to the first Great Exhibition, the vestal virgins who guarded the Temple of German Art confirmed both the real sacredness of the spot and its power to make the myth live (Figure 50).

Hitler had entrusted the realization of this temple to Troost, an architect with whom he shared a fascination with neoclassicism, which seemed to him to carry on the German tradition and also to blend with the buildings constructed in Munich by art patron Louis I. At the same time, in Paris, architects Louis-Auguste Boileau, Jacques Carlu, and Léon Azéma were justifying the neoclassicism of the new Trocadéro, which was to dominate the Universal Exhibition of 1937. They claimed to have "recovered for the new monument lines which, despite their modernism, well and truly belonged to the French monumental tradition and the harmony of Paris."[85] So their hope was "to bequeath to future generations one of the monuments that best expressed the spiritual and aesthetic tendencies of our time." Hitler meanwhile explained to Albert Speer that he was building "in order to bequeath to posterity the genius of his own age."[86]

It was likewise Troost who had already designed the Temples of the Heroes, whose example was supposed to exert its influence from the Königsplatz of Munich over the whole people—a fact that underlined the symbolic link that united these two eternal "guards": the dead people and living art. Behind the Neo-Doric colonnade inspired by sketches made by Hitler ten years earlier,[87] this temple was now to shelter annually the actuality of the eternal genius of the race, expressed in painted and sculpted forms.

The visible production of this eternal soul, of which the speeches of the Nazi leaders had been so full for the past four years, was no small undertaking. But so essential did it seem to Hitler that in every one of the speeches on art he had delivered since 1933, he had made it seem that the very survival of National Socialism depended on it. After reading the Führer's Nuremberg speech of September 1933, Thomas Mann noted, with some stupefaction, that never before had "the men of power . . . set themselves up in this way as the preceptors of their people, even of mankind." In Hitler he detected clearly enough "a typical product of the lower middle class, with a limited education and an acquired taste for philosophizing." He had "no doubt at all that for [Hitler], in contrast to types like Hermann Goering and Ernst Röhm, the main concern [was] not war but 'German culture'. . . . Neither Napoleon nor Bismark . . . would have spoken *ex cathedra* to proclaim a cultural theory for the nation or to outline a cultural program, although they were far better qualified intellectually to do so than this poor lout." Aghast, he observed that the totalitarian state was not only "a power base but a base for everything, and even dominates culture—culture above all—" and reduces it dictatorially, "sweepingly, to a few feverishly self-taught concepts based on terribly spotty reading."[88] Indeed, it was its very "spotty" or lacunary character that, so to speak, constituted the basis of the Nazi concept of culture. Perhaps this, in negative fashion, explains why so many intellectuals rallied to it. They filled in the gaps and incompletion of the Nazi world vision as they would have done on a Romantic sketch. That vision invoked the sublime to justify its failings and set itself the task of affirming an overwhelming plenitude that would compensate for them. But these lacunas were precisely the abysses to which Nazism banished everything alien to itself, just as its "steely Romanticism" eliminated all Romantic irony. We shall later see how the exhibition of "Degenerate Art," opened in 1937, just after the opening of the House of German Art, constituted a spectacular symptom of that lacunary culture.

The selection of the works judged worthy to figure in the first Great Exhibition of German Art followed the same logic as that which presided over the selection of the men who were to form the elite of the *Volksgemeinschaft*: purification in accordance with the Idea. Chaired by Adolf Ziegler, a jury of nine members, including among others Arno Breker and Gerdy Troost (Ludwig's widow), was supposed to effect a preselection of fifteen hundred works out of the fifteen thousand submitted. On June 5, having examined the jury's choice in the company of Hitler, Goebbels noted in his diary that although the sculptures seemed acceptable, many of the paintings were catastrophic. "Utterly disappointing examples of artistic Bolshevism were presented to me. . . . The Führer is spitting with rage." Hitler appointed his photographer Heinrich Hoffmann to oversee a reselection. On July 13, when Hitler paid another visit in the company of Goebbels, Gerdy Troost, Adolf Wagner, and of course Hoffmann, the "Führer's eye," the six hundred works that had been retained at last matched his expectations. Every trace of "Judeo-Bolshevism" in German art—that is anything that seemed to alter and undermine the identity of a racially healthy *Volksgemeinschaft*—had been eliminated.

The selection was intelligible, however, only if one understood that it was a matter, first and foremost, of taking a bet on time and eternity. To a large degree, the future of the Nazi myth was at stake here. It was necessary to ensure control over the imaginary representations of the people by means of the reproduction and massive diffusion of these images that were about to flood the whole of Germany. In 1939, French political analyst Anatole de Monzie wrote, "More than ever, people need images. They need them to orientate their curiosity, furnish their memories, sustain their enthusiasms and their approval."[89] That was precisely the role assigned to this temple: to recharge the memory of the German people so it would conform to these images when starting again. Merely to enter the sacred precinct was supposed to be enough to dispel its bad Jewish dream, thanks to the selection of images that were in conformity with the dreams of the "great Germans" who determined its destiny. An image therefore had to mediate in two ways: with the past and with the future of the race. It provided access to the dream of the genius and to the productive origin of its visions, and at the same time it was to be accepted as presenting and projecting its future and already visible destiny.

The temple thus sheltered this productive genius, which the Nazi lexicon called the eternal soul of the race. Walter Otto called attention to the Roman origins of the concept of *genius*: it was said to represent the immortal soul—that is, as Otto Rank added, the part of an individual that can "engender [*gignere*] what is immortal, be it a child or a work." Having originally been understood to have a strictly individual application, as an equivalent to the Egyptian *ka* or the Greek *daimon*, "in a culture founded on the rights of the father, *genius* had come to mean the community's power of reproduction, its ability to engender . . . and thus to ensure its immortality."[90] Whether or not the hypothesis was philologically valid, it was this concept of the eternal soul as a protective genius of the race that lay at the heart of the National Socialist doctrine—and that was at work primarily in art and as art.

Whereas sculpture in general offered only the human figure as the clothing of the genius, painting presented an opportunity for the genius to don the mantle of landscape to reveal itself to the people. Professor and architect Paul Schultze-Naumburg, one of the foremost *völkisch* ideologues of art, whose huge influence we shall be considering here, had as early as the beginning of the century formulated his theory of "a culture of what is visible (*Kultur des Sichtbaren*)." This culture incorporated "not only houses and monuments, and bridges and roads, but also clothing and social forms, forests, and stockbreeding, machines and the defense of the territory." For many decades, the people and the authorities had together fashioned the physiognomy of the country, giving it its unity. It was not a matter of a work of reason or logic, but of a spontaneous shaping (*Gestalten*) of reality in accordance with the Idea of the German *genius*. The long series of *Kultur-*

arbeiten that Schultze-Naumberg introduced adopted the goal of "opening the eyes" of the Germans to the fact

that our conscious gaze pronounces judgment not only on what is "beautiful or ugly," but also on what is "good or bad," in both senses [of the terms], that is to say, "practically useful or not useful" and "morally good or bad"; and also the fact that the eye does not need to base its judgment on language-expressed thought, in which we are accustomed to discover only "logical thought."[91]

Schultze-Naumburg accordingly based his works on photographic "examples" and "counterexamples" that were designed to educate the eye so as to ensure the preservation and propagation of German cultural productions, which only the German eye could judge to be beautiful, good, and useful to the German people. This was the first formulation of the normative principle of the *Entscheidung* (decision), which was to become the principle of the Nazi exercise of power.

Eminent historian of art Heinrich Wölfflin detected in fine arts productions "not only an individual style" but also "the *style of a school,* the *style of a country,* the *style of a race.*" To speak of a "national style," it was of course necessary to have first "fixed upon its durable characteristics," for the character of a particular period might modify certain aspects of it. But Wölfflin did not hesitate to conclude that certain "national characteristics" were permanent: "Visual schemata differ from one nation to another. In the art of presentation there is one manner peculiar to the Italians, another peculiar to the Germans, and they remain always the same throughout the ages." Any history of vision and presentation thus led "beyond art." For in the order of vision, all of these national differences were "more than simply a matter of taste." Rather, "[t]hey condition the principles that govern the image that a particular people constructs of the world, and they are conditioned by them." In the "revision in the guise of an epilogue" that he added to his *Fundamental Principles of the History of Art* in 1933, he denied that it was possible to establish an autonomous history of vision. He postulated, on the contrary, that there existed *national histories of vision,* determined by internal processes that were "always governed by the requirements of a particular time and a particular race."[92]

In its principles, Nazi discourse on art—in particular, Hitler's discourse—differed at once very little and very much from that of Wölfflin, who since 1929, along with a number of other eminent university professors, had been a patron of Rosenberg's Union Fighting for German Culture (*Kampfbund für deutsche Kultur*).[93]

The Nazi *Weltanschauung* certainly found in Wölfflin the credentials of nobility, given that the *Weltanschauung*, like him and many others, strove "to establish a national type of imagination."[94] But whereas Wölfflin prudently maintained that any vision was determined by "the spirit of the times" (*Zeitgeist*), Nazism insisted that it was determined purely by race, for which it postulated an eternity or a transhistorical identity of its own, which denied history. The *Zeitgeist* was totally absorbed by the *Volksgeist*, as in the 1927 declaration made by art historian Wilhelm Worringer to the effect that the Gothic style was "a phenomenon not belonging to any age but rather in its deepest foundations an ageless racial phenomenon."[95]

The inclusion of countless German landscapes (Figures 51 through 54) in the exhibitions in the Temple of German Art was a response to this determination to establish just such "a national type of imagination," one that was able to ensure the formation of a judgment that was at once aesthetic, ethical, and practical. The landscapes gave the people an image of the world that it had long fashioned through its work, in such a way that its genius had impregnated every feature of that image. As art historian Oskar Hagen proclaimed, the "German landscape is a self-portrait of the soul. The soul expresses all its beauty only when its body has been exhausted into annihilation."[96] Whereas the subjectivity of the Romantic artist turned a landscape painting into a veil through which his own individual genius could be glimpsed, here too, as in every domain subjected to the National Socialist ideology, what Romanticism declared about the links that united a landscape to an individual's spirit was shifted to apply to the collective spirit of the race, people, or nation.

As Jean-Claude Lebensztejn points out, Romanticism was "a desire and a strategy for organic fusion" so that "nature and feeling, and the subject and the object, could be indissolubly linked."[97] Nazi ideology certainly retained the Romantic fusion, but it did away with any kind of metaphor. For Hagen, Rosenberg, and Schultze-Naumburg, if there was a "German vision," it had to be expressed "body and soul" in the landscape, which was conceived as an organic extension of its genius. Through the centuries-long sacrifice of its labor, the German people had become incorporated in the landscape it had fashioned, transfiguring it into the collective body of its collective soul. (The banality of such statements—now commonplace in tourist guides to Europe—is simply a symptom of the banality of part of the *Blut und Boden* (blood and soil) ideology, which haunts the management of the perceptions of the masses that are avid for cultural idiosyncrasies and identities.)

Once landscape was defined as the self-portrait of the genius of a creative people, any landscape became acceptable provided that it had manifestly been worked on by man, who had remodeled it. Forest, mountain, and field landscapes were worked on by peasants; the marine landscape or that of a port bore the marks of the labors of fishermen, sailors, or dockers. But sometimes the mere presence of a symbolic figure—such as the eagles hovering above the territory over which they kept watch (*Wache*) (Figure 55) sufficed to transfigure an otherwise neutral scene into a self-portrait of the German spirit. Yet a landscape could likewise be of the "pure nature" that determined human destiny and that was presented both as a school for combat and as an object of domination. In 1941, Schultze-Naumburg revived the concept of the heroic landscape. Since the time of classical landscapes with figures by "the Norman Poussin and the Friburger [*sic*] Claude Lorrain," this kind of heroic landscape had, he declared, undergone a profound change: for example, the Italian landscapes by Hermann Urban, in which edifices constructed by men, who were never visible, fiercely stood firm against the forces of nature. "Heraclitus' saying, 'War is the father of all things,' acquires a new meaning in the light of our present *Weltanschauung*. We know that the whole of life is a battle, and the spectacle of nature as a whole shows us that no living being can keep on living without a battle."[98] And that battle fought for the life of the genius "founder of culture" was never better expressed than in the pictures of worksites established by the Third Reich. From the images of the huge quarries[99] that yielded the blocks of German stone destined to give body to the monuments of the eternal Reich (Figure 56), to those of the bridges and roads that composed the routes of the Führer (Figure 57), the even more heroic landscapes depicting these worksites clearly constituted a most sovereign affirmation of the theory of the landscape as a self-portrait and also of its validity. Thus there was no discontinuity at all between the more archaic "peasant" version of the values of the soil and the blood, and the modern version, which exalted the engineer.

One year before the Nazis accession to power, Ernst Jünger remarked that the surrounding world could be divided according to two distinct logics, which he set in opposition: the museum and the worksite:

We live in a world that, on the one hand, exactly resembles a worksite [and,] on the other, is just like a museum. . . . We have reached a kind of historical fetishism that is directly related to a lack of creative force. So it is consoling to think that, following the development of grandiose means of destruction, a kind of secret correspondence accompanies the accumulation and conservation of what is known as the cultural patrimony.

In the view of this "reactionary modernist"[100] who elaborated the figure of the worker while identifying with the nationalist trend of the *Tat* group and National Bolshevism, activity on the part of museums was just "one of the last oases of bourgeois security," a loophole used "to avoid political decisions." What the situation called for was not "talk about tradition, but the creation of one." Jünger nevertheless appealed to the "*living* form" of tradition, that which demands that one assume "responsibility not for the replicas of ancient images, but a direct responsibility for the original force that engenders them." He condemned "the attempts of a certain category of artists to transpose old recipes into a kind of *Weltanschauung* art," the "habitual loophole" for those lacking talent. In opposition to such artists, he set "the landscape of worksites, which demands sacrifice and humility from the generation that is consumed there," in accordance with a process that demanded "ever-closer fusion between organic forces and mechanical forces."[101]

Representations of that fusion, which Jünger called "organic construction," also enjoyed "members' rights" in the Temple of German Art. But whereas what Jünger had in mind was an art that would be a worksite in itself, incorporating "every domain in life," the temple offered the German people representations of its real worksites. All strategies designed to break with the past thus disintegrated, and continuity was reaffirmed: for far from opposing museum-based activity, pictures of worksite, on the contrary, prolonged it. Represented in its limited concrete form, the worksite found its place there, in the museum, and as such became integrated into the national patrimony, alongside the "replicas of ancient images." In his work entitled *German Art Today*, Werner Rittich could thus set side by side a view of Meissen, the *Albrechtsburg Fortress* by Karl Leipold, and the *Construction of the Hermann-Göring Factories of the Reich* by Franz Gerwin (Figure 96). For the regime's official history of art, as for Le Corbusier in France, chimney stacks and towering cisterns were the cathedrals and castles of the modern age.

The worksite became integrated into the general cult of work, which was an extension of the cult of art, encompassing it in the worship of "creative work" through which and in which the collective genius was confirmed. Images of the great worksites that factories were, and of the constructions and motorways of the Führer, thus exalted the power of the German creative genius, which realized itself as a landscape organically constructed so as to reflect its present dimensions. Such images by no means stood in opposition to images of a medieval village or a field ploughed by a carthorse; on the contrary, they constituted proofs of the continuity of the race's "Faustian spirit."

In a work devoted to images of the industrial universe that was under construction (published to mark the fiftieth birthday of reichsminister for armaments and munitions and engineer Fritz Todt), Wilhelm Rüdiger stressed the "eternal" links between art and technology:

These two powers produced from the same original roots and which, ever since they went their separate ways, seem to have confronted each other in irreconcilable hostility, are so close in Leonardo's technical drawings that they seem intertwined and united. . . .

For Leonardo, thinking and looking were not yet separate. . . . Out of the artist springs the technician, from one who looks comes one who thinks, from the creator [*Bildner*] comes one who calculates. The links are fluid; every representation is imperceptibly interplaying with others.[102]

That "fluid link" between the artist and the engineer was the very same as the link between the Idea and vision and their concrete realization. So the creative genius of the race could now become incorporated into the technological universe, just as it used to be in the landscapes of the Renaissance and the Romantic period. While National Socialist painting had a duty to preserve and repeat the images of the past, it also had to appropriate the new industrial landscape in order to show technology how to affirm at last its fidelity to its artistic origin: "The profession of the artist consists in rediscovering unity," so that an industrial building no longer seems "an alien body" in the landscape.[103]

However heterogeneous it may have been—both stylistically and thematically—the collection of German landscapes gathered together in the temple was thus charged with the task of forming a way of looking that, in return, would impart its unity to that collection. It was a way of looking for which Schultz-Naumburg had been praying as early as the beginning of the century—a way capable of pronouncing on what it judged to be "beautiful," "good," and "practically useful" for the future of the German people. Hitler too was convinced that "the nobility of the most exalted beauty lies in the last analysis only in what is logically most expedient."[104]

Although landscapes made up the greater portion of the painted works, sculpture as well as painting could exhibit or produce the collective genius in the lineaments of a human figure. It was clearly here that the racist concept of that genius was most manifest. The selection of figures seems to have been guided by the aim to gather together in the temple a body of examples of successive incarnations of genius in the course of history. If, as *Mein Kampf* declared, the *völkisch* Reich's task was to "embrace all Germans" and to "assemble and preserve the most valuable stocks of the basic racial elements in this people,"[105] the selection of present examples of the race had to be complemented by a selection of examples of German human beings who had been racially pure ever since their origins. Only artistic images could depict this epic of the Aryan genius through all its metamorphoses.

Accordingly, this genius had to be clothed in a body capable of immediately manifesting its eternal character. Throughout the regime, nudity was considered to be the most effective sign of that eternal character. In the first place, it was an obvious choice as a model for a community founded through and through on eugenism (the belief that the human species can be improved through selective breeding). Second, it presented the double advantage of visibly anchoring the history of the community in its Greek past and simultaneously lifting the image of the community out of any concrete historical temporality that would inevitably be conferred upon it by clothing. The bodies portrayed in Josef Riedl's *Ready for Battle* (Figure 58), Arno Breker's *Departure of the Fighter* (Figure 59), and Walter Hoeck's *Young Germany* (Figure 60) all showed how the same youth was always reborn, unchanged, to defend the Aryan culture, just as he had powerfully defended the culture of the Greeks in the past.

This first, summary clothing of the eternal soul was backed up by a second mode of signifying the Germanic-Nordic or Aryan sameness: namely, the accumulation of all the historical moments, all the different times believed to have manifested the visible essence of that sameness. Here, in contrast, clothing became the indispensable sign of the genius's unchanging identity throughout and despite history, for it could be identified only because of the appropriation of the successive stages of its deployment. The same Aryan nature was thus passed on from Wilhelm Dohme's vaguely Assyrian Middle Ages (Figure 61), through Willy Meller's classical Greece (Figure 62), then through the later Middle Ages of Rudolf Otto (Figure 63) and the at-once *völkisch* and revolutionary Renaissance of Albert Bürkle (Figure 64), eventually to inhabit the clothes of Elk Eber's *The Last Grenadier* (Figure 65). Setting out to conquer the eternity of the creative genius of the race, the artists ruled by the *Führerprinzip* were all seized by an irrepressible mimetic frenzy that led them to imitate every historical style in order to construct the myth of that eternity and to reproduce it in images.

As early as 1934—not long after the Night of the Long Knives (purge of the SA), which concluded the national revolution—Hitler wanted the art of the Third Reich to jettison both the Expressionist tendencies supported by Goebbels and the *völkisch* tendencies defended by Rosenberg and Himmler.[106] He issued a warning to the partisans of a "'Teuton art' [*theutsche Kunst*] generated by the bizarre world of their own Romantic representations of the National Socialist Revolution":

They never were National Socialists. Sometimes, in their hermitages, they inhabited a Germanic dream world that made even the Jews laugh; sometimes they trotted along, bravely and piously, in the middle of the sacred parades of a bourgeois Renaissance. . . . But what completely escaped their notice was that National Socialism rests on knowledge founded on the blood, not on archaic traditions. . . . Consequently, they are today offering us railway stations in the original style of the German Renaissance, street plaques typeset with authentic Gothic lettering, texts and songs freely adapted from Walther von der Vogelweide, fashion creations in the Faust and Marguerite modes, paintings in the manner of Säckingen's *Trumpet*, and possibly even defensive weapons in the form of axes and crossbows.[107]

But despite this public condemnation of the *völkisch* trend, less than three years later Hitler picked out not only *The Awakening* (into the myth) by his protégé Richard Klein, but also Hubert Lanzinger's *Portrait of the Führer*, which represented Hitler clad in armor, in the guise of a knight bearing on high the standard of German culture (Figure 66). Hitler's support for the largely *völkisch* parade of the Day of German Art and his delight in it, the selection of works for the Great Exhibitions of the years that followed, his unfailing fascination with the Wagnerian world—all of this testifies to the fact that, far from being excluded, this version of the Nazi myth continued to exist, in both its antiquarian and its modernist versions, in Hitler's imaginary representations as well as within the walls of the temple and throughout Germany.

It would be impossible to exaggerate the strictly functional nature of this coexistence of images, which was matched by the coexistence of three distinct types of architecture, which Hitler deliberately maintained side by side for the sake of the specific functions they were assigned in the new Germany. One day in 1938, when visiting a modern factory with Speer, Hitler "told him yet again that he was won over to the modern architecture of glass and steel":

Look at this facade over three hundred meters high. The proportions are very fine. It satisfies criteria quite different from those of a party forum. The latter, through their Doric style, express the new order, whereas here, inevitably, what prevails is the technological solution. All the same, if there is one of those so-called modern architects who would tell me that houses and town halls need to be built in the industrial style, I would say that he had understood nothing. That would be not modern but simply in bad taste, and would furthermore flout the eternal laws of architectonics. A place of work needs light, air, and functional installations; from a town hall I expect dignity, from a house to live in peace and quiet that can fortify me for the difficult struggle of life. Just imagine a Christmas tree against a wall of glass, Speer! Impossible! Existence has multiple needs: we must bear that in mind, both here and elsewhere.[108]

Hitler perceived no contradiction, nor even any tension between the three types. Far from characterizing Nazism, a similar "functionalism" was expressed in analogous terms by Fernand Léger that same year, 1938:

Is it possible to conceive of a habitation, a factory, and a monument using the same artistic formula for all three? . . . Architecture speaks to the average man. Let us follow him. He leaves his home, sets off for his factory or his office and, on the way, passes a palace or a monument or a factory. It is difficult for him to conceive that the three buildings resemble one another. What with the intimacy of his apartment, the rationality of the factory, and the monument's probable need to be spectacular, there is, I believe, room for three different styles.[109]

Under the Third Reich, neoclassicism was required to satisfy the need for "grandeur and nobility" in official buildings. The vernacular style, which was the architectural equivalent of *völkisch* painting, was recommended in the construction of farms, youth hostels, and insofar as possible, private houses (Figures 67 and 68). At last, as early as his 1933 Nuremberg speech, Hitler assigned to industrial buildings—whose modernity, even boldness, in some cases has never been denied (Figure 69)—the task of representing modern "spiritual monuments": "Using new materials such as steel, iron, glass, concrete, and so on, their evolu-

tion will inevitably follow a path in conformity with the purpose of the constructions and corresponding to the materials themselves."[110]

Throughout Germany, as in its temple, the totality of the genius of the race
was thus deployed, not so much in all its diversity but rather in its eternity,
which was understood as permanence. The multiple periods formerly dispersed
through history now coexisted in the same space, all together. The German,
Germanic-Nordic, or Aryan genius produced its self-portrait in dimensions that
combined with its power, giving visible form to what Hitler called its "living
substance." It was hoped that this genius, now unified, would at last feel "at one
with itself" within a culture that Hitler described as "founded on the Hellenic
spirit and German technology."[111] In all this there was no hint of eclecticism, but
rather an essential postmodernism: history vanished into the catalogue list.

The fact was that this list did not attempt to offer a complete representation of history. As with all objects it apprehended through their visible aspects,
Nazism exercised its judgment in order to preserve only what it reckoned to be
"beautiful," "good," and "practically useful" for the race. Its model for the fabrication of the ideal was that of neoclassical aesthetics: in accordance with the National Socialist Idea, it selected from its visible history only the fragments that
were necessary for the fabrication of "the German ideal of beauty" that would
embody its eternity. Once the body of the national god that had been frag-
mented by time was reconstituted, complete with all its healthy parts, this exhibition of the protective genius aimed to reproduce it intensively.

4

REPRODUCING THE GENIUS

> Whoever persists in seeing in National Socialism nothing but a political movement knows nothing about it. It is more than a religion: it is a will to create a new man.
>
> —Adolf Hitler, quoted in Hermann Rauschning, *Hitler Speaks*

One of the most remarkable aspects of Nazism was without a doubt the link it established between "the German ideal of beauty," which was supposed to have been developed over the centuries, and the fabrication of a superior human race, in accordance with knowledge and techniques provided by twentieth-century eugenics. Joachim Fest observed that with Hitler "all cynicism and calculation in the tactics of power were brought up short before this vision: the new man."[1] In *Mein Kampf*, Hitler lamented that as a result of "the open borders of our fatherland, [and] the association with un-German foreign bodies along these frontier districts," the German people "unfortunately is no longer based on a unified racial nucleus." He took comfort, however, from "the absence of complete blending." "Today in our German national body we still possess great unmixed stocks of Nordic-Germanic people whom we may consider the most precious treasure for our future." Without those pure reserves, "the highest goal of mankind" would have remained beyond the Germans, for "the sole bearer, whom Fate had clearly chosen for this completion, would have perished in the general racial porridge of the unified people."[2] Conscious of the fact that "such a unified mash . . . would expel all ideals from this world," the *völkisch* state had to "set race in the center of the community's life." Its twofold task was "to see to it that only the healthy beget children" (so that what would be created would be "images of the Lord and not monstrosities halfway between man and ape"), and through sterilization to forbid the reproduction of "all who are in any way visibly sick or who have inherited a disease and can therefore pass it on." An appropriate education was needed to enable the whole nation at last to participate in "the supreme blessing of a highly bred racial stock." Then men would be no longer *"concerned with breeding dogs, horses, and cats, but with breeding the human race."*[3] In the opening pages of *Mein Kampf,* however, Hitler defined the twofold task that fell to the *völkisch* state even more harshly: "To establish the deepest sense of social responsibility for the creation of better foundations for our development, coupled with brutal determination in breaking down unimprovable offspring." Instead of uselessly trying to "alleviate existing evil," it was better "to ensure from the start healthier channels for a future development."[4]

In 1935, Alexis Carrel, winner of the Nobel Prize for Medicine in 1912, published his *Unknown Man* simultaneously in Paris, New York, and London. The book was a huge popular success. This French doctor who had emigrated to the United States advocated "constructing man according to the rules of his nature." For him, as for Richard Walther Darré, leader of the peasants of the Reich (*Reichsbauernführer*) and minister of agriculture, the existence of social classes was "not due to chance or to social conventions." It rested "on a solid biological basis." However, even if heredity had assigned each person his or her place, it was now "imperative that social classes should be synonymous with biological classes." It was "the quality of [man's] tissues and his soul" that would trace out the destiny of individuals in the best of worlds: "Our efforts to render normal the unfit are evidently useless. We should then turn our attention toward promoting the optimum growth of the fit. . . . Modern nations will save themselves by developing the strong, not by protecting the weak." Alexis Carrel accordingly called for "the construction of an elite" by "voluntary eugenics," the only way to produce a "hereditary aristocracy." He was delighted by recent scientific discoveries: "For the first time in the history of humanity, a crumbling civilization is capable of discerning the causes of its decay." It would thus be in a position to "escape the fate common to all great civilizations of the past."

Carrel shared with Hitler the conviction that "as long as the hereditary qualities of the race remain present, the strength and audacity of his forefathers can be resurrected in modern man by his own will." But, he wondered, "Is he still capable of such an effort?" The "immense number of defectives and criminals" posed a problem: how to protect society, in an economical fashion, against the elements that so endangered it? The defectives and criminals "should be humanely and economically disposed of in small euthanasic institutions supplied with the proper gases." According to Carrel, "[m]odern society should not hesitate to organize itself with reference to the normal individual," for it was, after all, "the ultimate purpose of civilization" that was at stake.[5]

What distinguished this discourse from that of the Nazis was essentially the absence of nationalism and anti-Semitism, but it shared the Nazi conviction that the fabrication of the new man would not be possible without the elimination of what Hitler called "the mildewed parts" of the human race. In his preface to the 1939 American edition of his book, Carrel, drawing attention to J. Edgar Hoover's statistics—which estimated the number of criminals in the United States to be 4,760,000—reckoned that the country contained "30 to 40 million unadapted and unadaptable people." The preface closed with the following words borrowed from the book's eighth chapter: "To progress again, man must remake himself. And he cannot remake himself without suffering. For he is both the marble and the sculptor. In order to uncover his true visage he must shatter his own substance with heavy blows of his hammer."[6] The metaphor that, when used by Mussolini, had been applied to the body politic, was according to Carrel to be applied practically to the biological body of the whole of humankind.

The measures of legal sterilization recommended by Carrel for the mentally ill and certain criminals had already been in force, however, in the state of Indiana in the United States since 1907. By the late twenties, they were applied in twenty-eight American states and in one province of Canada. Fifteen thousand sterilizations had been carried out in the United States by 1930 and more than thirty thousand by 1939. In Europe, the pioneer countries in this field were Switzerland in 1928 and Denmark in 1929. Germany was next in 1933, followed by Norway in 1934 and Sweden and Finland in 1935. All of these countries adopted similar laws and were eventually followed by many other states throughout the world.[7]

In Nazi Germany, the first measures that were to realize the "negative" side of the eugenism program were taken on June 2, 1933. Wilhelm Frick, minister for internal affairs, announced the creation of a committee of experts to deal with questions of population and racial policies. This committee produced the so-called Sterilization Law of July 14, 1933. The aim of this law was "the prevention of hereditarily flawed progeniture" (*Gesetz zur Verhütung erbkranken Nachwuchses*). In the first year of its application, 56,244 decisions to sterilize were made by 181 "tribunals for hereditary health." Alongside some of the most influential figures in German medicine (one of whom was Ernst Rüdin, elected in New York during the preceding year as chairman of the International Association of Eugenic Societies), this committee of experts included Darré, race theorist Hans F. K. Günther, Reich SS leader and chief of the German police Heinrich Himmler, industrialist Fritz Thyssen, chief of the *Hitler Jugend* Baldur von Schirach, and architect Schultze-Naumburg. It was through the latter's works and lectures, and through the works and lectures of other members of the Saaleck Circle (a *völkisch* group opposed to modernism) one of whom was Darré, that the most direct and sometimes the most surprising links were established "scientifically" between art and race. Those links were an integral part of the Nazi *Weltanschauung*, which was presented as a system of bridges constantly thrown up between fantasy and reality. All of its metaphors were designed to be embodied, and all of those embodiments were supposed to correspond to the metaphors that defined them, to the point of conforming wholly with them. One reason, according to National Socialism, that art held such an eminent place among the "healthiest means" of improving the race was that a number of important figures in the regime invested it with a very real eugenic power.

Schultze-Naumburg and the Race's Self-Reproduction

Paul Schultze-Naumburg, originally a painter and sculptor who had linked his name with that of his birthplace, helped to found the Berlin and Munich secessions. Having subsequently diverted into architecture and interior decoration, he taught at the Weimar School of Arts until 1901, at which point he founded his own school of art in Saaleck. Connected as he was with Ferdinand Avenarius's art journal *Kunstwart*, which had published his "Kulturarbeiten," this founder (in 1904) of the League of Defense of the Homeland (*Heimatschutz*) naturally became, in the aftermath of the First World War, a part of the *völkisch* cultural movement, which was both nationalist and anti-Semitic. In the Wagnerian society of Bayreuth, Schultze-Naumburg met first Alfred Rosenberg then, in 1926, Hitler. Despite the intrigues directed against Schultze-Naumburg by Troost's wife, and despite Hitler's consequent irritation with Schultze-Naumburg, the master of Saaleck remained one of the regime's most faithful "cultural combatants." When he retired in 1940, he received a vibrant letter of appreciation written in the Führer's own hand, and Wilhelm Frick did not hesitate to declare that "his very name encompassed a whole program."[8] Cofounder in 1929 of Rosenberg's *Kampfbund für Deutsche Kultur* (Fighting League for German Culture), Schultze-Naumburg was appointed, following the elections of December 8, 1929, when the Land of Thuringe fell into the hands of the Nazis, director of the Weimar Advanced School of Fine Arts, Architecture, and Crafts, where his mission was to turn it into the "central point in German culture."[9] When he took office there on April 1, 1930, he immediately ordered the destruction of the painted murals that Oskar Schlemmer had painted for the buildings used by the Bauhaus. Once he was elected to the Reichstag as a representative of the NSDAP, Schultze-Naumburg managed to diffuse his influence from Weimar to Munich and throughout the whole of Germany. His objective was to develop, by means of examples and counterexamples, the "visual judgment" of Germans as to what was "beautiful," "good," and "practically useful" for the preservation of the future of their race: "The most elevated 'mission' of art was to provide 'goals' for the age, to render visible 'the image to be attained,' and to fashion the future image of the race. The sculptures of the cathedrals of Bamberg and Naumburg thus became the model for 'racial selection' in human stock-raising."[10] Schultze-Naumburg had been defending these theses for twenty years, elaborating them mostly on the basis of the work of his friends Hans Günther and Ludwig Ferdinand Clauss, two of the most popular Nazi race theorists, who nevertheless quarreled in the early 1930s over the validity of their respective racial criteria. Whereas Günther defended the idea of the decisive value of physical appearance in the determination of a "Nordic race," the "ideal type" of which was reflected in art,[11] Clauss countered this with the theory of a "racial soul," which claimed that a disjunction between the soul and the body was always a possibility; a Nordic soul could inhabit the body of a race that was not purely Nordic, which also meant that there was never a guarantee that a Nordic "corporeal configuration" sheltered a "psychic configuration" that was also Nordic.[12] This disjunction of the visible and the invisible, which was completely at odds with the Nazi dogma of their continuity, clearly presented the advantage of justifying whoever was the most powerful arbiter—the one who expressed himself with, for example, the formula that Göring took over from Karl Lueger (leader of the Christian Social Party and mayor of Vienna)—"I am the judge of who is Jewish"[13]—or who categorized people as "Jewish in spirit."

The principle of disjunction was never accepted, however, by any of the theories of art produced by the Nazi ideologues. On the contrary, they believed that only by casting a glance over the surface of the products of "degenerate art" they could read the souls of their creators like an open book. In *The Fight for Art*, Schultze-Naumburg reproduced photographs of a number of Expressionist paintings and set out the law of inference that justified their condemnation: "Whoever discovers the spirit of his own spirit here passes judgment on himself. He says just as much about himself as he does about the object he is evaluating."[14] The theory of the landscape-self-portrait that Schultze-Naumburg sketched in his *Kulturarbeiten* was now expanded into a general theory of art. It was in *Kunst und Rasse* (*Art and Race*), the most well-known of his works, however, that he formulated a complete explanation. It is worth setting out the premises on which this theory was based.

A race does not find expression in a particular form of state nor in a language, as was suggested by formulas such as "the French race," "the Italian race," or "the German race." This confusion, introduced by the historical emergence of the European nations, prevents one from seeing that a common language might represent a cultural group, but never "any racial, that is to say biological similarity of species [*Gleichartigkeit*]." Deprive a German of his language and transport him to a French or Italian cultural area and his "phenotype" might undergo a certain modification, "but his corporeal and spiritual properties will still be preserved by his descendants." All of this has now been illuminated by the laws of science: the environment does not alter hereditary characteristics. This biological heritage is what has always dominated an artist's relations with his environment. It is inevitably projected onto the natural subject he chooses to represent, whatever his choice. The *choice* of a subject is, of course, common to both photography and art, but the technical image simply mirrors the subject. In painting, the situation is quite different, for here what is reproduced is not the subject of the picture but the artist himself: "Spiritual creation, too, is a process of reproduction, and it is submitted to the same determining factors as purely corporeal reproduction."[15]

As will be remembered, Baldur von Schirach contrasted photographic "reality," which conveys only the present, to the "truth" of painting, which is oriented toward the future. In similar fashion, Schultze-Naumburg contrasted photographic objectivity to the image produced by an artist, which is "formed in the likeness of the world to which he aspires." It was therefore necessary to discover to what extent an artist's works were "flesh of his flesh" and how far that dependence was racially determined. If one commonly said that a woman resembled a Rubens or that a young girl was a "Botticelli type," one did not ever seriously try to find out what constituted the links between these types of art and the corporeal and spiritual properties of their creators. To speak of works of art as spiritual children was already to approach the mystery of the links that bind parents to their natural descendants. For "just as the body of a child can come only from the blood of its parents, so it is with spiritual children." Perusal of the portraits painted by the great masters before the invention of photography revealed that in the vast majority of cases they were self-portraits.[16] The figures painted by Raphael, Rubens, and Botticelli were thus always reproductions of their authors. To support his thesis, Schultze-Naumburg cited the following passage from Leonardo da Vinci's *Treatise*. Da Vinci had noticed that "the particular features of a painting correspond to the particular features of the painter himself," to such a degree that "most of the faces resemble their author":

Having frequently reflected on the cause of this defect, it seems to me that we must understand that the soul, which rules and governs the body, also determines our judgment even before we have made it ours. It is thus that the soul that forms the whole face of a man as it judges best, with a nose that is long or short or snub, similarly fixes his size and overall aspect. And that judgment is so strong that it moves the painter's arm and obliges him to copy himself, because it seems to the soul that that is the true way to paint a man, and that whoever does otherwise is misguided. And if it finds someone who resembles the body it has formed, it loves that person and falls in love with him or her. And that is why many people fall in love and take wives who resemble themselves, and often the children who are born from them resemble their parents.[17]

What da Vinci deplored, however, as being "the greatest defect of painters," which ought to be resisted by consulting the judgment of others, for Schultze-Naumburg constituted proof of a race's irresistible inclination to love itself. Whether or not he wished to, an artist was bound to reproduce his own racial *type*. According to Schultze-Naumburg, da Vinci had revealed a principle that related to the body (*leibliche Prinzip*). It was the principle of "the proper" and, as understood in legal terms, of what was "germane" or blood-related. In the last analysis, this was a racial principle (*rassische Prinzip*), by virtue of which no aesthetic judgment or judgment involving taste applied to a work of art could be "absolute, but only relative, conditioned by one's belonging to a particular race."[18] As Hitler told his audience at the 1933 Nuremberg Congress, "Only from such a [gifted] race can true genius arise, and it alone will be able to feel [*empfinden*] and understand it. . . . If the Greeks and the Romans are suddenly so close to the Germans, it is because all their roots intermingle in a basic race; and that is why the immortal realizations [*Leistungen*] of those ancient peoples still attract the descendants who are racially akin to them."[19] In *The Myth of the Twentieth Century*, Rosenberg wrote in a similar vein: "Giorgione's *Venus* acts unconsciously on us as does any other authentic beauty that is racially determined, that is to say, both organically and spiritually determined; [and that is why] the [Kantian] 'universality of judgments of taste can proceed only from a *völkisch*-racial ideal of beauty, and can be applied only to those who, consciously or unconsciously, carry in their hearts the same idea of beauty."[20] A Nazi art historian stated the same thing more simply, almost as though it were a commonplace: "German art is self-confession [*Selbstbekenntnis*]. It can be understood only by the nature [*nur aus der Wesensart*] of German man."[21] As for jurist Carl Schmitt, he too used the same "similarity of species" to illuminate the bonds of love that united the people with its long-desired Führer. In 1933, at the hands of this jurist, the concept of *Gleichartigkeit*, forged in 1928 by Schultze-Naumburg, turned into an *Artgleichheit*, a similarity of race or species that legitimated the concept of political leadership (*Führung*) that ruled out identifying the Führer as a dictator.

[The concept of *Führung*] is one of immediate actuality [*Gegenwart*] and real presence [*Präsenz*]. That is why it demands, as a concrete necessity, *an unconditional similarity of race between the Führer and those who follow him [die Gefolgschaft]*. It is this similarity of race that is the basis for not only the constant and unfailing contact between the Führer and those who follow him, but also their mutual loyalty. Only that similarity of race can prevent the Führer's power from becoming tyranny and arbitrary willfulness. It alone is the basis of the difference from the domination, however intelligent and profitable, of the will of a racially alien race [*eines fremdgearteten Willens*]. The *similarity of race* of a united people at one with itself is also the most nonnegotiable [*die unumgänglichste*] condition and basis for the concept of political *Führung*.[22]

Every word was loaded and designed to create an image "turned toward the Führer" so as to produce the most rigorous political theory of narcissism, shored up by the "friend/enemy polarity," which implied the exclusion of all those who were dissimilar; only he who is *artgleich* (racially similar) can be my friend. The mutual loyalty between the Führer and the *Gefolgschaft* pivoted on the same principle of similarity, so that any loyalty became primarily loyalty to oneself, and one had only to love in order to be loved in return. Given that this love was always love of the race by the race, Carl Schmitt could just as well have declared that all Germans, through their Führer, loved each other in their race, just as Christians said they loved each other in Christ. Schmitt's concept of political *Führung* corresponded on all points to Schultze-Naumburg's theoretical formulation of artistic *Führung.*[23]

Schultze-Naumburg went on to declare that an appreciation of the body was never better expressed than in the representation of a woman, in which "the erotic aspirations of the painter with regard to his partner take on characteristic forms." Venus, Leda, Diana, and Psyche, as painted by Botticelli, Giorgione, Titian, Tintoretto, Boucher, and Prudhon, were used to illustrate the axiom that "almost all representations of the nude feminine body constitute responses to that erotic aspiration, and show and awaken in us the dreams and desires [*Wunschträume*] that live in the artist." The sexual desire of the artist was a pure desire to survive himself. "Representations are almost always produced out of the human impulse that, after [the impulse] prompted by hunger, passes for the most powerful. It is love that guides the [artist's] paintbrush or chisel, for in his deepest subconscious slumbers the following desire: *it is in a human image such as this that you would like to survive.*" Schultze-Naumburg's discourse now took a remarkable turn, apparently suddenly mixing Neoplatonism borrowed from da Vinci with the most recent speculations of psychoanalysis. Without ever citing either source, Schultze-Naumburg now played off Freud against Kant. He must certainly have been familiar with Kant and there is no reason to believe he was totally ignorant of Freud's work. At any rate, his lexicon is that of psychoanalysis:

All the common considerations on the disinterestedness of art completely omit this internal coherence. The artist, like it or not, *cannot* escape his own body. However, this desire arises in him not only when he is experiencing feelings that are innate in him; even when, possibly constrained by academic rules, he has suppressed the representations that most originate from himself, these promptly return as soon as he feels himself free from constraint.[24]

What differentiated Schultze-Naumburg's discourse from that of Freud was the absence of any hint of sublimation in the process he described. Just as linguistic metaphors (a girl is a "Botticelli type," a work of art is the child of its author) for him became flesh and blood realities, so too the sexual desires and impulses of the artist were expected to be realized not only in art but also in the physical reality of the species. Indeed, sublimation had no place in this economy of reproduction, because no "person," no "individual," was involved, only the "racial heritage" that found in the image its medium of transmission. After all, what was the production of an image if not the process by which a genotype communicated and reproduced itself through its phenotype?

In Paul Westheim's critique "Racist Biological Aesthetics," published during his exile in Paris, he stressed that all Rosenberg talked about was an "aesthetic will," yet it seemed that the artist alone was without this; and that for Schultze-Naumburg "the creative agent was not a personality but the hereditary body of the race." One of the bases of the Nazi theory of art was indeed that the uniqueness of the artist faded away in the face of the racial community. It was a basis in harmony with the NSDAP principle according to which "the general interest takes precedence over individual interests." The god who inhabited an "inspired" artist in his work could not be a personal god but must be the national-*völkisch genius.* Westheim rightly compared the absence of any "aesthetic will" in the artist to the words pronounced by Goebbels on May 10, 1937, before the Chamber of Culture of the Reich: *"Der Künstler sei 'kunstbetreibend und nicht kunstführend'"* (The artist "exercises art, he does not direct it").[25] The "Rosenberg tendency" and the "Goebbels tendency," despite their rivalry, were thus certainly in agreement on this point: the genius of the German people was its hereditary patrimony and it was embodied first and foremost in the person of the Führer, the only true artist of the Third Reich.

When Hitler declared in Nuremberg in 1935 that "art, precisely because it is the most direct and faithful emanation of the *Volksgeist,* constitutes the force that unconsciously models the mass of the people in the most active fashion," he immediately added "on condition, however, that this art is a sincere reflection of the soul and temperament of a race and is not a deformation of it."[26] So if art held the power of autoformation for the race, it was indispensable that the *völkisch* state should control it: it had to be steered positively into the fabrication of the new man, and to exclude all risk of malformation. The effects of images on the generation of bodies had been a subject of intense speculation long before European thought came up with the idea of using them for eugenic ends controlled by the state. No doubt the Platonic city had not been unaware of eugenism, but it did not resort to the use of images because the philosopher had excluded artists from the city. On this point, National Socialism, which could not make that mistake because art was its very principle and guide, had been guided by predecessors.

Engendering Through Images

In the second chapter of *Laocoon*, Gotthold Ephraim Lessing drew attention to the fact that in the Greek city the civil authorities were "to force the artist to remain in his proper sphere." He observed that "the law of the Thebans commanded idealization in art and threatened digression toward ugliness with punishment." Lessing went on to explain that this law had not, as was sometimes claimed, been made in order to oppose artists who were inept, but to oppose "that unworthy artistic device through which a likeness is obtained by exaggerating the ugly parts of the original—in a word, the caricature." He then declared that we are wrong to laugh when we learn that among the ancients even the arts were subject to civil laws, because, first, "the ultimate goal of the arts . . . is pleasure, and this pleasure is not indispensable. Hence it may be for the lawmaker to determine what kind of pleasure and how much of each kind he will permit." Second, declared the thinker who produced *The Education of the Human Race,*

The plastic arts in particular—aside from the inevitable influence they exert on the character of a nation—have an effect that demands close supervision by the law. If beautiful men created beautiful statues, these statues in turn affected the men, and thus the state owed thanks also to beautiful statues for beautiful men. (With us, the highly susceptible imagination of mothers seems to express itself only in producing monsters).[27]

In a note in their critical edition of *Laocoon*, Jan Bialostocka and Richard Klein threw some light on the meaning of the last sentence. It alluded, they said, to "the ancient belief that the imagination of pregnant mothers can determine the conformation of their future children. The superstition lives on in the form of the commonly held belief that women horrified by some spectacle during their pregnancy may engender monsters."[28] A good example in an ironic mode of the persistence of that belief is provided by the satirical review of the 1877 Impressionist Exhibition by critic Louis Leroy. Condemning what he called Cézanne's "overexclusive love of yellow," he warned the public, "If you visit the exhibition with a woman in an interesting condition, pass quickly by M. Cézanne's portrait of a man. . . . That head, the color of boot soles, with such a strange look to it, might impress her too strongly and afflict her fruit with yellow fever before its entry into the world."[29] A caricature by Cham accompanied Leroy's article. In front of the entrance to the exhibition, a doorkeeper barred the way to a pregnant woman, exclaiming, "Madame, it would not be prudent. Please go away!" Lessing's remarks were certainly part of a long tradition, that of the myth of *engendering though images*, which at the end of the nineteenth century culminated in Oscar Wilde's paradoxical declaration, "It is not art that imitates life, but life that imitates art."

In Genesis 30:25–33, Jacob peels the green branches of poplar, hazel, and chestnut trees, revealing the white beneath the bark, so that the branches look "ringstraked, speckled, and spotted." Then he places the branches "in the gutters and the watering troughs when the flocks come to drink" so that the ewes in heat produce young that are "ringstraked, speckled, and spotted" just like the branches. In this way Jacob builds up a flock of speckled animals for himself from Laban's herds. According to surgeon Ambroise Paré, this tradition of engendering through images also affected the early days of Greek medicine: "Hippocrates saved a princess accused of adultery because she had given birth to a child as black as a Moor, whereas her husband and herself were white-skinned. She was absolved thanks to the persuasive words of Hippocrates, because the portrait of a Moor resembling the child customarily hung from her bed."[30] In his novel *The Ethiopica* (published in the late third or early fourth century), Heliodorus reversed the black-white relationship in a tale with the same structure that was apparently very popular among the Byzantines. In this story, Persinna, queen of Ethiopia, explains to her daughter, the child of black parents, why her skin is white:

Our family had as ancestors the Sun and Dionysus, among the gods, and among the demigods, Perseus and Andromeda. . . . Those who, depending on the circumstances, helped to build the royal palace adorned it with paintings depicting the stories of those deities. The paintings that represent them and their exploits are in the rooms used by the men and in galleries. Only the images of the heroes Andromeda and Perseus are to be found in the bed chambers. It was in one of these that Hydaspus and myself found ourselves. It was ten years since our marriage and we still had no child. We were taking a siesta, sleeping in the summer heat. Your father came and was united with me, swearing that it was in obedience to a dream. I immediately sensed that he had made me pregnant. During the period leading up to the birth there was a succession of public festivals and sacrifices to give thanks to the gods. The king was expecting an heir of his blood. You came into the world white; your fair coloring was not that of the Ethiopian race. I knew very well what the reason was. While my husband was embracing me, my eyes rested on a painting depicting Andromeda, completely naked, at the moment when Perseus was lifting her down from the rock, and the seed had unfortunately taken on a resemblance to the heroine.

When the king expresses doubts about the identity of his daughter, an old sage tells him, "If you wish for other proofs, you can easily examine the model, Andromeda: her image resembles this girl exactly."[31]

The myth, which figured in the third-century Neoplatonic debates on "the manner in which the embryo receives its soul," soon resurfaced in Saint Augustine. He wrote that Soranus "narrates that the tyrant Dionysius, because he was deformed and did not wish his son to be like himself, used at the time of intercourse to place before his wife a portrait of an extremely handsome man, so that she, desiring its beauty, might absorb it, and this effect might be transmitted to the offspring she conceived."[32] In the Christian Middle Ages, the myth was no longer associated with the reproduction of greater beauty, but on the contrary figured in treatises relating to monstrous births. The responsibility for a perverted resemblance to some model was usually attributed to the imagination of the woman: under the sway of Satan, she succumbed to the desire aroused in her by the image and subsequently gave birth to a creature marked by the wrath of God. The myth proliferated in the Renaissance thanks to the *vis imaginum*,[33] found a place in Montaigne's *Essays* ("On Imagination"), then reappeared in

Descartes and Nicholas Malebranche, and later still in Voltaire. The Baroque period was divided between "imaginationists" and "anti-imaginationists," who continued to hurl insults at each other until the emergence of teratology in the early
nineteenth century under the watchful eye of Isidore Geoffroy Saint-Hilaire.
Claude Quillet, an imagionationist, described the system that regulated the relations between images and the fetus. He found his inspiration both in the *simu-
lacra* of Lucretius and in the theory of animal spirits defended by Malebranche.
In *Callipaedia, or the Way to Produce Beautiful Children*, published in 1655, he no
longer regarded engendering through images as an accident, a monstrous way-
wardness punished by God. Every visible object was said to emanate continu-
ously and spread "subtle corpuscles and parts," "images of all kinds of things,"
which, "equipped with very light wings and rapid movement, love to insinuate
themselves through even the tiniest walls."[34] The beauty or ugliness of a yet un-
born child thus depended primarily on the objects the mother contemplated
during its gestation. The reason, however, that Giulio Mancini, in his *Considerazioni sulla pittura* (considerations on painting), recommended placing fine, las-
civious paintings in the chambers of spouses was "not because the imagination
imprints itself on the fetus . . . but because each parent, through the picture, imprints in their seed a similar constitution which has been seen in the object or
figure."[35] (Poet Gottfried Benn became Mancini's most direct successor when, in
1933, he declared that "propaganda reaches the reproductive cells."[36])

With Tommaso Campanella's *The City of the Sun*, engendering through images became the rule for the production of superior offspring, the normative nature of which was henceforth controlled by the state. Not only did the inhabitants
of this ideal city possess, as did Jacob, "magic ways of producing [animal] offspring of high eugenic value, [having animals copulate] in the presence of beautiful images or paintings of horses, sheep, or cattle," but they also knew how to
improve their own species: "They only copulate when digestion is completed and
after having prayed. Women are presented with the sight of fine statues of famous
men, after which they position themselves at a window and beg God in Heaven
to grant them fine offspring." Campanella went on to explain that in the City of

the Sun, "painting and sculpture preserve the memory of only great men, whom beautiful women contemplate when trying to ensure perfection for the race."[37] At this point the tradition underwent a remarkable shift of emphasis. Once and for all abandoning the sphere of monstrous births provoked by guilty gazes on the part of mothers, it began to speculate on a possible way for the state to use images for eugenistic ends, just as Lessing would suggest a century and a half later.

Ten or so years before Lessing, in 1766, wrote *Laocoon*, however, Johann Joachim Winckelmann remarked, "We know what pains they [the Greeks] took to have handsome children." He criticized Quillet: although his *Callipaedia* considered a variety of ways to conceive beautiful children, it "falls far short of their [the Greeks'] expedients." For the ancients, Winckelmann declared, "even attempted changing blue eyes to black ones." What he seemed to be saying as he emphasized that "diseases which are destructive of beauty were moreover unknown to the Greeks"[38] was that we were more beautiful when we were Greek. Nevertheless, for him the links between real bodies and imaginary bodies were not unequivocal. Sometimes the masterpieces of the Greeks outstripped nature because they received "certain ideal beauties . . . produced by images drawn purely by the artist's understanding." Sometimes real bodies could, through physical exercise, attain to the perfection of art. When this happened, "the bodies acquired the great virile contours that the Greek masters gave their statues." Sometimes in Winckelmann's writings, however, all the frontiers between real bodies and those of fiction became blurred. He began by asserting the purely spiritual nature of the ideal model: it was "according to those ideas, exalted above the pitch of material models, [that] the Greeks formed their gods and heroes." He then immediately added that they did so "without indulging their fancy too much" when they drew the beautiful profile of a god or a goddess. Given that such a profile was also to be found on coins representing the heads of famous women, it had to be supposed that "this profile was as peculiar to the ancient Greeks as flat noses and little eyes [were] to the Calmucks and Chinese."[39] So, in the past, certain natural bodies must have been privileged to establish some communication between human beauty and divine beauty; and that ideal beauty, which had previously been thought to be either purely fictitious or else achievable by dint of physical effort, now appeared to be the most physical of all the properties of the Greeks, whose art, in the last analysis, simply reflected it.

Lessing dismissed all such hesitations. His hypothesis of a reciprocity of effects between real man and man as portrayed in art prepared the way for the modern view that was inaugurated by Baudelaire, who stressed the power exerted by the ideal, which was capable even of modeling our bodies: "A man's idea of beauty is imprinted on his whole turn-out [equipage], softens or stiffens his clothes, makes his gestures rounded or angular, and even subtly eventually penetrates the features of his face. The man ends up resembling what he would like to be."[40] The real turning point certainly came in the nineteenth century. The power of the image as a model was now celebrated for its happy effects directly on the bodies of human beings, even without mediation by the female sex. Hippolyte Taine, who had no qualms about declaring that "the genius of masters lies in creating a physical race," invited his contemporaries to contemplate the bodies painted by Andrea del Sarto, Raphaelo, and Rembrandt, and then exclaimed, "Those are the bodies we ought to have; alongside that race of men, the rest are weak or soft, crude or unbalanced."[41] At this point, along came Oscar Wilde, who in paradoxical mode, and on the express basis of the myth of engendering through images, reversed the classical and Aristotelian tradition of imitation. He protested against the naturalism of his contemporaries and "the decay of lying": "Life imitates Art far more than Art imitates Life," he declared, and

A great artist invents a type, and Life tries to copy it, to reproduce it in a popular form, like an enterprising publisher. The Greeks, with their quick artistic instinct, understood this, and set in the bride's chamber the statue of Hermes or of Apollo, that she might bear children as lovely as the works of art that she looked at in her rapture or her pain.

He concluded that "the true disciples of the great artist are not his studio-imitators, but those who become like his works of art. . . . In a word, Life is Art's best, Art's only pupil."[42]

The myth thus underwent a considerable transformation: the woman lost her mediatory function as mother in the engendering of the new human race.

The image's engendering power was now such that it appeared to operate, without mediation, on everyone so that the whole human race acceded to the radical passivity once reserved for women. In a more modern version of the myth, the image propagated by publicity or propaganda confirmed the constant validity of the hypothesis of a process of self-engendering: each individual became capable of becoming pregnant with a being resembling the image that seemed to correspond to his or her desire. A new man was now born every time there was an acting out in accordance with the image.

Schultze-Naumburg never cited Genesis or Heliodorus or Montaigne, or even Lessing or Taine; and the irony of Wilde's paradoxes were certainly well beyond him. Nevertheless, he seems to have embraced all their theses and been determined to verify them by trying them out on the body of the German-Nordic people. A certain similarity between his line of thought and that of Winckelmann was also perhaps detectable in his efforts to get "the race's ideal of beauty" to coincide with its real body.

It was, however, his friends Hans F. K. Günther and Walther Darré who produced the clearest formulations of this function of the image that was to make possible the realization of the ideal Reich. Their writings, more than any others, reveal most clearly what was really at stake in the identification of art and politics. For they explained the real meaning of Hitler's and Goebbels's diatribes against art for art's sake. Art *by* the people and *for* the people, which they opposed to *art for art's sake*, simply meant that it fell to the people to fabricate its own ideal image or type that would constitute the model and guide capable of propelling the people toward its own salvation. Neither the state, said Hitler, nor propaganda, said Goebbels, were goals; they were simply means. No more was art ever a goal in itself. The ultimate goal was not the production of the Reich as a work of art, but the fabrication of a people composed of new men.

Walther Darré: Breeding According to Type

It was as a guest of Schultze-Naumburg's in Saaleck that Walther Darré wrote his principal work, *Race: The New Nobility of the Blood and the Soil,* which was published in the same year (1930) as his friend Rosenberg's *The Myth of the Twentieth Century*. It was Darré who persuaded Heinrich Himmler to select his SS according to "rigorous" racial criteria—Aryan ancestors stretching as far back as the seventeenth century—and to keep a close eye on their marriages.[43] Darré persuaded Hitler to hold a festival of the German peasantry for 500,000 spectators. The first festival took place on October 1, 1933. The 1934 festival attracted 700,000 people, and the 1935 festival attracted one million. Darré's writings, even more than Schultze-Naumburg's, reveal the connections between the generating function of images and the formation of a racial elite, itself designed to be the model adopted by the entire people.

Darré, born in Argentina, studied at King's College, Wimbledon, and held a diploma in agronomic engineering, acquired in Germany after the Great War. He then turned his attention to raising livestock and soon became engaged in the study of human races. He too was convinced that only the German-Nordic race was endowed with "creative" virtues, and he believed these had degenerated each time the race turned away from agriculture, deserting the land for the town. Any process of regeneration thus depended on the reconstitution of a "new nobility" that would combine both peasant and warrior virtues—the virtues that had always characterized the Indo-German Nordic nobility.

According to Darré, a Teuton noble used to consider himself "a guardian of the divine order, established by the energy, perpetuated in himself, of the actions of his divine ancestor." With his conversion "to Christianity, that is to say to the doctrine of the acquisition of qualities through Unction," his bases were undermined: his value no longer depended on his birth because "in the race toward heavenly happiness, every individual became the equal of the noble."[44] Besides, the sacrament of baptism confused all the boundaries of a community founded on race. Despite Christianity, however, "the whole of German morality has for fifteen hundred years been based on a conscious concept of selection" designed to protect the hereditary qualities of the purest elements of the race.[45]

Since, as Clauss declared, "the body is the soul's field of expression," the soul must be allowed to express itself in a perfect body. It was therefore a duty to "liberate a people from all the impurities likely to disturb the body of an individual and hence also souls." This was possible only if one "observed the laws of heredity and eliminated all that was undesirable."[46] While Darré shared with Hitler, Alexis Carrel, and many others the modern conviction that "no medical treatment can regenerate masses of decomposing seeds," he was distinguishable from them because he cited Euripides and Plato, the better to establish the profoundly "Greek" nature of selection, to which the Germans, the Greeks' natural heirs, were also the spiritual heirs. According to Euripides' *Heraclidae*, "No treasure is more precious for children than being born from a noble and virtuous father, and marrying into other noble families. Woe to whoever is so imprudent as to be overcome by passion and enter into union with bad partners, leaving to his children dishonor in exchange for the guilty passions he has enjoyed!" Darré then cited Hans F. K. Günther, who had just published *Platon als Hüter des Lebens* (Plato, the Guardian of Life): "It was Plato who gave the word 'Idea' its philosophical meaning and who, through his doctrine, became the first founder of idealism . . . ; and it was he who attributed to the sway of the Idea an absolute value that dominates everything. And as an idealist, that same Plato came to conceive of the idea of selection."[47]

It was precisely on the interpretation of the *Idea* not only as something whose essence consists of being able to be visible but also as something that ought to *become* visible that National Socialism rested. To make the Idea visible was thus to produce a *type* that would function as the goal for a program of selection. It was in the following terms, which Himmler was soon to repeat to the Hitler Youth organizations, that Walther Darré expressed the first of the rules of selection that presided over the raising of horses, and that he intended to apply likewise to the "breeding" of his new nobility:

One *establishes a type to be realized by selection, in order first of all to fix the goal* to be attained. For the raiser of livestock this serves as a kind of compass. This example should train the eye to perceive defects and find reference points. [This type] can be used in the reality of raising livestock more or less as Plato's definition of the perfect sovereign is used.

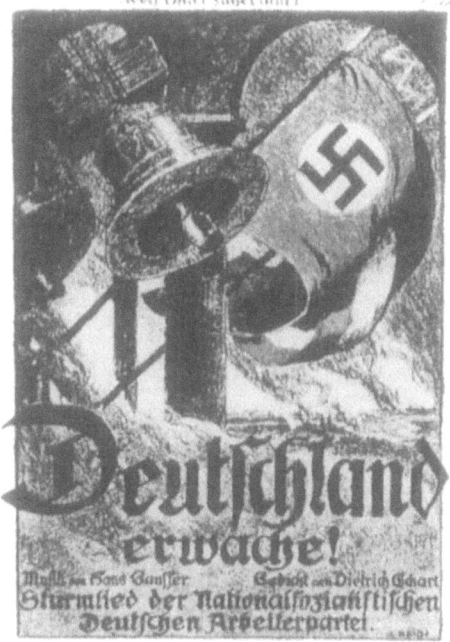

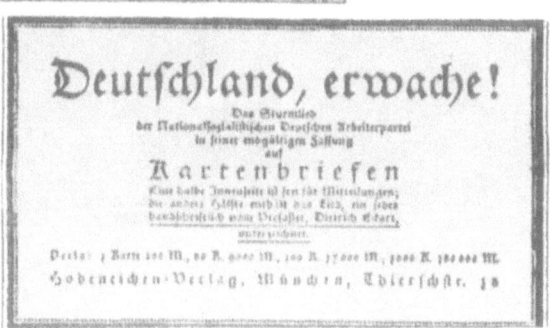

33.   Albert Reich, cover for *"Deutschland erwache!"* 1923.
Published in A. Reich and O. R. Achenbach, *Vom 9, November 1918 zum 9, November 1923* (Munich: Eher, 1933), p. 78.
Author's collection. Photo preserved in the Bibliothèque de
l'Institut d'Histoire de l'art, Strasbourg.

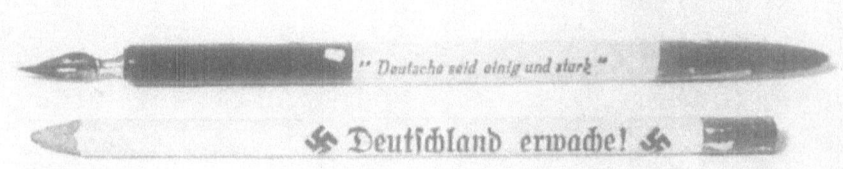

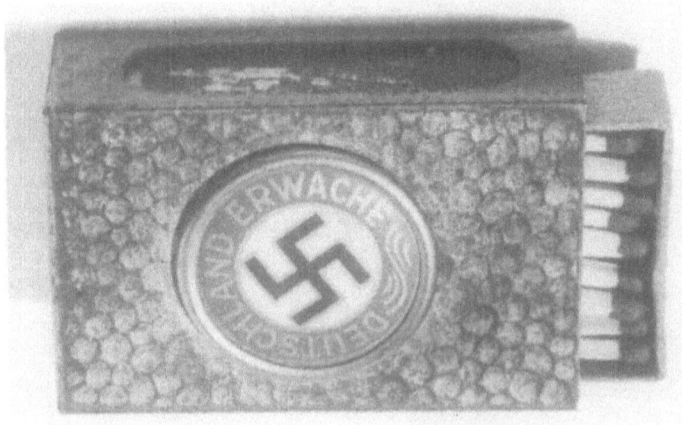

34. *(top)* Pencil and pen holder. Photo by Württembergisches Landesmuseum, Stuttgart.

35. *(above)* Metal matchbox. Photo by Württembergisches Landesmuseum, Stuttgart.

36. Pfullingen church: "The window of the choir, above the altar. The shape of the swastika reproduces that of the wooden swastikas of popular art." Published in *National-sozialistische Monatshefte*, May 1938, no. 98, illustration 4 (between pp. 424 and 425). Document preserved in the Bibliothèque de l'Institut d'Histoire de l'Art de Strasbourg.

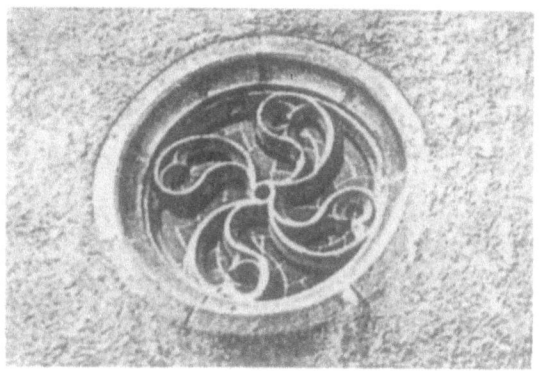

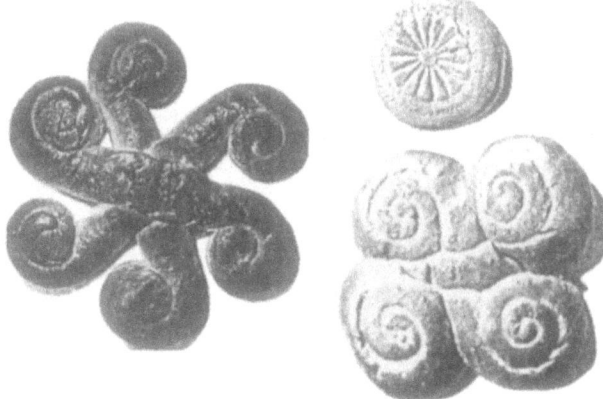

37. "Christmas cakes from central Germany: Their shapes show clearly how essential the solar wheel is to the Christmas festival." Published in *Nationalsozialistische Monatshefte*, December 1937, no. 93, illustration following p. 1096. Document preserved in the Bibliothèque de l'Institut d'Histoire de l'Art de Strasbourg.

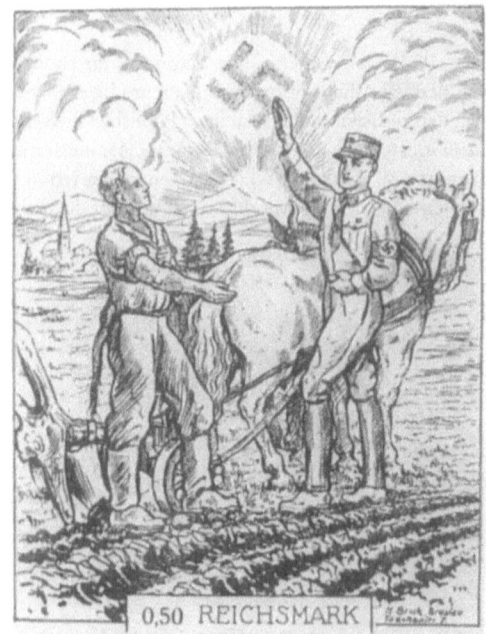

38. *(right)* A supportive postcard, n.d. Photo by Württembergisches Landesmuseum, Stuttgart.

39. *(below)* Richard Klein, *The Awakening* (oil on canvas), 1937. Published in *Kunst und Volk*, 1937, no 8, p. 229. Photo by Zentralinstitut für Kunstgeschichte, Munich.

0,50 REICHSMARK

Nun endlich ist die Zeit gekommen
Da unser deutsches Volk erwacht;
Am deutschen Bauern soll's nicht liegen
Er steht schon längst auf seiner Wacht.

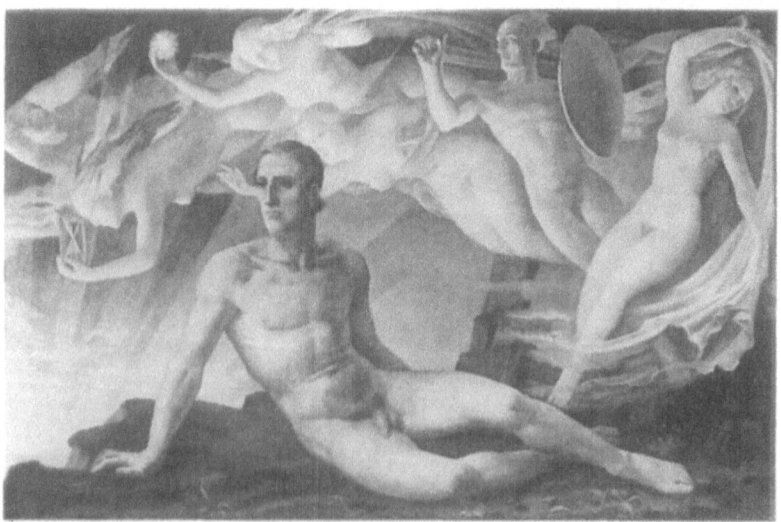

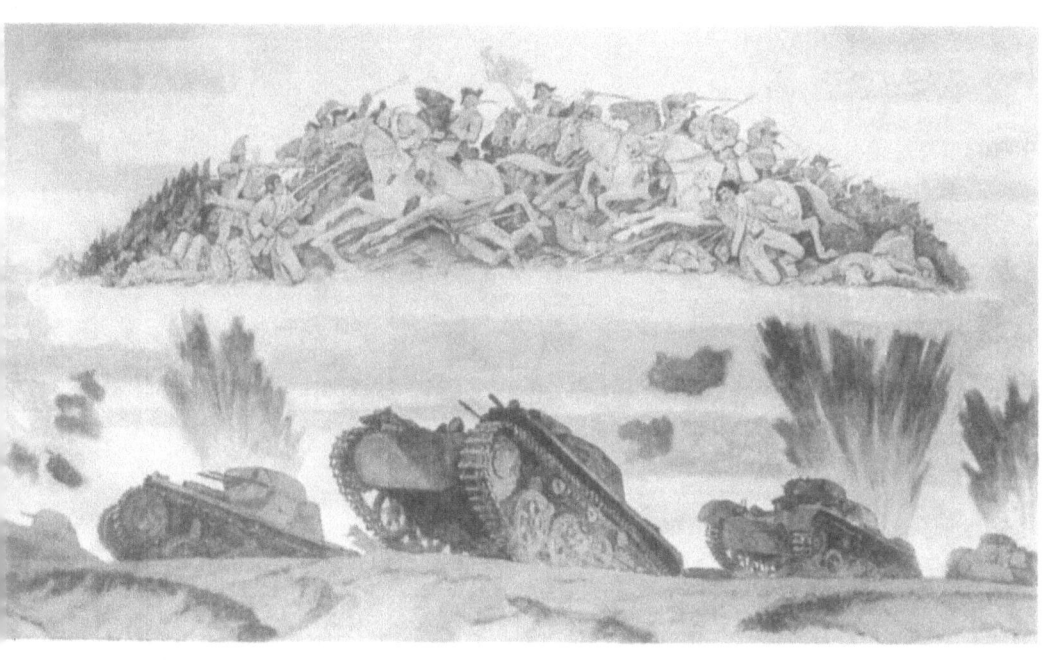

40. Ferdinand Spiegel, *Tank* (wall painting), circa 1938–1939. Published in *Die Kunst im dritten Reich*, 1939, no. 3, p. 85. Photo by Zentralinstitut für Kunstgeschichte, Munich.

41. *(right)* The First Day of German Art, Munich, 15 October 1933: The Gothic float. Published in *Die Kunst*, December 1933, vol. 69, no. 3, p. 84. Document preserved in the Bibliothèque de l'Institut d'Histoire de l'Art de Strasbourg.

42. *(below)* The First Day of German Art, Munich, 15 October 1933: The Bavarian Rococo float. Published in *Die Kunst*, December 1933, vol. 59, no. 3, p. 81. Document preserved in the Bibliothèque de l'Institut d'Histoire de l'Art de Strasbourg.

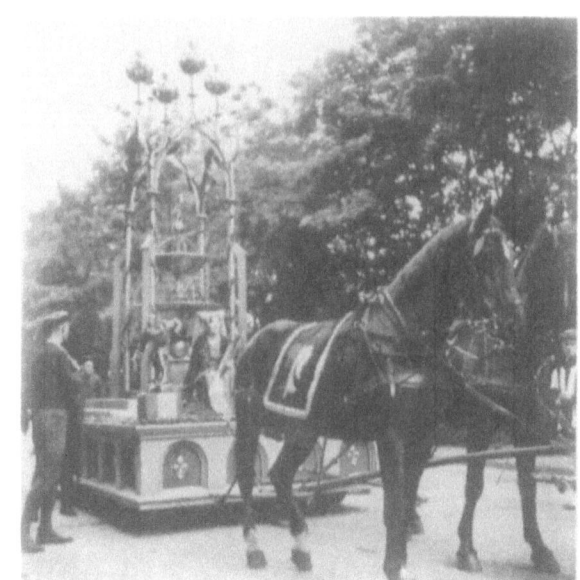

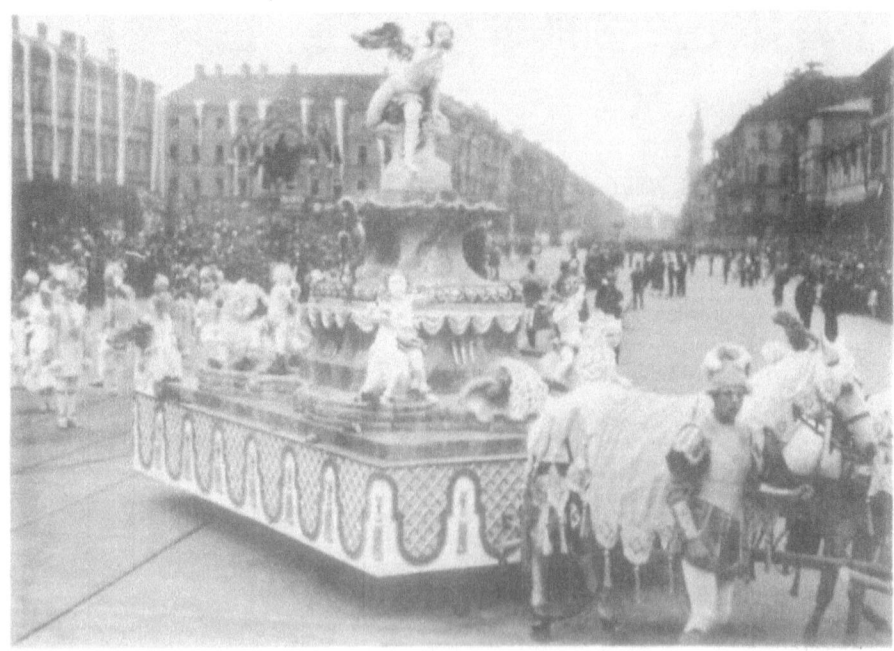

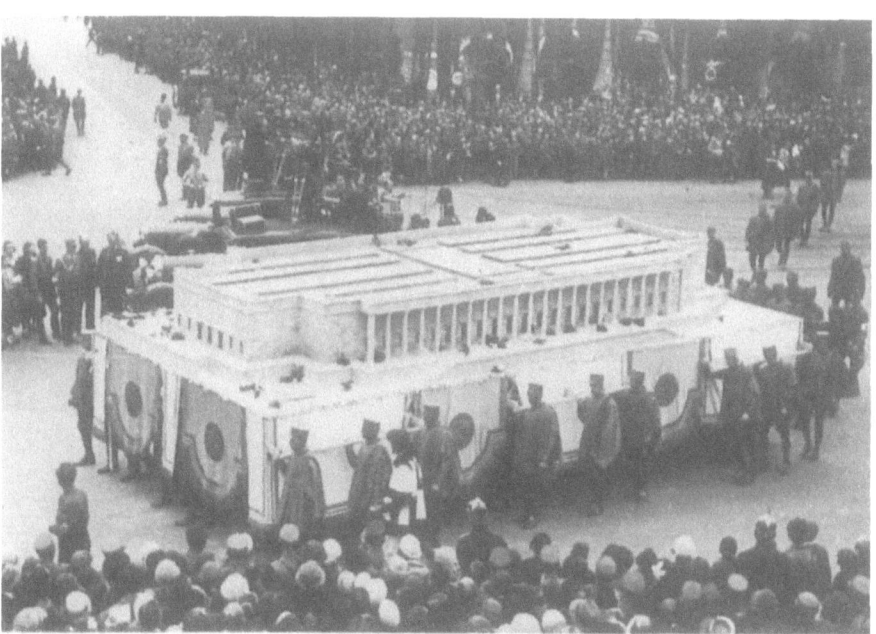

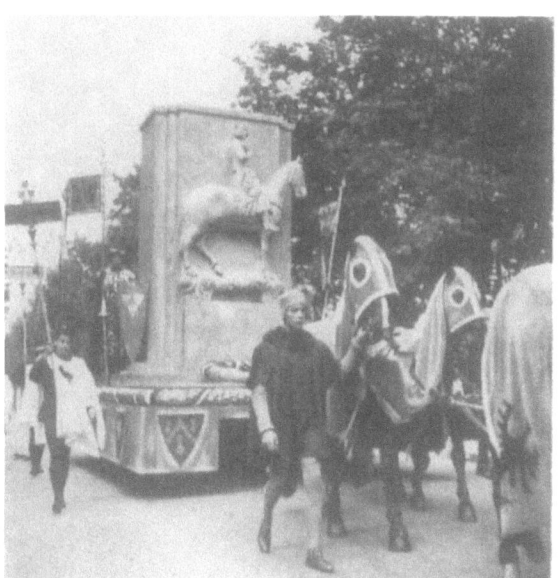

43. *(above)* The First Day of German Art, Munich, 15 October 1933: The House of German Art float. Photo by Landeshauptstadt München-Stadtarchiv.

44. *(left)* The First Day of German Art, Munich, 15 October 1933: The German Art float. Published in *Die Kunst*, December 1933, vol. 69, no. 3, p. 83. Document preserved in the Bibliothèque de l'Institut d'Histoire de l'Art de Strasbourg.

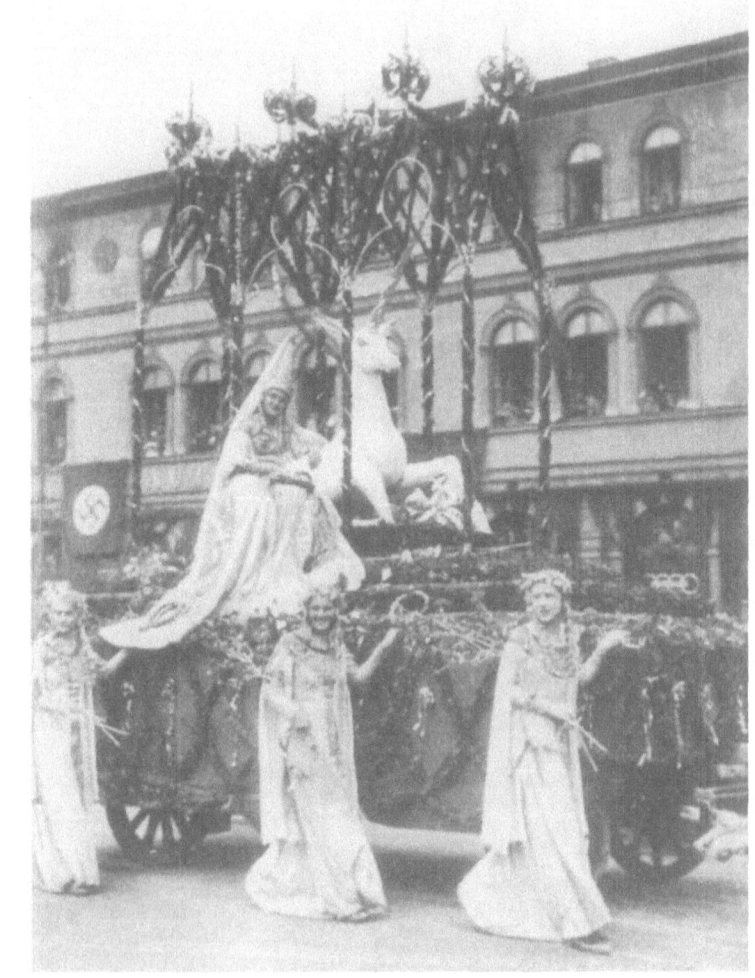

45. The First Day of
German Art, Munich,
15 October 1933: The
German Fairy Tales
float. Published in *Die
Kunst*, December 1933,
vol. 69, no. 3, p. 84.
Document preserved in
the Bibliothèque de
l'Institut d'Histoire
de l'Art de Strasbourg.

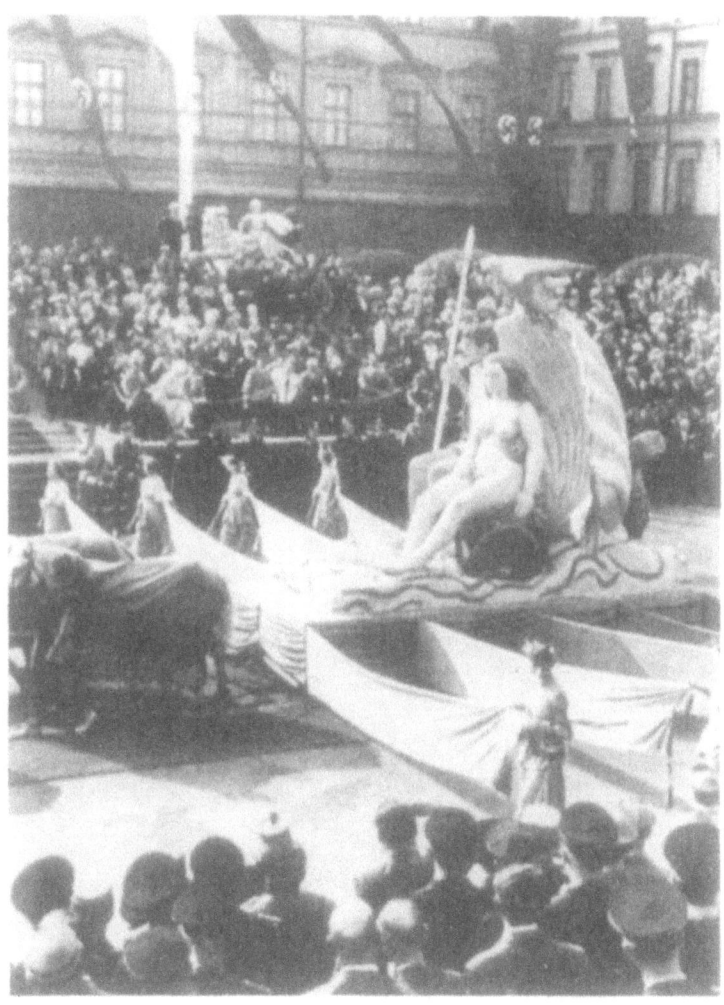

46. The Second
Day of German Art,
Munich, 18 July 1937:
The Germanic Age
float. RR.

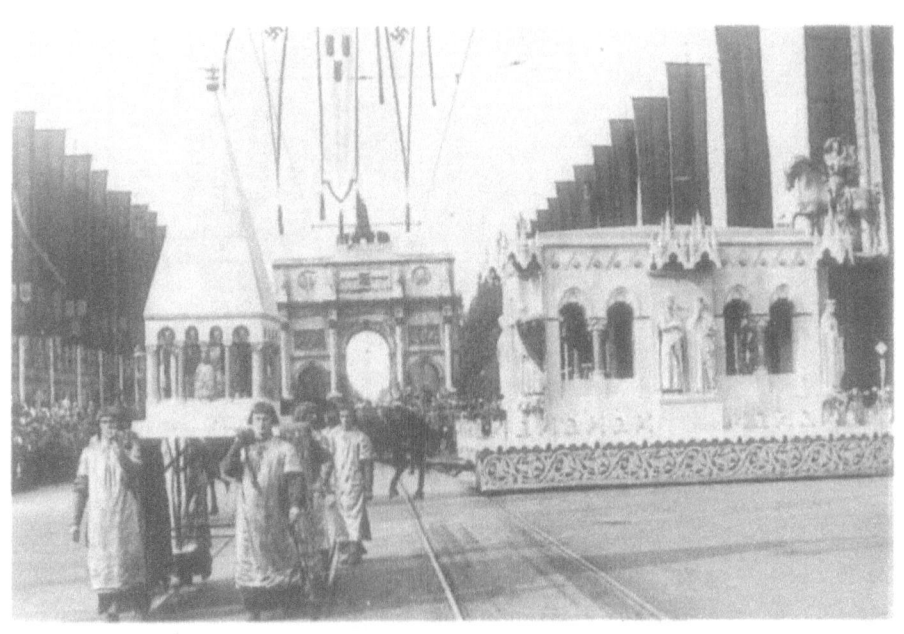

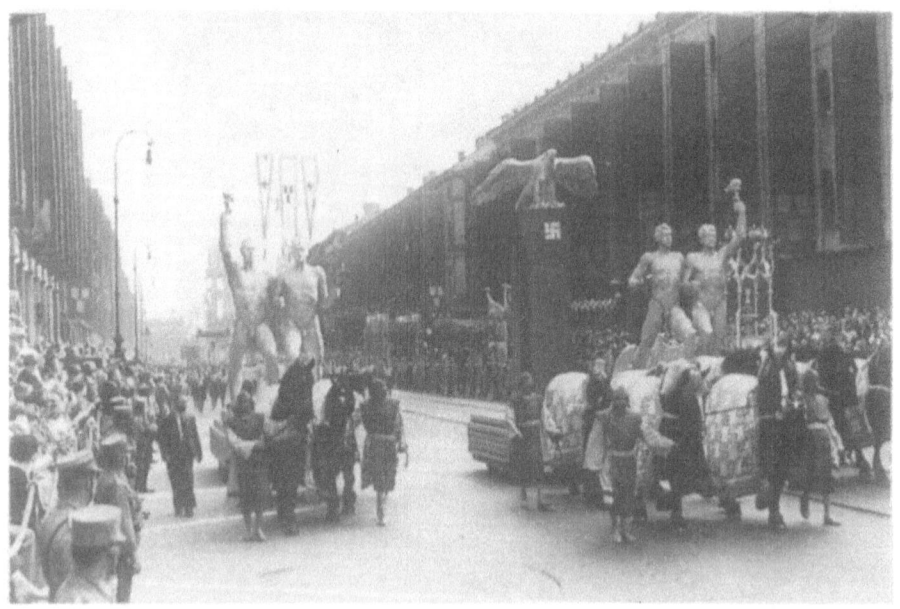

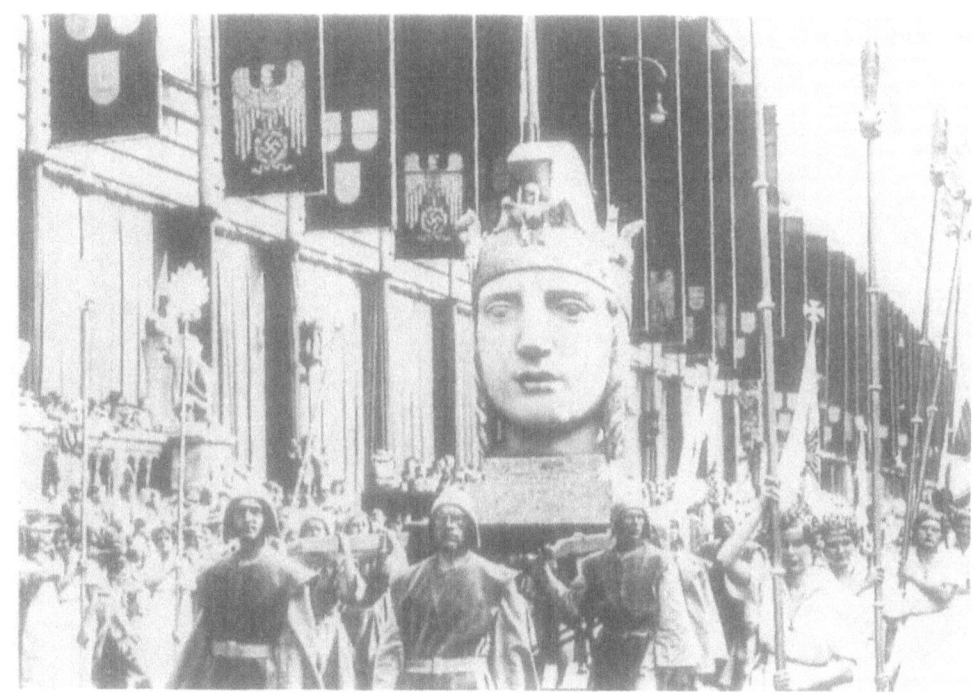

47. *(opposite, top)* The Second Day of German Art, Munich, 18 July 1937: The Gothic Age float (The Founders of Naumberg). Photo by Landeshauptstadt München-Stadtarchiv.

48. *(opposite, bottom)* The Second Day of German Art, Munich, 18 July 1937: The New Age float (Faith and Fidelity). Photo by Landeshauptstadt München-Statdtarchiv.

49. *(above)* The Second Day of German Art, Munich, 18 July 1937: Pallas Athena, carried by Teutons. RR.

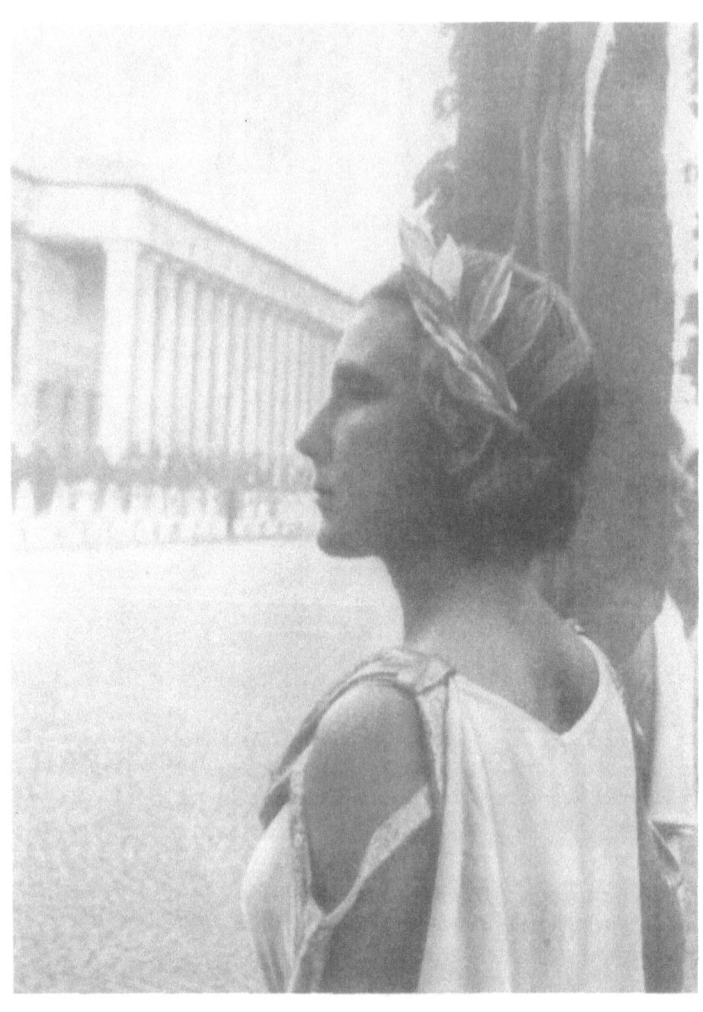

50. The Guard of the Temple of German Art on the occasion of Mussolini's visit, Munich, September 1937. Photo by Heinrich Hoffmann. Published in Hoffmann, *Mussolini erlebt Deutschland* (Munich: Heinrich Hoffmann Verlag, 1937), p. 45. Document preserved in the Bibliothèque de l'Institut d'Histoire de l'Art de Strasbourg.

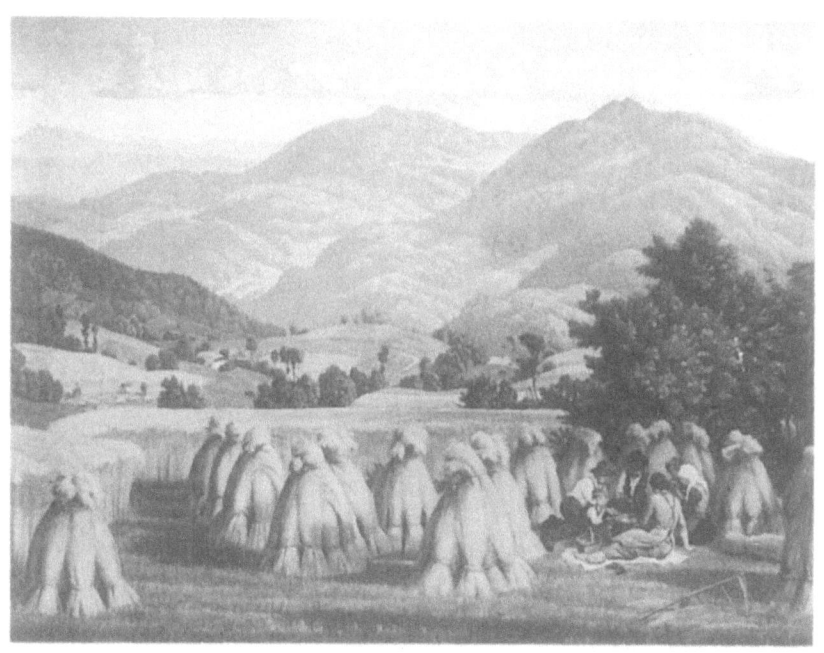

51. Karl Alexander Flügel, *The Harvest* (oil on canvas), circa 1938. Photo by Zentralinstitut für Kunstgeschichte, Munich.

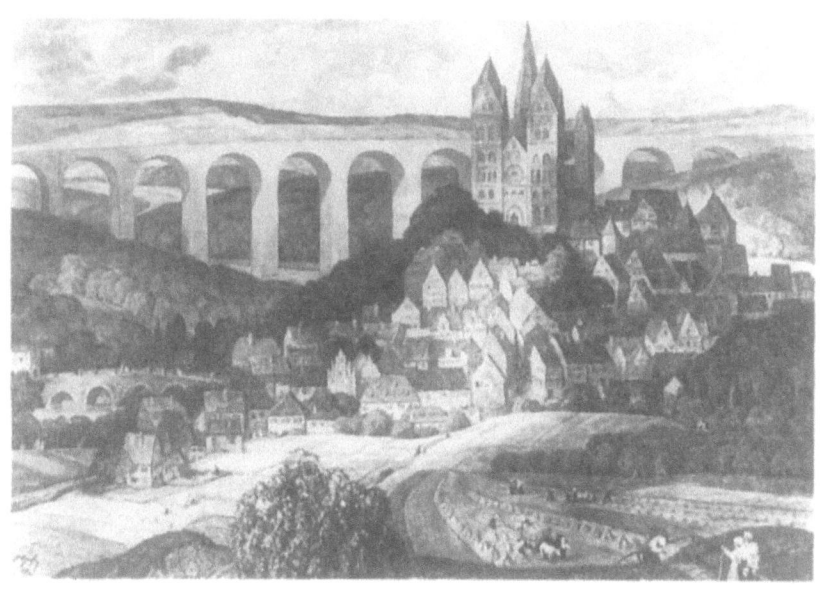

52. Oskar Graf, *Limburg an der Lahn*, circa 1940. Photo by Zentralinstitut für Kunstgeschichte, Munich.

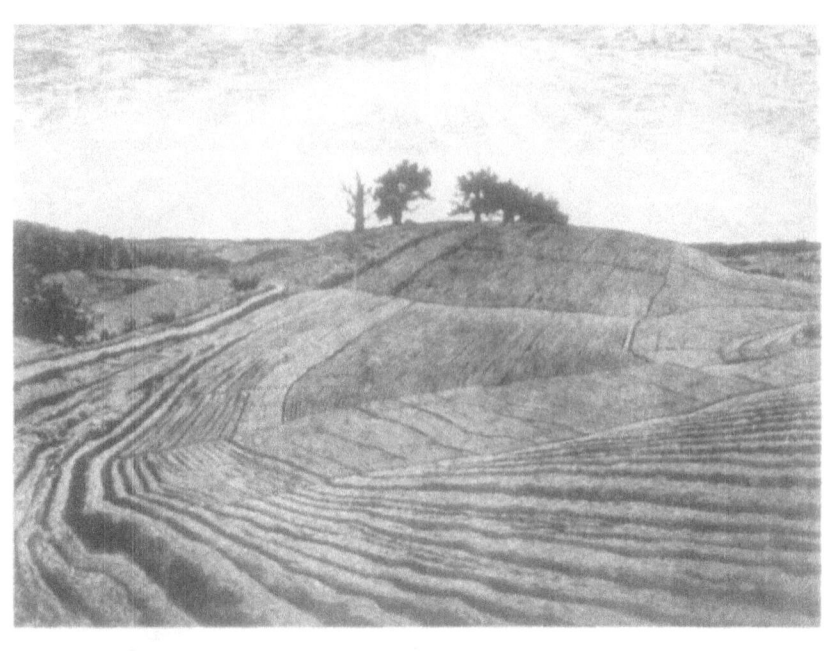

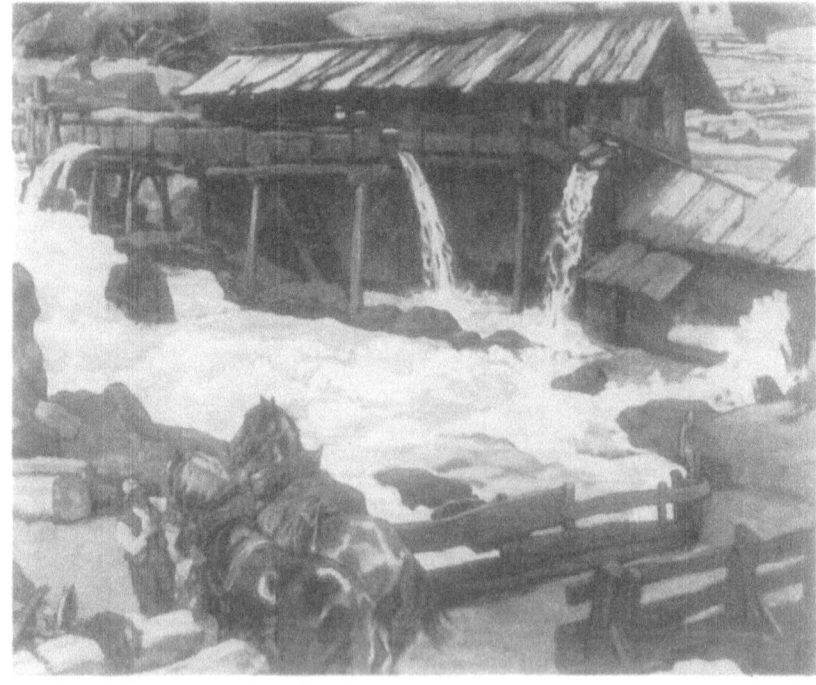

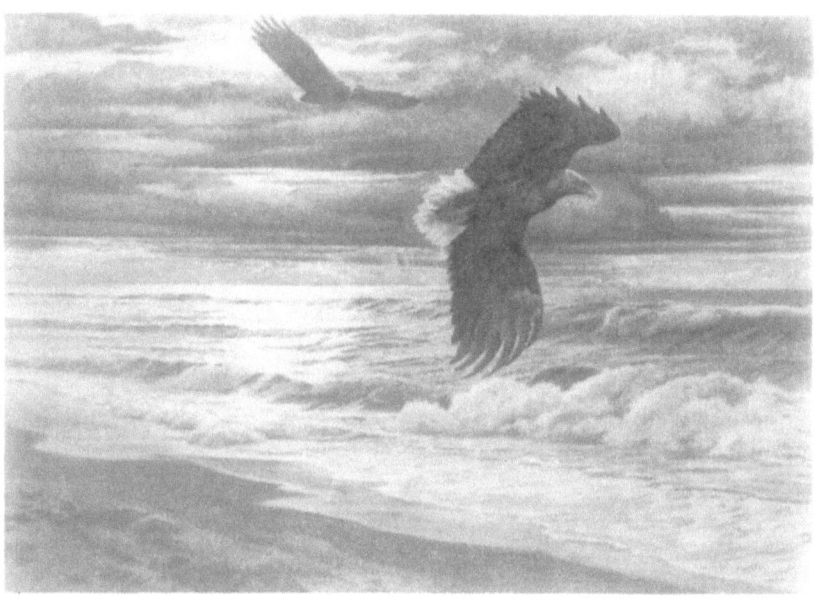

53. *(opposite, top)* Karl Hennemann, *Ploughed Field* (woodcut), n.d. Published in Werner Rittich, *Deutsche kunst der Gegenwart* (Breslau: Hirt, 1943), vol. 2, p. 131. Document preserved in the Bibliothèque de l'Institut d'Histoire de l'Art de Strasbourg.

54. *(opposite, bottom)* Erwin Puchinger, *Mountain Sawmill* (oil on canvas), n.d. Published in *Die Kunst im deutschen Reich*, 1943, no. 1, p. 27. Document preserved in the Bibliothèque de l'Institut d'Histoire de l'Art de Strasbourg.

55. *(above)* Michael Mathias Kiefer, *North Sea* (oil on canvas), 1942. Published in *Die Kunst im deutschen Reich*, 1943, no. 1, p. 15. Document preserved in the Bibliothèque de l'Institut d'Histoire de l'Art de Strasbourg.

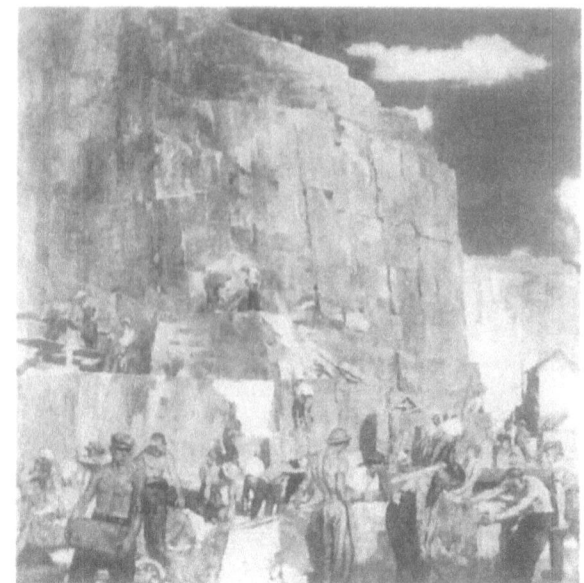

56. *(right)* Albert Janesch, *The Quarry* (oil on canvas), circa 1940–1941. Published in *Die Kunst im deutschen Reich*, 1942, no. 1, p. 26. Document preserved in the Bibliothèque de l'Institut d'Histoire de l'Art de Strasbourg.

57. *(below)* Carl Theodor Protzen, *Motorway Bridge Near Cologne*, n.d. Published in Wilhelm Rüdiger, *Kunst und Technik* (Munich: Verlag der deutschen Technik, 1941), plate 16. Document preserved in the Bibliothèque de l'Institut d'Histoire de l'Art de Strasbourg.

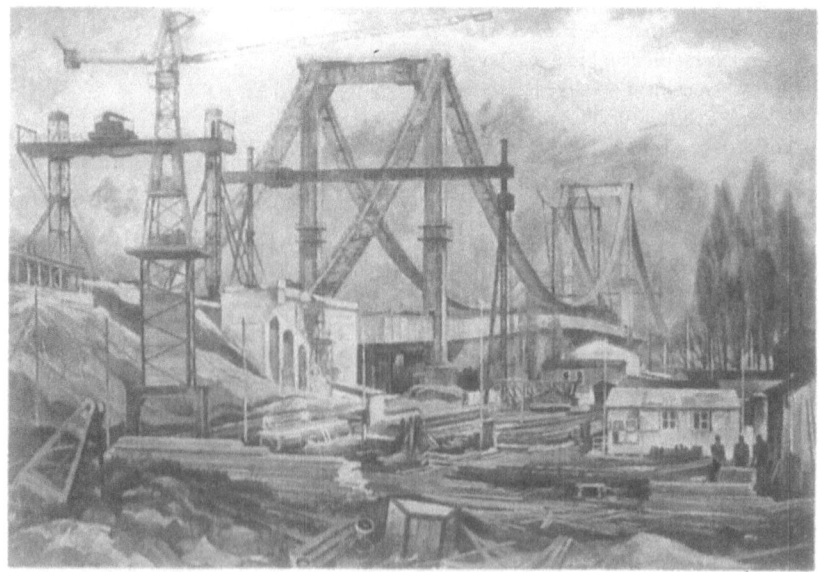

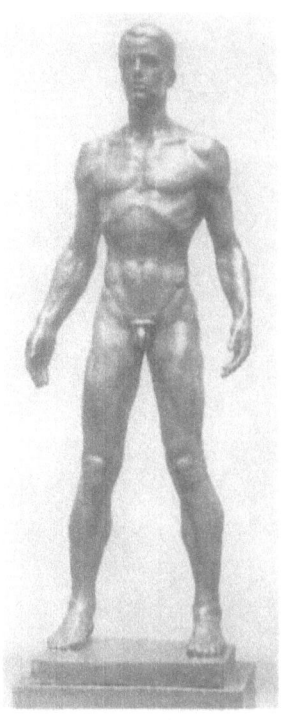

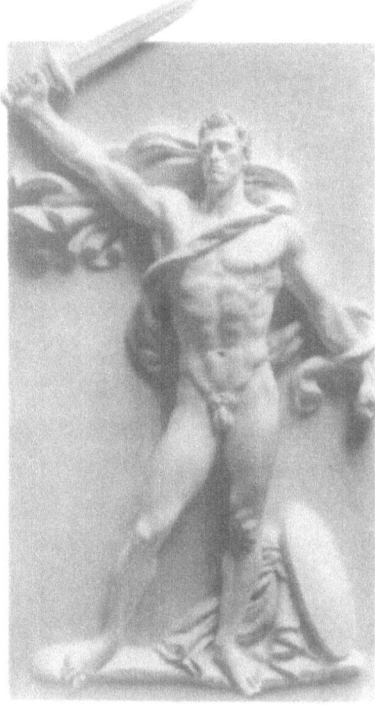

58. *(top, left)* Josef Riedl, *Ready for Battle* (bronze), n.d. Published in *Die Kunst im deutschen Reich*, 1942, no. 12, p. 294. Document preserved in the Bibliothèque de l'Institut d'Histoire de l'Art de Strasbourg.

59. *(top, right)* Arno Breker, *The Departure of the Fighter*, circa 1940 (plaster for a stone bas-relief). Published in *Die Kunst im deutschen Reich*, 1942, no. 1, p. 7. Document preserved in the Bibliothèque de l'Institut d'Histoire de l'Art de Strasbourg.

60. *(bottom)* Walter Hoeg, *Young Germany* (painting for the Hall of Lost Steps, Braunschweig railway station), n.d. Photo by Zentralinstitut für Kunstgeschichte, Munich.

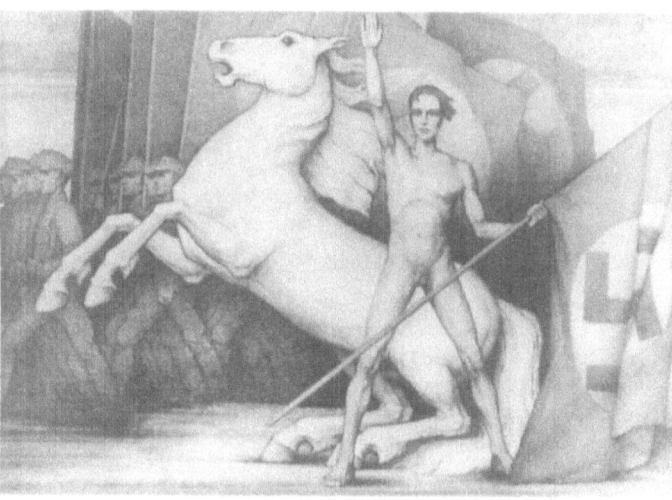

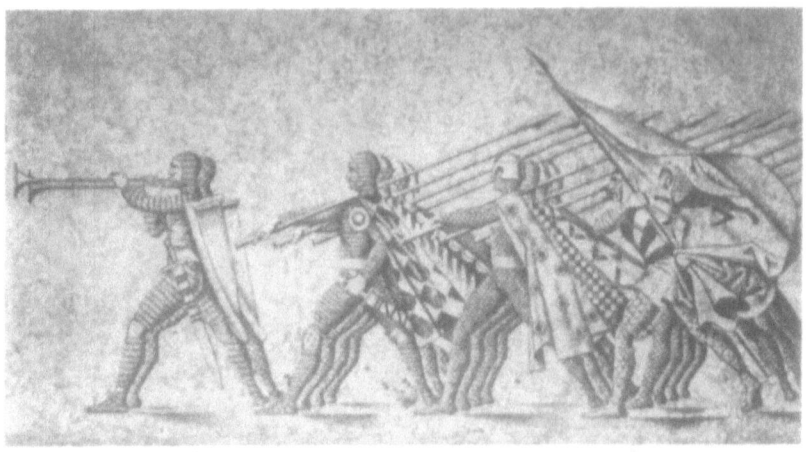

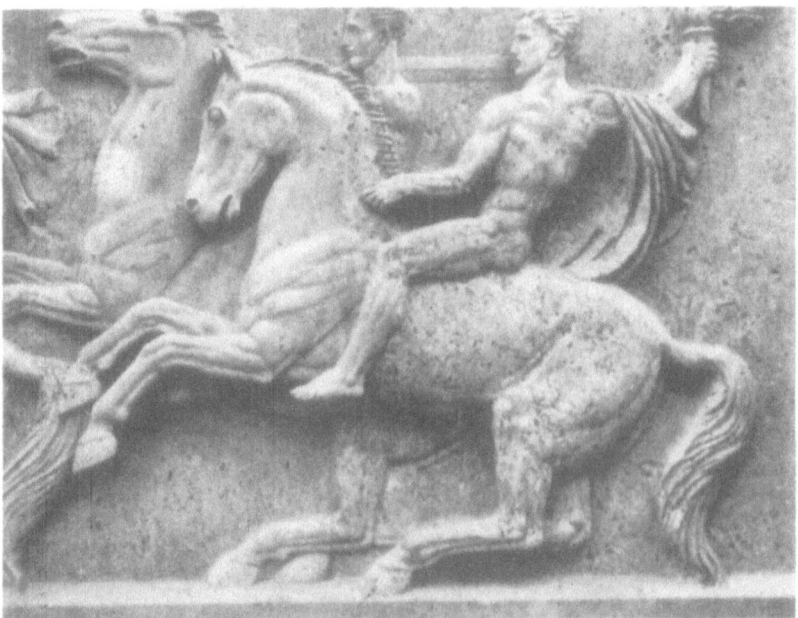

61. *(top)* Wilhelm Dohme, wall engraving in Braunschweig Cathedral (detail), n.d. Published in Werner Rittich, *Deutsche Kunst der Gegenwart* (Breslau: Hirt, 1943), vol. 2, p. 85. Document preserved in the Bibliothèque de l'Institut d'Histoire de l'Art de Strasbourg

62. *(bottom)* Willy Meller, detail from a bas-relief in the entrance hall of the Ordensburg of Crössinsee, 1939. Published in Werner, *Die deutsche Plastik der Gegenwart*, vol. 2, p. 85. Document preserved in the Bibliothèque de l'Institut d'Histoire de l'Art de Strasbourg.

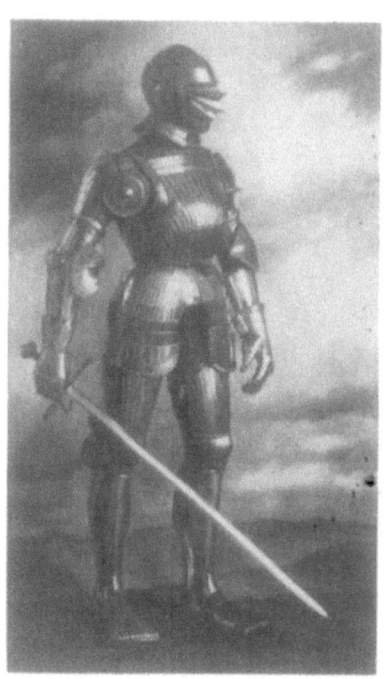

63. Rudolf Otto, *Ready for Battle* (oil on canvas), n.d. Photo by Oberfinanz-direktion, Munich.

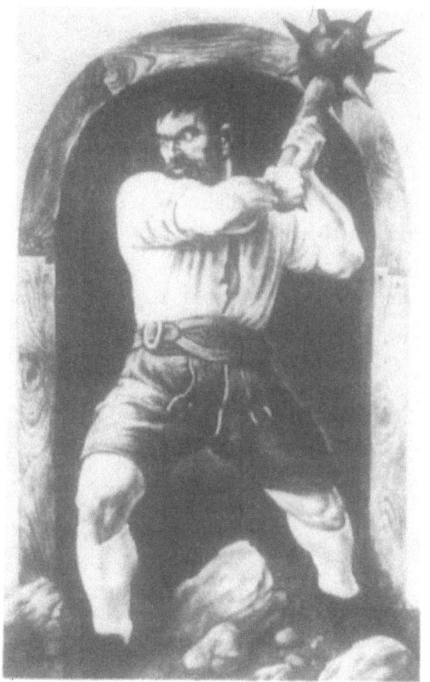

64. Albert Bürkle, *Fighting Peasant* (oil on canvas), n.d. RR.

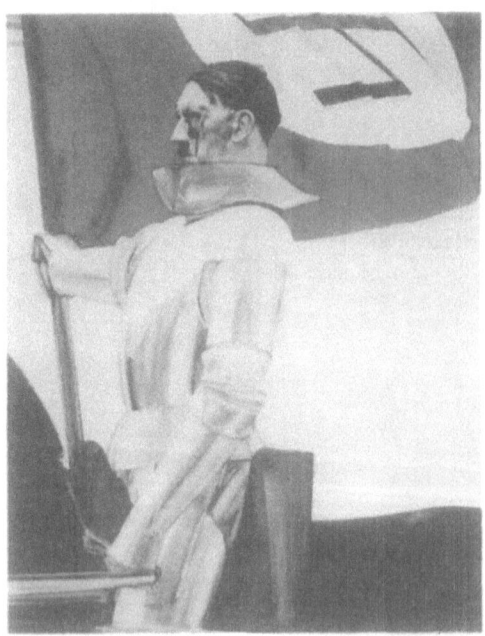

65. Elk Eber, *The Last Grenadier* (oil on canvas), 1937. Published in Rittich, *Deutsche Kunst der Gegenwart*, vol. 2, p. 70. Document preserved in the Bibliothèque de l'Institut d'Histoire de l'Art de Strasbourg.

66. Hubert Lanzinger, *Portrait of the Führer* (*The Protector of German art*) (oil on canvas), 1934 or 1936. Photo in U. S. Army Art Collection, Washington.

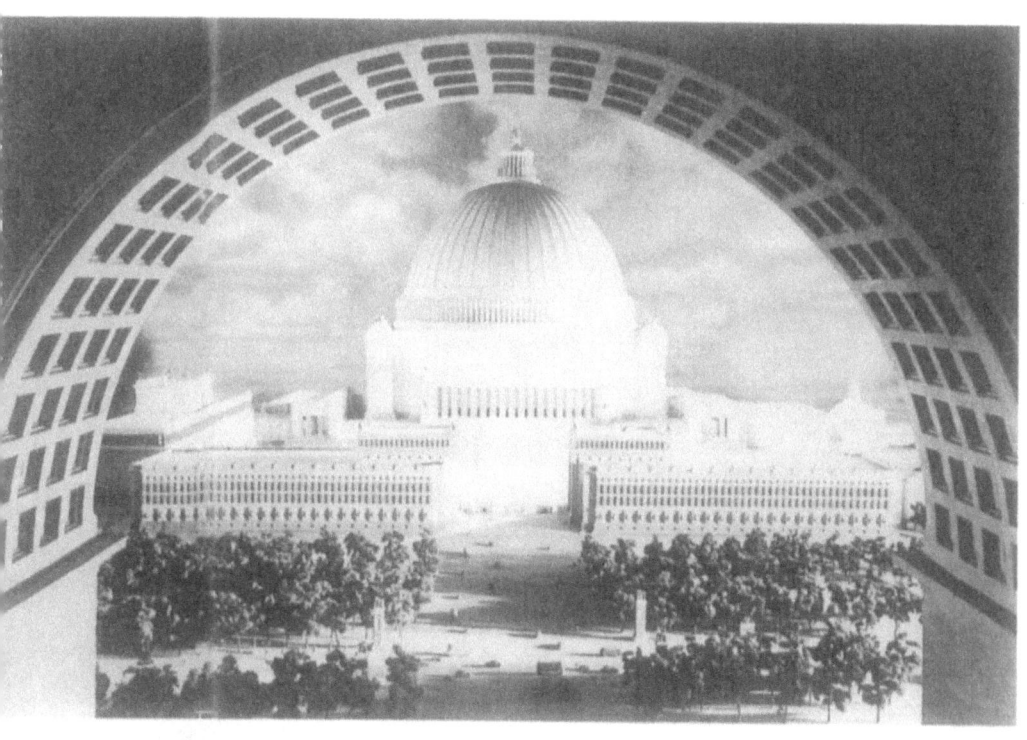

67. Albert Speer, Model for the
Great Dome of Berlin-Germania,
spring 1940 (Plan 2848). RR.

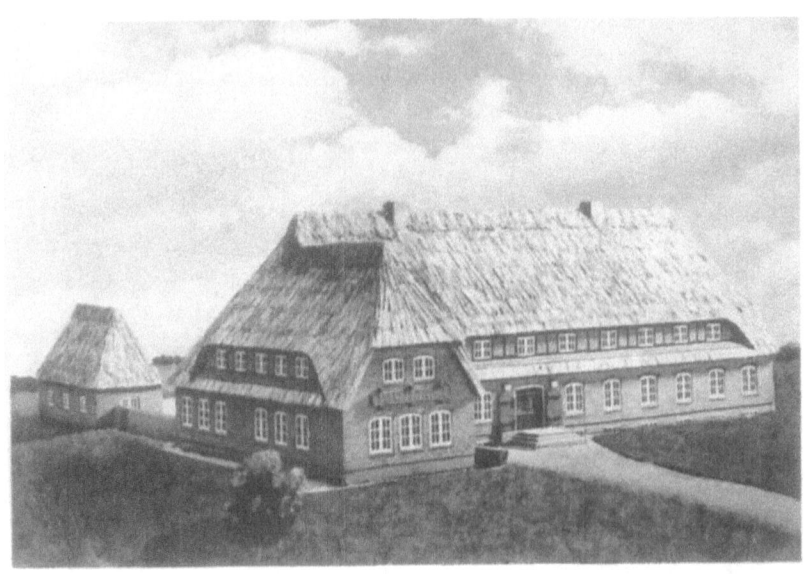

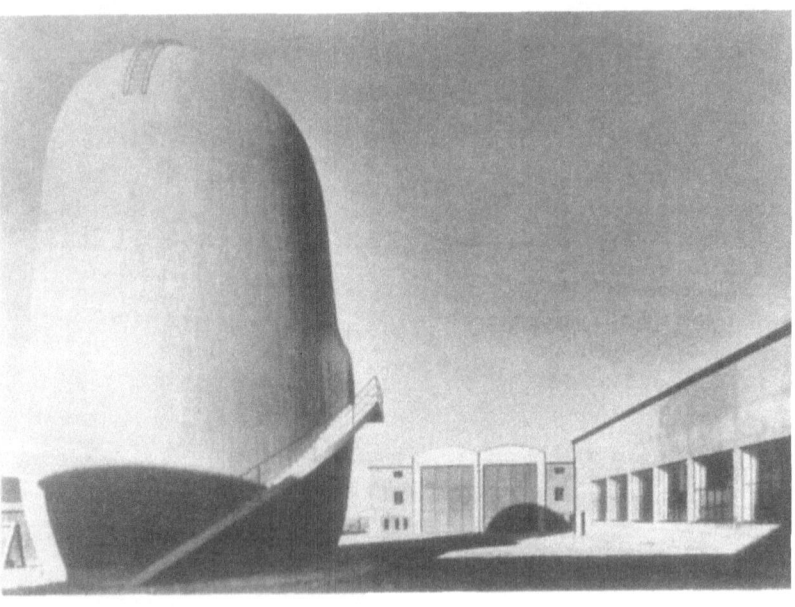

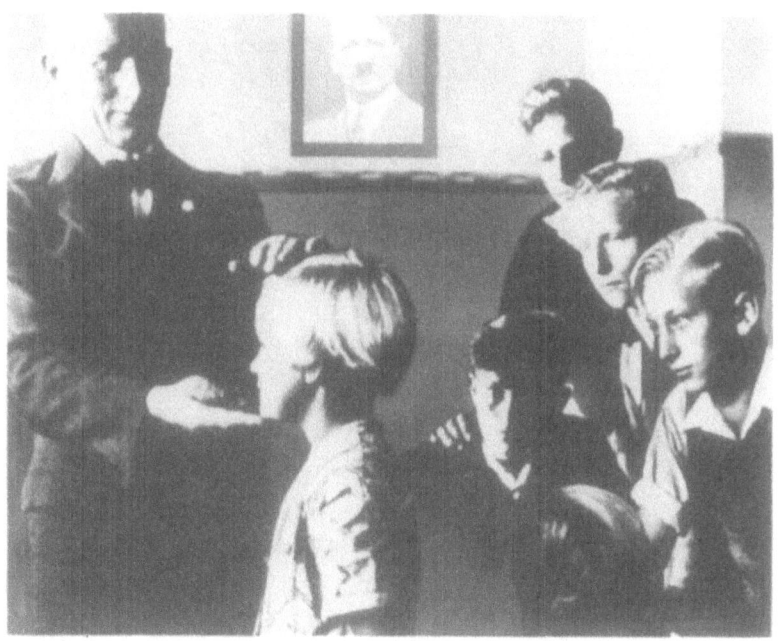

68. *(opposite, top)*   Karl Schönig, Youth Hostel, Husum. Published in Gerdy Troost (ed.), *Das Bauen im neuen Reich*, p. 49. Document preserved in the Bibliothèque de l'Institut d'Histoire de l'Art de Strasbourg.

69. *(opposite, bottom)*   Hermann Brenner and Werner Deutschmann, *Center for Aeronautical Trials: The Turbine and the Assembling Hall.* Published in Rittich, *Architektur und Bauplastik der Gegenwart* (Berlin: Rembrandt, 1938), p. 158. Document preserved in the Bibliothèque de l'Institut d'Histoire de l'Art de Strasbourg.

70. *(above)*   A "racial science" lesson: Measuring skulls at school. Photo by Bilderdienst Süddeutscher Verlag, Munich.

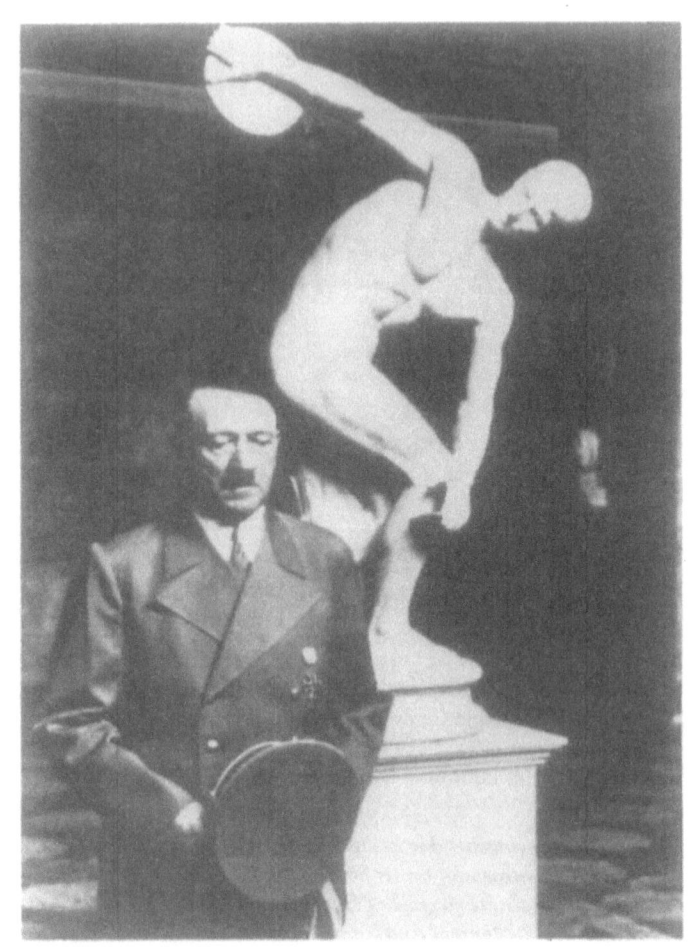

71. Hitler at the installation of the copy of Myron's *Discus Thrower*, in the Munich Glyptotech, July 1938. RR.

One certainly does not expect a sovereign to conform exactly to Plato's definition, but all the same it is an excellent criterion for assessing real sovereigns and maintaining the rules governing their functions.[48]

In defining this type, the raiser of livestock had to rely on his memory as much as on his eye, in order to be able to tell "exactly which form is indispensable for a particular result and which is useless." In this the raiser of livestock resembled the sports trainer, who "likewise must trust his eye and his memory."

When applied to human breeding, the type had to be elaborated from "the German past," from "the essential being of the [kind of] man who has been the upholder of German morality and history." Fortunately, tradition had preserved "the memory of certain precious human symptoms, which are worthy of being preserved in the body of the people." It was thus possible to know, with "absolute certainty," thanks to science, "who has been a champion of Germanism in history."[49] The first thing to do in breeding Germans of superior quality was to "create a sense of race in the people" and therefore "educate it to know how to recognize racial differences *by sight.*" Once an appropriate breeder had memorized a "purely schematic" image or "ideal," he would be able to pick out "defects and deviations" and go on to gauge the value of each specimen.

Upon acceding to power, the Nazis immediately put this program into action by introducing the teaching of *Rassenkunde* (racial science) in German schools. These lessons encouraged every pupil to reconstruct the racial myth for himself or herself from images and texts, in order to prepare him or her "to cooperate actively in everything that can strengthen the Nordic membership of the German people," as the decree that instituted this teaching put it. As well as practicing "assessing racially alien faces," every pupil had to measure the brain pan (top and back of the head) of his or her schoolmates in order to learn how to recognize the specimens that most closely approximated the ideal German-Nordic type (Figure 70).

Pressing on with his methodical exposition, Darré, having reminded the reader that "in every matter of conservation, the most elementary goal is the destruction of whatever is undesirable," cited race theorist Kurt Hildebrandt, author of *Norm und Entartung des Menschen* (Norm and Degeneration in Man), in order to explain the function of desire:

Education [*Bildung*] is the sense of life, so *love of education* is the sense of *events*. It is through education that secret desire receives its visible image. Together with a presentiment of one's own form, obscure instincts develop, and that *glimpsed form becomes the criterion for all action, the measure of all beauty.*

No doubt it was not yet possible to "assert that such an image of the goal of selection would be successful among our people." Nevertheless, even if the experience of animal selection did not prove "the possibility of its realization at the human level," it did make it "very probable."[50] Darré could therefore consider *Kultur* to be a process of "ennobling innate dispositions" and declare, along with his friend F. K. Günther, that one should use "corporeal and spiritual *Kultur* as a tangible image" in order to achieve the goal: "To arouse the desire for *realization*, there must be *something to accomplish.* The tension of present reality straining toward the image not yet fixed in time is enough to spark active life." In this way the Nordic movement could "recover the Hellenic joy of the hero with a joyful body."[51] Baudelaire had the intuition that "man ends up resembling what he would like to be." Now it was a matter of rationalizing the process so as to make that link represented by desire for the model methodically productive.

Since the late twenties, however, the genetic approach to race had seriously undermined the kind of physical anthropology that was founded on racial typology. So most of the race theorists committed to Nazism knew perfectly well that racial types were pure fiction. In 1929, one of them admitted, "We so far have no proof of the reality of these 'racial types' on which we base our theories." The following year, he denounced as pure fantasy the opposition postulated between the cross-breeding of the present and a purer past.[52] In a book on "racial hygiene," which Hitler read while in prison, geneticist Fritz Lenz did not hesitate to declare that "at the beginning of everything there is myth. . . . Yes, race is a myth, not so much a reality of the experimental world as an ideal to be attained."[53] Armand Zaloszyc has shown that a similar reversal of perspective had already occurred in the attitude toward degeneration in nineteenth-century

France. Whereas in 1857 Benedict Augustin Morel had defined it as "a sickly deviation from an initial type," Valentin Magnan, in the great synthesis on *Degenerates*, which he published in collaboration with Maurice Paul Legrain in 1895, declared, "It is not possible to conceive scientifically of a perfect type at the origin of our species . . . and it is at the opposite pole to the origin of the species that we should seek the ideal type, that is to say, at its end."[54] Almost immediately, Houston Stewart Chamberlain adjusted this Neo-Darwinism to pan-Germanist Germany: "Even if it were proved that there never was an Aryan race in the past, we want there to be one in the future: for men of action, that is the decisive point of view."[55]

It was precisely in this respect, however, that racial science stemmed from art: belief in the mythical character of the racial type and its definition as an *ideal to be accomplished* were initially features of the aesthetics of neoclassicism. Conversely, the task of an artist was now considered to be related to that of a scientist, because they shared a common goal: to define an ideal type and make it real.

Erwin Panofsky claimed that the father of neoclassical aesthetics was Giovanni Pietro Bellori, "precursor of Winckelmann," who in 1672 published *L'Idea del Pittore: dello Scultore e dell'Architetto*. This treatise of Neoplatonic inspiration was not content simply to declare, following the ancients and the Renaissance, that an artist "should draw beauty from the most beautiful parts of the most beautiful bodies" in order to make up his figures; nor did it simply compare the artist "to God, in order to make artistic creation heroic." Bellori furthermore declared that the author of nature, "in fashioning his marvelous works, looked deeply into himself and constituted the first forms, called Ideas, in such a way that each species was expressed by that original Idea, giving form to the marvelous context of things created." But while the celestial bodies above the moon were not subject to change, and remained eternally beautiful and ordered, sublunary bodies were, on the contrary, subject to change and to ugliness: "Because of the inequality of matter, the forms change, and human beauty is especially disarranged, as we see from the infinite deformities and disproportions that are in us." For this reason, "painters and sculptors, imitating that first maker, also form in their minds an example of superior beauty, and in beholding it they emend nature with faultless color or line."

The moment of the reversal of the Neoplatonism emphasized by Panofsky came with the totally new definition of the Idea, which now stemmed from man's intuition of nature through the senses: "*Born from nature, it overcomes its origin and becomes the origin of art.*" The Idea had become *reality itself* in a purified form, and was transformed into an "ideal."[56] To put this another way, the model was no longer the eternal essence that, in Plato, presented itself to the mind. Now it was the form that, purged of all accidents of contingency, forced itself upon the eye. The notion of the Idea as an ideal spread through Germany, England, and France and was eventually taken over by Sir Joshua Reynolds, who thought the greatness of art lay in one's ability to rise above all particular forms and accede to "that *central form* . . . from which individuals deviate only to fall into difformity."[57] In his commentary on Quatremere de Quincy's *Essay on the Nature, the End, and the Means of Imitation in the Fine Arts*, critic Jean-Claude Lebensztejn pointed out that Quatremere's originally empirical theory of the ideal carried with it a theory of nature: "Each natural individual is an accidental deviation, a particular divergence from the ideal center of nature, from its original design, its law." So it was that Quatremere could write that "individuals should be . . . means for studying the species; and it is through the species that one must learn to rectify the individual."[58] The artist's task was always to "correct nature" or to "rectify the individual" on the basis of an ideal now identified with the law of nature, a law embodied in the *type*.

In its racial policy, Nazism was based on this kind of rationality far more than on the irrationality to which it so loudly laid claim and that is so readily attributed to it. If irrationality did play a part, it lay not in the method but in the decision to apply it to "human material," with man defined as a being of desire, modeling himself on his ideal. As we have seen, the belief that the rules of art produced by neoclassicism could be transposed to the art of human breeding found paradoxical expression in the late nineteenth century through Oscar Wilde: "A great artist invents a type and Life tries to copy it, to reproduce it in a popular form, like an enterprising publisher."[59] For Nazism, which set out to give body to every metaphor, the artist's task was to fathom the spirit of the Germanic people, observe its various physical manifestations, and from this extract the precious ideal type that would serve as model in the process of reproduction. Working "toward the Führer's" and "responding to the Führer's desire," Nazi artists who regarded Hitler as their master and as the best connoisseur of the Spirit of the people produced not a *völkisch* but a "Hellenic" type, the one that the Führer had always detected in his people, beneath all the historical strata and all the successive stages of cross-breeding.

In his 1934 Nuremberg speech, after pouring scorn on the *völkisch* art defended by certain retrograde figures, Hitler explained the "internal link" that justified the incarnation of present-day Germans in the Greek type and ideal:

Hellenism found a particular way of artistically reproducing man and woman that should not be regarded as merely a Greek manner, in the same sense as the African manner in which a negro tribe represents man and woman; it must furthermore be considered, abstractly speaking, as clear, that is to say, as right. For that representation expresses not only certain particularities that are conditioned by race, but also the race's own comprehension [of] the absolute rightness of the formal representation of the bodies of woman and man. It is thus and not otherwise that each of them must be if they are, anatomically at least, to accomplish their supreme tasks. Just as the image of the man expresses the greatest virile force, thereby showing that it conforms to his essence and natural vocation, so too the image of the woman exalts the ripeness of life and the sacred mother, in conformity with woman's highest goal. That well-understood and well-reproduced conformity with this goal constitutes the ultimate measure of beauty. If other peoples do not understand this beauty, it is simply because they are incapable of any perception of that most lofty conformity with the goal.[60]

The identification of the Idea with an ideal form reached its culmination in neoclassical thought, but Nazi thought was the first to identify the ideal endowed with the form of reality.[61] Hitler confused the figures of art with his living people because he too was convinced of the power of the (racial) type: in the ideal figure of art, the very signs of fertility were fertile, just as signs of fighting were themselves forms of fighting. What the nineteenth century had pronounced to be the ideal of art now became true in real life: it consisted primarily of potentiality and power. This dogma of immanence was also a way of reconnecting with the Christian dogma of the *real presence* immanent in the host. Even if active power was called *genius* or *idea*, its presence in the form of the *type* or the *ideal* was regarded no longer as symbolic but as real. Analyzing our modernity, philosopher Jan Patočka has found another way of expressing this thought: "The possible is no longer that which *precedes* reality; rather, it is becoming reality itself in its creative process."[62]

In his speech delivered at the opening of the Great Exhibition of 1937, Hitler criticized artists who were content to express their "solid will" and their "inner experience" (*inneres Erlebnis*) verbally, "for above all, what we call will interests us far less than power." That almost direct quotation from Wagner introduced a remarkable passage in which Hitler insisted at length that "*the new age [was] working to produce a new type of man.*" Recalling the radiant bodies seen the previous year at the Berlin Olympic Games, he declared, "Never has humanity been so close to the ancients as today, in both appearance and feeling."[63] The original type was no longer reserved for art, but was beginning to imprint itself upon life.

Prodigies and Monsters

On his visit to Italy in 1938, Hitler was so struck by the sight of a Roman marble copy of Myron's *Discus Thrower* that Mussolini decided to give it to him as a present. The Führer in turn "offered" it to the German people and had it placed in the Munich Glyptotech. Inaugurating the second Great Exhibition of German Art that same year, Hitler wound up his speech by speaking of that "fine, immortal work" (Figure 71).

May none of you fail to visit the Glyptotech, for there you will see how splendid man used to be in the beauty of his body, and you will realize that we can speak of progress only when we have not only attained such beauty but even, if possible, when we have surpassed it! And at that sight may artists realize how miraculously the vision and power of that Greek Myron is revealed to us today—that Greek who created this work almost two and a half thousand years ago, and before the Roman copy of which we stand today in the deepest admiration! And may you all find in that work of art the measure of the tasks and achievements [*Leistungen*] of today! May you all aspire to what is beautiful and sublime and so be able, in the people as in art, to face up to the critical evaluation that will be passed in thousands of years to come![64]

That Greek vision and power were thus to be perpetuated *in the people, as in art*, and if the Führer condemned the art of his own time, it was because, in contrast to Myron's *Discus Thrower*, it was endeavoring to "remove the past from the eyes of the present."[65] The "ideal of Nordic beauty," identified with its Greek model, continued to obsess Hitler, Himmler, and Darré, as it also did Schultze-Naumburg (who considered the ideal to have been resuscitated in the Bamberg Horseman)[66] and all the artists most committed "toward the Führer." Even Rosenberg and Goebbels, whose initial preferences inclined, respectively, to the *völkisch* style and Expressionism, had to rally to that Nordic ideal from 1934 on, by reason of the *Führerprinzip*. One of Hitler's most deeply held convictions was that "the highest ideals always correspond to a deep vital necessity, just as the canons of beauty lie in the last analysis only in what is logically most expedient."[67] He shared with his own neoclassical age not only an evident fascination with Greek art but also, in his own way, a functionalist vitalism: life, understood to be the supreme function, as it developed determined the ideal form of beauty that was the most useful to it, that is to say, the one that best ensured its reproduction and perpetuation. Hitler thus set out "as an axiom, not only that man lives in order to serve the highest ideal, but also that that perfect ideal, in its turn, constitutes a condition of man's existence. The argument thus comes full circle." And right from the dawning of the Nordic-Aryan culture, that circle encompassed the reciprocal relations between the race's art and its life, and their mutual engendering for all eternity. In this circular process, any intrusion by a body alien to that race and that art inevitably threatened their eternity, whether that "racially alien" (*artfremd*) body was ideal or real.

One of the most remarkable aspects of Nazism was the way in which, throughout its reign, it meted out the same treatment to both men and works that were judged to be "weak and mildewed"—what Hitler called *das Schwache*—

treatment that ranged from exclusion to cremation. Conversely, all the measures for "the protection of the race" were matched, under the Third Reich, by measures for the protection of art. The year 1933, which saw the introduction of the first anti-Jewish measures and the sterilization law, was also the year of the exhibitions of "degenerate art" (*entartete Kunst*), which were organized first in April in Mannheim, then in Karlsruhe, Nuremberg, Chemnitz, Stuttgart, Dessau, Ulm, and Dresden. Only the last of these exhibitions was actually called *Entarte Kunst*, after Hitler, in his first speech on art, delivered in Nuremberg, repeated several times that "humanity would degenerate" (*würde entarten*) and *Kultur* would become retrograde if it were left in the hands of "elements that were decadent or alien to the race."

As for the ban imposed on the works of Jewish artists, at first it was legally distinct from the ban affecting the "degenerate" artists; but on the eve of the major exhibition of "degenerate art" in Munich in 1937, in which Jewish and non-Jewish artists alike were condemned, sterilization on racial grounds began to be implemented against the *Rheinlandbastarde* ("Rhineland bastards"), children born from unions between German women and black soldiers during the French army's occupation of the Ruhr. This sterilization program, prepared long in advance, was first put into operation on June 30, 1937, in the Protestant hospital of Cologne and was followed by about five hundred other programs.[68] The reason that "artistic sterilization" was considered so important by the Nazis was that they believed that "Negro art" produced by Jewish and "degenerate" artists was a threat to the future of the German-Nordic race, just as the "Rhineland bastards" were.

Ever since the publication in 1928 of *Art and Race*, Schultze-Naumburg had been repeating the same warning: not only were the destructive effects of cross-breeding on art to be feared, so too were its converse effects: degenerate art would engender monstrous human beings. The circle always closed upon itself, whatever the ideal—be it of redemption or corruption—from which it received an impulse. The famous plates that illustrated Schultze-Naumburg's text (Figures 72 through 75) were by no means intended to show that the modernists had taken as their models flesh and blood monsters[69]—quite the contrary: "It goes without saying that it should not be supposed that such patients served as models for the painters. Our parallel is designed not to find a faithful concordance in every case, but to show a truth that more or less corresponds to what is represented in those images."[70] And what was that truth?

Schultze-Naumburg, who was far less naive and stupid than is, for reasons of convenience, suggested today, maintained that roughly up until the death of Goethe in 1832, there existed a dominant *Weltanschauung* that assigned to morality and to the deity the task of "repressing evil . . . , a process on which the future of mankind and *Kultur* depended." Evil was, to be sure, not liquidated, but "simply expelled from consciousness," and in proportion to the strength of the moral personality, "the conscious won out over the unconscious and its dark instincts." Of course, the latter did reappear from time to time, but all that was needed was "a little tap on the nose" to return them to their lair. Then, however, countless demagogues suddenly began to announce: "You do not have to repress your instincts with your morally constrained consciousness. For they are a part of yourself, and you should 'liberate' them." This slogan, which encouraged every individual to "express himself or herself" (*sich ausleben*), threw open "Pandora's box," allowing its howling demons to escape and spread. Schultze-Naumburg believed that contemporary art mirrored this process, which opened up the way for "subhumans," incapable of repressing their destructive instincts. Amid this chaos there developed an "infantile predilection" for social outcasts and "an almost perverse desire" for alien races and their way of behaving.[71]

The Nazi condemnation of contemporary art was thus explicitly founded on the following conviction: *Kultur* was no longer fulfilling its traditional function of repressing destructive instincts. That this art might simply be presenting (sometimes with critical intent) modern barbarity rather than encouraging it was precisely what Nazism could not accept, given that it rejected all sublimation and, on the contrary, postulated the ability of any image to actually transform reality. What justified the condemnation of contemporary art was that by allowing what was repressed by *Kultur* to resurface within it, this art was setting the repressed in the place of the ideal. Goebbels, along with the other ideologues of the regime, attributed this eruption of repressed instincts to the Jews, who had no "sense of beauty" and whose talent was "more suited to purely intellectual doubt than to revealing natural beauty and aesthetic harmony." But there did exist "a typically Jewish art": "It practices the glorification of all vices and monstrosities. It raises to the level of an artistic ideal whatever is nonheroic, ugly, sick, and decomposed. This pathological anomaly in the life of culture is what we call degenerate art."[72] This eruption into art of what used to be repressed and its replacement of the ideal were precisely what Hitler was condemning in Nuremberg:

That which poses as a revelation of the "cult of the primitive" is not the expression of a naive, unspoiled soul but of a degeneracy that is utterly corrupt and diseased. . . . It is not the function of art to remind men of the forms taken by degeneracy but rather to combat those forms by pointing to that which is eternally healthy, eternally beautiful. When destroyers of art of this type presume to desire to give expression to "the Primitive" in the consciousness of a people, they should remind themselves that our people at least, some thousands of years ago, had already long grown out of such "primitivism."[73]

Some ideologues tried to elaborate an aesthetic Darwinism, among them Ludwig von Senger, who contrasted the "nordic three-dimensional feeling of art" to the "Eastern two-dimensional feeling," which was clearly to be found in Bolshevik art.[74] The success of such efforts remained limited, however, for it was the effects of art that were at stake, not its causes. Hitler went on to say that the mission of art was to "demonstrate the vital necessity of that which is good and useful, [not to] ensure the triumph of that which is harmful . . . , to dig about in muck, out of a love of muck, and not to paint mankind only when it is degenerate, presenting to the eye women suffering from cretinism, who are turned into symbols of maternity, or crippled idiots who are turned into examples of energy."

As ever, Hitler failed to differentiate life from its image. To his mind, just as the ideal of Greek art ought necessarily to be embodied in his people, so too it was at all costs necessary to prevent degenerate art from engendering monsters. Nazism thus set up an extremely conventional opposition between the two poles of the sacred: on the one hand, the exhibitions of "degenerate art" encompassed all that Nazism believed to stem from the forces of death and destruction; on the other hand, the Great Exhibitions of German Art brought together all the positive powers that were supposed to ensure the continuity of the German-Nordic *Kultur*. This fantasy of a possible clear-cut division between the pure and the impure naturally enough created for the Nazi authorities as many problems pertaining to art objects as to "human material."

By condemning the new art that made room for what *Kultur* had repressed up until the beginning of the twentieth century, Hitler acquired legitimate grounds for championing the legacy of the traditional values on the basis of which that *Kultur* had been maintained. In doing so, Nazism of course refused to recognize the nature of the split that had irremediably separated the ends of art and those of *Kultur*, despite the fact that it had been perfectly capable of diagnosing that split, which *Mein Kampf* dated at one point to 1910 and at another to the late nineteenth century. Schultze-Naumburg, for his part, dated it symbolically to the death of Goethe. It will be remembered that when Edouard Manet lamented the negative reception of his sacrilegious *Olympia* at the 1865 Salon, Baudelaire ironically wrote to him, "You are just the first in the decrepitude of your art."[75] None of these diagnoses was totally false. It is true that the mirror that modern art held up to a *Kultur* founded on repression did indeed set criticism of that *Kultur* in the place formerly occupied by the ideal that upheld or was the basis for that *Kultur*, and the reason that Nazism condemned modern art was certainly that this art, sometimes despite itself, mirrored what Nazism set out to repress to the point of rendering it invisible.[76]

When Schultze-Naumburg stigmatized the "infantile predilection" for social outcasts and the "almost perverse desire" for alien races, he was, with considerable perspicacity, simply drawing attention to the desire for otherness—a desire that certainly was incompatible with the demand for reproduction of "the same," and with the will for self-reproduction and self-formation (*aselbstgestaltung*), which at long last was supposed to fix in place the community's internal links for a thousand years to come.

All the ideologues of National Socialism based their theories on the postulate that man is a being subject to desire. Throughout their reign they endeavored to provide that desire with one exclusive object. In this respect, Nazism's competition with Modernist art was similar to its rivalry with Christianity. In both cases what was at stake was the position of being the object of desire. Rosenberg was always saying that every race had a nostalgic desire (*Sehnsucht*) for its own type or god, and Darré maintained that "the secret desire received its visible image" in the type. Replacing Christ with a racially similar (*artgleich*) Führer, or replacing the critical image of modern artists with an image of "the Nordic ideal" was always a matter of directing the desire toward the object that would justify all sacrifices in the name of the eternity of the race. In her memoir of being a young Catholic Berliner won over by Nazism, Melita Maschmann reflected that after the end of the war it took her twelve years to realize that she had served "an idol avid for blood": "We had locked ourselves into a kind of idolatry for our people, a sentiment the counterpart to which could be only scorn and hatred for other peoples. . . . In this way, we had acquired closed minds, fit for a savage tribe that imagines that its tribal gods are the most powerful in the world."[77] This self-idolatry, manifested as much through the mediation of the artistic German-Nordic ideal as through that of the Artist-Christ-Führer, implied that the desires of the people were exclusively endogamous.

Few theorists of Nazism expressed the endogamous nature of that amorous bond better than Carl Schmitt. His work, which provided the new regime with a juridical basis in the shape of the *Artgleichheit*, concluded with the following words:

We are seeking an attachment (*Bindung*) that is more sure, more alive, and deeper than a deceptive attachment to the falsifiable letter of thousands of articles of the law. Where could that attachment lie if not in ourselves and in our own *Art* (race, species, nature, way of being)?[78]

Schmitt set in opposition to the letter (*Buchstabe*) of the law "our own way of feeling today" (*unser heutiges Enpfinden*), which was more organic and biological. Without this *Artgleichheit*, this attachment of the community to its own species or race (*Art*), "the whole of the Führer's state" would be unable to "survive for a single day."[79] It is true that National Socialism survived thanks only to the extreme fluidity and the constant changes of its legal texts, the counterpart to which was the embodiment of the law in the race and its immanent image—a beautiful form identified with the Messiah. The absence of a written and stable constitution that established intelligible and legible links was offset by "the real presence" of the image immanent in the race. This image, which created bonds of feeling, embodied the law of desire, which prescribes ignoring or destroying the "other." The law of the image delivered the German people from the ancient law.

It was possible, however, to pair desire with the law in the legal texts themselves or in the directives conveyed by official speeches, which thus came to seem remarkably like the slogans of propaganda. It will be remembered that one decree urged individuals "to respond to the Führer's desire" and that a leader would explain that the duty of every individual was "to work toward the Führer." Such pronouncements were matched by slogans that opened or closed the space and time of the desire, at the same time assigning to it its object: "Give a child to the Führer," "Die for the Führer," or "We were born to die for Germany," which was prominently displayed in every Hitler Youth camp.[80]

Hannah Arendt correctly noted that, for all their claims to explain everything, totalitarian ideologies "have the tendency to explain not what is, but what becomes, what is born and passes away."[81] Even as they set limits to the desires of individuals, these slogans, by affirming the perpetuation of the race beyond the limits set for the individual, sanctioned the infinity of the desire. The cult of the Führer was thus identified with the cult of the race, enclosing the latter in a self-idolatry that, as Melita Maschmann observed, did indeed cause it to serve "an idol avid for blood."

Accelerators

In the House of German Art, the call to sacrifice raised by all those bodies that were *available* and *ready for combat* insisted that, if it were to be heeded, the human material (*Menschmaterial*) capable of the supreme sacrifice must simultaneously be renewed. That is how the works that urged the reproduction of life came to be inseparable from those that were calling on men "to die for the

Führer." Arendt observed that "total terror, the essence of totalitarian govern- ment, "is supposed to provide the forces of nature or history with an incompa- rable instrument to accelerate their movement, . . . but to accelerate them to a speed they would never reach if left to themselves."[82] Nazi imagery was an es- sential element in that terror: it constituted a veritable *accelerator of passions* that tended to precipitate the natural cycle of birth and death in a general mobiliza- tion of the *Volkskörper*. The industrial character of the extermination, today re- garded as one of the most distinctive features of the Nazi horror, was in fact in- separable from the determination to industrialize the production of the new man. The industrial production of death on the one hand and life on the other constituted two aspects of one and the same process of selection according to the National Socialist Idea, although it quite clearly produced far more death than it engendered life.

One element in this industrial realization of the Idea was the fabrication of paintings and sculptures that served as prototypes in a process of selective re- production on a grand scale: catalogues, specialist reviews, the daily and weekly press, and postcards from the House of German Art were distributed in many thousands or hundreds of thousands of copies. The mechanical reproduction of works of art was placed at the service of the organic reproduction of the genius in such a way that, to paraphrase Walter Benjamin, it seemed that the genius had reached the era of its technical reproducibility.

"What do we want our people to resemble?" asked one racial education specialist. He suggested juxtaposing two sets of images: the first would present "faces and bodies of a definitely Nordic type," the second "a group of Jews who could either be ordinary contemporaries or 'Jewish personalities' such as most of the Bolshevik leaders. . . . It is precisely by collecting examples of the two types that we shall get children to identify instinctively with one group and violently reject the other."[83] Using the same ploy of examples and counterexamples, the efficacy of which had long ago been demonstrated by Schultze-Naumburg, this pedagogue made the aim of the contrasting exhibitions of "degenerate art" and "German art" abundantly clear: attraction to the Nordic type and repulsion of the antipeople (*Gegenvolk*) were supposed to become progressively natural reflexes for all members of the community. Given that the condition for the race's eternal life was its improvement through purification, it was necessary to lead every individual back to the natural reflex of love for his or her own racial type and to detach him or her from any "perverse inclination" for alien races. Needless to say, the nude bodies, painted or sculpted, that were exhibited each year in the Temple of German Art made sense only in view of the role they were expected to play.

The female type illustrated in Ivo Saliger's *Diana at Rest* (Figure 76) represented an ideal of Nordic beauty produced by a remarkable montage. Against the background of a landscape of "eternal Germany," three contemporary faces were attached to bodies resembling photographic nudes but arranged in poses that were inspired by classical iconography. The most glorious past of the race was here united with the beauty of fashion magazines. All the same, the relative virility of the forms in these paintings was in many cases matched by a feminization of the masculine bodies offered by, for example, Arno Breker's statues. The conventional distribution of sexual features was here confused in order to promote an image of plenitude and health that the public was supposed to absorb to its very marrow. *The Judgment of Paris* (Figure 77), also by Saliger, again transported the Greek myth to the German countryside. The same montage of faces and feminine bodies was evident, and Priam's son, clad in shorts, was turned into an apparent member of the Hitler Youth (*Hitler Jugend*) organization. Although seated on a rock, he seemed to be making a gesture of retreat when faced with the naked body of Aphrodite. Was she advancing to fight him or to love him? Her posture, which seemed to suggest, contrary to legend, that coupling was imminent, was also implicitly reminiscent of certain sculpted bodies "ready to fight" or "ready for sacrifice" (Figure 78). With the battle on the "birth front" already in the offing, Hera and Athena, rejected by Paris, were reclothing themselves beneath a Germanic oak tree that had been substituted for Mediterranean pines. The male spectator may have been able to identify with Paris, who was seen from the back, but the impossibility of his coupling with the depicted fig-

ure of Aphrodite reestablished the truth of the myth. What all of this really involved, however, was the shaping of taste and vital reflexes to ensure that Paris's
choice in the image would be reproduced in life.[84]

The group of statues entitled *The Judgment of Paris,* by Josef Thorak (Figure 79), was almost always photographed from Paris's point of view. In fact, sometimes the camera lens was quite simply substituted for the Greek hero, so that the
judgment to be made on the respective racial qualities of the three ancient god-
desses fell to the spectator. In his 1936 speech to the Hitler Youth organization,
Himmler rejoiced at this: "The Germans, in particular the German young, have
learned anew . . . how to look at bodies and judge this God-given body, this God-
given life, and this race according to their value or lack of value."[85] The sexual object of desire, the woman, was constantly present in history, as was the man, the
eternal fighter for the race. Whether or not they were simultaneously present in
the image, they were inseparable partners in the fight for the eternal life of their
race. As early as 1934, Hitler proclaimed, "The sacrifice made by man in the struggle of his people is also made by the woman, who sacrifices herself in the struggle
for the preservation of this people in each of its cells. What the man deploys in
heroism on the field of battle, the woman deploys in devotion, suffering, and endurance with an eternal patience. Every time she brings a child into the world, she
emerges victorious in a battle for the being or nonbeing of her people."[86]

Occasionally our heroes abandoned their original Greekness in favor of a
Germanized Renaissance symbolism (such as *Mars and Venus,* by Saliger, Figure
80). But the fecundity of the Greek myths soon drew them back: Saliger's *Leda*
(Figure 81), voluptuously stretched out on a ground cloth that protected her from
the German pine needles, awaited the arrival of the swan that was approaching to
engender heroes with her. Hitler, however, preferred the version by Paul Mathias
Padua (*Leda and the Swan,* Figure 82), which he acquired for his personal collection. No doubt the neck of the swan into which Zeus had transformed himself
seemed to Hitler more suited to magnify Hitler's power. "Your body does not belong to you, but to your lineage [*Sippe*] and your people [*Volk*]," the brochures of
propaganda on natality were forever repeating.[87] Clearly the Führer, the virile in-

carnation of the people, was the symbolic father of all the children born to German women mindful of their duty.

The female nudes, which accounted for one-tenth of all the works exhibited in the Temple of German Art, not only constituted models of the type or ideal of Nordic beauty, but also provided models of the sexual behavior that was supposed to attract the race's masculine elite. The body language of stereotyped seduction that was repeated time and again in paintings and sculptures (Figures 83 through 85) owed very little to the iconographic tradition of "the great Nordic style," but corresponded far more closely, as did the female faces depicted, to the images found in fashion magazines and advertisements. In the speech cited earlier, Himmler rejoiced at the change in social behavior that was imminent. In the past, "a young girl of lesser racial value" who was "more attractive" would be invited to dance, while "the girl who was racially valuable was always a wallflower, because our people's ideal had changed very much for the worse. . . . But now things are changing. I think we are entering a period when the Nordic girl will be the bride, not the other one."[88] The effects expected from these model images were indeed those described, even before Oscar Wilde, by Baudelaire, when he spoke of the "kept girls" who "tried hard to resemble the images of Gavarni."[89]

In theory, these representations of purely sexual objects did not contradict the numerous portraits of honorable mothers, for in this art it should have been possible for the blatant eroticization of the female body and the glorification of maternity to coexist, even if they could not do so in traditional bourgeois morality and life. The sexual object, which was invariably racially typecast, was not an end in itself, but on the contrary was supposed to draw attention to the role that fell to it, namely to transmit and reproduce the Aryan genius. Just as all sterile enjoyment of sex was opposed by the demand that the Nazi Idea be made a reality, so too was the purely aesthetic enjoyment of works of art, which were invariably simply "means to an end," just as the state was for Hitler and propaganda was for Goebbels. This theory was formulated in exemplary fashion in the journal produced by the NSDAP's Bureau of Racial Policies. It denounced the doctrine of "art for art's sake" for being "typically Jewish and homosexual," as was proved by the fact that its defenders excluded themselves either as Jews from the *Volksgemeinschaft* or as homosexuals from the process of reproduction.[90] Meanwhile, Himmler was also at pains to warn his SS generals of the dangers of the homosexuality that was rife among their troops:

The destruction of the state begins the moment an erotic principle intervenes (and I say this in all seriousness): for when a principle of sexual attraction between men exists in this state of men, professional qualifications and output no longer play their role. . . . Homosexuality thus ruins all output [*Leistung*] and any system based on output; it destroys the very bases of the state.[91]

Yet there was no reason to believe that the heterosexual soldiers who took to the front postcards of female nudes published by the House of German Art always used these postcard simply to guide their choice of female reproducers of the Aryan genius. "There is no task that exists for its own sake" was at any rate the watchword for the SS, which never ceased, along with Himmler, to reiterate "the absolute necessity for understanding the futility of everything that is an end in itself."[92]

According to this logic of the instrumentalization of bodies or *Mensch-material*, every image of a desirable young woman ought to have been regarded as anticipating the image of a mother and, in the longer term, the eternity of the race. In reality, however, there was a manifest break between the two statuses of women presented by paintings, as indeed there was in real life under the Third Reich. Arthur Ressel's *Future Mother* (Figure 86) testified to the immediate de-sexualization of a woman once she passed from the status of desirable object to that of mother. That daunting physical transformation, however, did not prevent a massive response to the appeal made by Reichsfrauenführerin Scholtz-Klink[93] in Nuremberg in 1936 to a "people subject to the race" (*artgebundenes Volk*).[94] That year, more than one thousand girls returned from the congress pregnant.[95] The sporting and paramilitary framework provided for the young did not deflect the libido from its sexual goals, as some are mistakenly inclined to believe.[96] On the contrary, the preparations for war and the policy of *Bevölkerung*, populating the east, which was intended to make the "vital German space" a reality, insisted on the coupling of racially pure young people. So each time a joint gathering of units of the Hitler Youth organization and the Bund Deutscher Mädel (BDM), the League of German Girls, was in the offing, the girls' *Führerin* would harangue her troops as follows: "You cannot all find husbands, but you can all become mothers."[97] The situation was such that the BDM was soon nicknamed *Bald Deutsche Mutter* (Soon a German Mother). The battle that Hitler was encouraging on the "birth front" was also spreading to the countryside, where BDM camps were often situated close to those for young men in the Labor Service. Paintings such as *The Time of Ripening* (*Reifezeit*) by Johannes Beutner (Figure 87) and *Summer* by Wilhelm Hempfing (Figure 88) were no doubt responses to the *Blut und Boden* (blood and soil) Mother Earth ideology; but they also illustrated the song that celebrated the organization of leisure pursuits for the Labor Front, the KdF (*Kraft durch Freude*, Strength through Joy): "In the fields and on the heath / I lose my strength through joy."[98]

With the advent of war, discourse on natality became noticeably more authoritarian. In 1940, the principal of a girls' school in reconquered Alsace impressed on his pupils that they should remember they were "true Germans, and that the principal duty of a German woman [was] to give the Führer as many children as possible, one a year if that was what he ordered." Marriage was for decadent peoples, so they should never repulse the advances of young Aryan men; on the contrary, they had "a most strict duty" to have "intimate relations with them as often as possible."[99] A decree dated October 28, 1935, called this arrangement "biological marriage," which was a significant part of the *Führerdienst*, one's service to the Führer. As for the *Lebensborn* (Source of Life) organization founded by Himmler in the same year, it was considered the crowning touch to the apparatus for the production of the new man. The Sources of Life were places where "the best specimens of Nordic women" were selected for their reproductive capacities so they could be united with the SS elite and ensure the rational breeding of *SS-Kinder* (SS children). One day in January 1941, Himmler, who kept an eye on the progress of these institutions, became incensed at the lackadaisical atmosphere that prevailed there. To remedy this, he decided "to install a mother-and-

child statue in front of every center, to testify clearly to the role of the Lebensborn, and without delay [to] hang in a suitable place a picture of 'a mother breast-
feeding.'"[100] Himmler certainly believed, as did Wilde, that "Life imitates Art far
more that Art imitates Life." It was, after all, just a matter of making use of the old
power of *examples*, just as Baldur von Schirach did when, addressing the Hitler
Youth members whose Führer he was, he spoke of his faith in "the power of the
model that leaves its imprint on everything."[101] However narrowly doctrinaire
Nazi formulations generally were, it is clear that they were able to rally people so
successfully thanks only to the deep well of ideology into which they tapped.

All of the Nazi ideologues declared that art must once again become the
"vital power" it had been in the past, but it was Wolfgang Willrich, one of the
painters who enjoyed the protection of Himmler and Darré, who carried breeding according to an ideal type into its critical phase. His work entitled *The Purification of the Temple of Art*, published a few months before the opening of the
1937 Great Exhibition of German Art and the exhibition of "degenerate art,"
seemed to suggest that the new man of National Socialism could be engendered
only through art—and art of the purest kind.[102] He declared essentially that art
would be able to break the chain of natural causes of degeneration if it proved
possible to implant in the Germanic body a graft of the pure ideal of the ancients,
which had been preserved in art as well as in certain specimens of Germans. It
was as if, given that racial medicine was not yet effective in the biogenetic fabrication of the new man, it fell to art to implant a graft in the imaginary representations of the German race.

In Willrich's opinion, "the most noble task of artistic creation" was to define
"the healthy man of the Nordic race." In opposition to the degenerate art that
had to be expelled from the temple because it "offered as a model a caricature instead of an ideal,"[103] he set about seeking in the works of art of the ancients and
of the Middle Ages—in both "art which creates types" and in the bodies of his
compatriots—for "the ideal German face" that would serve as a type. Reminding
his readers that racial doctrine aspired "to the health of the people, the purity of
the race, and the eternity of the species [*Art*] of the German people," he declared

that images could propagate this more effectively than words. He then produced his own version of the myth of engendering through images, basing it on the doctrines of Darré:

Through the selection of the best specimens from the point of view of heredity, and with these submitting freely to breeding for the race, racial doctrine is endeavoring to create a new German nobility, to serve as a guide to the people, as a species and in action, through its superior will and its valorous example. To awaken the German people's nostalgic desire for such a nobility, to establish the beautiful and sublime clearly and engrave this in a compelling way within it, not simply as a privilege of the gods in whom it is impossible to believe, but as a human possibility and as the ultimate goal of regeneration (*Aufartung*) . . . [w]hat a sublime task that is for art![104]

To become gods again: art, which guided healthy men to their own divinity could also enable them to overcome death. For art—which according to Willrich was founded on knowledge of the natural laws of death, life, and heredity—made it possible to be done with the old representation of a personal life after death and "definitely to dispel the dread of personal punishments and rewards." In effect, this was the old Roman doctrine of genius, as described by Otto. Willrich explained that racial doctrine taught the need "to go forward to meet personal death in a desire for suprapersonal survival—not in some beyond but in one's children and [in] the children of those children, and in creative realizations [*Leistungen*] here on our own Earth."[105] One of the ploys used constantly by Nazism was indeed to invoke salvation here on Earth, accessible through the works produced by the German race. Through art it was possible to act on the powers of destiny, by guiding and orienting people's judgment. What was this divine aspect to the laws of nature if not "a power, a secret full of promises, destined to plumb man's reason to its very limits"? The limits of reason were marked not only by words but also by the images of photography, which were too attached to "the now" to guide the race along the path of the regeneration to come. This is why racial doctrine needed more than just the words and photographs of its handbooks if it were to propagate itself in concrete fashion. "Neither words nor photography have the power to call forth at once the clearest representations and enthusiastic participation. Only the plastic arts can do that." To set the racial body in enthusiastic motion, it was necessary for the object proposed as its desire to somehow automatically arouse it: "When it comes to feeling, and above all to the eye's judgment as to whether a feature is noble or mean, words and concepts are far too inadequate masters. The art of the painter or the sculptor, in contrast, can convey directly to the subconscious what should be worshiped and what should not, and can do so with insistent penetration."[106]

The frontispiece to Willrich's book (Figure 89) depicted the object presented for the people's automatic adoration clearly enough. It was one of his own works, entitled *Die Hüterin der Art* (The Guardian of the Species), which he was later to place at Himmler's disposal for "the decoration of whatever space is worthy of it."[107] Willrich, who advocated renovating ancient figures from mythology and recasting them as *credible* symbols, thus reused the virginal figure of Mary in his painting intended for the modern altar of the Nazi faith. Just as the *Madonna del parto*, painted by Piero della Francesca in Monterchi, Italy, still carried in her womb the child who would come to deliver men from sin, the Guardian of the Species, radiant in the center of Willrich's picture, clasped her hands over the belly that was soon to produce a child for the Führer. The new law set out to preserve and renew the old. Just as among the Nazis who were most hostile to Christianity there were some, such as Reich Minister for Church Affairs Hans Kerrl, who admitted that they had nothing "to put in the place of Christian morality," so too were there some among Christians, such as Cardinal Michael von Faulhaber, who confessed that they "had no objections to an honest study of race, nor to a policy to safeguard the race."[108] However, even if the Guardian of the Species restored the virginal figure of Mary the mother of God, that productive body also appeared in the guise of an armed maternal body. A second version of the painting with the same title (Figure 90) changed the figure into a guardian of the "Germanic hearth." So one and the same mother was resuscitated with two functions: to engender god and to act as the vestal virgin watching over the temple that sheltered the genius of the German race, thereby symbolizing the self-purification of the temple of art that she herself represented.

This temple, which Hitler had dedicated to "the goddess of art," where "the seeds of a new and superior culture" were to be deposited, was without a doubt the maternal deity within which the German people could find refuge and at the same time purge themselves until they felt "at one with themselves."[109]

Gottfried Benn or the Endogenous Image

Symptomatic of the competitive spirit that prevailed among the fanatics of purification was the fact that Willrich, one of the artists most fiercely attached to the purity of the maternal image, was also the most violent detractor of the very poet who strove the hardest to restore that image.[110, 111]

"Expressionism was an art, the last art in Europe," wrote Gottfried Benn, the poet and doctor whose rallying to Nazism in 1933 rocked the foundations of the entire intellectual class. In that year, in a mixed state of extreme lucidity and visionary exaltation, Benn proclaimed that what was then beginning with the new regime was "no longer art," about which he would no longer speak except as of "a phenomenon of the past" (to borrow Hegel's expression). In response to the attacks launched against the Expressionist movement—to which he had belonged—by Rosenberg and the *völkisch* groups, Benn described it as "a European style" produced by "a wide, united front of artists of exclusively European and Aryan heredity." All its manifestations had been devoted to "the destruction of reality" (at that time perceived as a "capitalist notion") and to promoting the spirit's return to "its own inner reality, its being, its biology, its structure, its interactions of a physiological and psychological nature, its creation, its radiance." Benn's deeply held conviction was that after Expressionism there would no longer be any art "in the sense of the past five centuries." Now was a time of "metamorphosis": "a new race is about to be born for Europe." Although he was finally rejected by a number of the Nazi authorities to whom he had offered his support in a blaze of publicity, Benn was one of the most authentic of the Nazi intellectuals, by reason of the force with which he asserted the genetic nature of the links that united art with race. To the "friends" of National Socialism who viewed the matter of racial selection "with skepticism," he replied unhesitatingly:

Propaganda reaches the genes, words touch the sexual glands. There can be no doubt that the hardest reality of nature lies in the fact that the efforts of cerebral life are felt by the constitution of the cellular plasma; [no doubt] the spirit is a dynamic element that creates forms in the process of historical evolution. There is a unity here: *whatever is imprinted by politics is produced by the organism.*

And what is imprinted by politics will be not art but a race of a new species, which is already clearly recognizable.[112]

Seldom can the basis of National Socialism have been so clearly expressed as here, where Benn not only anticipated all the ideologues appointed by Nazism but moved far ahead of them with regard to the far-reaching implications of what Hitler glorified as "the implacable logic of the Idea." It is true that similar formulas were produced by all of them. For example, in October 1933, Wilhelm Rüdiger wrote, "For art, in its happening, is not an aesthetic affair but a biological one."[113] And when Benn declared that "art constitutes the preservation of a people as a species, its definitive hereditary continuity," he was indeed simply repeating Hitler. But only Benn, as a doctor-writer could attempt, on the basis of Novalis's definition of "art as progressive anthropology," to retrace the grandiose epic that, starting with animals, led to the species that we now call human:

Eras end up with art, and the human race will end up with art. First the saurians, the lizards, and then the species endowed with art. Hunger and love: those are paleontology; and even among insects there is domination and division of labor. But *they* made gods and art, and then, later on, just art.[114]

Benn's commitment to Nazism, which was complex and not without contradictions, rested on his belief in the absolute necessity, at once historical and biological, of a truly physical mutation of the human species. In 1930, the question of what the subject of man's dream is ran through his essay on the problems of poetic creation. In answer to the question, "Who dreams the dream?" he replied, the body, because "[i]t holds a dream that has come from far away. . . . " The historical necessity for a mutation in the species was based on a body that had the essential property of dreaming, and that could be defined only as a dreaming substance: "The body is the last constraint and the depth of necessity; it carries the presentiment, it dreams the dream." At this time, however, Benn conceived of this union between dream and substance only in the solitude of one thinking body, that of a single individual unbound from close envelopment by a political or mystical body:

There is only the solitary individual and his images, now that there is no longer any Manitou to bring deliverance within the clan. It is over, that mystical participation thanks to which reality was absorbed, sucked in like a drink and turned into dreams and ecstasies; but the memory of that totalization lives on eternally. Only the individual exists; subjected beneath the constraints of repetition to the individually decreed law of becoming in the game of necessity, only he is there to serve that immanent dream.[115]

Almost a century earlier, Edgar Allan Poe used Newton's universal law of gravity as a metaphor for the tendency of every atom to rally, not to a concrete or abstract *place* but to a principle: "The source lies in the Unity principle. That is the father that they have lost. That is what *they seek* always, immediately, on every side, wherever they may find it, even partially; in this way they in some measure appease their indestructible tendency, as they progress toward their final absolute satisfaction."[116] In 1930, Benn still felt he belonged to the postmonarchical age in which a head no longer dominated a body politic mystically soldered together in all its parts, and in which no Manitou stood for any salvationary dream. But in that same year, "the structure of one's personality" came to seem, to him, to be governed by "the law of an unimaginable metamorphosis."[117] Two years later, a meditation on Goethe and the natural sciences led him to attach the image to a vaster and more primeval body: "What is envisioned is the *gene*, the idioplasma, the mothers, the ancestors, the primordial phenomenon from which an inherent image emanates."[118] In a radio broadcast on April 24, 1933, Benn described that body no longer as "solitary" but as a protoplasmic mass discharging its most advanced pseudopods into time. Benn now announced "the appearance of a new typological variety" that was "the only criterion of historical value." And just as Hitler was soon to confide to Rauschning that the new man was *already there*, Benn added, "That type, it must be said, is already present." It was history, however, that created this new type, in accordance with its own internal necessity, not the type that generated a break within history. "History does not proceed democratically, but in an elemental fashion, always elemental at its turning points. It does not pass by way of the urns, but projects its new biological type out ahead."[119] The same argument resurfaced in his reply to writer Klaus Mann, who from exile publicly asked Benn what motive could have induced him to place himself "at the disposal of individuals whose nullity is absolutely unprecedented in history and whose moral ignominy provokes the disgust of the entire world." In his response Benn implicitly identified new forms of art and new biological types:

How do you suppose that history moves? . . . How, for example, do you picture the twelfth-century transition from Roman sensibility to Gothic sensibility? Do you think that there was any discussion about the matter? Do you think . . . there was a *vote* to decide between Roman art and Gothic art—that people *thrashed out* the matter of arches: round ones or polygonal ones?

In opposition to such a "literary" concept of history, he preferred to see in history "the elemental, inevitable phenomenon of a surge." His retort to Klaus Mann ran as follows:

[History] owes you nothing! But you owe it everything! It knows nothing of your democracy or the rationalism that you may so painstakingly have revered. Its only method or style is, at each of its turning points, to produce a new human type drawn from the inexhaustible womb of the race, a type that will have to make its way by fighting, and build into the matter of time the idea of its species and generation, never drawing back, but struggling and suffering as is decreed by the law of life.[120]

It was thus history that produced art forms and styles, just as it produced human types—with no discussion, no vote, no recourse to that democracy of which it knew nothing—simply by obeying the law of life. It seems hardly necessary to point out that it was only by denying, in the face of all the evidence, the fantastic scope of all the debates that had, each time, preceded and accompanied the emergence of new forms of art in the western world, that Benn could thus reduce history to a purely organic process, an activity produced by a matrix; and it was likewise only by abruptly denying any internal debate on the part of the artist, by denying that every word or every dab of paint placed alongside another resulted every time from a yearning to resolve a tension, a question, or a conflict—only by denying all this could he identify the birth of a style with the birth of a biological type, in accordance with a continuous process of violent and necessary engenderings.

In 1943, by which time everyone in Germany was beginning to see that the war would be lost and that the Nazi dream would never be realized, Benn wrote *Provoked Life*, a strange text that clearly betrayed a disappointment in Nazism. He half-retracted his former words: images of the great primordial dream might sometimes become art and make their way in this world, but equally they might sometimes simply remain thoughts or ecstatic dreams. How fortunate primitive peoples were, with their collective trances and drugs that engendered a "provoked life," a *"reality sprung in all its purity from the cortex."* In 1943, however, it seemed to Benn that there was no law that dictated how to choose—from the mass of what he called *endogenous images*, "our last possibility for happiness"—between those images that were destined to be realized and those that were not. He claimed to stand on a spiritual level that "recognizes no reality whatever, and no history either; at certain temporal intervals, and that's all there is to it, certain brains, through recollection, realize their dreams, which are images of the great primordial dream."[121] "That's all there is to it"—it was as if nothing ever determined which images would acquire lasting form, or which would remain latent, as if they were lying below any visible surface. After the war, Benn saw more clearly and concluded that the determining law was the natural and historical law of violence.

The necessity for violence was his ultimate justification when, while writing *Double Life* in 1950, he recalled Klaus Mann's accusatory letter and his own trenchant reply. Seventeen years later he was still producing that same reply to the question of "how history operated" to justify his support for Nazism:

It must be said, briefly and using today's vocabulary: history does not proceed in a democratic fashion, but by violence. But that faces us with an insoluble question: What exactly is violence? Where does it begin? Wherein lies its essence? Birth—that is violence! The ice age was violence! And so are fights between animals! And the extermination of crime! Every policeman is violence. So is all order.

In the last analysis, when one reflected that Christianity—"the religion of humility"—had produced more victims "with its religious wars of popes, emperors, of thirty years' duration, its inquisitions, its witch-hunting, and its edicts" than two world wars, "what was one to say? It is insoluble. *Understanding is no longer a matter of thinking.*"[122]

Five years after the collapse of the Nazi regime, the same old fundamental denial was still going strong. That violence began at birth and ended in all kinds of order *was not a question addressed to thought*. By this Benn indicated, even more clearly than in the 1930s, the religious nature of Nazism, in which *understanding* was not a matter for thought but meant feeling, in one's body and soul, one's own belonging to some type of primeval body, to a dreaming substance committed to a struggle in order to realize its vision.

Benn wanted to see Expressionism as a displacement of Kant's question, How is knowledge possible? He claimed that this question had been taken over by the aesthetic field: "How is the creation of forms possible? . . . In other words, what an enigma, what a mystery it is that man should produce art, need art; what a unique happening at the heart of European nihilism!" Nazism had whispered a twofold solution to him—"Art has always meant birth"[123]—and birth presupposes violence; also, "All eternity needs art, absolute art, form,"[124] for this brings rest. The need for art was simply a need for eternity and rest, and the whole of history became a struggle to achieve tranquil eternity. This struggle was always that of a body at work, whether in war, in a factory, at a writing table, or on a birthing table. And work with words was itself entirely at the service of that huge labor, which meant that every body that produced words contributed to the production of a new body that matched the type originally dreamed of.

Benn had not waited for Nazism's accession to power to formulate his reduction of language to a phenomenon of biological production and reproduction; for as early as 1930 he had sought to regard poetry "as a primary phenomenon encompassed by the biological process."[125] Consistently enough, three years later he invoked Pavlov in support of his affirmation to the effect that "the word is the strongest physiological stimulus known to the organism and, it must be said, also the most unpredictable."[126] It was on the grounds of that *unpredic-tability* that Benn justified the control and censorship that the new state had to exercise over language: freedom of thought was one of "the great fantasies of the bourgeois age" because it took no account of the inherent unpredictability of the effects of language on the body. Thus, when he declared, "Propaganda reaches the genes, words touch the sexual glands," he was expressing the heart of his commitment to Nazism, his commitment as a writer conscious of belonging to a primordial body, and his conscious of owing everything to it. When he said that "fundamentally, thinking has only ever been done by history, and by history alone,"[127] he meant that there had never been any history of a *debate* because de-bate was impossible within a biological process. In short, the only history was the history of nature, because history itself was a natural body, a protoplasmic body intent on reproduction, thinking or dreaming of its own reproduction. "Being, nature: there are no explanations to be wrested from it; it is everything. I leave everything to it. Let it do what it will with me, I praise it in all its works."[128] According to Benn, history was the process of natural reproduction dreaming of itself—a process in which Benn himself was not the subject, but the dream and the instrument.

The Images Underlying Words: Purification

This desire for a language that was one with the organic matter of which it was the dream—a dream through which the matter regenerated itself—was clearly expressed by Hans Friedrich Blunck, president of the Chamber of Literature of the Reich. According to Blunck, the desire was to be done with the *nonorganic* impurity of the mother tongue. Speaking of the introduction of foreign words and foreign ideas, through which some had claimed to establish equality at the heart of the German people, Blunck declared:

The experiment has failed. In the future we shall try to choose another way forward: re-turn to the purity of the images that underlie words, accessible to all, images that must help—and can help in a decisive manner—to prevent the formation of another prole-tariat in future generations.[129]

The inevitable failure of articulated language to loosen its hold on the body was used to justify the destruction of that language, in the name of the superior efficacy of the images underlying it. One and the same thinking ran through and linked together the themes of the type, the organic, and a language that would finally be restored to its body and at last be *natural*. "The purity of the images underlying words" thus became a guarantee against any proletarian degeneration—that is to say, any degeneration that went against nature. The image underlying words was ultimately called on to oppose the rationality of critical discourse for the same reasons as pure visibility was always preferable to legibility. As Benn observed, words, the strongest physiological stimulus known to an organism, were also the most *unpredictable*, and on that account might need to be censored. An image, conversely, did not suffer from the defect that was inherent in language: affecting bodies in a mimetic (imitative) way, it acted on them through visible contamination and consequently always governed them within the space of what could be foreseen and was foreseeable. An image, which was the model for controlled anticipation and for the engendering of the same by the same, was par excellence the language to use for the governing of bodies. They had, in their own ways, all said the same thing—Benn, Schmitt, Hitler, and Schultze-Naumburg —the last of whom, when laying the foundations of his "culture of what is visible," had insisted that "the eye does not need to base its judgment on thought expressed in language, in which we are accustomed to discover only 'logical' thought."[130] Restoring the purity of the image underlying words meant reducing language to its most summary assertive function, so that each of its judgments appeared to state an unquestionable reality. Above all, it meant reducing language to its archaeological and etymological dimensions, turning it into nothing but an exhumation of the *etumos*, a truth that was buried deep in language itself. That is why this language, which Victor Klemperer called the LTI (*Lingua Tertii Imperii*),[131] was presented as the language of reminiscence. It was supposed to take Germans back to the images of their common dream—those that Benn called "the images of the great primordial dream," and that Rosenberg described as defining the German destiny once and for all. The *etumos* of the Third Reich, its most true, authentic, and real element, lay in the *Uralter Traum, den wir geträumt* (the age-old dream that we have dreamed).[132] For it to become "a destiny," that language had to remain as close as possible to the mythical point at which dreams and visions were inseparable from the primitive body; only thus could it restore the people to its *Uralter Traum* and to an impulse that drove it to make the images of that dream real. The fact that the *etumos* characterized a state of language and a way of using it that no longer existed was altogether in accordance with Nazism's compulsion to resuscitate the past.

The nature of the link that, in some fantastical way, united word and image in an original dreaming and maternal substance explains something essential about the structure of National Socialism—namely its constant denial that the loved object might have been lost. In contrast to the "cultural pessimism" (*Kulturpessimismus*) that *believed* that object to be lost and, like Oswald Spengler, declared that the decline of the West was irreversible, Nazism maintained that it *knew* that the beloved object had been preserved in language, in the blood and the soil, in art and above all in the species (*Art*). The sole role of Nazi "science" was to provide proofs that this object, far from belonging only to the past, had always been dormant. As Baldur von Schirach said, "In Germany, there is nothing more alive than our dead."[133] The immense effort of realization (*Leistung* and *Verwirklichung*) that was sweeping a whole people toward its ideal Third Reich was certainly quite the reverse of the work of mourning. It was the work of anamnesis that asserted itself as faith in one's own power to reawaken the lost object. Werner Hamacher forged an apt expression to describe the Fascism of Benn, who labored at that task. He called it *necro-materialism*.[134] The aim of Nazism was to conjure into reality this defunct object, now found only in the *Wunschtraum*, the dream and the desire to resuscitate what was dead. Nazism called this return the concrete realization of the Idea by dint of an effort the goal of which was "to be at one with oneself," as Rosenberg, citing Meister Eckhart, put it. Not one of the many funerary rites of Nazism—ranging from that of November 9 at the Feldherrnhalle, with its roll-call of the dead, across the board to the annual ceremonies of the Nuremberg Congress—was ever intended to be an act of mourning for part of its people. On the contrary, the constant aim was to restore the dead to a ghostly life. It was not a matter of discharging a debt to the dead so they would not return to trouble the world of the living. Rather, the community set out to cancel its own debt by restoring life to its dead, in exactly the same way as Benn sought to bring the "protoplasmic mass" back to life. The climax in the staging of such events was the roll-call of the dead conducted by the living, which realized the *autonomy* of the community. This roll-call was the ritual of self-appropriation through which the community laid down the law for itself—the law of restoration and resurrection of the "substance of the people" and of its reproduction in its reincarnation. Himmler expressed this law altogether unequivocally: "A people that believes in rebirth and that honors its ancestors—thereby honoring itself—always has children and so lives eternally."[135]

If the union of "oneself" with whatever had become detached involved sight more than any of the other senses, it was because only sight seemed able to guarantee the "real presence" of the lost object and its strict contemporaneity manifested in the reunion of the people with the embodied Idea now made visible. In contrast, the trouble with words was that they might obscure the *present* restitution of space and time and instead screen the visible and keep it at a distance, thereby sanctioning doubts as to its reality and reintroducing the temporal distance that an image wiped out.

Even within the *Lingua Tertii Imperii* it was thus necessary to decide clearly between, on the one hand, the words capable of rendering visible the now refound lost object and, on the other, those that lacked the power to do this. Alfred Bäumler, one of the regime's accredited philosophers, did wonders in this respect:

Whether one speaks of "Hitler" or of "the Idea" is by no means a matter of indifference. Whenever one simply says the "Spirit" or the "Idea," we may conclude that this implies a philosophy of idealism without images (*des bildlosen Idealismus*), a philosophy that claims that the Idea in itself is more than a man, more than any realization (*Verwirklichung*). . . . Hitler is not less than the Idea; he is more than the Idea, because he is real (*wirklich*).[136]

The censoring of words was encouraged by Benn on the grounds of their "unpredictable" nature. Bäumler now claimed to exclude from the LTI all words that "were without images," words that referred one to the invisibility of the Idea instead of reducing their distance from reality and making it possible to, so to speak, *touch* reality in its immediacy. The superiority of Hitler over the Idea was the superiority of a concrete ideal that was at once symbolic *and* real; it stemmed from its visibility, which made it a concrete "phallophany,"[137] and manifested the power that was now restored.

The fact that the Führer was commonly called the Savior, whose appearance had been prepared for and hailed by the resurrection of all the myths about "the sleeping emperor," turned him into a living negation of the loss of the beloved object. The fact that he was also called the artist of all artists, the only one capable of restoring to his people a Germany believed to be defunct, placed him immediately at the heart of the Western tradition that assigned to art that most decisive of functions: namely, to repair the loss of the object by representing it, that is to say, by restoring it to a presence. As Leon Battista Alberti wrote:

Painting possesses a truly divine power in that not only does it make the absent present (as they say of friendship), but it also represents the dead to the living many centuries later, so that they are recognized by spectators with pleasure and deep admiration for the artist. . . . We should also consider it a very great gift to men that painting has represented the gods they worship, for painting has contributed considerably to the piety that binds us to the gods, and to filling our minds with sound religious beliefs.[138]

The further step taken by Nazism, which was never satisfied with a purely symbolic way of making the lost object present in a work of art, was to deploy all means of technical rationality to give the object body and life in the figure of the new man. Correlatively, Nazism deployed a violence reinforced tenfold by technology against all those who were likely to place in doubt that the lost object could be resurrected in the race and in art.

"Woe to those without faith!"[139] was not a vain imprecation but a death sentence pronounced on whoever, by refusing to profess his faith in the image, resisted the process of autosuggestion that was supposed to restore the *Volk*'s lost oneness with itself. Hitler, who was aiming for a culture "founded on the Hellenic spirit and German technology," pointed out in *Mein Kampf* that the goal of

Nazism did not, "like that of bourgeois parties, consist in a mechanical restoration of the past, but in an effort to erect an organic folkish [racist] state." He claimed that in order to accomplish this *organic* restoration of the past, the movement had, right from the start, "espoused the standpoint that its Idea must be put forward spiritually, but that the defense of this spiritual platform must, if necessary, be secured by strong-arm means." He defined this project as a replica of and reply to Bolshevism, which he described as "*Weltanschauung* enforced by terror."[140]

National Socialist terror was thus employed against all those who, in reality as well as in the Nazi imaginary representations, opposed its *Weltanschauung*, its compulsion to realize the Idea, that is, the artistic erection of a figure embodying the lost object. Benn wrote, "All things become inverted, all notions and categories are changed in character as soon as they are considered from the point of view of art, when it is art that disposes of them, and they are placed at its disposal."[141] Of all the inversions generated by the primacy of the "point of view of art," belief in the possible reversibility of time was perhaps the most essential, because therein lay the condition for refound happiness.

One year before the Nazis came to power, Ernst Jünger already saw that inversion was likely to occur as soon as "the world of work" was deliberately placed under the guardianship of art: "As soon as we become aware of our own particular productive force, nourished by sources of a different nature, a complete reversal of the vision of history and the appreciation and administration of historical performances will become possible."[142] The awareness to which Jünger referred in fact became confused with the moment of the Nazis' assumption of power, which he felt to be imminent. This awareness was thus also identified with the hold that art assumed not only over the world of work but also over people's consciousness of time and history. Jünger went on to say, "We should . . . know that it is the victor who writes history and who determines his genealogical tree."[143]

Victorious art dictates its own laws: that was also the message of the ban imposed on art criticism (*Kunstkritik*) by order of Goebbels on November 27, 1936, and by its replacement with the "artistic review" (*Kunstbericht*). Words now had to preserve intact the purity of any work that "worked toward the Führer," in order to "allow the public the possibility of forming its own judgment."[144] In other words, the unpredictability of words should never be allowed to obscure the expected effects of identification. (As Hitler wrote, "a piece of literature never knows into what hands it will fall."[145]) Besides, as one ideologue explained, criticism in its modern sense was a Jewish invention: its sole criterion of judgment was subjectivity, never the higher interest of the race. Because "the general interest took precedence over individual interests," it was necessary to be done with the *Ich-Tyranneides Kritikers*, the "tyranny of the critic's ego," that destructive power that disintegrated the image of the community and undermined its self-confidence.[146]

Just as Hitler had confided to Rauschning that "conscience is a Jewish invention,"[147] he also set the sovereignty of art, which imposes silence, in opposition to a critical conscience expressed in words: "Nothing is more likely to reduce the petty critic to silence than the eternal language of great art. Before its manifestations, the centuries bow down in respectful silence."[148] In the same vein, he declared, "Beauty must exercise its sway over man, subjugate him to its power."[149]

This was also the meaning of the radical inversion to which Benn and Jünger referred: the power to impose silence was now said to be immanent in the work of art itself, the law of which was deployed in order to destroy "the critic's ego." The recourse to force was clearly a sign and confession that works of art were unable to wholly provide the community with an identity and to procure for it the promised satisfaction signified by silence. The weakness of works of art was palliated, however, by the force of man. The circle of terror thus closed on itself; those who confessed their faith in the Artist (Hitler) and in the art that was supposed to regenerate them were the very same people who silenced the miscreants and the degenerates. In this way they too, like the Artist himself, used their hammers and chisels to strike away "the weak and mildewed part" of the people so that, casting off the words of critical conscience, the splendid figure of the community could at last arise.

We have already noted the text dictated to certain Munich schoolchildren in which a parallel was drawn between the Passion of Christ and that of the Führer: "Whereas Christ was crucified, Hitler was made Chancellor." The inefficacy of the sacrifice and death of Christ was set in contrast to the survival and triumph of Hitler. Hitler himself clearly set out the basis of his own superiority as a savior: "I am doing away with the dogma of the redemption of men through the death of the divine Savior, and propose a new dogma . . . : the redemption of individuals through the life and action of the new Legislator-Führer, who comes to relieve the masses of the burden of liberty."[150] There could be no better formulation of the link between liberty and the loss of the beloved object. The pact offered by Hitler was clear: only at the price of renouncing individual liberty could the lost object be restored and instituted as law.

In 1927, Hugo von Hofmannsthal clearly defined what moved the members of the conservative revolution: "What they have gone off to seek is not liberty, but bonds. . . . Never has the Germanic struggle for liberty been more ardent and consequently more determined than the struggle of the thousands of souls of this nation to find a true constraint, or than this refusal to accept constraint that was not sufficiently constraining."[151] One century earlier, François Guizot, in the name of reason, had already stigmatized man's desire to find "a power that had an immutable and certain right to his obedience" and "the hope finally to obtain a master who could never fail him and whom one would never need or have the right to repudiate."[152] A little later, Thomas Carlyle similarly regarded the French Revolution as "an invincible revolt against sovereigns and masters who lied." "As a philanthropist," he saw this revolt as "a quest, a very unconscious yet serious quest for true sovereigns and true masters."[153]

It was because Hitler himself perceived this quest as the motivating force behind most human actions that he could claim "to relieve the masses of the burden of liberty." Sometimes he formulated this idea very simply, in terms that would even have won the approval of Freud: "There can be no culture without constraint or the individual's renunciation of individual liberty,"[154] or "The whole of life is simply a renunciation of individual liberty."[155] The corollary to this idea was the death sentence for anyone who preferred to bear that "burden of liberty" and to expose himself to doubt by renouncing the restoration of the sought-for object. Conversely, among the "elect people," whoever professed his faith in

Hitler forthwith obtained the satisfaction of recovered certainty. As Robert Ley, head of the Labor Front, said, the foundation (*das Fundament*) of the National Socialist edifice was faith, because faith in Hitler gave one faith in oneself and in one's people.[156] But it was in Nuremberg that Ley explained most clearly how faith relieved one from liberty: "We have faith in Adolf Hitler and in his Idea. This faith is converted into obedience. Whoever does not obey has no faith!"[157] This was another replica of Hobbes's *Leviathan*, which had made faith in Christ and obedience to the law the two virtues necessary for salvation.[158] The same process was summed up in Goering's famous "I have no conscience! My conscience is called Adolf Hitler."[159] This statement conveyed exactly how Nazi law stemmed from this faith. In line with all of this, a new version of "the categorical imperative in the Third Reich" was elaborated as early as 1936 by Hans Franck, head of law in the Reich: "Whenever you make a decision, ask yourself, 'How would the Führer decide in my place?'." In 1942, Franck rephrased this as, "Act in such a way that the Führer, if he knew of your actions, would approve of them."[160]

Christianity, which in the Passion retraced the loss of the object through which man is abandoned to his liberty, sought to make both that loss and that liberty bearable through the *certitudo salutis*, or present certainty of salvation in the beyond.[161] Later on, the doctrine of the image as a new incarnation of the *Logos* was evolved, a restorative and reparational incarnation that renewed the promise and pointed to the way ahead. At a time when the world came to be deserted by the certainty of a salvation promised by a dead god, faith in a living and visible god—who in his life and in his *present* works brought salvation here and now—was suddenly able to relieve every member of the community of his freedom to judge and also to choose, which was now made by the permanent decision of the Führer.

In payment for that relief, however, every individual had to work to resurrect the ideal past that was identified with the *Volksgeist* or primordial dream embodied by Hitler. Every individual thus became "a soldier of the Führer," who in and through his work realized a community that was redeemed by its guide. It was a continuous process that did away with culpability and cancelled out all debts and responsibilities—a process designed to produce a people from which not one of its members would ever again be divided socially, by time, by space, or above all by conscience.

The production of the new man truly was a process of self-purification designed to realize the fantasy of total man finally delivered from the culpability that in the past had been all that prevented him from acceding to divinity.

5

IMAGES OF NAZI TIME:

ACCELERATIONS AND IMMOBILIZATIONS

> There are two deadly human sins from which all the rest stem: impatience and laziness. They were ejected from Paradise because of their impatience, and they cannot return there because of their laziness. But perhaps there is really only one deadly sin: impatience. They were ejected because of their impatience; because of their impatience, they cannot return.
>
> —Franz Kafka, "Reflections on Sin, Suffering, Hope, and the True Way"

As we have seen, the National Socialist *Weltanschauung* was presented as a structure that constantly anticipated its own end, that is, the realization of the movement's mission. This is why it would be misleading to see in National Socialism's constant use of religious vocabulary and, correlatively, of the redemptive image no more than a simple, cynical exploitation of a ready-made Christian fund of words and images.

At a deeper level, Nazism seems to have repeated the same link between faith and sight that is central to Christianity, within the same structure of anticipation as that constituted by Christian eschatology. The fact that Hitler one day declared that "faith" had "restored the sight" of the German people cannot be explained simply as "a deliberate blasphemy." It seems, rather, to have been a response to growing pressure from an eschatological movement that he had certainly helped to create but that to a large extent eluded his control. It is no exaggeration to say that Nazism constituted an almost exact realization of the situation that Georges Sorel had hoped for, described, and theorized about when even before the Great War he appealed for a myth that, like the Christian myth of salvation, would, through images more than words, be capable of speeding up the march of the masses toward deliverance.

Images and Anticipation

As early as February 1, 1933, Dietrich Bonhoeffer recognized and denounced the messianic role that was being assumed by a führer who claimed to embody the spirit of the people (*Volksgeist*), to bring with him a Reich that was "close to the eternal kingdom," and to start fulfilling the ultimate hope of one and all. We should remember, however, that once Nazism was in power, it never ceased to declare that it had *already* brought the Germans the hoped-for salvation, yet simultaneously promised a salvation *yet to come*. The Third Reich declared itself to be eternal as soon as it was born, yet it insisted that the *Volkskörper* should construct its own eternal life. It claimed that the people's spirit was restored by being embodied in the Führer, who was the incarnation of "the eternal soul of its race"; at the same time it urged the *Volkskörper* to take part in the building of the eternal Reich. It offered the people salvation, yet salvation remained to be won. The paradox was not new, and it has to be seen in the light of the paradigmatic role played by Christianity. In this respect, a short digression will be helpful at this point.

Although Christ "obtained eternal redemption" (Heb. 9:12) for men and "became the author of eternal salvation unto all them that obey him" (Heb. 5:9), after his death people continued to live in expectation of salvation: "For we are saved by hope" (Rom. 8:24). Yet the coming of the Messiah, a visible event in history, had brought individual salvation for the inner man: "Behold, now is the accepted time; now is the day of salvation" (2. Cor. 6:2). Rudolf Bultmann has repeatedly underlined this paradox of the earliest Christian communities: "The authentic, true life is already present," but Christian existence is above all eschatological, "for it consists in living for the future," for the second coming of

Christ, which makes the present, as it were, a "between time," a time between "no longer" and "not yet."[1] History thus became absorbed into eschatology. Salvation, which the ancient law had promised for the end of history, was suddenly, through faith, being granted *now* to the believer: faith and faith alone could liberate man from that law which had always proved powerless to ensure salvation (Gal. 3). According to Bultmann, however, the fact that the second coming of Christ did not happen as soon as had been predicted clearly caused "great disappointment and doubt" among the early Christians. Although the disappointment was neither sudden nor universal, it made it necessary to defer the second coming to an indeterminate future and to call for patience while reaffirming the power of faith even more vehemently. This tendency, which began with Paul, became even more prevalent, deeply transforming the Church from an eschatological community into an institution for salvation in which the cult proclaimed the presence of Christ and the sacraments anticipated the eschatological event and guaranteed the salvation that was to come.[2]

Paul asked for "much patience" in distress (2 Cor. 6:4) between the first and second comings of the Messiah, in order to sustain hope, "for we walk by faith, not by sight" (2 Cor. 5:7). The Epistle to the Hebrews, however, although inspired by the writings of Paul, modified this opposition between faith and sight. What Paul presented as a relationship of radical disjunction was now shifted into a relationship of marked temporal dependence. "Faith is the substance of things hoped for, the evidence of things not seen. For by it the elders obtained a good report" (Heb. 11:1–2). Faith, a confident anticipation of the future, always made visible in advance that which did not yet exist. Abel, Enoch, Noah, Abraham, and Sarah "all died in faith, not having received the promises but having seen them from afar, and were persuaded of them and embraced them" (Heb. 11:13). Faith, finally, was what made one act "concerning things to come" (Heb. 11:20).

In a world liberated from the ancient law but still waiting for the second coming of Christ, the temporal vector that linked faith to sight underwent an important modification. Bultmann noted that this change was given lexical expression as early as the beginning of the second century: the words *epiphaneia* (apparition) and *parousia* (coming), which originally designated the future coming of Christ, began also to designate his coming on Earth in the past.[3] This development was in response to the perception that doubt about the epiphany that was promised was expanding into doubt about the epiphany of the past. Reassurance on the reliability of that founding moment had become as necessary as reassurance on the reliability of the future.

This ambivalence about the temporal vector soon affected the earliest Christian images, which sometimes reactivated the past and sometimes anticipated the moment of salvation. Their sudden proliferation under the Severan dynasty (193–235 A.D.), a period that coincided or immediately followed the appearance of Jewish iconography, signaled the rivalry between the two religions of salvation, which until then had remained aniconic. Both sought to strengthen the believer in his faith and to guide him in the practice of his religion. The Jewish community was tolerated but dispersed; the Christian community was threatened by persecution. It has been supposed, reasonably enough, that both resorted to images so as to ensure and preserve the identity of their respective faiths in a strongly iconized pagan world. We need not examine here all the differences that, despite mutual exchanges and influences, later affected the iconographical programs of Jewish and Christian places of worship. We should note, however, one of those differences, because it seems to be essential. Christianity regarded the "present life as an offering to the Lord in response to the granted salvation, the accomplishment of which was prophesied for the kingdom of paradise." Mosaics, with their narrative content, proceeded outward from the altar situated in the church's apse in the same way that historical time proceeded outward from the Word of God.[4] In Christian churches, the images of paradise evolved toward a Eucharistic symbolism so that the already present time of individual salvation merged with the Messianic time yet to come. In contrast, the iconographical programs of synagogues, which were never narrative, focused entirely on the expectation of the Messiah, in accordance with the Torah.[5] Although both iconographies were oriented toward the Messianic future, Jewish iconography represented it as a collective event in life on Earth at

the end of history, whereas the Christian images tended to identify the present individual salvation, bestowed in the past by the incarnation of the *Logos* and now
repeated by the sacraments, with the final salvation at the time of the second coming and the Last Judgment, which together would give the people access to eternal life. In Byzantium, this contraction of the two periods was given visible expression, which Andre Grabar hails as one of the main successes of Byzantine
iconography and one of the most stable. On the cupolas and later on the tympa-
nums of Western churches, the figure of Christ Pantocrator represented the Son
and the Father simultaneously.[6] This image of the Word of Christ ("He that seeth
me seeth him that sent me," John 12:45) expresses the full power of anticipation
that lies in the figurative image. Whereas from the sixth century on an icon of
Christ had been understood as a reactivation of the past Incarnation, which
brought it into the present, Christ Pantocrator projected the beholder into the future, to the end of his earthly life. The represented Incarnation placed him in the
presence of the God who was reputed to remain invisible until the day of the Last
Judgment.[7] Christianity thus pulled together through its imagery that which was
separate; by merging the mediator with the terrible God, the visible with the invisible, it reconciled the object of love with the object of fear. The image com-
pressed the recollection of a blessed past and the anticipation of a feared future,
merging them into the pure presence of the salvationary image. Telling no story, it
stood in contrast to narrative images in the same way that eternity stands in contrast to history. It seemed endowed with the power to extend the present indefi-
nitely. Because it contained the threat of death, which it seemed to suspend or defer, it asserted its protective power; it was a *nunc stans* that overcame death, beyond
time, like the eighth day of the week or "an eternal Sunday."[8]

The function that Christianity attributed to the image preserved its value as
a paradigm because it provided an incomparable solution to the tension of an existence pulled one way by salvation already bestowed and the other way by salvation that remained to be won,[9] one way by a faltering memory of past felicity, the
other by an aspiration toward future happiness. It was no longer faith that aroused
the image of what did not yet exist; rather, it was the image that sustained faith.

The temple was the factory that produced the new man, plunging the faithful into a liturgy that enabled them to relive the whole history of salvation, from the memory of the Incarnation of the Son all the way to the vision of the Father. Thus, what Paul declared would be made visible by faith but seen only from afar and remain unobtainable was rendered present by the Christian image that, at the same time, indicated the path to follow in order to reach what had been promised. In this way, life according to the image was already life within the image. The new man was yet to come but was already present.

Accelerations

Within this structure of recollection and anticipation, the desire to accelerate the moment leading to eternal beatitude was clearly not peculiar to Nazism; in fact, it is generally agreed that the latter was innovative very little or not at all. The desire for acceleration of the end, which was in truth a constitutive element in the whole structure, was always associated with the toppling of the established order, the deception and imposture of which were perceived as obstacles to the accomplishment of the prophecy.

As is well known, because of the marginality of the social strata from which it was originally recruited and because of the mystic charge it attached to the term *Third Reich*, Nazism was an avatar of revolutionary millenarianism, up to and including the much-proclaimed asceticism of the Führer. Usually, however, such groups resorted far less to images than to force and violence in their bids to accelerate the movement of the history of salvation and to install the reign of God on Earth as soon as possible.[10] In fact, in such groups the destruction of images was, on the contrary, often inspired by the desire to be done with the imposture of the order that images represented and upheld.

The coexistence of images and the force that guaranteed their power had in the past more often been characteristic of the European monarchies and empires. In their cases, however, the spiritual and temporal authorities, whether in alliance or merged, had on the contrary generally endeavored, through the combination of both images and force, to slow down any historical change and thereby ensure their own stability. In the aftermath of the French Revolution and the announce-ment of "the death of God," a new feeling took hold of European consciousness: "What used to move at a walking pace now moves forward at a gallop," wrote Ernst Arndt as early as 1807.[11] History seemed to be speeding up of its own ac-cord. In 1831, Chateaubriand noted, "I was writing ancient history, and modern history was knocking at my door. In vain I cried, 'Wait, I'm just coming'. It passed on, to the sound of cannon fire, seeping away three generations of kings."[12] The nineteenth century's writers described it as an "entirely new historical expe-rience of acceleration"; relations between the old and the new seemed to change with "an incredible rapidity," and the present was judged "too rapid and provi-sional" not only to provide a stable point of view on recent events, but even more to illuminate the future, which on that account seemed all the more elusive.[13] This was also the moment when declining faith in Providence and the whole sys-tem of divine foresight was replaced by faith in progress, which was considered to be immanent in nature, and by a belief that it was possible for knowledge to in-crease even more and thereby increase terrestrial happiness so that happiness would eventually achieve perfection.

It was not, however, until the end of the nineteenth century that there emerged a veritable intuition that a combination of images and the application of force could be used to accelerate history. It was during the 1890s that the first theories appeared on managing the masses by means of images. Such a theory about the link between the masses and images was formalized above all in France, which as Zeev Sternhell has shown was the real laboratory of the fascisms of the twentieth century. Gustave Le Bon, in *Psychologie des foules* (The Crowd) (1895) and Georges Sorel, in *Réflexions sur la violence* (Reflections on Violence) (1907) both regarded the image as the most powerful means for the mobilization of the masses. Both fought against parliamentary democracy, but Le Bon did so in the name of conservative authoritarianism, refusing to regard a parliamentary assembly as anything other than a suggestible crowd easily influenced by images and "simplistic ideas." Sorel, conversely, did so in the name of revolutionary trade-unionism, which when mobilized by the image of a "catastrophic myth" analogous to that of the early Christians would succeed in "suppressing the parliamentary socialism" that was holding back the movement of history. These two theories became models for the theories of those, ranging from Mussolini to Hitler and from Wyndham Lewis to Carl Schmitt, who ascribed more weight to images than to words for accelerating the movement of the masses. Let us pursue this thread for a moment, without becoming distracted by the links between it and the racism and nationalism of such authors.[14]

Le Bon declared that crowds, "are everywhere distinguished by feminine characteristics. . . . Unable to think except in images, they can be affected only by images. Only images terrify or beguile them and become motives of action."[15] It was hard to tell, however, whether he meant that an image contains an immanent principle capable of setting a crowd in motion, or whether he thought a crowd, being by nature always "impulsive and mobile," needed only the image to direct its own movement. At any rate, maintaining that images and the "word-images" of orators and leaders had the ability to arouse the unconscious desires of the crowd, Le Bon declared that such arousal led to an acting out that prompted violence: "Like a savage, it [a crowd] is not prepared to admit that anything can come between its desire and the realization of its desire. It is less capable of understanding such an intervention as a consequence of the feeling of irresistible power given by its numerical strength."[16]

Between the crowd and the realization of its unconscious desire, the image that turned that desire into a conscious one thus created an unacceptable gap. The reason the image generated violence was that it gave rise, seemingly automatically, to a wish to plug that gap. In this way the crowd became the agent of the image's own impulse toward effective and violent self-realization. The crowd's extreme sensitivity to the order of images made it socially threatening, for any image that reflected its desire was liable immediately to set off that violent process of realization. Probably for the first time, the image was conceived to be the most effective accelerator of the passions corresponding to "the era of crowds."

It was on precisely the above theses that Georges Sorel, ten years later, founded his theory of "social myths" capable of generating the violence that he believed to be necessary for the European West to accede more swiftly to true Socialism.

These results could not be produced in any very certain manner by the use of ordinary language; use must be made of a body of images which, *by intuition alone* and before any considered analyses are made, is capable of evoking as an undivided whole the mass of sentiments which corresponds to the different manifestations of the war undertaken by Socialism against modern society.[17]

Both Sorel and Le Bon were fascinated by the idea of reducing the thought expressed in language to images. But what for Le Bon remained simply a source of terror and scorn for the crowd became for Sorel a cunning ploy adopted by reason: it was the "secret virtue" that animated the masses and made history move on. For Sorel, the "Socialist myth" implied "the organization of images" whose value was primarily instrumental. He regarded them as "a means of acting upon the present."[18] Invariably speaking of myth in terms of "motivating images" (*images motrices*), he was quick to acknowledge his debt to Henri Bergson. It was from Bergson that he learned that perception was by no means aimed purely at disinterested knowledge or some kind of contemplation, but was in itself, by nature, active. The actuality of our perception, Bergson said, consists "in the movements that prolong it. . . . The past is just an idea, [but] the present is an ideomotor."[19]

Sorel depended on that motivating force immanent in the present image to produce the masses' "march toward deliverance."[20] But as he saw it, it mattered very little whether or not one knew "what the myths contain in the way of details which will actually form part of the history of the future . . . ; they are not astrological almanacs; it is even possible that nothing which they contain will ever come to pass—as was the case with the catastrophe expected by the early Christians."[21] The discrepancy between announced ends and realized ends was unimportant because the purpose of the myth was "to act on the present."

Mussolini's Fascism shared Sorel's admiration for "the fully developed and completely armed pessimism" of early Christianity,[22] and it was consciously inspired by his notion of an apocalyptic myth composed of "motivating images" that set the masses moving toward the promised deliverance. In the speech he delivered in the autumn of 1922, shortly before the March on Rome, Mussolini announced, "We have forged a myth; a myth is a faith, a noble enthusiasm; it does not need to be a reality; it is a spur and a hope, faith and courage. Our myth is the nation, the great nation that we wish to turn into a concrete reality."[23] Carl Schmitt cited these words in *Parliamentarianism and Democracy*, which was devoted to "irrational theories of the immediate use of violence" and in which he produced a long analysis of Sorel's *Reflections on Violence*. He agreed with artist and writer Wyndham Lewis, who regarded Sorel as "the key to all political thought today," and concluded that "the most powerful myth lies in the national myth," the myth founded on "representations of race and lineage," on language, tradition, and the awareness of a common culture and common destiny. All of this seemed to him inevitably to generate opposition between nations, each of which was moved by its own myth; and for the political theology he was defending, those national religions possibly threatened a new polytheism. The myth was a reality that could not be ignored, however, particularly because it testified to the fact that "the era of discussion" was past.[24]

As for Nazism, we should remember that in the early days of the regime, Alfred Rosenberg rejoiced that the German nation had at last found "its style of life." "It is the style of a marching column, and it matters little whether and for what purpose that column is marching."[25] What he was expressing obviously related to the "revolutionary" moment of the movement—the moment that assumed as its immediate goal "the awakening" of Germany. But the Nazi myth was not that of a nation whose concrete realization did not necessarily entail the destruction of others. It was the myth of a unique race that embodied the "creative genius" that would soon find realization through a murderous self-purification. The eschatological nature of the process that was now set in motion led not to an eternal march but rather to an accelerated march by the *Volk*, which would continue until such time as it was immobilized in the promised eternal purity that Hitler called "the visible immortality of the nation."[26]

The Führer was constantly declaring his sense that the time allowed for him to complete the mission with which he felt he was invested was limited. Biographer Joachim Fest relates that in the spring of 1932, Hitler declared that he had "not time to wait, not a year to lose. I must take power very soon in order to be able, in the time left to me, to accomplish the gigantic task that falls to me. I must! I must!"[27] He was constantly lamenting that he had "not much time left" and feared that he would "soon disappear." He also marveled at the progress of medical science, which was speeding up the effects of treatments for prolonging life. Having briefly feared that he was suffering from cancer of the larynx, he took a particular interest in the treatment for this disease. One day he said, "Radium has become completely useless for its treatment because of a remarkable invention that uses a kind of X-ray: one application of between ten and fifteen minutes to the seat of the disease is all that is needed."[28] On another occasion, he expressed his irritation at the Church's resistance to evolution in its dogmas: "Humanity is progressing with a slowness of which one is ashamed." Then came the following remark, which conveys all of his fears of never seeing what he called "the accomplishment of his *oeuvre*": "One often finds oneself deploring having to live at a time when one cannot clearly see the shape of the world to come."[29]

The *Weltanschauung* of Hitler and his "visions," which had been realized in Nazi imagery, did not merely anticipate "the shape of the world to come" and bring relief to the period of waiting; they were also supposed to speed its realization in the manner in which he himself recognized to be that of publicity images, as he confessed to his entourage one evening in 1942:

The Führer then spoke of the virtues of advertising. Throughout one entire year the Odol company had its name publicized [beneath the image of a bottle], without commentary, on the walls of his little town—and everyone, intrigued, wondered what it meant. Then, when the name and the bottle beneath which it was positioned had become a very familiar sight, the following commentary appeared: "Odol, the best water for dental hygiene." The success was startling. Such an advertisement should not be banned simply because it is Jewish. By making such a useful article indispensable, it spares a whole generation from working.[30]

In this petty and possibly invented apology, Hitler does seem to set out a few of the major principles of his vision of the world, which was invariably determined by his fascination with "startling success." Its symbolic value therefore makes worthwhile pausing to consider it for a moment. In his description of the fabrication of "expectant attention,"[31] which took place in a situation of expectation that produced movement, he first made clear that publicity and commercial propaganda worked in exactly the same way as the "social myth" described by Sorel. Second, he explained how the image, by arousing desire, could engender a new man who took shape acting out the purchasing and thus the appropriating of both an object and a name. Finally, he drew attention to the work-saving that resulted from the very process of suggestion.

This last point is quite important. The work-saving clearly had nothing to do with the work necessary to acquire the product, but referred to the work that would have been necessary for the company to sell its product had it not resorted to the power of the image. The economic point of view that Hitler put before the members of his general staff was that of a company manager anxious to increase the power of his business with a minimal investment of energy, which certainly suited his own laziness. But if the image was able to produce such a great added value, it was because, he explained, it spared "a whole generation" from working. The miraculous power of the image thus also had to do with the acceleration of human time: between the seminal moment of the appearance of the image and the birth of the new man, the productive function of maternal mediation became unnecessary. (Oscar Wilde appeared to have been right: art created a type that life, "like an enterprising publisher," tried to reproduce in a popular form.) The fact is that the publicity image itself provided the productive mediation that ensured at once the transmission of the product's name and its own perpetuation.

The first imperative, however, was something to motivate the masses. Until they were set in motion, nothing could happen. After a period of expectant attention, the desire aroused in them was, once again, for purification. The Odol company promised that anyone who undertook the sacred ablutions carried out in its name would be cleansed of all impurities. From the point of view of the masses set in motion by an image, the economic principle was similarly by no means indifferent. Hitler believed, quite simply, that "a picture, in all its forms up to the film" possessed greater persuasive power than a written text, even when reduced to a proclamation on a poster:

Here man needs to use his reasons even less; it suffices to look, or at most to read extremely brief texts, and thus many will more readily accept a pictorial presentation than read an article of any length. The picture brings them in a much briefer time, I might almost say at one stroke, the enlightenment they obtain from written matter only after arduous reading.[32]

For the masses who wished to accede to knowledge of a better world, an image thus had the obvious advantage of sparing them intellectual work and fatigue. The immediacy of the demonstration furthermore saved an incomparable amount of time, easily and rapidly inspiring faith in the promised world. "That is what I call publicity!" Hitler exclaimed in Vienna before the image of a woman with "very long Lorelei-like locks," promoting her miraculous hair cream; he added, "We must manage to turn propaganda into a faith, so that it is no longer clear what is imagination and what is reality. . . . Propaganda is the essential basis of every religion, whether it be a matter of heaven or of hair cream."[33] Around this time he tried his own hand at a poster design: to induce faith in the virtues of Nigrin shoe polish, he used words only to extend the shine of a dazzling boot.[34]

Here too faith kept alive the desire for the object that gave access to this different world. However, because the very nature of desire prevents it from finding total satisfaction in immediate acquisition, a certain disappointment was inevitable. The movement of the masses prompted by the myth-image might then be converted into either revolt or work. Under the Third Reich, either force and constraint directed the violence of revolt toward those who were declared to be obstructing the complete realization of the desire, or they suppressed all movement that had not been converted into work, thereby ensuring the all-powerful impact of the image.

Movement converted into work certainly made access to the all-powerful world of the image possible, but it also deferred this access. Although salvation was already granted to the creative race on the grounds of blood, the National Socialist sanctification of "creative work" made such work the instrument and guarantor of the salvation yet to come. Quite soon, however, access to the world of the image was reserved for the rare few who were the elect. By 1933, the performance and productivity (*Leistung*) policy for work introduced the Reich's professional competitions (*Reichsberufswettkampf*), the winners of which "were treated like Olympic athletes or film stars, brought to Berlin, and photographed with [head of the German Labor Front Robert] Ley and Hitler himself.[35] In the system of selection and competition that was set in place, the most intensive work could thus speed up entry into the world of the image, the world of the living gods. In that world, the Führer of the party and of Germany appeared also as the Führer of the community of work (*Arbeitsgemeinschaft*) of the Germans. So the propaganda was not constructing a world that was different from the real one; on the contrary, it was that world's very essence, revealed its structure, and provided a purified image of it.

Ernst Jünger explicitly presented this "reactionary modernism" as a process of acceleration. It was a movement, however, designed to work itself out and lead back to the state of repose that was immanent in it: "The more we devote ourselves to movement, the more we must become deeply convinced that behind it there is concealed a Being of calm, and that all the speeding up merely translates an imperishable original language."[36]

On the eve of the Nazis' accession to power, this movement seemed to Jünger to be that of a battle that could not "be interrupted at will" but possessed "its firmly delimited goals." However, only an elite clearly understood those strict limits, so the force of the current that carried the blind masses along in "total mobilization" justified restricting to an elite the responsibility for this onward movement with no turning back: "The more 'individuals' and the masses grow weary, the greater the responsibility that falls only to a few. There is no way out, no shortcut, no doubling back. Rather, it is important to intensify the force and speed of the process into which we are locked. So it is good to feel that beneath the excessive dynamism of the time, an immobile center lies hidden."[37]

Jünger would have liked to examine his fellows with the eye that an entomologist casts on extinct species. His cold hatred was provoked by the human impossibility—his own—of "contemplating one's time with the eyes of an archaeologist to whom its secret meaning is manifest." He yearned for "a gaze liberated by its cosmic distancing from the contradictory interplay of movements." But such a way of seeing was accessible only to "heroic realism," which alone could make it possible "to be not simply material but also a dispenser of destiny." To regard oneself as "the representative of the figure of the worker," the only true form of the will to power, was to understand that "any demand for liberty within the world of work is therefore possible only if it takes the form of a demand for work." Contrary to those who, by transposing the "biblical curse to the material relationship between exploiters and exploited" sought only to shake off an evil and so could conceive only of a negative liberty, he appealed to a more lofty concept, worthy of "the age of the worker" in which, under the domination of art,

nothing could exist that cannot be conceived as work. Work is the rhythm of the fist, of thoughts, of the heart, life day and night, science, love, art, faith, cult, war; work is the vibration of the atom and the force that moves the stars and the solar systems.

Aware that he stood "on the brink of transformations such as no redeemer ever dared to dream of," Jünger dreamed of a space "in which work occupied a religious level" and to which performance (*Leistung*) would give total expression. Then would appear what was already heralded by the desire for technological perfection: "the replacement of a dynamic and revolutionary space by a static and extremely ordered space," which would bring about "a switch from change to constancy."[38] This was precisely the dream that Nazism tried to realize.

Artists, Workers, and Soldiers: Total Mobilization

The notion of "creative work" certainly lay at the heart of the whole National Socialist system. On the one hand, it claimed to be the basis of Nazi racism, which opposed the Aryan "creator of culture" to the Jew, who was "a destroyer of culture"; on the other hand, it formulated the deep transformation of the very notion of work that Nazism was trying to bring about. For the regime never ceased to boast about this: thanks to Nazism, work at last sloughed off the weight of the biblical curse and became fully identified with artistic activity. Each and every laborious activity now became part of the vast process of the race's self-redemption, at a stroke wiping out sin and culpability as it built the city of God on Earth. Between those two poles, sin and redemption, the people, through its own effort, became an *Arbeitsgemeinschaft*, a self-forming "community of work" whose activity established its own profile.

It was perhaps once again Gottfried Benn who formulated most clearly how work that was identified with art contained an incomparable power of liberation from the ancient law. On May 1, 1933, on the occasion of the first Festival of Work, which was immediately followed by the dissolution of the trade unions, Benn announced the new gospel:

The Festival of National Work and art: what do the two have in common? Can it be that the vibrant surges of this day give actuality to art—art with all its strict laws and its slow maturations? Art always feels actualized and stimulated wherever it perceives greatness, whether it be in nature or in history, and this is certainly a great historic moment: work is about to find itself delivered from the defilement of being a yoke, a kind of punishment, a proletarian evil, which has afflicted it over past decades. Now, through it, we are celebrating the alliance of the people, the pact made by a newly emerging community. In work we celebrate the creative virtue that, throughout the entire series of all the transformations of peoples, has never ceased to forge human society in ever-new cultural units, snatched from history by work.[39]

This was indeed a historical moment if, thanks to its *creative virtue*, work could at last redeem that proletarian evil and "actualize" art by snatching from history the birth of a new community purged of all defilement.

In its 1920 manifesto, the National Socialist Party of German workers had already quite purely and simply assimilated all work into creative activity: "The first obligation of every citizen is to *create*, either with his mind or with his body."[40] In his speech of May 1, 1933, Hitler likewise assigned to work the same tasks he was to assign to art in the months that followed: the self-formation, self-purification, and self-liberation of the German people: "We also know that all human work will ultimately be vain unless it is illuminated by the blessing of

Providence. But we are not the kind of people who lazily leave everything to the beyond. . . . The German people have come to themselves. They will not endure people among them any more who are not for Germany. . . . We do not pray to God 'Lord, make us free.' We shall work. . . . "[41]

Like art, work became a process of self-purification and self-liberation for the German people, here and now. It became a continuous movement of *Entscheidung*, of trenchant decision by which it separated itself in the present from the curse of the past and outlined its future. On October 24, 1934, Hitler set as the goal of the Labor Front "the formation of a veritable *Volks und Leistungsgemeinschaft* (community of people and performance) of all the German people."[42] In *Mein Kampf* he wrote that "the idea of creative work . . . always has been and always will be anti-Semitic,"[43] which meant primarily that the movement of creative work assured the people of liberation from the ancient law and of the conquest of its own autonomy. But *Arbeit macht frei* (work makes one free), the inscription set above the entrance to the Auschwitz camp, meant not only the destruction of the Jews who embodied that law—*Arbeit macht Judenfrei* (work eliminates the Jews)—but also, given that "the Jew still resides within us,"[44] and that "as long as we have not annihilated the Jew within ourselves, our survival will remain in the balance,"[45] it ultimately also meant *Arbeit macht Menschenfrei* (work eliminates people), the self-destruction of Germans in the purity of the realized Idea.

In a speech entitled "Our community must be clearly defined, clean, and well disposed!" Ley stressed how that "work and art belong to one another" because "they stem from a single root: the race."[46] Later, when it became a matter of "defending the race's community," Goebbels stressed the identity of the struggle of the soldier, that of the worker, and that of "the creator of culture": "Art is not a distraction for times of peace; rather, it too is a spiritual and trenchant weapon for war."[47]

On October 15, 1933, the laying of the foundation stone of the House of German Art in Munich was saluted in terms that clearly indicated that the party was as much the party of German art as it was the party of the German workers.

Adjutant Gauleiter Otto Nippold declared, "The Day of German Art will serve to restore the cultural life of the community and our sense of the community. That is why the ideal value of this day does not reckon it to be subsidiary to the Day of German Work [May 1] but must and does make it its necessary complement."[48] But National Socialism did far more than simply complement the glorification of national work with that of national art: it also united them within one and the same cult, served first and foremost by soldiers, whether these were military, artists, or workers. As Jünger wrote, "To see the word *work* with its new meaning, you need new eyes."[49] And those eyes were the eyes of artists capable of providing the people with a view that combined elements of "heroic realism" with Goebbels's "steel Romanticism."

"Work ennobles" (*Arbeit adelt*) was one of the regime's slogans that painters and sculptors could most easily flesh out. Except for a few solitary peasant figures—such as those of Werner Peiner's laborer sculpting *The German Land* of which he is a part (Figure 91) and Heinrich Berann's *Winnower* (Figure 92), dominating the landscape with his sublime efforts—painters generally preferred to produce images of the collective labors of peasant families or communities. The same went for other forms of laborious activity, in which the rhythmic repetition of the gestures of work taken up by one body after another represented a "typification" of the community at work. Ria Picco-Rückert's *Unified Strength* (Figure 93) thus depicted the construction of a railway thanks to the combined efforts of a whole cluster of bodies. "Steel Romanticism was clearly even more manifest in Arthur Kampf's *The Rolling Mill* (Figure 94), which according to art historian Werner Rittich revealed "a new relation to work": "Both through the powerful strength of the workers and through the atmosphere surrounding the work, this is a symbol that concentrates both the will to work and high performance [*Leistung*]."[50] The victorious struggle against fused matter was reminiscent of both Saint George overcoming the dragon and Wagnerian drama.

It was in the representation of industrial landscapes, however, that painting, moving far beyond all mythology borrowed from the past, produced the real image of the modern myth of work that Nazism, from 1939 on especially, wished to present. What *Ship Under Construction* by Curt Winckler (Figure 95), *The Hermann-Göring Factory Under Construction* by Franz Gerwin (Figure 96), *The Oil Refinery* by Richard Gessner (Figure 97), and *The Great Coking Plant with Adjacent Installations* by Dirk Van Hees (Figure 98) showed was not so much that "concrete work remained invisible,"[51] but rather the disappearance of the actual workers, who were either swallowed up by a technical environment of gigantic dimensions or totally absent. Once again, the image did not so much falsify reality as tell the truth about the Nazi dream. In 1937, the review *Kunst und Volk* (Art and the People) thus praised "the human work of art in which even the tiniest details spoke of the work involved without you seeing the worker."[52] The ideal for which the National Socialist cult of work aimed was without a doubt total absorption of the workers into the productive oeuvre that would speak in the name of the community.

In the painting by Ferdinand Staeger entitled *Wir sind die Werksoldaten* (We are the soldiers of work) (Figures 99a and 99b), Robert Ley's "soldiers of work" bore the imprint of the "type" so dear to Wolfgang Willrich, Walther Darré, and Ernst Jünger. In its upward, rhythmic march, "the new nobility of work," the soldiers silhouetted against the sky of the Third Reich shouldered their spades as if they were rifles. The Labor Front was engaged in the same struggle for eternal Germany as were their soldier-comrades. That struggle shaped anonymous faces and bodies, testifying that "art progresses from the individual to the type."[53]

Sculptor Fritz Koelle specialized in the representation of the figure of the worker. Ever since the late 1920s, his perception of the working class had become increasingly heroic. His miners, boilermakers, steelworkers, and rolling-mill workers did not all have the same face, but they all did have the same air of determination. As art critic Ernst Kammerer commented, "They all speak of the serious nature of work."

Koelle's men are impregnated by work. There can be no doubt that, without their work, they would have other faces and other shapes. Day after day, month after month, year after year, they have been shaped by work. . . . They have become men of iron. Tenacity, endurance, and inflexibility are their virtues. They show what a man can do. They are giants. One countenance speaks for many others [*ein Gesicht steht für viele*]. The same hard will lives in all their faces.[54]

The expression of that "hard will" grew, however, as the years passed. Koelle's *Miners*, produced in the twenties, were hardly more than one meter tall; by 1932, his *Blacksmith* was two meters; by 1937, his *Miner from the Sarre* had grown to three meters; and in 1939, the latter was supplanted by an *Isar Raftsman* (Figure 100), who stood three meters and sixty centimeters tall. The more monumental the body of the worker was, the better it expressed the effacement of the real workers in their battle for the overall oeuvre. "For what these figures convey is a battle," Kammerer said. "Just as there is an unknown soldier, so too there is an unknown worker. The sculptor Fritz Koelle has devoted his life to honoring the unknown worker."[55] The cult of work was now identified with that of the heroes who had already fallen in the same battle to build the ideal Reich. The superpower symbolized by these artistic works was thus not the power of work or of the worker but of a death anticipated by the artist's vision. Koelle showed exactly how monumental sculptures could represent an assumption of the dynamism of total mobilization. Their very real technical perfection made visible what Jünger called "the replacement of a dynamic and revolutionary space by a static and extremely ordered space," thereby satisfying the desire "to move on from change to constancy."

Effecting that transition from dynamic movement to static order involved first producing the type that would be instrumental in asserting its domination. In the eyes of Jünger, warfare remained the model of every work space and every work process in which "the national effort leads to a new image: the organic construction of the world." "The hero of this process, the unknown soldier" already displayed the qualities that were to characterize the figure of the worker: "His virtue lies in the fact that he can be replaced and that behind each man slain his replacement is already holding himself in readiness. His criterion of reference is that of objective performance [*Leistung*], [that is,] performance without fine speeches; so he is, in a very special sense, the bringer of a revolution *without words* [*sans phrase*]."[56] Jünger could just as well have described his worker using the words applied to Koelle's silent worker: "*Ein Gesicht steht für viele*" (One countenance speaks for many others). This statement constituted a veritable slogan, for which Staeger produced the ultimate image in his *Political Front* (Figure 101).

Jünger's concept of "organic construction" was quite the reverse of utopian, because it was simple enough to be realizable by Ley's Labor Front. Albert Speer, who headed the Bureau for the Beauty of Work (*Amt Schönheit der Arbeit*)—the slogan of which was "the German working day will always be beautiful"[57]—announced the advent of "a new face for the German factory." It was, to be sure, partly a matter of convincing the worker that the achievements of the beauty-of-work organization "would free physical work from the curse, damnation, and inferiority that have dogged it for centuries,"[58] but first it was important to create a healthy, modern, luminous, clean, and "beautiful" environment, so as to increase the productive yield amid joy: *Je höher die Leistung, um so grösser die Arbeitsfreude*" (The greater the performance, the greater the joy in work).[59]

Following an agreement reached in 1936 between the Chamber of Plastic Arts of the Reich and the Bureau for the Beauty of Work, artists were invited into the factories. "The daily contact with artists and the fact of living with their creations"[60] was supposed to awaken the workers to the beauty of their own work. More and more art exhibitions were held in work places, and frescoes and decorations invaded not only the adjacent spaces but even the workshops themselves,[61] so that, just as Sorel had planned, the worker could come to understand that "art anticipates work as it should be practiced in a regime of extremely high production."[62]

Meanwhile, the shortage of manual workers that followed the rapid fall in unemployment[63] at the end of the crisis caused Ley to keep the workers themselves in good working order, because any weakness on the part of individuals might endanger the general productivity. Every "soldier of work" was accordingly also regarded as a technical organism, each element of which had to be replaceable from a stock of spare parts that would guarantee the continuity of the process:

We shall give power to the *Volk*. At fixed periods we shall give every German a medical overhaul, just as we overhaul engines. We renovate engines but leave men sick. Until now, nobody has bothered about this. But who can continue to accept this when men are worn out at the age of forty? Where can we find more men to replace them? It is not a lack of raw materials that may prove fatal to us, but the lack of men. The way that an individual lives is not his private affair. Each one is a soldier of the Führer and must be watchful of his health and his performance, in the interests of the *Volk*.[64]

These words of Ley were pronounced just as the new four-year plan, which established a war economy, was introduced; they also coincided with the trials of the first prototypes of the *Volkswagen* (people's car, or VW) in response to the Führer's expressed desire, in 1933, to undertake "the motorization of the German people."[65] Hitler, who had asked Ferdinand Porsche to see that the "people's car" looked like "a beetle," had sketched a model of it in the restaurant of the Osteria Bavaria in Munich in August 1932 (Figure 102).[66] Although the total mobilization of the German people never did include its total motorization, because the VW was not mass-produced until after the fall of the regime, it was nevertheless Hitler who constantly linked the fate of the German people to that of its motors. In an interview given in July 1933 to the *New York Times*, he declared that he wanted to pull Germany out of its paralysis, revive industry, and develop a new spirit by first motorizing the nation. The reason he admired Henry Ford was not because Ford had pioneered standardized production but because he produced for the masses: his little car had done wonders for "destroying class differences."[67] The VW was supposed to restore the lost unity of the *Volkskörper* in similar fashion. If the theaterization of daily life had turned the *Volksgemeinschaft* into a "lived experience" (*Erlebnis*), the people's car was to be its most advanced technical instrument: soon everyone would be able to experience "eternal Germany," striking deep into its forests, at one with the German soil, at last all brought together, and with Mother Earth reawakened by new irrigation. The VW was thus in no way alien to the *Blut und Boden* (blood and soil) ideology but was the instrument of its technical realization.

On March 1, 1933, Hitler declared that it was not enough to restart (*anzukurbeln*) production; it was also necessary to develop the consumption capacity: "So much blood has been drawn off its economic life by foreigners over recent years that the circulation has been stopped."[68] On September, 23, opening the worksite of the Frankfurt-Heidelberg motorway, he rejoiced at this creation of "new arteries for traffic": "This is not merely the hour in which we begin the building of the greatest network of roads in the world; this hour is at the same time the road toward the building up of the German *Volksgemeinschaft*." For in truth the automobile was part of the very stuff of the German people: "The motor-car had been invented in Germany." In February 1935, at the opening of the Automobile Salon in Berlin, he declared, "Fifty years ago, it was a German who realized the old dream of a vehicle that would move by its own forces." Assuredly, the destiny of "the German substance" was likewise to realize the dream of propelling itself. In 1938, in a climax of self-suggestion designed to promote self-starting and self-firing, Hitler boasted of the dynamic effects of the propaganda favoring motor cars, automobile races, and the construction of roads and considered soon introducing a badge for automobile sports that, when distributed yearly, would spur on the motorized youth of Germany.[69] At that point, the vision of the new man that Hitler had announced three years earlier would be fulfilled: "The German youth of the future must be slim and slender, swift as the greyhound, tough as leather, and hard as Krupp steel. We must educate a new type of manhood so that our people does not go to ruin among all the degeneracy of our day."[70] The people's car had the requisite material and qualities.

Organic construction was a concept according to which the past was linked to the future through the present mobilization that would ensure the temporal homogeneity of the Reich. At the beginning of the century, the protofascism of Filippo Tommaso Marinetti's early futurism claimed to be breaking under the crushing weight of the past. It celebrated "the beauty of speed" as an acceleration through time and space that was capable of tearing man free from the weight of history: "A racing car with its boot adorned with great snaking pipes with explosive breath . . . a roaring automobile that looks as though it is running on grapeshot . . . is more beautiful than the *Victory of Samothrace*."[71] But National Socialism did not exalt motion in itself. For the Nazis, the speeded-up movement of history, like everything else, was but a "means to an end." As engineer Karl Arnhold explained to the youth of Germany, "Technology has made old, very ancient dreams come true"—seven-league boots, the cannon ball of Baron Munchhausen, the dream of Icarus—"all that used to be desires and dreams is now realized by technology!" But he took good care to make it quite clear that "creative technology works only when it lies in the blood!"[72]

If German youth had to be the swiftest in the world, it was so they could be the first to win the promised deliverance, the first to make the original dream of the race a reality, the first to construct at last the organic eternity of this Aryan *Kultur* founded on "Hellenic spirit and German technology."[73] This reactionary modernism was expressed in exemplary fashion in the poster for the International Automobile and Motorcycle Exhibition held in Berlin in 1939, which showed two roaring racing cars, seemingly emerging from a neoclassical edifice, about to conquer the globe (Figure 103).

"Youth must be guided by youth"—the message conveyed by this slogan of Baldur von Schirach's Hitler Youth organization was that the eternally young Aryan genius was essentially *self-propelled*; the genius could remain in motion amid immobility, at the heart of "a German way of life determined with precision for a thousand years to come."[74]

A Pure Present

At a moment when the promises of happiness made by the zealots of rapid technological progress contrasted so violently with the uncertainty that hung over the immediate future, the Nazi *Weltanschauung* presented itself as the possible means of conciliating the most rapid of movements with the most assured stability. It was above all in 1934, when a halt was called in the "revolutionary" movement and the German mode of life was "precisely determined for a thousand years to come," and thereafter that it seemed that the movement was supposed to coexist with a pause, violence with calm, life with death. And as we have seen, that coexistence was inseparable from the self-purification of the German people and the Reich, which the National Socialist *Weltanschauung* sought to obtain by dint of both constraints and motion governed by an image of eternity.

In the speech he delivered in Nuremberg on September 11, 1935, Hitler de-

veloped one of his favorite theses on art: a people and its art were never temporally finite to the same degree. Speeding through the centuries and the millennia
in his usual bold way, he drew from his meditation on the ruins of the past a lesson that was neither that of a historian nor that of a philosopher contemplating
the decline of empires and the vanity of all power. Rather, it was that of an artist
attempting to gauge his own chances of surviving through the immortality of his
oeuvre:

What would the Egyptians be without their pyramids and their temples, . . . the Greeks
without Athens and the Acropolis, Rome without its monuments, our generations of
Teutonic emperors without the cathedrals? . . . That there was once a Mayan people is
something we would not know or would neglect were it not for the fact that such powerful town ruins and vestiges of legendary peoples forced themselves upon our attention
and demanded scholarly investigation. No people survives beyond the testimonies of its
culture [*Kein Volk lebt länger als die Dokumente seiner Kultur*]![75]

Having enchanted himself with the above formula, two years later Hitler
had it engraved on a bronze plaque designed to be placed over the entrance to
the House of German Art. Through this bronze plaque that would survive him,
Hitler testified to the eternal "truth" of his words, in which the press was quick
to detect "the bases of National Socialist creation."[76] But that saying of the
Führer's assuredly held an inner meaning over and above a simple injunction to
his people to take pleasure in the new works of the thousand-year Reich. To be
sure, as the visitor who entered the sanctuary of German art surrendered to the
images that urged him on to both productive coupling and heroic sacrifice, he
laid himself open to experience those accelerators of the passions that were supposed to renew the human material (*Menschmaterial*) and ensure the immortality of his people. But that pronouncement set above the very portals of the temple called on every individual to respond as a member of a community that itself
was mortal and would survive only collectively and through its art. It nevertheless left room for a veritable transubstantiation of the community beyond its
mass disappearance and its mass resurrection in its art—a transubstantiation that
would occur when a people produced by the same blood would be able to un-

derstand it all over again. Every individual thus had to learn to face up to this common destiny, anticipating his own personal death and constructing a *vita nova* (new life), the superior and eternal life that would animate the art of the community.

That sentence of the Führer's on its own imparted full weight to Walter Benjamin's famous thesis on the links that the "aestheticization of politics" practiced by Fascism maintained with the theory of "art for art's sake." Clearly the former did not simply mean the subjection of art to political ends. For on that basis it would be very hard to distinguish Fascism from all the other regimes—and history has seen many of them—that have used and still use art in a similar fashion. Benjamin's target was a *particular kind* of aestheticization of politics: he was condemning a mankind whose "self-alienation has reached such a degree that it can experience its own destruction as an aesthetic pleasure of the first order. That is the kind of aestheticization of politics practiced by Fascism."[77] What Benjamin had in mind, however, was Italian Fascism, which as its herald Marinetti put it was expecting "from war the artistic satisfaction of sensitive perceptions modified by technology." In this Futurist and Fascist aestheticization of politics, which found realization in warfare, Benjamin detected "the consummation of art for art's sake."

National Socialism, however, for its part, never directly identified the state of war with the realization of the eternal Reich. War was not an end in itself; for National Socialism, war remained, in the same way as propaganda, art, and politics, "a means to an end." Warfare was far more directly identified with the process that led to the "realization of the Idea," so that in the Nazi *Weltanschauung* it had the same function as all its other "battles." Like the "battle for art," "the battle on the birth front," and the "battle for production," it was part and parcel of "the battle for life" that was to lead to the realization of the essence of the German people. Warfare too thus played a role as an accelerator of passions that was supposed to speed up the fulfillment of the primordial dream. After the *Blitzkrieg*—the lightning war of 1939 to 1940 waged by concentrating the most modern motorized means on one single point of the front—a triumphal repose still

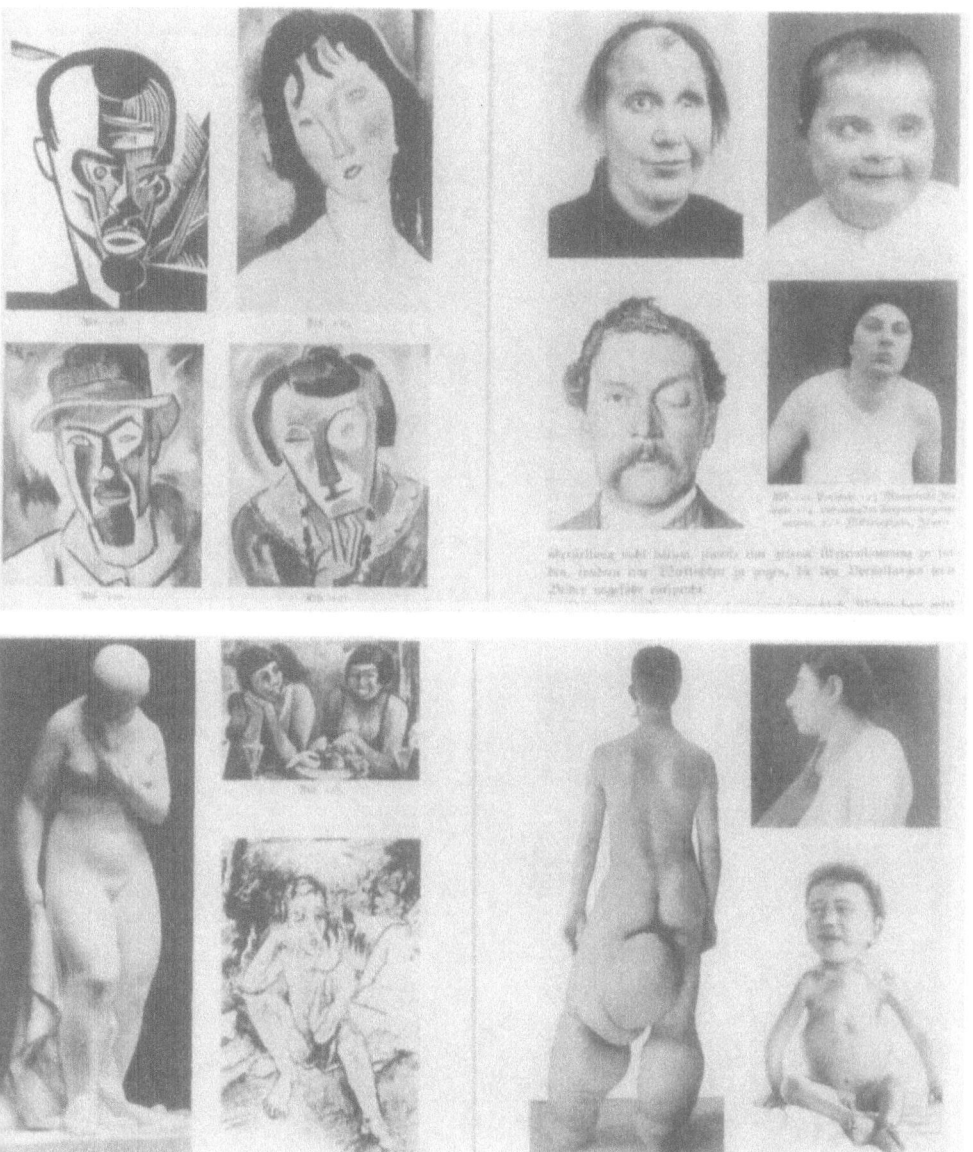

72.

73.

72. to 75. Paul Schultze-Naumburg, plates from *Kunst und Rasse* (Art and race) (Munich: J. F. Lehmanns), 1928, pp. 106–15. Document preserved in the Bibliothèque de l'Institut d'Histoire de l'Art de Strasbourg.

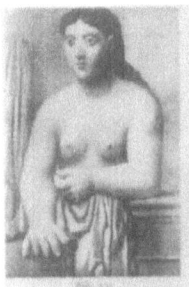
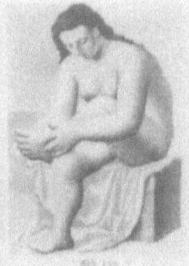

Abb. 138.

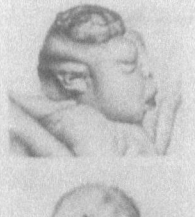
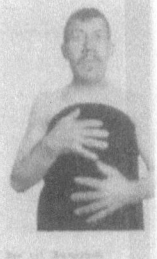

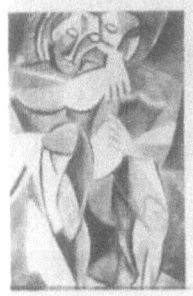

74.

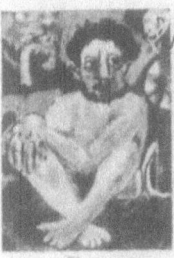
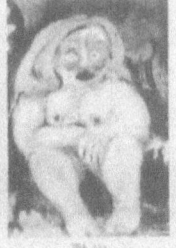

Abb. 141. Abb. 142.

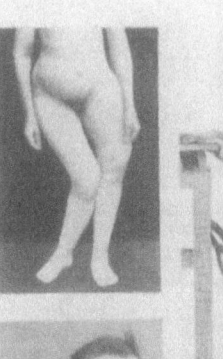
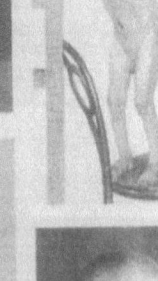

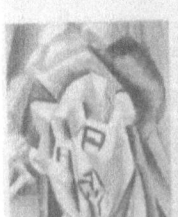
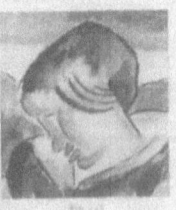

Abb. 143.

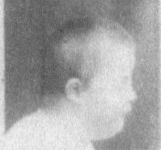

75.

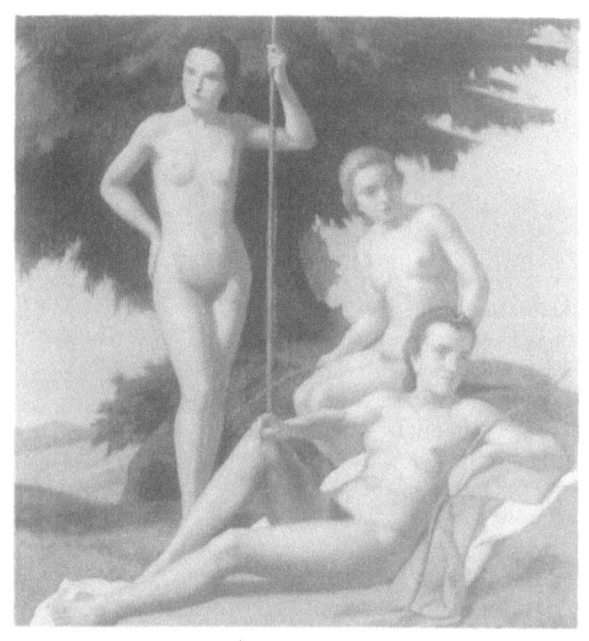

76. Ivo Saliger, *Diana at Rest* (oil on canvas), circa 1939–1940. Photo by AKG, Paris.

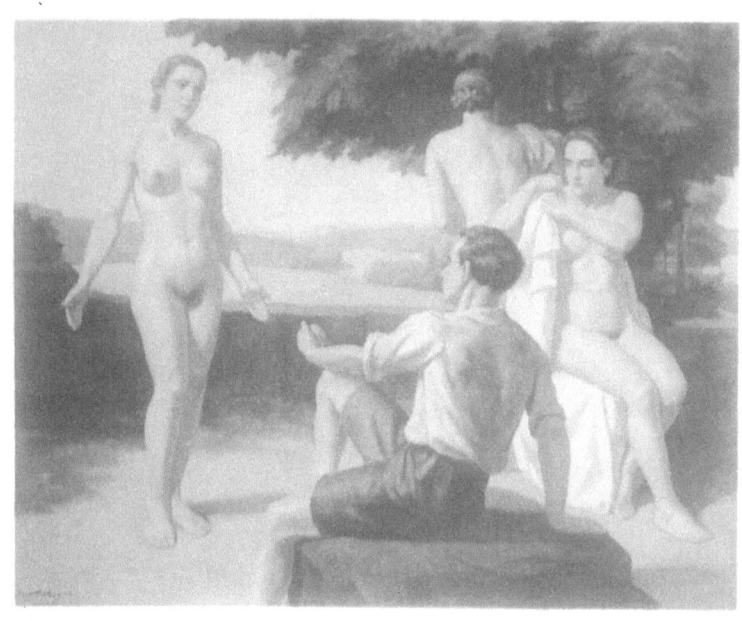

77. Ivo Saliger: *The Judgment of Paris* (oil on canvas), circa 1938–1939. Property of Germany. Photo by AKG, Paris.

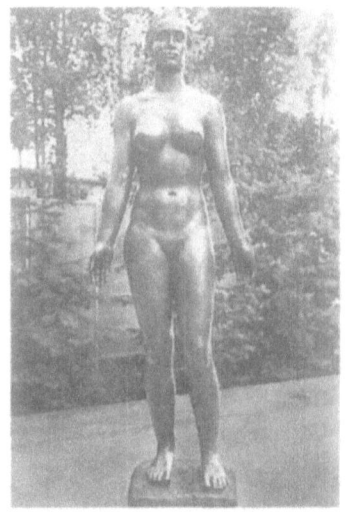

78. Georg Kolbe, large statue of a woman (bronze; Height: 2.15 m.), 1934. Published in Wilhelm Pinder, *Georg Kolbe: Werke der letzen Jahre* (Berlin: Rembrandt, 1937), p. 49. Document preserved in the Bibliothèque de l'Institut d'Histoire de l'Art de Strasbourg.

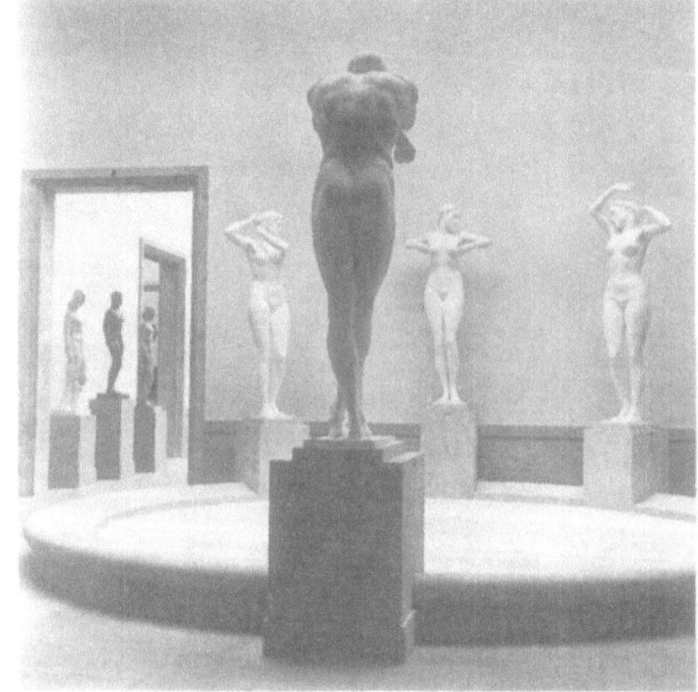

79. Josef Thorak, *The Judgment of Paris*, 1941. Published in Kurt Lothar Tank, *Deutsche Plastik unserer Zeit* (Munich: Raumbild Verlag, 1942), illustration no. 114. Document preserved in the Bibliothèque de l'Institut d'Histoire de l'Art de Strasbourg.

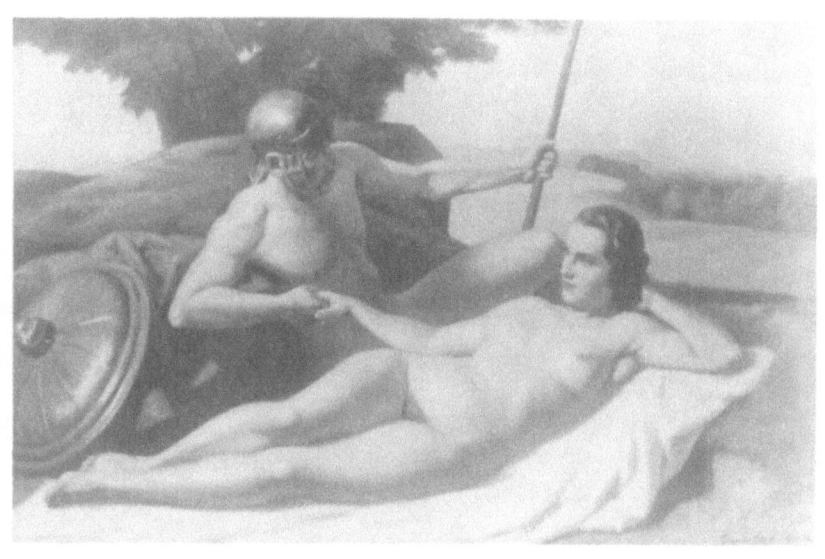

80. Ivo Saliger, *Mars and Venus*, n.d. Photo by AKG, Paris.

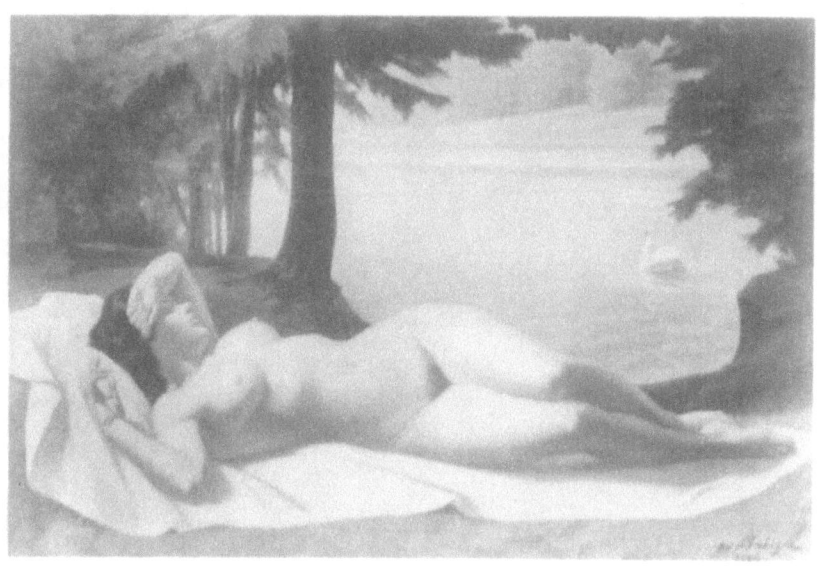

81. Ivo Saliger, *Leda* (oil on canvas), n.d. Photo by AKG, Paris.

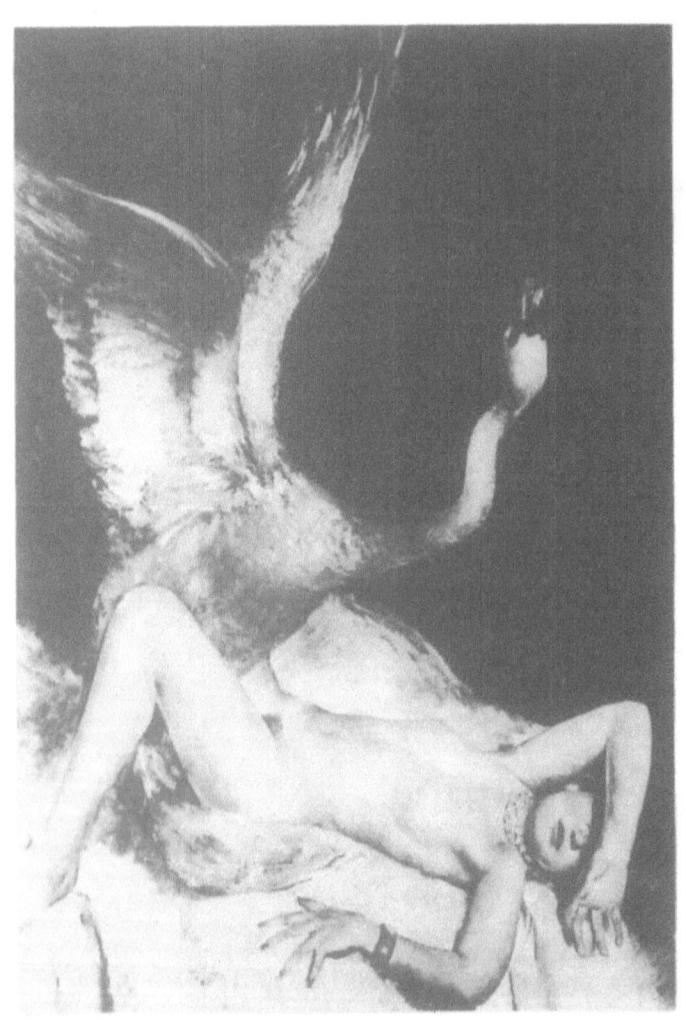

82. Paul Mathias Padua, *Leda and the Swan* (oil on canvas), n.d. RR.

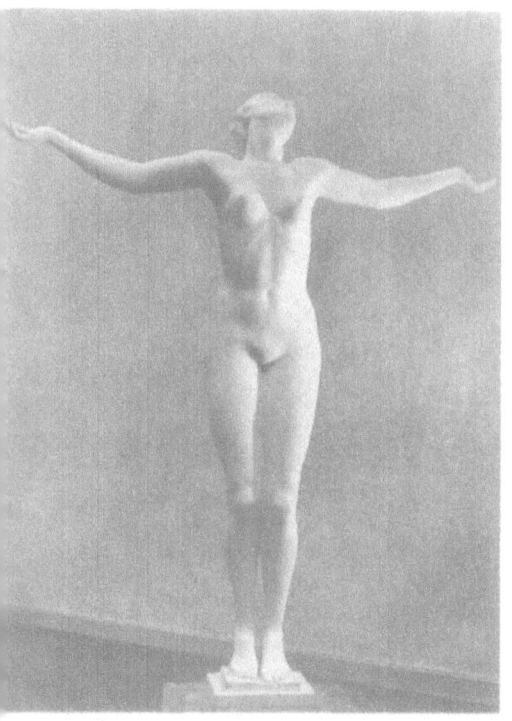

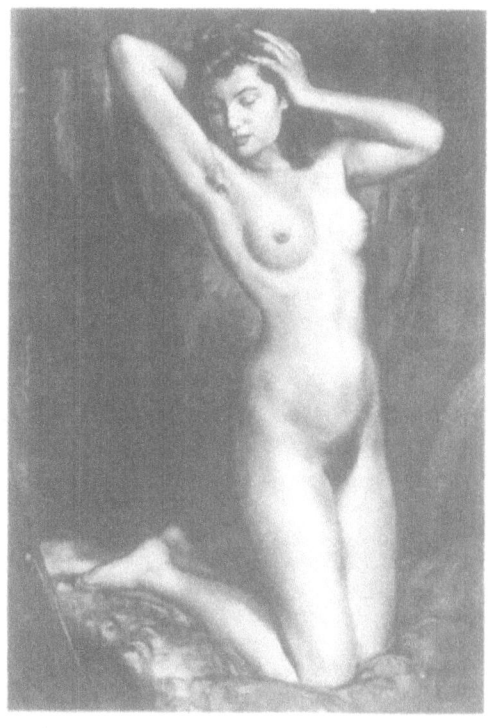

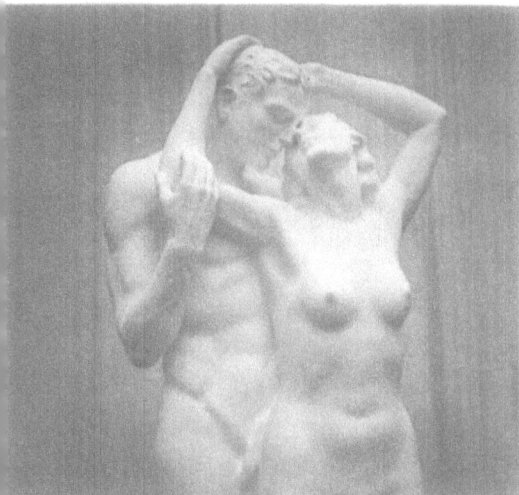

83. *(top, left)* Josef Thorak, *With Passion (Hingebung)*, plaster cast for a bronze, 1940. Published in Werner, *Die deutsche Plastik der Gegenwart*, p. 152. Document preserved in the Bibliothèque de l'Institut d'Histoire de l'Art de Strasbourg.

84. *(top, right)* Wilhelm Hempfing, *Kneeling Nude*, n.d. Postcard from the House of German Art. Author's collection. Photo preserved in the Bibliothèque de l'Institut d'Histoire de l'Art de Strasbourg.

85. *(left)* Josef Thorak, *Two Human Beings* (detail), n.d. Published in Tank, *Deutsche Plastik unserer Zeit*, illustration no. 99. Document preserved in the Bibliothèque de l'Institut d'Histoire de l'Art de Strasbourg.

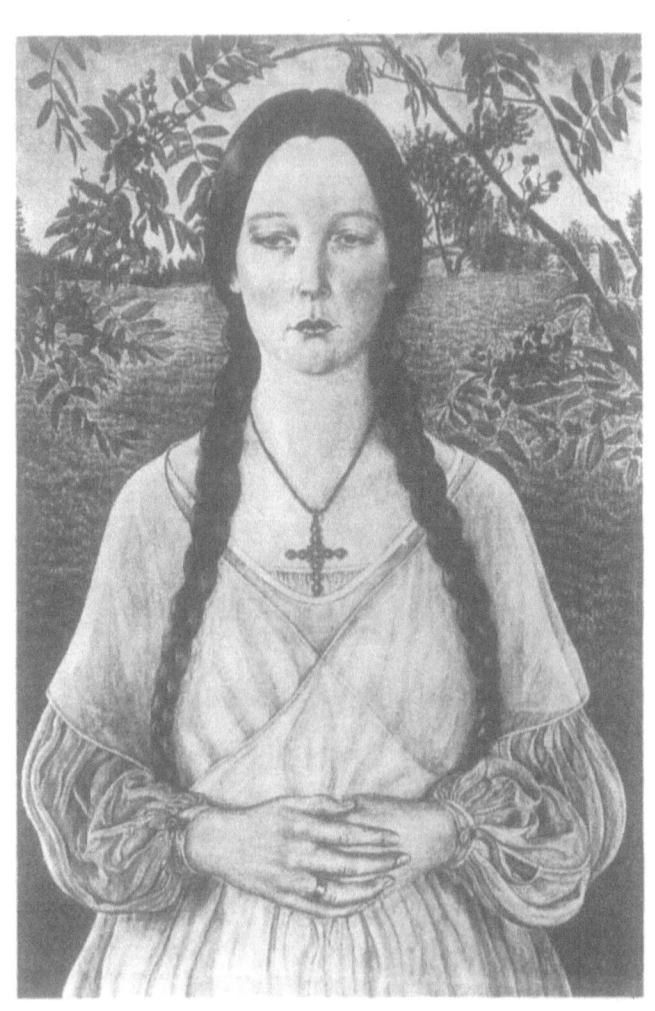

86. Arthur Ressel,
Future Mother, n.d.
Photo by Zentral-
institut für Kunst-
geschichte, Munich.

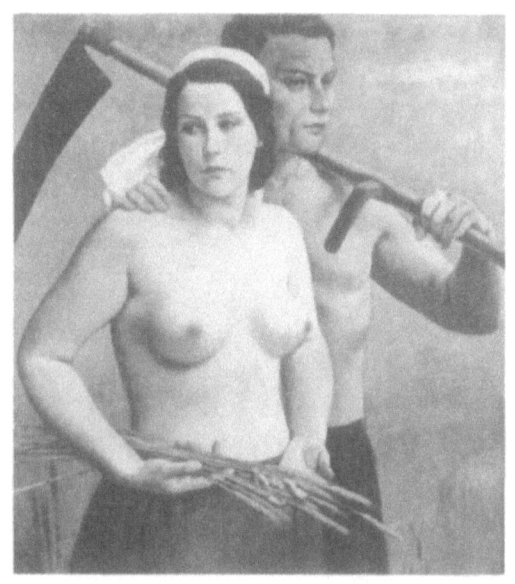

87. Johannes Beutner, *The Time of Ripening*, n.d. Photo by Bilderdienst Süddeutscher Verlag, Munich.

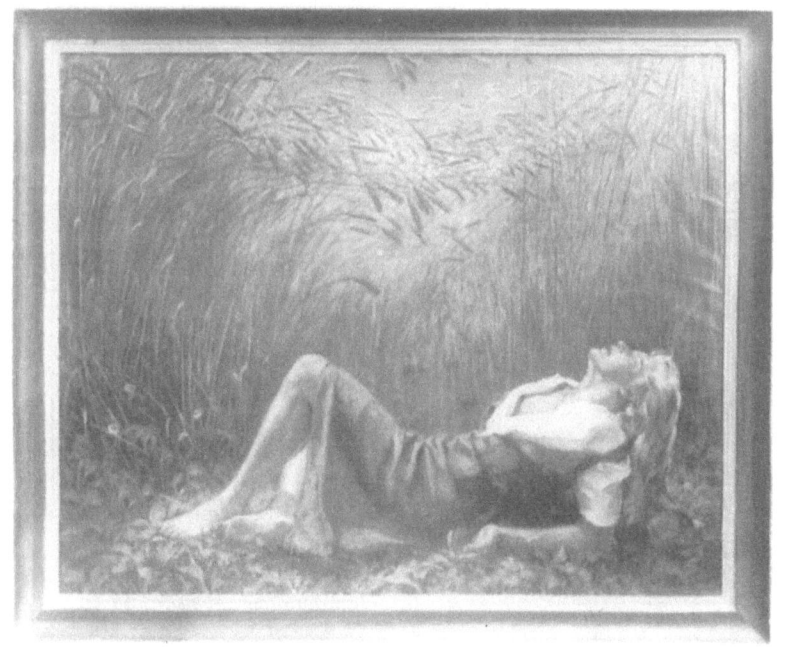

88. Wilhelm Hempfing, *Summer*, n.d. Photo by Bilderdienst Süddeutscher Verlag, Munich.

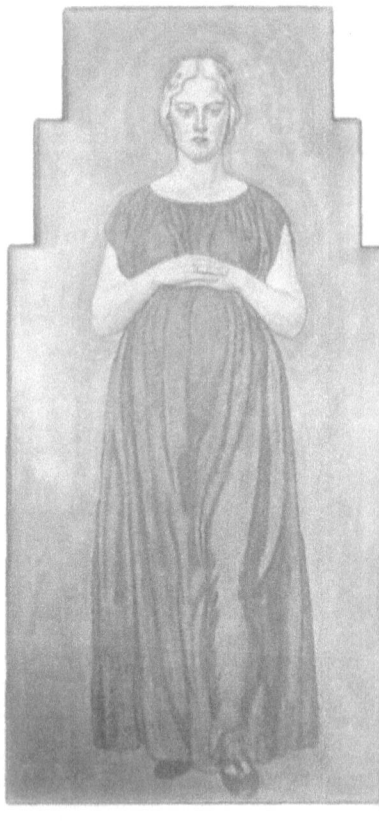

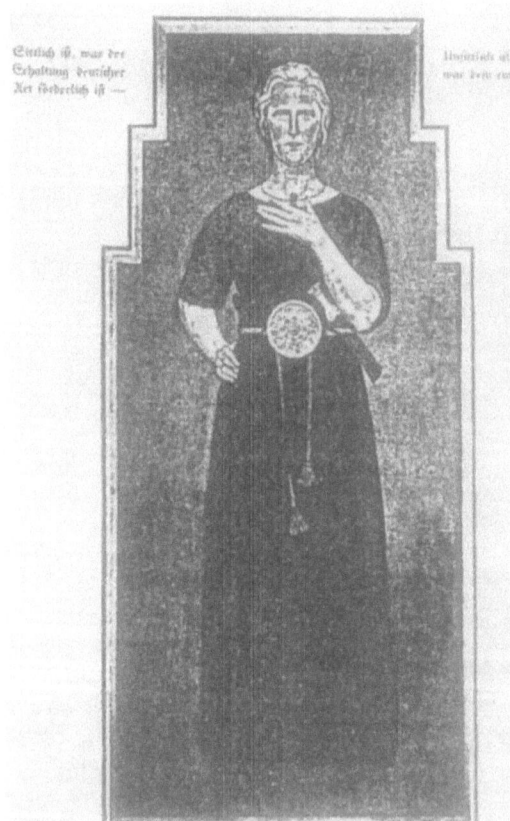

89. *(above)* Wolfgang Willrich, *The Guardian of the Species,* frontispiece to *Die Säuberung des Kunstempels* (Munich/Berlin: J. F. Lehmanns, 1937). Photo by Zentralinstitut für Kunstgeschichte, Munich.

90. *(left)* Wolfgang Willrich, *The Guardian of the Species,* circa 1937. "Whatever is useful for the preservation of the German species is moral. Whatever opposes it is immoral"—Walter Darré. Published in *Rasse: Monatsschrift der Nordischen Bewegung,* 1937. RR.

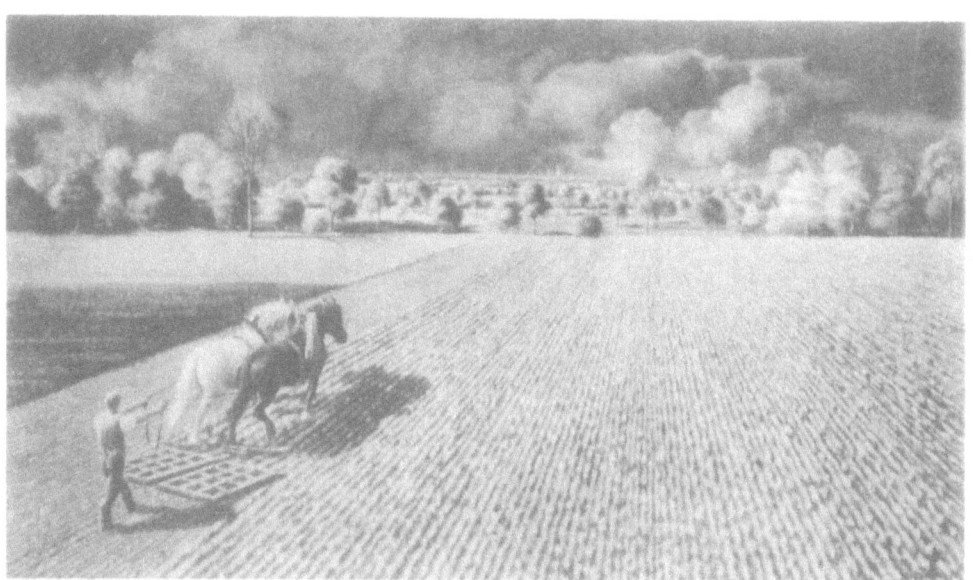

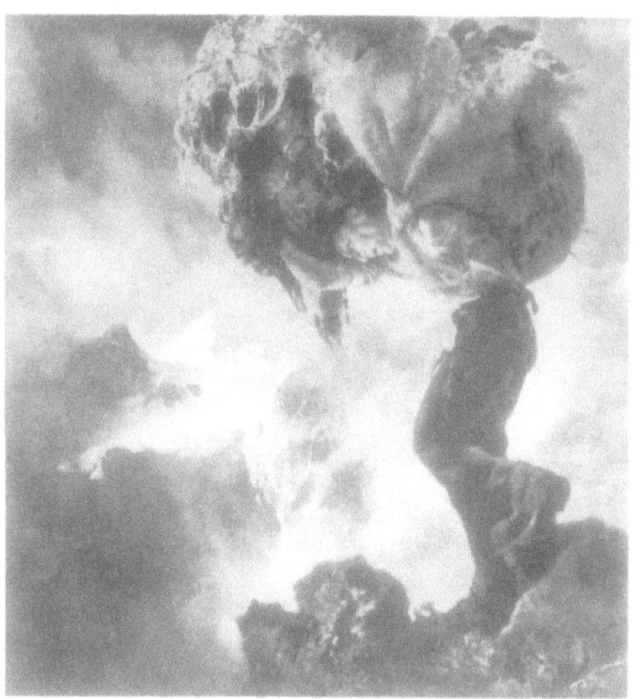

91. *(above)* Werner Peiner, *German Land* (oil on canvas), 1933. Published in Rittich, *Deutsche Kunst der Gegenwart*, vol. 2, p. 40. Document preserved in the Bibliothèque de l'Institut d'Histoire de l'Art de Strasbourg.

92. *(left)* Heinrich Berann, *The Winnower* (oil on canvas), circa 1943. Published in *Kunst dem Volk*, 1943, special "GDK" issue, p. 31. Document preserved in the Bibliothèque de l'Institut d'Histoire de l'Art de Strasbourg.

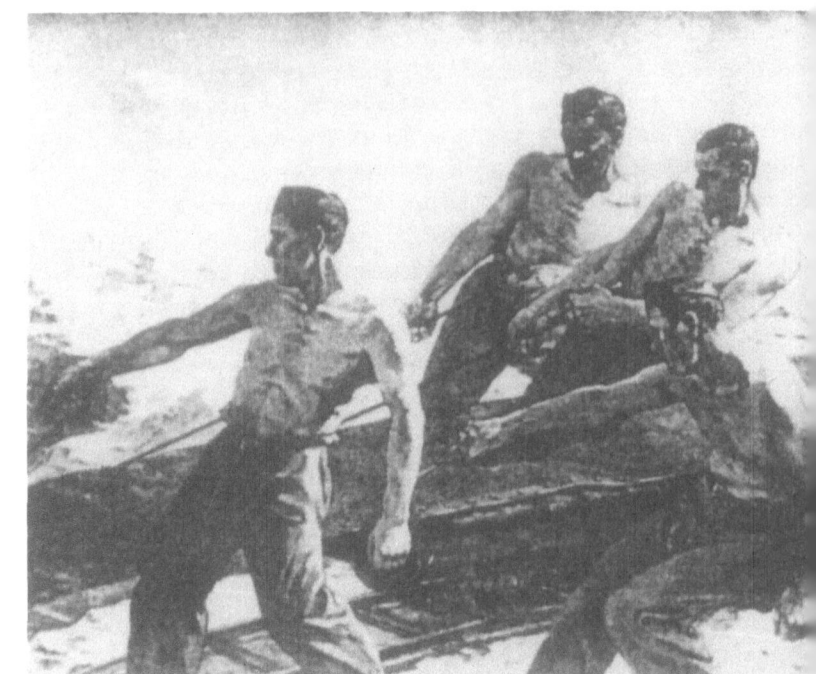

93. *(right)* Ria Picco-Rückert, *United Strength* (oil on canvas, 160 x 200 cm.), 1944. Photo by Bayerische Staats-gemäldesammlung, Munich.

94. *(below)* Arthur Kampf, *The Rolling Mill* (oil on canvas), 1939. Published in Rittich, *Deutsche Kunst der Gegenwart,* vol. 2, p. 64. Document preserved in the Bibliothèque de l'Institut d'His-toire de l'Art de Strasbourg.

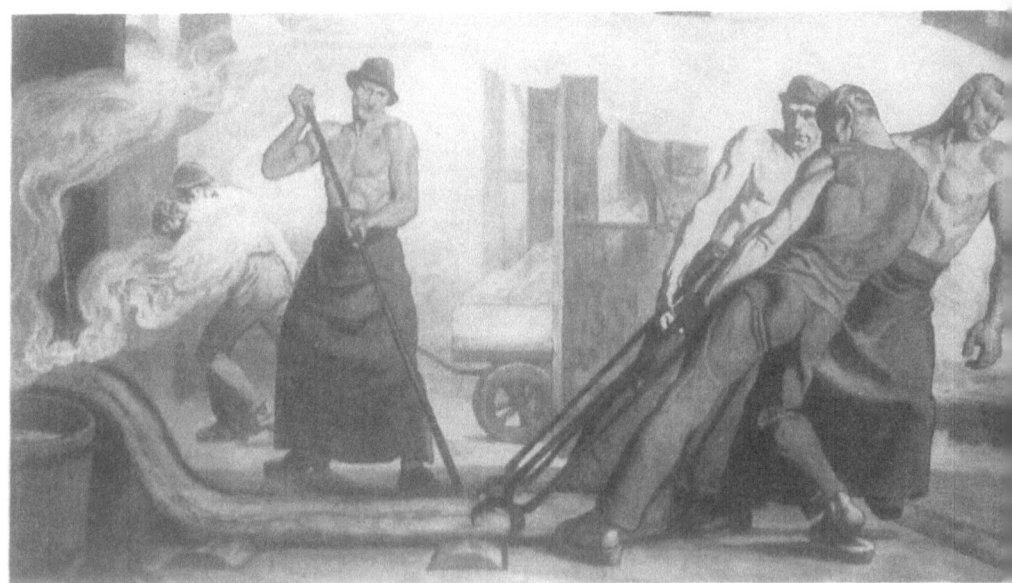

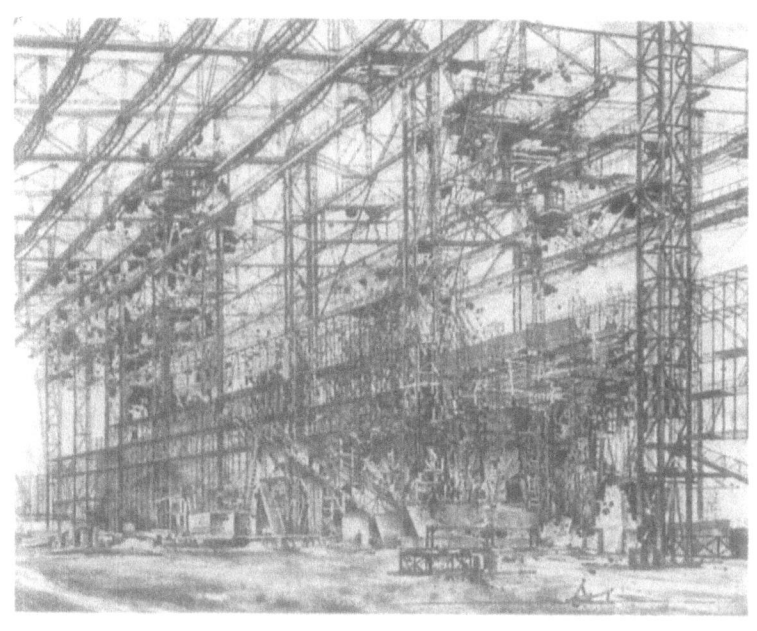

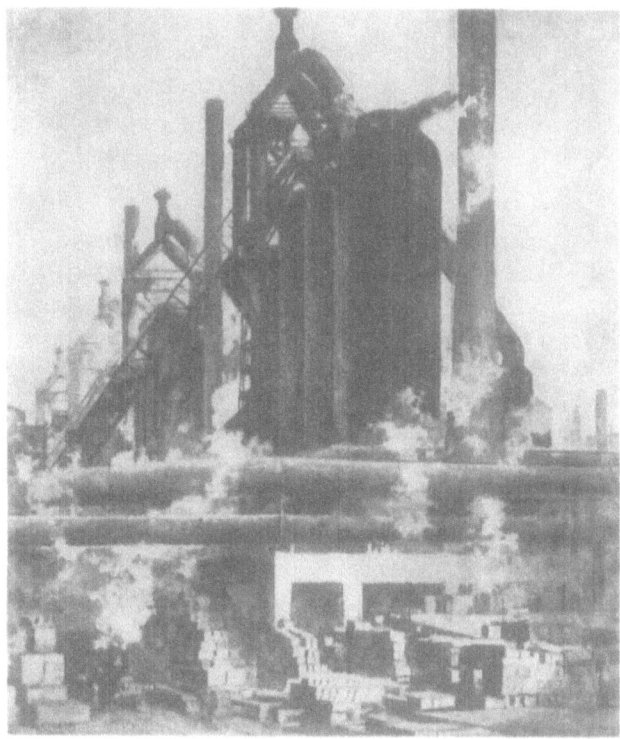

95. *(above)* Curt Winckler, *Ship Under Construction* (lithograph), n.d. Published in Rittich, *Deutsche Kunst der Gegenwart*, vol. 2, p. 133. Document preserved in the Bibliothèque de l'Institut d'Histoire de l'Art de Strasbourg.

96. *(left)* Franz Gerwin, *The Hermann-Göring Factory Under Construction* (oil on canvas, 180 x 155 cm.), 1940. Published in Rittich, *Deutsche Kunst der Gegenwart*, vol. 2, p. 133. Document preserved in the Bibliothèque de l'Institut d'Histoire de l'Art de Strasbourg.

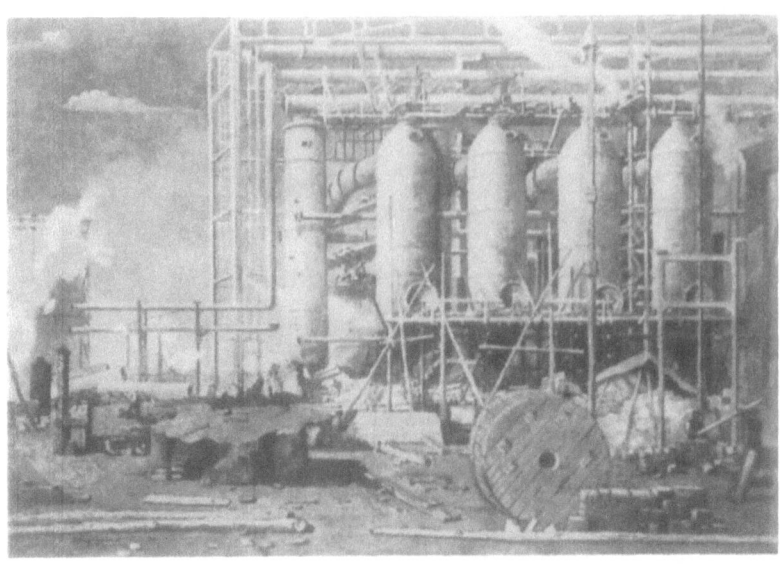

97. *(above)* Richard Gessner, *The Oil Refinery*, 1941. Published in Rüdiger, *Kunst und Technik*, plate 38. Document preserved in the Bibliothèque de l'Institut d'Histoire de l'Art de Strasbourg.

98. *(right)* Dirk Van Hees, *The Great Coking Plant, with Adjacent Installations* (drypoint etching), n.d. Published in Rüdiger, *Kunst und Technik*, plate 38. Document preserved in the Bibliothèque de l'Institut d'Histoire de l'Art de Strasbourg.

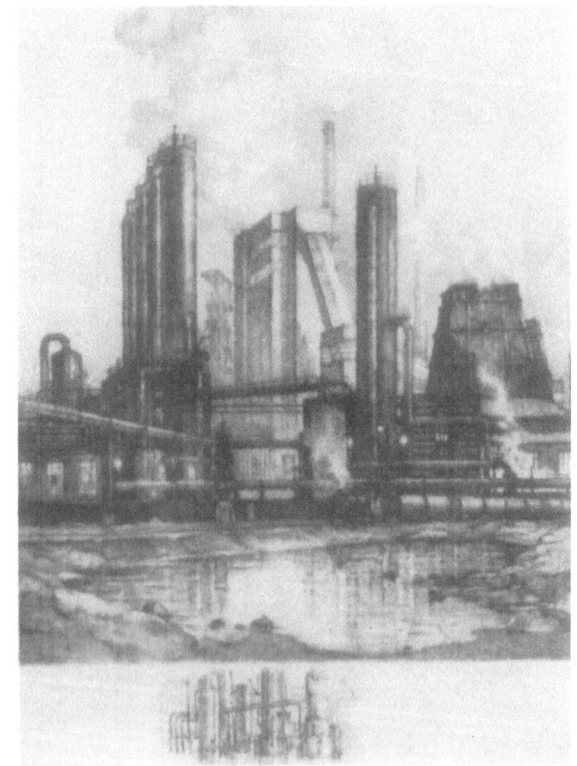

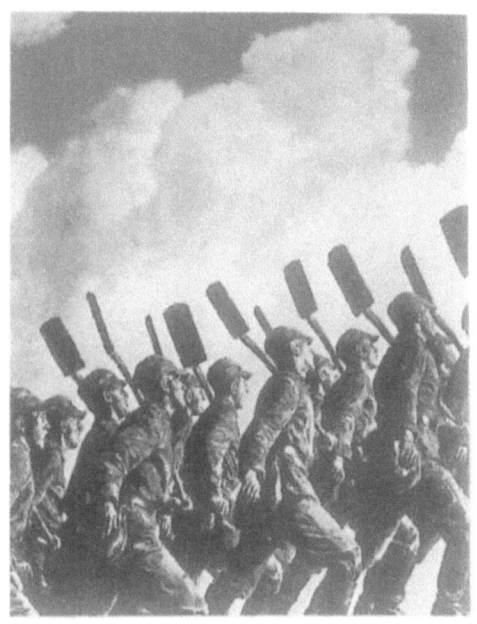

99a. *(left)*   Ferdinand Staeger, *We Are the Soldiers of Work* (oil on canvas), 1938. RR.

99b. *(below)*   "The younger generation lines up to form a gigantic pacific army" (photograph), circa 1935. Published in Schemm, *Deutsches Volk, Deutsche Heimat*, p. 228. Author's collection. Photo preserved in the Bibliothèque de l'Institut d'Histoire de l'Art de Strasbourg

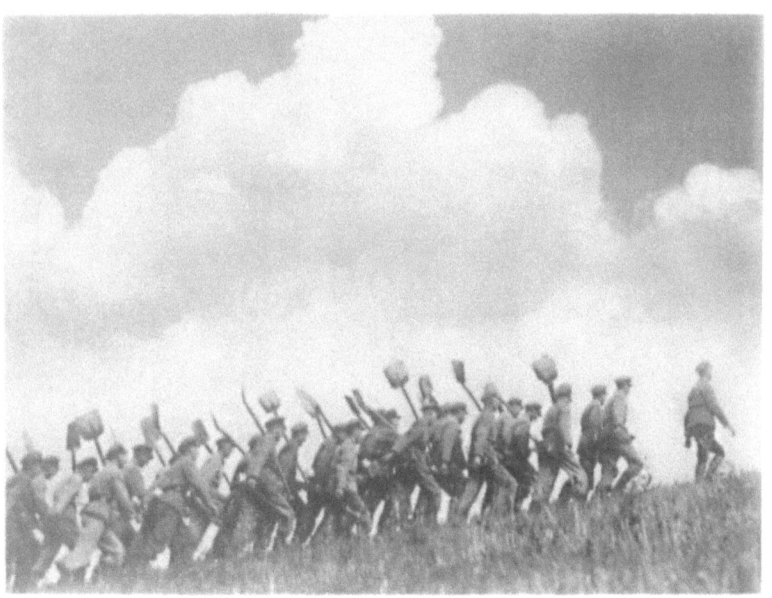

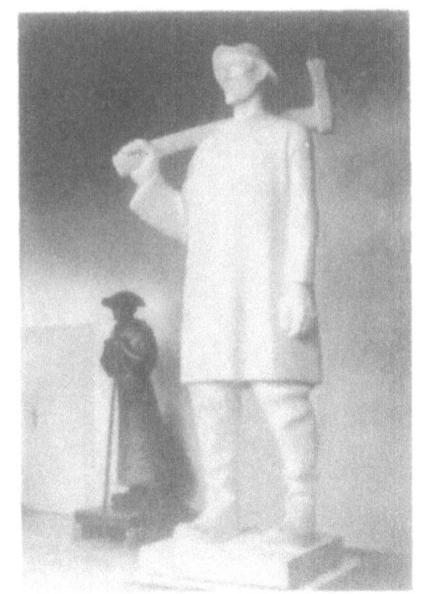

100. *(right)* Fritz Koelle, in the background, *The Foundry Worker* (bronze, height 3 m.), circa 1939; in the foreground, *The Isar Raftsman* (plaster, height 3.60 m.), 1939. Photo by Bildarchiv Preussischer Kulturbesitz, Berlin.

101. *(below)* Ferdinand Staeger, *Political Front* (oil on canvas), n.d. RR.

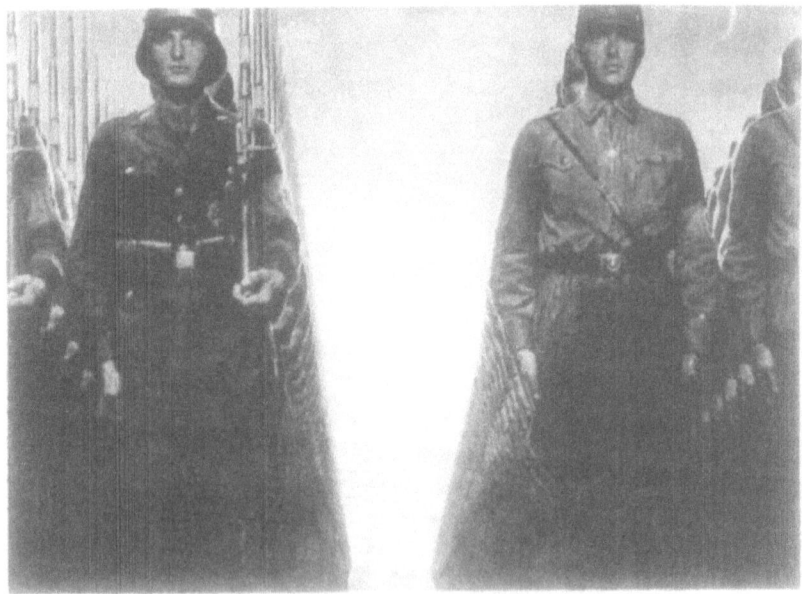

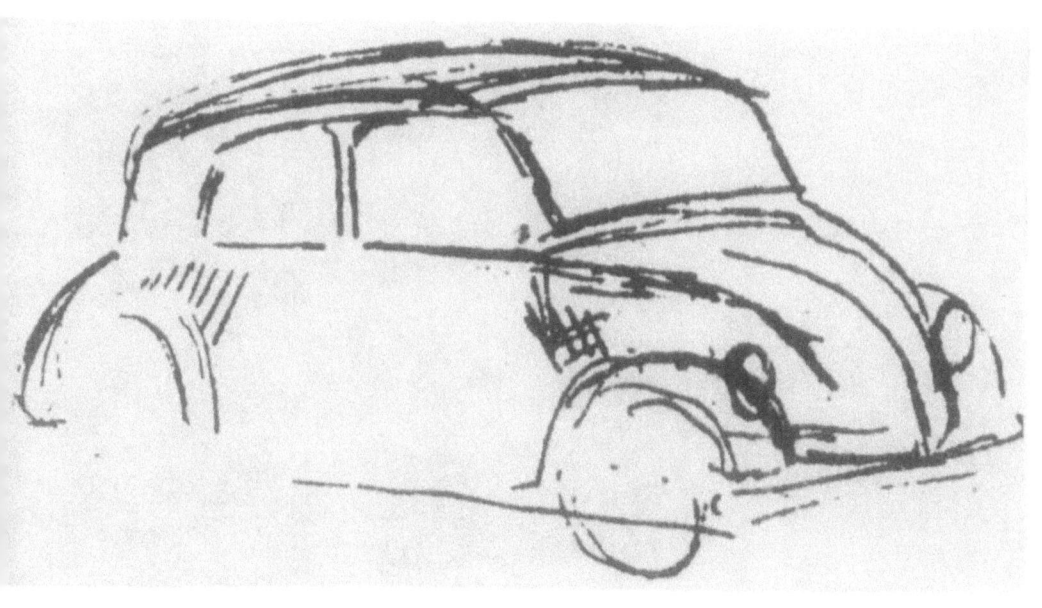

102. Adolf Hitler, sketch for a car
shaped like a "beetle," 1932. RR.

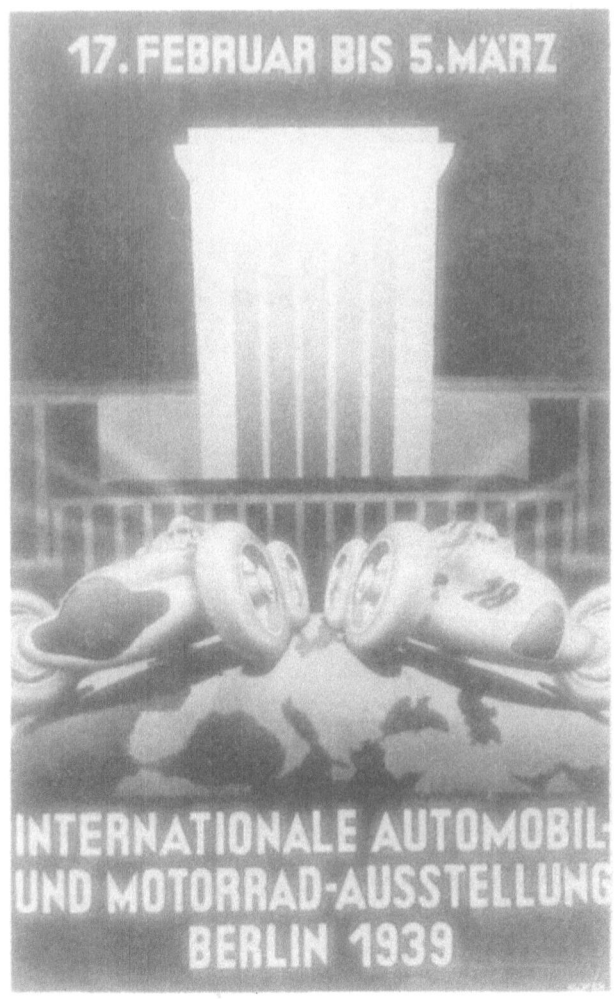

103. Poster for the International Automobile and Motorcycle Exhibition, Berlin, 1939. RR.

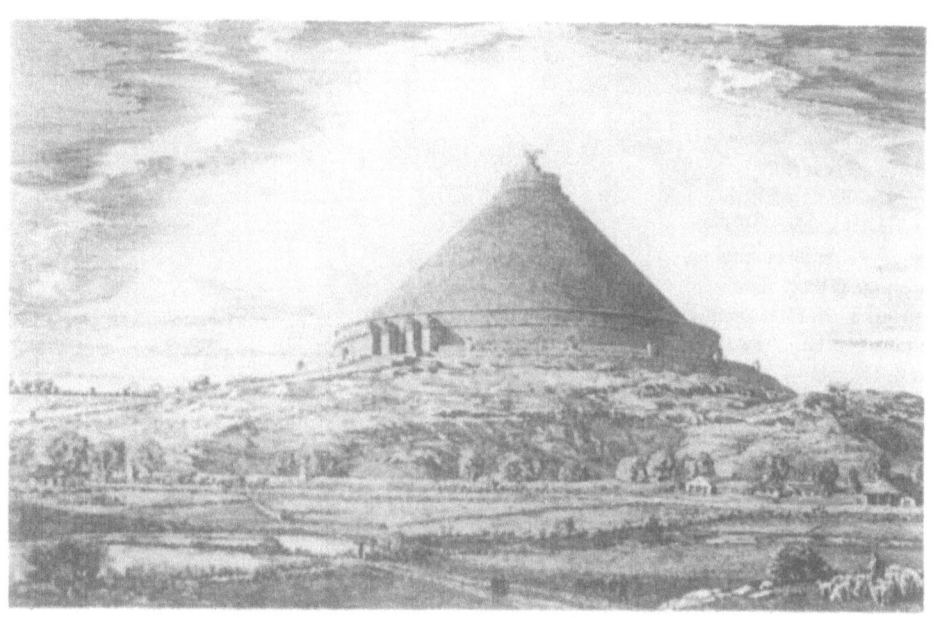

104. Wilhelm Kreis, *Great Memorial in Russia*
(ink drawing), circa 1942. Published in *Die
Baukunst: Die Kunst im deutschen Reich*, 1943, no. 3,
p. 52. Document preserved in the Bibliothèque de
l'Institut d'Histoire de l'Art de Strasbourg.

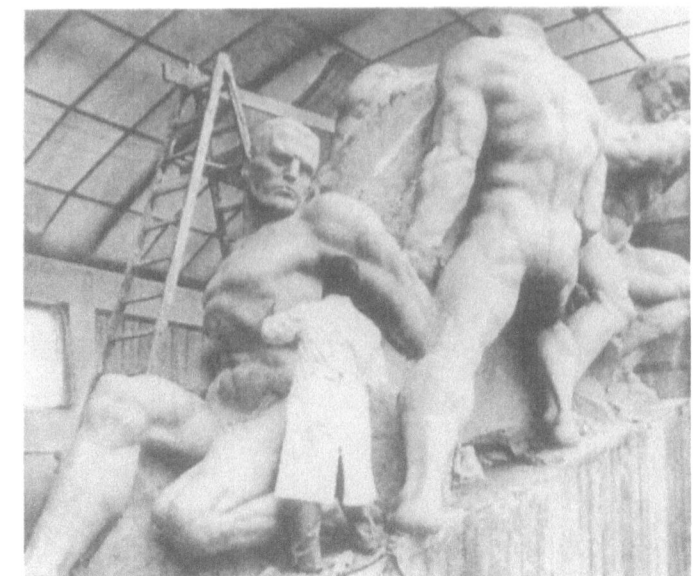

105. Josef Thorak with his *Monument to Work on the Motorways of the Reich* (plaster model), 1938. Published in Tank, *Deutsche Plastik unserer Zeit*, illustration facing p. 104. Document preserved in the Bibliothèque de l'Institut d'Histoire de l'Art de Strasbourg.

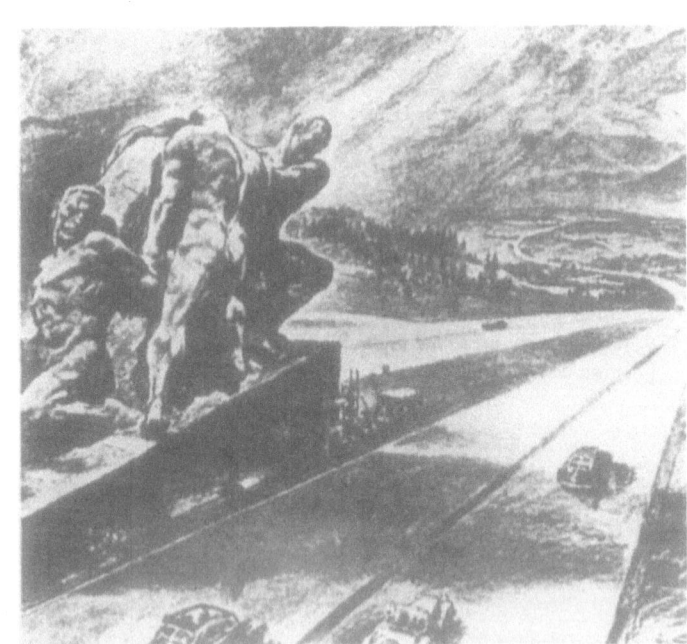

106. Josef Thorak, *Sketch for a Monument to Work on the Motorways of the Reich*, 1938. Published in *Kunst im 3. Reich: Dokumente der Unterwerfung* (Frankfurt: Frankfurter Kunstverein), 1975, p. 179. Photo Jonas Verlag, Marburg.

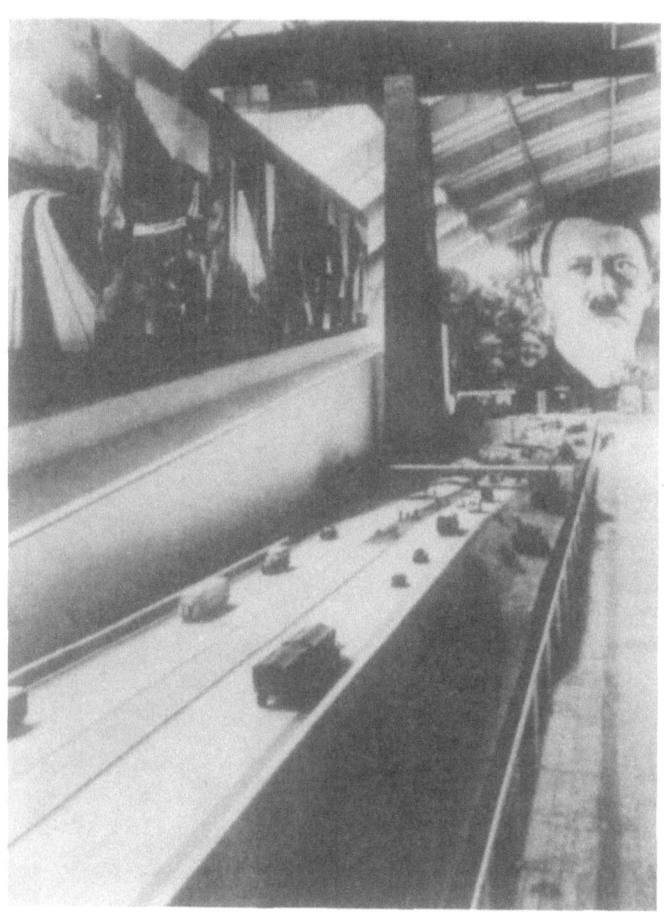

107. "All Roads Lead to Hitler." Exhibition devoted to the "Adolf Hitler roads." Published in Hellmut Lehmann-Haupt, *Art Under a Dictatorship* (New York: Oxford University Press, 1954), illustration no. 36. RR.

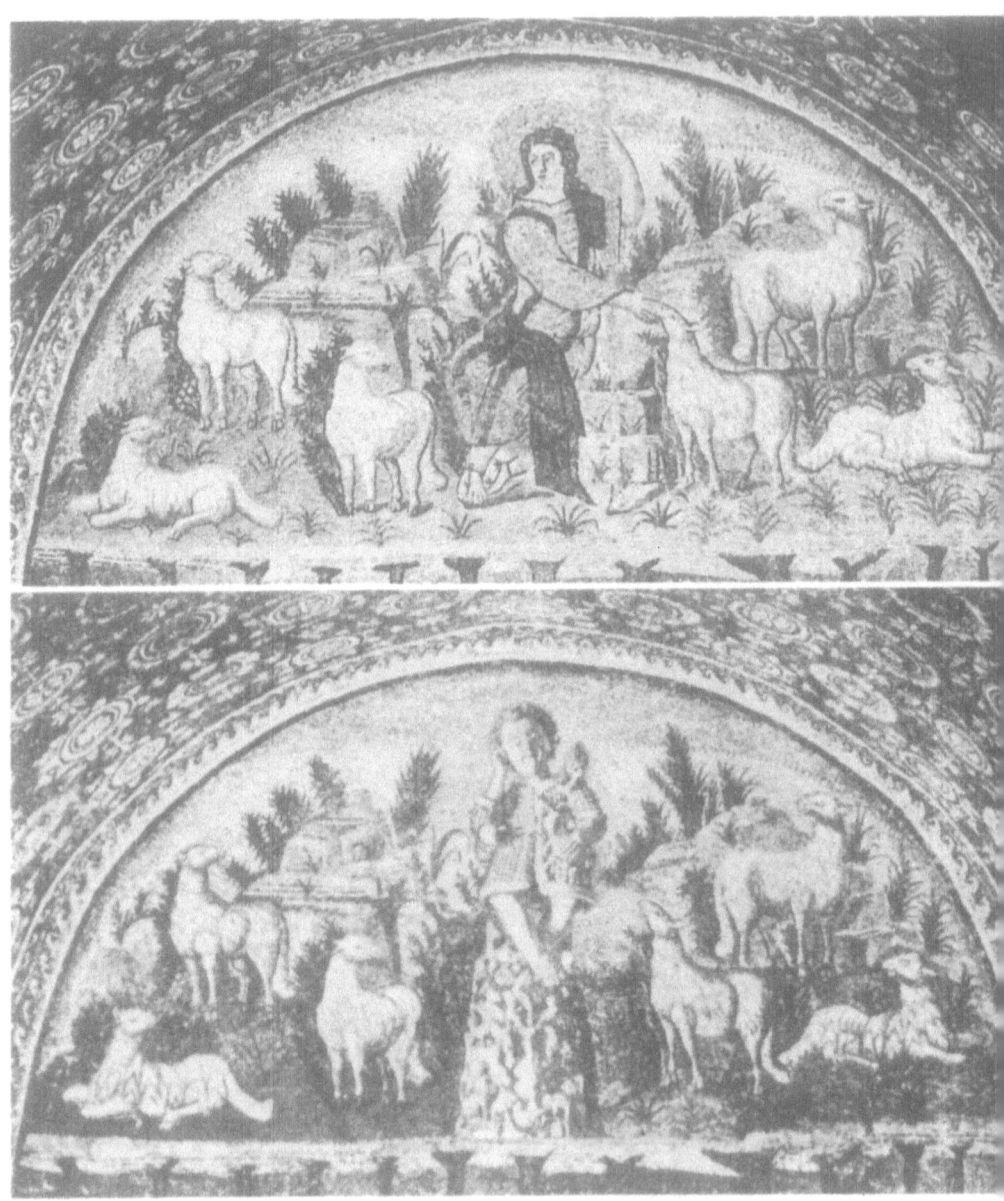

108a. *(top)* *The Good Shepherd* (mosaic mural), Mausoleum of Galla Placidia, Ravenna. Photo by Alinari Anderson-Giraudon, Vanves.

108b. *(bottom)* Josef Strzygowski replaces "the King of the Jews" of the Mausoleum of Galla Placidia in Ravenna with a Yima of "Aryan" origin. Published in Strzygowski, *Das indogermanische Ahnenerbe des deutschen Volkes und die Kunstgeschichte der Zukunft* (Vienna: Deutscher Verlag für Jugend und Volk, 1941), p. 69. Document preserved in the Bibliothèque de l'Institut d'Histoire de l'Art de Strasbourg.

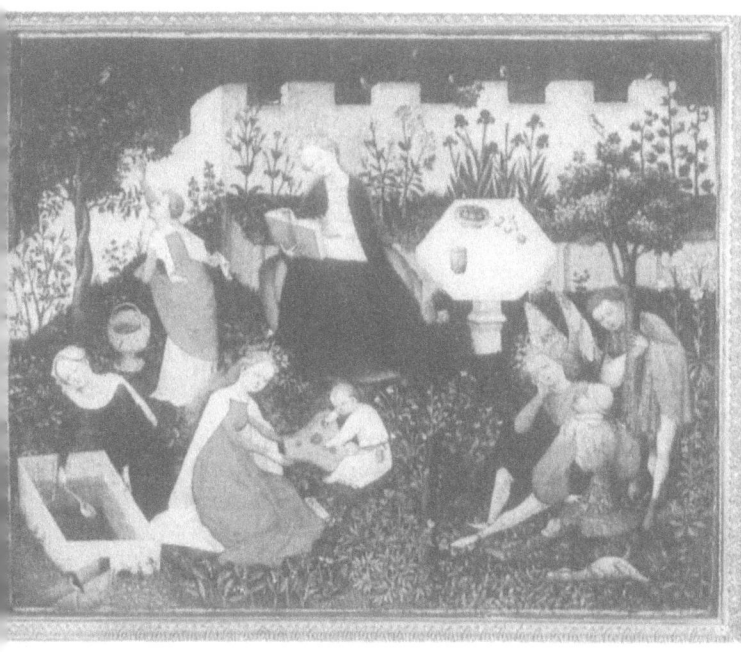

109a. *(left)* Rhineland School, *The Garden of Paradise*, circa 1420. Frankfurt: Städelsches Kunstinstitut. Photo by Bridgeman-Giraudon, Vanves.

109bc. *(below)* Josef Strzygowski cuts out the Virgin and Child and adds a "Nordic" fountain of life. Published in Strzygowski, *Das indogermanische Ahnenerbe des deutschen Volkes und die Kunstgeschichte der Zukunft*, p. 74. Document preserved in the Bibliothèque de l'Institut d'Histoire de l'Art de Strasbourg.

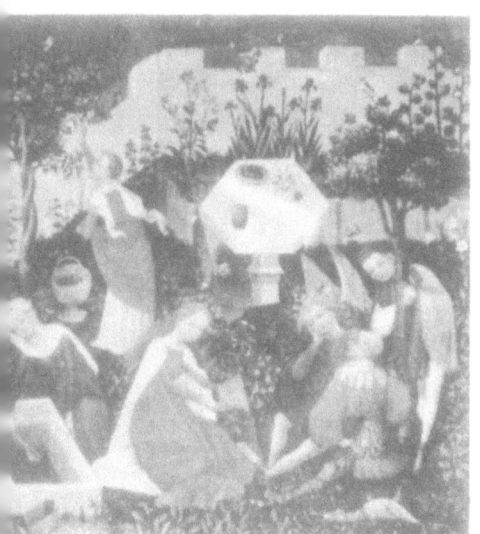

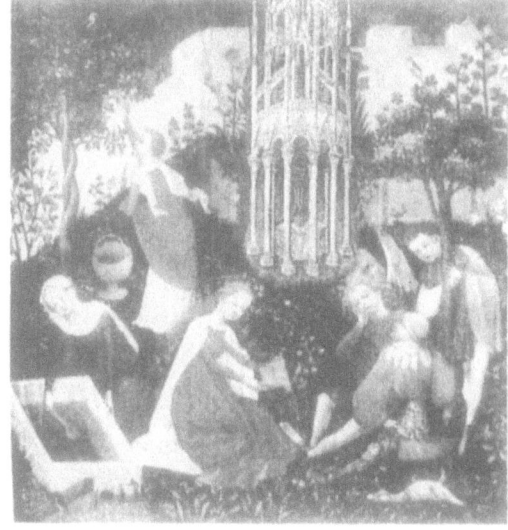

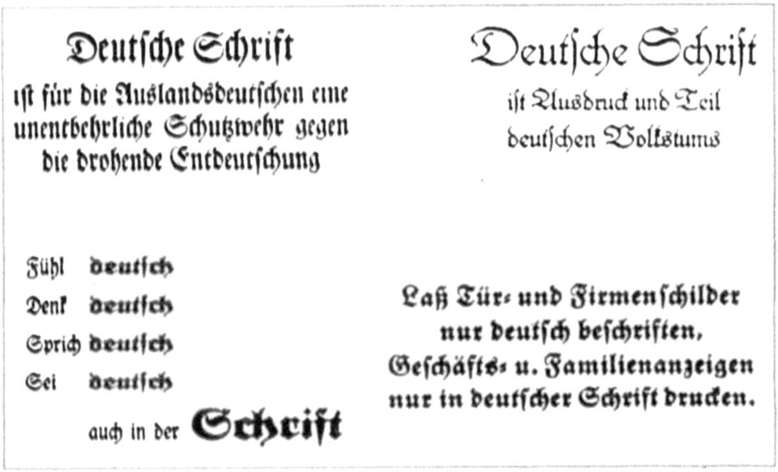

Deutſche Schrift

ist für die Auslandsdeutschen eine
unentbehrliche Schutzwehr gegen
die drohende Entdeutschung

Fühl deutsch

Denk deutsch

Sprich deutsch

Sei deutsch

auch in der **Schrift**

Deutſche Schrift

ist Ausdruck und Teil
deutschen Volkstums

Laß Tür- und Firmenschilder
nur deutsch beschriften,
Geschäfts- u. Familienanzeigen
nur in deutscher Schrift drucken.

110. "German writing is an expression of the German people, a part of it." Published in Lehmann-Haupt, *Art Under a Dictatorship*, p. 171. RR.

seemed a possibility. For, over and above all its tumults, the war was primarily intended to restore the calm and radiant vision of the eternal Reich that lay as a dream in the heart of the *Volksgeist.*

Arthur Moeller van den Bruck wrote, "The idea of eternal peace is certainly the idea of the Third Reich. But its realization must be obtained through combat and the Third Reich wants to be more firmly established."[78] The old Augustinian truth that "every man is in quest of peace, even in waging war," if only to change it to suit himself,[79] was certainly not unfamiliar to Hitler. Even when the battles were raging most fiercely, he delighted in evoking his visions for a Europe that he would have pacified: "Wars pass. Only the works of culture never pass away. Hence my love of art."[80] With the tranquil assurance of those who see culture as the highest achievement of man, he always reckoned that the life of a people could be justified only by its art.

Initially, however, according to Hitler, the National Socialist revolution could justify its right to interrupt the decline of history only by visibly realizing, in art, the Idea by which it was guided. That was certainly what he meant in his Nuremberg speeches of 1933, when he was preparing to remodel first the Munich Königsplatz, then the architecture of the whole of Germany:

Even if a people fades away and its men fall silent, the stones will speak. . . . That is why every great political period in the history of the world will establish its right to existence by the most visible justificatory evidence of its value that it can possibly produce: *its cultural realizations [Leistungen].*[81]

But two years later it was not just a historical political right that found legitimization in art, but the right of the race or people, now restored through its politics. Certainly Hitler again declared that "the Nationalist Socialist movement . . . must strive by every means to transform its *claim* into a *legitimate demand* through its creative cultural realization [*Leistung*]." It was first a matter of pursuing the movement of self-suggestion through art—in other words, "to get the people to believe with conviction in its mission in general and the party's mission in particular, through the demonstration of its superior cultural gifts and their visible effects."[82] But the suggestion also had other aims. Of course Hitler was targeting neighboring nations, but also, beyond the perception of his contemporaries, the judgment of history itself:

The more the vital and natural needs of a nation are unrecognized, repressed, or simply challenged, the more important it is to bestow upon those natural needs the character of a superior right, by means of visible demonstrations of the highest values of the people—demonstrations which, as the experience of history shows, are what remain, even after centuries, as the indestructible evidence not only of the greatness of the people but, on that account, also of its moral right to live [*Lebensrecht*]. Yes, even if the last living witnesses of an unfortunate people were to fall silent, the stones would begin to speak. A people that has not placed the construction of its own monument among the values of its culture is deemed by history to be hardly worthy of mention.[83]

Hitler expected history to look upon the National Socialist oeuvre—*his* oeuvre—with the same eyes through which he himself looked upon the Greek, Egyptian, and Roman past. For the Führer certainly held in high esteem those monuments that testified to the greatness of the peoples of the past, thereby *a posteriori* justifying their existence. For the German people, in its turn, to deserve the attentive gaze of history, it had to prove itself, likewise, capable of anticipating its own death in a monument that would embody it worthily. But because it was only once it was dead that a people could attest to its greatness through its monuments, that people had to be totally taken over by what Hitler called *das Wort aus Stein* (the word of stone).

It was in this respect that Nazism, more than Italian Fascism, confirmed—despite its denials—that it was a perfect realization of art for art's sake. For the Third Reich to be in a position to declare itself eternal, it had to be able to look at itself as an artist, with eyes from beyond the tomb. Such was precisely the anticipatory movement that Théophile Gautier, who one century earlier had been the first theorist of art for art's sake, demanded of the artist:

Tout passe. L'art robuste
Seul a l'éternité,
Le buste
Survit à la cité.[84]

Everthing passes. Robust art
Alone is eternal.
The bust
Survives the city.

To be sure, the theory of art for art's sake was also, or perhaps primarily, a theory of the artist's immortality through art and his own oeuvre. But Gautier also opposed the fury of war to the calm eternity of art, which is produced away from that warfare:

Pendant les guerres de l'empire,
Goethe, au bruit du canon brutal,
Fit *Le Divan occidental.*
Fraîche oasis où l'art respire.
. . .
Sans prendre garde à l'ouragan
Qui fouettait mes vitres fermées,
Moi, j'ai fait *Emaux et Camées.*[85]

During the wars of the Empire,
Goethe, to the sound of the brutal cannon,
Wrote *Occidental-Oriental Poems,*
A fresh oasis where art can breathe.
. . .
Heedless of the hurricane
That battered at my closed window,
I, for my part, wrote *Enamels and Cameos.*

Far from setting the artist in opposition to the soldier, as Gautier did, National Socialism conferred the dignity of the artist upon all the combatants of the *Volksgemeinschaft,* whether they fought on the military front, the labor front, the art front, or the birth front. The most noble of tasks fell to them all: to outlive themselves in the eloquent stones of the eternal Reich. For this to happen, the entire *Volkskörper* had to be mobilized, with its faith placed in Providence (*Vorsehung*), its aim being to flesh out "the Führer's vision."

But over and above the fashion for neoclassicism that swept through the official architecture of the thirties in both Europe and the United States, these buildings imitated not just one but many styles from the past. While the vernacular style was reserved for model farms, and functionalism for factories, the community embodied itself in stone by imitating Athens or Babylon; the fortress of Castel del Monte, built by Frederick II; or the Colosseum of Rome. This was not only so as to enable the *Volksgemeinschaft* to identify itself by appropriating the fragments of its race's eternal soul that history had dispersed. The point of imitating the styles of the past was also and above all to make something into the past, to pass something off and make it pass away. It was to provide visible and tangible proof, *hic et nunc,* of the greatness of the community, which had become a work of art; to provide proof of the already present yet simultaneously historic power possessed by this community that was embodied as if it were already a part of history. Just as the gaze of the artist, who expects to be judged purely by posterity, anticipates his own death and considers his work from the point of view of history, the gaze with which the Führer contemplated his people was that of an artist considering his *finished* work.

> Sculpte, lime, cisèle;
> Que ton rêve flottant
> Se scelle
> Dans le bloc résistant![86]

> Sculpt, polish, chisel;
> Let your floating dream
> Be sealed
> Within the resistant marble block!

In 1933 art historian Hubert Schrade described the *human architecture* constituted by the orderly Nuremberg masses. But in 1939 he considered that human architecture to be more closely linked with stone, now that the Zeppelin esplanade had been built, with "the Führer's place" positioned at the center of the main tribune:

All, in the *same* posture, with the *same* costume, lined up toward a *single* goal, must feel that the strict positioning of the columns expresses the order beneath which they have set themselves. Alongside the stone [*am Stein*] they must sense the same will for form that has also seized hold of them, living men. Between themselves and the architecture they sense a total harmony. And within this harmony, art appears as it should: both as a service and as something with the power to intensify. . . . Whoever wishes to build as National Socialism does must ensure duration. Only that which is calculated to last for centuries can really claim to have been constructed.[87]

The mobilization of the masses was thus designed to produce their sublime petrification—sublime primarily in the sense that Hitler gave to the word when he claimed for art "a sublime mission that calls for fanaticism," but also sublime in the Hegelian sense, for the National Socialist Idea, as it phenomenalized itself in stone, did not find fulfillment in the stone itself but, on the contrary, gnawed away the matter until it brought about its ruin. Hegel declared that sublimity "forces the matter in which sublimity appears to disappear. Matter is expressly conceived as not being in conformity with sublimity."[88]

There was one architect who came to see that matter "given form" could never be in conformity with either the National Socialist Idea or the desire for sublimity of a Führer who identified with time. After Ludwig Troost's death, Albert Speer became Hitler's favorite Master of Works, and one day he blew up the reinforced concrete hangars positioned on the site where the great Nuremberg tribune was to be built. It was upon seeing that "the iron reinforcements protruded from concrete debris and had already begun to rust" that he hit upon his famous "theory of ruin value":

Buildings of modern construction were poorly suited to form that "bridge of tradition" to future generations that Hitler was calling for. It was hard to imagine that rusting heaps of rubble could communicate these heroic inspirations that Hitler admired in the monuments of the past. My "theory" was intended to deal with this dilemma. By using special materials and by applying certain principles of statics, we should be able to build structures that even in a state of decay, after hundreds or (such were our reckonings) thousands of years, would more or less resemble Roman models.

To illustrate my ideas I had a romantic drawing prepared. It showed what the reviewing stand on the Zeppelin Field would look like after generations of neglect, overgrown with ivy, its columns fallen, the walls crumbling here and there, but the outlines were still clearly recognizable.[89]

Delighted by the "luminous logic" of this sketch, Hitler ordered that in the future the Reich's most important buildings should be constructed according to "the law of ruins." Speer had hit the bull's eye by responding "to the Führer's desire" in this way and, on his behalf, anticipating the moment when "men fell silent." That moment would come long after the movements of the community's fighters had been frozen and immobilized in stone, and when history would at last recognize them as a people of artists and founders of culture (*Kulturbegründer*) who had constructed their own monument.

This desire to speed up the final redemption of the people was also detectable in the gigantic cities of the dead that had been planned as early as 1940 by Wilhelm Kreis. According to Kreis, these cities, which were supposed to mark out the frontiers of the new Europe that stretched from the Atlantic to the Urals and from Norway to Greece, were not simply to be "sites to honor the dead." They were to be symbols that gave meaning to "the great historical turning point" and that constituted "an eternal reminder . . . of the unification of Europe under the leadership of its core people, the Germans." These monuments contained "the tombs of the generation of warriors of German blood who had, as they had so often done for two thousand years, defended the cultural world of the West"; they spoke "a language that was understood by every man of the same blood shed here"[90] (Figure 104).

In Nuremberg it was as if the Führer could see an accelerated version of the whole film of his people, from the point when it entered history to the point where it left it:

Who can fail to be moved by the thought that the thousands of men parading before us at this moment are not only individuals moving through the present, but the eternal expression of the vitality of our people, both in the past and in the future? . . . The path they are following is the one that our people has followed for centuries, and if we but close our eyes for a moment, we can imagine that we hear the onward march of all the ancestors of our race.[91]

The *Gleichschaltung* was not just a synchronization of bodies in movement; it was also a synchronization of temporalities: the future was marching with the past, in the eternal present of the race, and the movement was leading toward the immobility of stone.

Ever since the building of the first Temples of the Heroes—left open to the skies in the square of the Bavarian capital, which had been rebaptized as the capital of the movement—the community had been hastening, through the struggle of its creative work, to reach out to the cities of the dead that would mark out the borders of the future "vital space" (*Lebensraum*). Through this accelerated movement toward the ultimate consecration, it was *visibly* exiting from history in order truly to enter it.

The rapid motorization of the community, which brought continuous supplies of the blood needed to mark out its frontiers, was now bringing into physical being the primordial *Lebenstraum* (vital dream) that was becoming a reality in the *Lebensraum*. The same atemporality that filled the dream permeated the space of the eternal Reich: the motorways that linked one point with another, with all the desired speed, overcame the obstacles in their path with bridges built sometimes of stone, sometimes of steel, which resembled now Roman edifices, now futuristic ones. The vast enterprises of Fritz Todt's organization, responsible for the Führer's roads, were building these monuments "for eternity": they were to be "the pyramids of the Reich." Josef Thorak was sculpting the model for his Monument to Work (Figures 105 and 106), which was intended to be positioned alongside one of the Reich's motorways; it represented an ancient and lordly people hewing out rocks, naked and colossal geniuses opening up the paths of eternity for the motor's people. Time seemed to come to a halt and be converted into space. But as Todt said, to see the goal was in itself to concentrate and master time and space: "The new Adolf Hitler motorway, the *Autobahn*, matches our National Socialist nature. We wish to see the goal far ahead of us, and we wish to reach it rapidly and directly."[92]

One exhibition demonstrated that all roads now led to the Führer, just as they had once led to Rome (Figure 107). Meanwhile Inge Capra was also singing, "My Führer, you alone are the way and the goal!"[93] National Christianity, eternally at the cutting edge of the technology that realized its creative essence, also knew how to wipe out the distances that separated its Christ from each member of the community: "The time has now come for us to begin to implant Your Image, my Führer, in all German hearts, deeply and ineffaceably, by means of the National Socialist television."[94] Engineers and propagandists alike were jubilant: "If we so desire, tomorrow all Germans will be able to look toward Nuremberg!" Was not that precisely the Führer's wish? At the last congress he had said, "If today the entire German people could see you, I believe that even the last remaining skeptics would be converted and convinced that the foundation of a new nation, the community of our people, is not just words but reality" That was why both engineers and propagandists were now beaming with joy:

If anything more persuasive than speech exists, it is certainly seeing with one's own eyes! . . . If you work for the launching of television, you will be working for the total and irreversible victory of the National Socialist Idea! Carry the image of the Führer into every German heart! . . . Long live the Führer! Long live our dear movement! Long live the reawakened Germany, which has now recovered its sight![95]

If in the image space had been made to contract in the communion of one and all, time seemed to have dilated into an "eternal Sunday." And as space confirmed the extension of the *Lebensraum*, it seemed to absorb history, establishing a purified present.

But the work of purification was never-ending, for the battle for an eternal life and an eternal art was in truth a battle against time. Two kinds of eternity were constantly thrown into opposition: that of the Aryan *Kultur* and that of the *ewige Jude*, the "eternal Jew" who gnawed away in advance at every messianic figure. Even if the Aryan eternity had proved capable of absorbing both its past and its future, these still had to be purged of all defilement in order to ensure the perennial present. From start to finish, this was the raison d'être of the eternal Reich.

On the occasion of the *auto-da-fe* of May 10, 1933, at the sight of the books in flames, Goebbels exclaimed, "The period of paroxysmal Jewish intellectualism is now over. . . . You are quite right, in the deepest darkness of this night, to consign the evil spirit of the past to the flames."[96] But even at the end of the war, the past was still contaminating the present. In August 1944, correspondence and photographs were exchanged between the Institute for Research on the "Jewish question" and the office of Rosenberg: in the museum of Wasserburg am Inn, an ancient wooden Christ with a strongly Jewish cast of features had been discovered.[97] And on October 21, 1944, an office in the Einsatzstab Rosenberg sent a pressing request for clarification to the Central Bureau of the "supranational forces" in Berlin. Ludwig van Beethoven had sent certain letters to a Viennese publisher beginning with the salutation "Esteemed Brother." It was "important" to know whether Beethoven had been a Freemason.[98]

A little earlier, eminent professor of the history of art Josef Strzygowski, whose early works are still considered authoritative, was busy purifying all existing images of a past the Jews had contaminated. First he attacked the mausoleum of Galla Placidia in Ravenna. The mosaic at the entrance, which depicted "The King of the Jews as a Good Shepherd," was clearly a perversion of the Iranian Yima (first man). A photographic montage enabled Strzygowski to put an end to the imposture, restore the throne of the Parsee figure, and return Paradise to its original Aryan condition (Figures 108a and 108b). Next he attacked an anonymous painting of the German fifteenth century (Figure 109a) on the grounds that it deceptively showed "the destiny of Christ between birth and death in a *Garden of Paradise*." Armed with scissors, Strzygowski relieved the image of its Judeo-Christian Virgin and Christ (Figure 109b); then, returning to "the legacy of our ancestors," he placed in the centre of the picture a fountain of youth borrowed from the very "Nordic" *Heures de Chantilly* (Figure 109c) so as to reconstitute an authentic and pure image of a "sacred wood" (*Schicksalshain*) in which the "Aryan destiny was at stake.[99]

Gothic writing itself was soon to become a vector of contamination, despite the fact that in June 1933 the *Berliner Lokal-Anzeiger* was boasting that "the characters known as German" were "incomparably richer and more beautiful than those known as Roman!" Whoever, free of prejudice, was set before the German and Roman runic alphabets placed side by side would at a mere glance discern which was the intruder. But vigilance was necessary on the part of the press, in which the frequent use of Roman characters testified to the extent of the Jewish influence.[100] By 1937, the situation on this front was indecisive, but it was not yet certain that the Roman alphabet would triumph throughout the world, overcoming all that fell within its field. For what was at stake here was certainly the liberty of eternal Germany: "For us, the German characters mean much more than the Roman characters mean to others. *For us, they express our very being, our own German being, which words do not suffice to describe.*"[101]

As we have seen, in opposition to the *Buchstabe*, the "letter," Carl Schmitt set "our feeling of today," something more organic and biological, as the foundation for a new German law. But now it was Gothic writing that, in and through its visible materiality, was guaranteeing the togetherness and identity of the community of feeling. The intelligible aspect of the writing mattered little compared to its sensitive powers. The old opposition of *muthos* to *logos* had been repealed; and myth had finally absorbed language.

Calligraphy competitions were organized in schools and the efforts of the winners were published in magazines (Figure 110), on calendars, and in the specialist press: "Feel German, think German, speak German, and in writing too be German." Forgetting the international origins of Gothic writing, in 1940 the town of Nuremberg celebrated the five hundredth anniversary of the Gutenberg printing press with an exhibition entitled "Writing, a German Art."[102] But suddenly, on January 3, 1941, a confidential letter from Martin Bormann sounded the alarm:

What follows is brought to general attention by order of the Führer: it is mistaken to consider or describe the writing known as Gothic as German. In reality, what is called Gothic writing are Jewish characters known as Schwabach writing. Exactly as they were later to take possession of the press, the Jews of Germany seized the printing presses [after the invention of the procedure] and that is how the massive introduction of the Schwabach characters in Germany came about.[103]

Bormann's orders issued from the Obersalzberg were therefore that the font used by the German press, which was already circulating its publications abroad, was to be changed immediately. There then followed a hard-fought controversy in which the history of typography clashed with the interests of propaganda. But from that day on, even the Führer's speeches were printed in Roman characters.

It was no doubt Goebbels who pressed for the switch to be promptly made, for his first concern was to ensure the propagation of the National Socialist Idea beyond the frontiers of Greater Germany. The extension of the Third Reich to so many countries where the Gothic characters were considered illegible made the rationalization of writing unavoidable.

Clearly the writing that was supposed to mirror the German spirit had not been sapped from within by the "eternal Jew"; it was crumbling of its own accord, as if gnawed away from the inside, having supposedly absorbed the influence of a "foreign nature (*artfremd*)" that here seemed to impose its own law. In truth, the very demand for efficient communications that had made the success of the Third Reich possible also fueled its decline. Efficient communications, which at first had been necessary for the constitution of the German Reich, then later for its extension, and then finally for its circulation within its conquered eternity, were now altering its very Germanity (*Deutschtum*). In the name of efficiency and *Leistung*, it was now necessary to forgo the self-referentiality of German *Kultur* and the visible *Deutschtum* of its writing and instead adopt the instruments of the "civilization" described as Roman, liberal-plutocratic, or Bolshevik. The more performance was victorious, the more it reintroduced what it was supposed to eject; the more effective it was, the more the anticipated moment of "being at one with itself" receded.

The same insistence on efficient communications was formulated by Hitler across the board, from the domain of natality to those of engines and architecture. For him, the frequent propagation of life guaranteed activity, extension, and superiority. "The child will be our salvation!" he exclaimed in the train taking him to Berlin in January 1942. "The fact of always having a surplus of births will give us our chance, for that will create needs, and needs force one to be active. We do not run the risk of becoming arrested at a stage of development that obliges us always to remain at the cutting edge of technological progress. In itself this ensures our progress forward."[104] Two months later he expressed his delight that the war would provoke "a vast normalization in the technological domain." The proliferation of engine types in Germany at the time created a need for "a wide diversity of spare parts, whereas in the United States they are largely standardized." The Führer therefore urged the creation of "*a single engine* that would be *easily interchangeable* and would suit all vehicles, both on the ground and in the air."[105]

But the efficient nature of communication through architecture was certainly what excited Hitler the most, for he once wished to be the greatest architect of all time. At the age of sixteen he wanted to add one hundred meters to the length of the frieze of the Linz Museum, which was already one hundred and twenty meters long, so that his hometown should possess "the longest sculpted frieze in the world." Later he installed in his Obersalzberg house the largest pane of retractable glass in the world in order to enjoy the most beautiful panorama in the world. He was always designing and hoping to realize the largest tribunes, the highest domes, and the most gigantic triumphal arches in the whole world and "of all time."[106] Elias Canetti noticed this: "Each of his projects and each of his deepest dreams are dictated by the need to surpass. You could even call him *a slave to surpassment*. But he is not alone in this. If you had to sum up the essence of our age in a single feature, all you might find is this: the need to surpass."[107] The architecture of the excessively gigantic public buildings that Hitler planned with Speer seemed to him to have the power to dilate the present infinitely and thus to contain the whole of "the eternal substance of the people." He had giant models of these buildings paraded in the processions of the Days of German Art, while in books and reviews devoted to presenting the achievements of the new Reich, photographs of existing buildings were shown alongside photographs of the models. Here again, what had already been accomplished coexisted at the same level as what would be realized in the future. The present always had to be visibly surpassed in advance, ahead of itself, in order to demonstrate that the promised eternity was not a matter of vain words but a reality that was already there. Such a desire to extend the present infinitely, as if to enter eternity, could find a semblance of satisfaction only through an extension of the German space.

In 1933, Julius Petersen exclaimed, "Now tomorrow has become today. The end-of-the-world atmosphere has been transmuted into a beginning. The new

Reich is set up. The Führer ardently longed for and announced has appeared."[108] By the end of the regime, the motivating image (*image motrice*) of the Führer had accelerated the production of motor roads, cannons, acropolises, suspension bridges, engines, seaside resorts, television projects, "cities of the dead," ruins, and worksites, all of which coexisted in confusion. Many had believed that Hitler's image would enable them to accede more speedily to the eternal Reich, the very name of which had changed. In order that there should be no doubt as to its eternity, the Reich was no longer the "Third"; it was the "German Reich." The switch, which took effect on July 10, 1939, on the order of the Führer,[109] indicated that at long last the succession of empires and times was over and the Germans were entering into the eternal German substance. The redemptive image had wrested an entire people from its melancholy and restored its faith in itself.

In *Mein Kampf,* Hitler wrote, "Only when an epoch ceases to be haunted by the shadow of its own consciousness of guilt will it achieve the inner calm and outward strength to prune off brutally and ruthlessly the wild shoots and tear out the weeds."[110] He may not have read Freud, but he had at least understood that the image of a past purified by its organic and technical resurrection dissipated the accusatory shadows of that past and, through its "real presence," which promised the power of complete happiness, provided the strength to destroy without culpability.

REFERENCE MATTER

Notes

The complete references for works cited several times are given in the bibliography at the end of the volume.

The references to *Mein Kampf* are to the English edition (E) and the German edition (D), followed by the page numbers.

ABBREVIATIONS

Baynes: Baynes, *The Speeches of Adolf Hitler*
G. S.: Wagner, *Gesammelte Schriften*
Hinz: Hinz, *Die Malerei im deutschen Faschismus*
Mythus: Rosenberg, *The Myth of the Twentieth Century*
Principes d'action: Hitler, *Principes d'action*

POSITIONS

1. Jaspers, *La Culpabilité allemande*, p. 165.
2. Richard, *Le nazisme et la culture*, p. 176.
3. Closing speech at the Nuremberg Congress, September 1933; Hitler, *Die Reden Hitlers am Reichsparteitag 1933*, p. 37.

1. ARTIST AND DICTATOR

1. Goebbels, *Michael*, pp. 21, 41.
2. Joseph Goebbels, *Combat pour Berlin* (Paris: Société de Presse et d'Editions, 1966; originally published 1931), chap. 2, p. 38.
3. Lehmann-Haupt, *Art Under a Dictatorship*, p. 45.
4. Paul Valéry, "L'idée de dictature," Preface to Antonio Ferro, *Salazar: Le Portugal et son chef* (Paris: Grasset, 1934); Paul Valery, *Regards sur le monde actuel et autres essais* (Paris: Gallimard, 1945), p. 82.
5. Pierre Joseph Proudhon cited by Georges Sorel, *Reflections on Violence*, p. 156, n. 27.

6. Ludwig, *Talks with Mussolini*, p. 128.

7. Cited by Annette Malochet, "Novecento: Point d'ordre?" *Le Retour à l'ordre dans les arts plastiques et l'architecture, 1919–1925*, eds. J.-P. Bouillon, B. Ceysson, and F. Will-Levaillant (Cierec: Université de Saint-Etienne, 1975), p. 206.

8. Ludwig, *Talks with Mussolini*, p. 128.

9. Arendt, *The Human Condition*, p. 204.

10. Maximilien de Robespierre, "Sur les rapports des idées religieuses et morales avec les principes républicains et sur les fêtes nationales," speech given on May 7, 1794, published in *Textes choisis*, ed. J. Poperen (Paris: Editions sociales, 1958), vol. 3, p. 157.

11. Louis XIV, *Mémoires et Lettres* (Memories and letters) (Paris: Plon, 1942), p. 46. Clearly these pronouncements by the monarch should be tested against *Le Portrait du roi* (Paris: Minuit, 1981), in which Louis Marin has shown how the regime of representation was "at once the *means* of power and its *basis*" (p. 11).

12. J. Goebbels, 11 April 1933, cited by Brenner, *La Politique artistique du national-socialisme*, p. 274.

13. Hitler, *Die deutsche Kunst als stolzeste Verteidigung des deutsches Volkes*, p. 14.

14. Paul Valéry, "Lettre sur la Sociétés des Esprits," in *Oeuvres*, ed. J. Hytier (Paris: Gallimard [Pléiade], 1962; originally published 1933), vol. 1, p. 1140 (italics in original).

15. See, for example, Jochen Schmidt, *Die Geschichte des Genie-Gedankens in der deutschen Literatur, Philosophie und Politik, 1750–1945*, 2nd ed., 2 vols. (Darmstadt: Wissenschaftliche Buchgesellschaft, 1988; and, from France, Édouard Pommier, *L'Art de la liberté* (Paris: Gallimard, 1991), pp. 247–84.

16. Louis Vitet, *Le Globe*, 2 April 1825.

17. Victor Hugo, *Oeuvres Complètes, Poésie, I*, eds. J. Seebacher and G. Rosa (Paris: Robert Laffont, 1985), p. 411; Adolphe Thiers, "Le Salon de peinture de 1824," *Le Globe*, 1824, vol. 1, p. 80.

18. Jules-Antoine Castagnary, "Le Salon de 1868," *Salons (1857–1870)* (Paris: Bibliotheque-Charpentier, 1892), vol. 1, p. 291.

19. Albert Léon Gleizes and Jean Metzinger, *Du cubisme* (Sisteron: Présence, 1980; originally published Paris: Figuière, 1912), pp. 74–75.

20. Umberto Boccioni, Carlo D. Carrà, Luigi Russolo, Giacomo Balla, and Gino Severini, "Les exposants au public," in *Futurisme: Manifestes, Documents, Proclamations*, ed. G. Lista (Lausanne: L'Age d'Homme, 1973; originally published 1912), pp. 170–71.

21. Gleizes and Metzinger, *Du cubisme*, p. 74.

22. Victor Hugo, *Notre-Dame de Paris*, ed. L. Cellier (Paris: Garnier, 1967; originally published 1831), p. 202.

23. Wassily Kandinsky, *Du spirituel dans l'art, et dans la peinture en particulier* (Concerning the spiritual in art, and painting in particular), trans. N. Debrand and B. du Crest (Paris: Denoël, 1989; originally published 1912), chap. 3, p. 69.

24. Filippo T. Marinetti, "Contro l'amore et il parlamentarismo," in *Futurismo e Fascismo*, Foligno, Franco Campitelli, 1924; originally published June 1910), p. 47. Marinetti dedicated this collection of manifestos *"al mio caro e grande amico Benito Mussolini"* (to my beloved and great friend Benito Mussolini).

25. Fernand Léger, "Les origines de la peinture et sa valeur représentative," *Montjoie*, May 29, 1913.

26. Eugen Weber, *L'Action française* (The French Action), trans. M. Chrestien (Paris: Fayard, 1985), pp. 132–33.

27. Guillaume Apollinaire, "Orphée," *Oeuvres poétiques*, eds. M. Adéma and M. Décaudin (Paris: Gallimard, 1965; originally published 1917), p. 683.

28. Kasimir Edschmid, "Expressionismus in der Dichtung," *Die neue Rundschau*, March 1918, cited in Richard, *D'une apocalypse à l'autre*, p. 78.

29. Mann, *Reflections of a Nonpolitical Man*, pp. 182–83, 290.

30. Wagner, "Die Kunst und die Revolution," in *G. S.*, vol. 10, pp. 33, 40, 35.

31. See Armin Mohler, *Die Konservative Revolution in Deutschland, 1918–1932: Ein Handbuch* (The conservative revolution in Germany, 1918–1932: A handbook), 4th ed. (Darmstadt: Wissenschaftliche Buchgesellschaft, 1994; originally published 1950).

32. Kantorowicz, *The King's Two Bodies*.

33. See Ernst Kantorowicz, "The Sovereignty of the Artist: A Note on Legal Maxims and Renaissance Theories of Art," *De Artibus Opuscula XL: Essays in Honor of Erwin Panofsky*, ed. M. Meiss (New York: New York University Press, 1961), pp. 261–79.

34. Georg W. F. Hegel, *The Philosophy of Right*, trans. T. M. Knox (Chicago/London: William Benton, 1952), p. 94, para. 279.

35. François Guizot, *Histoire de la civilisation en Europe (1828–1830)*, ed. P. Rosanvallon (Paris: Hachette, 1985), p. 98.

36. *Mein Kampf*, E 471, D 579–80. See Jäckel, *Hitler idéologue*, p. 109.

37. Richard Wagner, *Les Maîtres chanteurs de Nuremberg*, trans. G. Pucher, in *Guide des opéras de Wagner*, ed. M. Pazdro (Paris, Fayard, 1988), act III, scene V, p. 430. In *The Suffering and Greatness of Richard Wagner* (*Wagner et notre temps*; Paris: Hachette, 1982; originally published 1933), Thomas Mann protested, "There is no justification for ascribing to Wagner's nationalistic gestures and declarations their present meaning—the meaning they would convey today. That would be to twist them, misuse them, and taint their Romantic purity. . . . In those days the national Ideal was poetry and spirituality, a free value for the future . . . " (p. 120). Mann, who regarded himself as a guide for Germany, refused to recognize the great movement toward the realization of the idea that was at work in Europe, particularly in Germany.

38. Arendt, *Between Past and Future*, p. 121.

39. Arno Breker, cited by R. Müller-Mehlis, *Die Kunst im dritten Reich*, pp. 93–94.

40. See Kantorowicz, *The King's Two Bodies*, passim.

41. *Principes d'action*, p. 134.

42. See Fest, *Hitler*, book 4, chap. 1.

43. The semantic field of *Volksgeist* is hard to pin down. According to Johann Gottfried Herder, the *Volksgeist* was at once the soul, spirit, genius, and daimon of the *Volk*—the people—but sometimes also of the nation, defined in terms of language, customs, taste, physiognomy, and genetics. See, for example, Johann Gottfried Herder, *Sämtliche Werke*, ed. B. Suphan (Berlin, 1877–1913), vol. 24, pp. 43–46; and vol. 14, p. 38: "Wunderbare, seltsame Sache überhaupt ists um das, was genetischer Geist und Charakter eines Volkes heisset. Er ist unklärlich und unauslösslich: so alt wie die Nation, so alt wie das Land, das sie bewohnte." Under National Socialism, *Volksgeist* became, through contamination with *völkisch*, the spirit of the people in the sense of "a community by blood and race [*Bluts-und-Artsgemeinschaft*]." The semantic field of *Volksgemeinschaft* likewise evolved. Ferdinand Tönnies (*Gemeinschaft und Gesellschaft* [Community and society], 1887) opposed the natural and organic character of the community as *Gemeinschaft* to the rational and historical character of society or collectivity as *Gesellschaft*, a term used by National Socialism to set a society of classes in opposition to the unity of a "community by destiny." See Berning, *Vom "Abstammungsnachweis" zum "Zuchtwart"*; and Hilde Kammer and Elisabet Bartsch, *Nationalsozialismus: Begriffe aus der Zeit der Gewaltherrschaft, 1933–1945*. Reinbek bei Hamburg: Rowohlt, 1992.

44. Julius Langbehn, *Rembrandt als Erzieher: Von einem Deutschen* (Rembrandt as educator: By a German) (Leipzig: Hirschfeld, 1891), pp. 267, 265.

45. H. Rauschning, *Hitler m'a dit*, p. 206. Since 1972, the trustworthiness of Hitler's pronouncements recorded by Rauschning has been brought into question (see T. Schneider, *Hermann Rauschnings "Gespräche mit Hitler": Eine Geschichtsfälschung* [Ingolstadt, 1984]). They have therefore been used in the present work only when they correspond to Hitler's pronouncements elsewhere.

46. *Mein Kampf*, E 391, 357; D 435, 433.

47. *Der Kongress zu Nürnberg*, p. 110.

48. Houston S. Chamberlain, *Immanuel Kant: Die Persönlichkeit als Einführung in das Werk* (Munich: Bruckmann, 1905); and *Die Grundlagen des 19: Jahrhunderts* (Munich: Bruckmann, 1899; *La Genèse du XIXe siècle*, French trans. R. Godet [Paris: Payot, 1913]).

49. See Marthe Bibesco, *Images d'Epinal* (Paris: Plon, 1937).

50. Vermeil, *Doctrinaires de la révolution allemande*, p. 64.

51. Hermann von Keyserling, *Das Spektrum Europas* (Heidelberg: Niels Kampmann, 1928); *Analyse spectrale de l'Europe* (Paris: Stock, 1930).

52. Thomas Mann, "Warum Hindenburg, nicht Hitler?" *Kölnische Zeitung*, 8 April 1932; cited by Walter Struve, *Elites Against Democracy: Leadership Ideals in Bourgeois Political Thought in Germany, 1890–1933* (Princeton, New Jersey: Princeton University Press, 1973), p. 312. I have borrowed much information and also the following quotations from

this remarkable work, chapter 9 of which is devoted to Keyserling ("Count Hermann Keyserling and His School of Wisdom: Grand Seigneurs, Sages, and Rulers," pp. 274–316). Struve does not mention the text in which I am interested because it falls outside the historical framework he has adopted.

53. Hermann von Keyserling, "Bücherschau" and "Zum Problem von Blut und Geist," published in the review of the School of Wisdom, *Der Weg zur Vollendung*, April 1932, vol. 20, pp. 13–14; and November 1932, vol. 21, pp. 5–6; cited by Struve, *Elites Against Democracy*, p. 3112.

54. Hermann von Keyserling, *La Révolution mondiale et la Responsabilité de l'esprit* (Paris: Stock, 1934), p. 136. The Letter/Preface by Paul Valéry is dated 12 January 1934.

55. Hermann von Keyserling, "Utopistes et prophètes," *Sur l'art de la vie*, pp. 107–11.

56. *Mein Kampf*, E 193–95, D 229–32. See Jäckel, *Hitler idéologue*, pp. 7–10.

57. Cited by Fest, *Hitler*, book 5, chap. 3.

58. Cited by Neumann, *Béhémoth*, p. 106.

59. Cited by Brenner, *La Politique artistique du national-socialisme*, p. 274.

60. Speech of 1 August 1923, Munich, Baynes, vol. 1, p. 75.

61. The quotations from "La vie est un art" are taken from Keyserling's collection *Sur l'art de la vie*, pp. 247–76.

62. Cited by Langbehn, *Rembrandt als Erzieher*, p. 65.

63. Cited by Mann, *Reflections of a Nonpolitical Man*, p. 406.

64. *Mythus*, p. 529 (p. 331 in English translation).

65. F. Lüke, *Das ABC der Rasse* (Bochum, n.d.); cited by Mann, *Dix millions d'enfants nazis*, p. 130.

66. Ferdinand Hoffmann, *Sittliche Entartung und Geburtenschwund* (Politische Biologie, no. 4; Munich/Berlin: Lehmanns, 1939), pp. 78–79.

67. Petronius, *Fragments*, 27, 1: "It is above all fear that created the gods."

68. Richard Wagner, "Das Kunstwerk der Zukunft," *G. S.*, vol. 10, p. 61.

69. Johannes Hohlfeld, *Dokumente der Deutschen Politik*, vol. 2, ed. P. Meier-Benneckenstein (Berlin: Junker und Dünnhaupt, 1939), p. 324.

2. THE ARTIST-FÜHRER: A SAVIOR

1. Dietrich Bonhoeffer's speech of 1 February 1933, cited by F. Stern, *Dreams and Illusions*, p. 224.

2. Baynes, vol. 1, p. 569.

3. These words of Paul de Lagarde are cited in *Mythus*, pp. 457–58.

4. In his second book, written in 1928, Hitler declared, "The government of our people, in the face of and against all eternal historical truth, and fully aware that it is a mistake, still allows the thesis of our culpability in the war to prevail and burdens our whole people with it (*L'Expansion du III Reich*, p. 108).

5. Mann, *Reflections of a Nonpolitical Man*, pp. 189, 21.

6. Moeller van den Bruck, *Das dritte Reich*, p. 322.

7. On this essential moment, see the classic and seminal work by Stern, *The Politics of Cultural Despair*.

8. *Mein Kampf*, E 28, D 31.

9. Thomas Mann, "Discours à des ouvriers de Vienne," speech given 1932, published in *Les Exigences du jour* (Paris: Grasset, 1976), p. 145.

10. Cited by Viereck, *Metapolitics*, pp. 144, 155, 164.

11. Cited by Fest, *Hitler*, book 4, chap. 3.

12. Mann, *La Haine*, p. 23.

13. Otto Dietrich, *12 Jahre mit Hitler* (Twelve years with Hitler). Munich: Isar-Verlag, 1955, p. 178.

14. *Mein Kampf*, E 660, D 781.

15. Hitler, speech given 16–17 January 1942, published in *Libres propos sur la guerre et sur la paix*, vol. 1, p. 212.

16. Goebbels cited by Roger Manvell and Heinrich Fraenkel, *Goebbels, sa vie, sa mort*, trans. J. and S. Ouvaroff (Paris: Robert Laffont, 1960), p. 56.

17. Cited by Viereck, *Metapolitics*, pp. 157–58. It was Funk who later chose Liszt's *Preludes* to announce the 1941 military victories against the Soviet Union (see Speer, *Inside the Third Reich*, p. 280).

18. Comments made midday on 10 May 1942; cited by Picker, *Hitler, cet inconnu*, p. 365.

19. Mann, *La Haine*, p. 33, italics added.

20. Manvell and Fraenkel, *Goebbels, sa vie, sa mort*, p. 392, n. 9.

21. Friedrich Nietzsche, "Reconnaissance Raids of an Untimely Man," in *Twilight of the Idols*, trans D. Large (Oxford/New York: Oxford University Press, 1998; originally published 1888), p. 55.

22. Guillaume Apollinaire, *Méditations esthétiques: Les peintres cubistes* (Paris: Hermann, 1965; originally published 1913), p. 47.

23. Fest, *Hitler*, book 1, chap. 4.

24. *Mein Kampf*, E 374, D 456.

25. Hitler, *Die Reden Hitlers am Reichsparteitag 1933*, p. 12.

26. Ibid., pp. 32–33: *"zu seiner dauernden Selbstbehauptung."*

27. "Rede Hitlers auf der Kulturtagung des Reichsparteitages in Nürnberg 1935," Hinz, pp. 140–42; Baynes, vol. 1, pp. 571, 572–73.

28. Hinz, p. 143; Baynes, vol. 1, p. 574.

29. Novalis (Friedrich von Hardenberg), *Schriften* (Stuttgart: Kohlhammer, 1960–75), vol. 3, p. 569 (*L'Encyclopédie*, trans. M. de Gandillac [Paris: Minuit, 1966], p. 318, fragment 1426).

30. "Kunst als Grundlage politischer Schöpferkraft: Die Aquarellen des Führers," in *Völkischer Beobachter*, Münchener Ausgabe (Munich edition), 24 April 1936, p. 1.

31. The autoproductive structure of the myth related by the Nazis has been well demonstrated by Philippe Lacoue-Labarthe and Jean-Luc Nancy in "The Nazi Myth," trans. B. Holmes, *Critical Inquiry 16*, 1990, 291–312. But Lacoue-Labarthe and Nancy still regard Nazism as "a specifically German phenomenon" (p. 27), as Nazism itself loudly claimed to be, in order to lend weight to its radical autonomy.

32. Comments made on 10 May 1942, cited in Picker, *Hitler cet inconnu*, p. 365, italics added.

33. Georg W. F. Hegel, *Lectures on Fine Arts*, trans T. M. Knox (Oxford: Clarendon Press, 1975), vol. 3, p. iii.

34. H. F. Blunck, *Wille und Macht*, 1 May 1934, p. 17, cited in Wulf, *Literatur und Dichtung im Dritten Reich*, p. 196.

35. A formula often used by Goebbels as early as 1933 and right up until 1943; see Herf, *Reactionary Modernism*, pp. 195–97.

36. Novalis, "Faith and Love, or King and Queen," *Philosophical Writings*, trans. M. M. Stoljar (New York: State University of New York Press, 1997), pp. 95–96, para. 39.

37. Cited by Joachim Fest, "Die Unfähigkeit zu überleben," in *Nationalsozialistisches Diktatur, 1933–1945: Eine Bilanz*, eds. K. D. Bracher, M. Funke, and H.-A. Jacobsen (Bonn: Bundeszentrale für politische Bildung, 1986), p. 790.

38. *Der Kongress zu Nürnberg, vom 5, bis 10, September 1934*, p. 216.

39. Kantorowicz, *The King's Two Bodies*, pp. 383–450.

40. Judith E. Schlanger, *Les Métaphores de l'organisme* (Paris: Vrin, 1971).

41. *Mein Kampf*, E 435–36, D 536–37.

42. Cited by Kershaw, *Hitler*, p. 51.

43. Stern, *Hitler*. A good description is provided by Fest, *Hitler*, book 4, chap. 3.

44. *Mein Kampf*, E 428, D 527.

45. Femininity has become a classic topic, mainly thanks to Gustave Le Bon. *Mein Kampf* also contains the following variant: "The people in their overwhelming majority are so feminine by nature and attitude that sober reasoning determines their thoughts and actions far less then emotion and feeling" [E 167, D 201].

46. Speech of 30 January 1936, cited by Fest, *Hitler*, book 1, chap 2.

47. Stern, *Hitler*, p. 28.

48. Ibid., p. 74.

49. *Der Kongress zu Nürnberg, vom 5. bis 10, September 1934*, p. 87.

50. *Mythus*, pp. 234, 273, 394.

51. Stern, *Hitler*, p. 26.

52. Kershaw, *The Nazi Dictatorship*, p. 142.

53. Broszat, *L'Etat hitlérien*, p. 49.

54. Krockow, *Les Allemands du XXe siècle*, pp. 169, 174.

55. Hanns Kerrl, Minister for the Churches of the Reich, in 1940, cited by Broszat, *L'Etat hitlérien*, p. 355.

56. Joseph Goebbels, "Erkenntnis und Propaganda," in *Signale der neuen Zeit*, p. 34.

57. Jaspers, *La Culpabilité allemande*, p. 118.

58. Jacques Ellul, *Propagandes* (Paris: Armand Colin, 1962), pp. 36–39.

59. Cited by P. Reichel, *La Fascination du nazisme*, p. 178.

60. Fest, *Hitler*, p. 747, book 8, chap. 2.

61. Rudolf Herz, *Hoffmann und Hitler: Fotographie als Medium des Führer-Mythos* (Munich: Klinkhardt & Biermann, 1994), pp. 107–13.

62. *Mein Kampf,* E 310, D 375–76.

63. Marcel Mauss, *Oeuvres*, ed. V. Karady (Paris: Minuit, 1974), vol. 2, p. 117.

64. J. Goebbels, "Erkenntnis und Propaganda," in *Signale der neuen Zeit*, pp. 29–30.

65. Kershaw, *Hitler*, p. 52.

66. Arendt, *Between Past and Future*, p. 131.

67. We should bear in mind the influence that Carl Schmitt exerted (particularly through *Der Hüter der Verfassung* [Tübingen: Mohr, 1931]) upon the Constitution of the Fifth Republic in France. René Capitant, who wrote a review of this work ("Le rôle politique du Chancellier du Reich," *Politique*, 1932, pp. 216–29) and later visited Schmitt and became friendly with him, was responsible for the "semi-presidential" form of the regime, the very considerable powers of decision (*Entscheidung*) accorded to the president, and the all-too-famous "article 16" of the constitution, which allowed the president to take action in what Schmitt, in *Political Theology*, called "exceptional situations." See A. Baring, "Ein Hüter der Verfassung? General de Gaulle und die fünfte französische Republik," *Deutsches Verwaltungsblatt*, February 1961, vol. 76, no. 3, pp. 101–8; and Piet Tommissen's introduction to the German translation of René Captitant's "L'Etat national-socialiste" in *Schmittiana-1, Electica*, nos. 71–72 (Brussels, 1990; originally published 1934), pp. 119–20. I am grateful to Antonia Birnbaum for having drawn my attention to these sources. See also Jean-Louis Schlegel's introduction to Schmitt, *Théologie politique*, p. xi.

68. Schmitt, *The Concept of the Political*, p. 38.

69. Schmitt, *Théologie politique*, pp. 15, 23, 46.

70. Rauschning, *Hitler m'a dit*, p. 278.

71. *Mein Kampf,* E 431–32, D 531–32.

72. Decree R. Min. Amtsbl., 1935 S. 43 RU II C 5209, cited by Mann, *Dix millions d'enfants nazis*, p. 126. The "desire of the Führer" to which all teachers were exhorted to respond was one he expressed in *Mein Kampf* as follows: "The crown of the folkish state's entire work of education and training must be to burn the racial sense and racial feeling into the heart and brain of the youth entrusted to it. No boy and no girl must

leave school without having been led to an ultimate realization of the necessity and essence of blood purity. Thus, the groundwork is created by preserving the racial foundations of our nation and through them in turn securing the basis for its future cultural development" [D 475–76, E 389].

73. Cited by Kershaw, *Hitler*, p. 8, n. 14.

74. *Völkischer Beobachter*, 16 August 1934, cited by Richard, *Le Nazisme et la Culture*, p. 187.

75. Stern, *Hitler*, p. 101.

76. Gottfried Benn, "Le monde dorien: Recherche sur les rapports de l'art et de la puissance," in *Un poète et le monde*, p. 216.

77. Goebbels cited by Stefan Priacel, "L'art et la propagande," in *Encyclopédie française* (Paris, 1935), vol. 16, pp. 64–68.

78. *Der Kongress zu Nürnberg, vom 5, bis 10, September 1934*, p. 28.

79. Viereck, *Metapolitics*, p. 132; *Mein Kampf*, E 194, D 232; Rauschning, *Hitler m'a dit*, p. 257.

80. Cited by Speer, *Journal de Spandau*, 7 February 1948, p. 108.

81. Alfred Roller, a former collaborator of Gustave Mahler, created the scenery and was criticized for his "sickening close relations with international Jewry." Hitler admired him and made unsuccessful advances toward him during his Viennese years; see C. Delage, *La vision nazie de l'histoire*, p. 207.

82. Himmler, *Discours secrets*, p. 46.

83. Hitler cited by Fest, *Hitler*, p. 499, book 6, chap. 1.

84. Wagner, "Die Kunst und die Revolution," *G. S.*, vol. 10, p. 44, italics added.

85. Ibid., pp. 41–42.

86. Wagner, "Das Kunstwerk der Zukunft," *G. S.*, vol. 10, p. 79.

87. *Mein Kampf*, E 345, D 419; Hitler, *Die Reden Hitlers am Reichsparteitag*, p. 30; Baynes, vol. 1, p. 573.

88. Secret order of 6 June 1941, partially cited in W. Hofer, *Der Nationalsozialismus*, p. 160, doc. 88a; the complementary passage is cited by Wulf, *Martin Bormann, l'ombre de Hitler*, p. 121, italics added.

89. Hillel and Henry, *Au nom de la race*, p. 37.

90. Schmitt, *Staat, Bewegung, Volk*, p. 42.

91. Ernst Bloch, "Amusement Co., Horreur et Troisième Reich," in *Héritage de ce temps*, p. 58.

92. Cited by Ayçoberry, *La question nazie*, pp. 45–46.

93. Cited by Kershaw, *The "Hitler Myth*,*"* p. 109.

94. Eric Voegelin, *Rasse und Staat* (Tübingen: Mohr, 1933).

95. Vermeil, *Doctrinaires de la révolution allemande*, p. 313.

96. Voegelin, *Les Religions politiques*, pp. 96–97.

97. Thomas Hobbes, *Leviathan* (London: J. M. Dent and Vermont, Charles E. Tuttle, 1994), chap. 34, p. 237.

98. *Mythus*, p. 529 (p. 331 in English translation).

99. *Mein Kampf*, E 336, D 406.

100. Elmer Davis, *Not to Mention the War* (New York: Bobbs-Merrill, 1940), pp. 205–6; cited by Viereck, *Metapolitics*, p. 139.

101. Hans Schemm, "Dem deutschen Künstler zum Gruss! Die Totalität des künstlerischen und politischen Genius" (Salute the German artist! The totality of the German artistic and political genius), *Völkischer Beobachter*, 15 October 1933, p. 1.

102. Hans Schilling, "Richard Wagner's ethischer Nationalsozialismus," *Nationalsozialistische Monatshefte*, notebook 40, July 1933, p. 297.

103. Wagner, "Die Kunst und die Revolution," *G. S.*, vol. 10, pp. 46–47.

104. Ibid., vol. 10, p. 14.

105. Gamm, *Der braune Kult*, p. 169; Schoenbaum, *Hitler's Social Revolution*, p. 76.

106. See Kershaw, *The "Hitler Myth,"* pp. 26–27.

107. Fest, *Hitler*, book 2, chap. 2. Curiously enough, Fest here repeats comments made by Hitler that he cites later, "comparing the situation of the party, its persecution, and its hardships to the situation of the early Christians (ibid., book 3, chap. 3).

108. Baynes, vol. 1, p. 78.

109. The sixteen comrades mentioned here were the NSDAP members who fell at Hitler's side in the course of the failed putsch of 9 November 1923. They occupy a central position in the Nazi blood myth. Hitler had the architect Paul Troost build two Heroes' Temples in their memory in a square in Munich. See p. 64, "The *Erlebnis* in Painting."

110. Cited by Hofer, *Der Nationalsozialismus*, p. 128, doc. 64b, 16 March 1934.

111. National Archives of Munich, cited by Fest, *Hitler*, book 3, chap. 3.

112. Cited by Fest, *Hitler*, book 5, chap. 2. An analysis of the complex positions adopted by the various churches faced with Nazism is clearly beyond the brief of this book. On this point, see, among hundreds of other studies, the recently reprinted work by Denzler and Fabricius, *Christen und Nationalsozialisten*.

113. Cited by Broszat, *L'Etat hitlérien*, p. 341.

114. Ibid., p. 346.

115. Erich von Hartz, *Wesen und Mächte des heldischen Theaters* (Berlin: Langen-Müller, 1934), p. 28, cited by Brenner, *La politique artistique du national-socialisme*, p. 157, from whom I quote.

116. Vondung, *Magie und Manipulation*, pp. 180–81.

117. *Bauamt und Gemeindebau*, vol. 16, p. 1, cited by Wulf, *Theater und Film im Dritten Reich*, p. 182.

118. Cited by Brenner, *La Politique artistique du national-socialisme*, p. 162.

119. "Entwicklung der Thingspielarbeit," *Das Deutsche Volkspiel*, vol. 1, 1933–34, p. 174, cited by Vondung, *Magie und Manipulation*, p. 153.

120. Hans Johst, *Schlageter* (Munich: Langen-Müller, 1933), p. 82.

121. Richard Euringer, "Thingspiel: Thesen I," *Völkischer Beobachter*, 20 June 1934, cited by Wulf, *Theater und Film im Dritten Reich*, pp. 184–85.

122. Fest, *Hitler*, book 5, chap. 2.

123. Gamm, *Der braune Kult*, pp. 141–44.

124. Vondung, *Magie und Manipulation*, pp. 83–85, 155–83.

125. *Mein Kampf*, D xxix (Dedication at beginning of German edition).

126. "Die Erde war mit eurem Tod zu Ende,/mit eurem Ruhm fängt unser Leben an/ . . . Führer, schreite nun aus der Helle des Ruhms,/lösten sich von dir die Schatten der Nacht,/da du die Fackel hielst an den Stufen des Todes;/Trage den Glauben uns zum Lichte voran,/dass die Steine erzittern von der Gewalt deines Schrittes" (*Gesänge unter der Fahne: Vier Kantaten*; Munich: Eher, 1935, pp. 44, 48); cited by Vondung, *Magie und Manipulation*, pp. 156, 161.

127. Hermann Burte, *Die Dichtung im Kampf des Reiches* (Hamburg: Hanseatische Verlag, 1943), p. 71; cited by J. Hermand, *Der alte Traum vom neuen Reich*, p. 285.

128. *Die neue Gemeinschaft*, 1943, p. 466; cited in Vondung, *Magie und Manipulation*, p. 167.

129. G. Troost (ed.), *Das Bauen im neuen Reich*, p. 10 (photographs from the Ehrentempel accompany the cited passage).

130. Georges Bataille, "Architecture." In *Oeuvres complètes*, ed. D. Hollier. Paris: Gallimard, 1970, vol. 1, p. 172.

131. Troost, *Das Bauen im neuen Reich*, pp. 10–14.

132. Rittich, *Architektur und Bauplastik der Gegenwart*, p. 32.

133. I. Capra, "Bekenntnis zum Führer," *Musik in Jugend und Volk, 1937–1938*, p. 227; cited by Wulf, *Literatur und Dichtung im Dritten Reich*, p. 412.

134. Roland Barthes, *Camera Lucida* (London: Vintage, 1993), pp. 87, 90, 92.

135. Rittich, "Die Werke der 'Grossen Deutschen Kunstausstellung 1942' im Haus der Deutschen Kunst in München," *Die Kunst im dritten Reich*, August-September 1942, p. 205.

136. Umberto Boccioni, Carlo D. Carrà, Luigi Russolo, Giacomo Balla, and Gino Severini, "Les exposants au public," in *Futurisme, Manifestes, Documents, Proclamations*, ed. G. Lista (Lausanne: L'Age d'Homme, 1973; originally published 1912), pp. 170–71.

137. R. Scholz, "Kunst und Gemeinschaft: Zur Grossen Deutschen Kunstausstellung 1942," *Die Kunst im dritten Reich*, August-September 1942, pp. 200–204.

138. Werner Rittich, "Malerei im Haus der deutschen Kunst, II," *Die Kunst im dritten Reich*, November 1942, p. 270. For a rather different interpretation of the role of color in the painting of the Third Reich, see André Gunthert (whose remarks have largely

stimulated my own), "Détruire la peinture: Logique de l'image totalitaire," *L'Ecrit-voir*, 1985–86, no. 7, pp. 66–75.

3. EXHIBITING THE GENIUS

1. *Mein Kampf*, E 357, D 432–33.
2. Hitler in Nuremberg on 11 September 1936, cited by Fest, *Hitler*, book 4, chap. 2.
3. *Mein Kampf*, E 185–87, D 223–25.
4. Ibid., E 263 and 269, D 318 and 325.
5. Ibid., E 268, D 324.
6. Ibid., E 270–72, D 327–31.
7. Rauschning, *Hitler m'a dit*, p. 264.
8. *Mein Kampf*, E 234–35, D 282–83. Emphasis added.
9. Ibid., E 206, D 246. Emphasis added.
10. Baynes, vol. 1, pp. 21, 30.
11. *Mein Kampf*, E 275–77, D 332–34.
12. Édouard Drumont, *La France juive* (Paris: Marpon et Flammarion, 1885), vol. 1, p. 10; Léon Poliakov, *Histoire de l'antisémitisme* (Paris: Le Seuil, 1991; originally published 1955), vol. 2, p. 291; Zeev Sternhell, *La Droite révolutionnaire: Les origines françaises du fascisme, 1885–1914* (Paris: Le Seuil, 1978), p. 154.
13. Cited by Margarete Plewnia, *Auf dem Weg zu Hitler: Der "völkische" Publizist Dietrich Eckart* (Bremen: Schünemann, 1970), p. 47.
14. *Mythus*, p. 32.
15. *Mein Kampf*, E 270–72, D 326–28.
16. Johann Gottlieb Fichte, *Addresses to the German Nation*, trans. G. A. Kelly (New York: Harper and Row, 1968), pp. 227–28, end of Address 14.
17. *Mein Kampf*, E 60, 262, 348, 356, D 70, 316, 421, 432.
18. Stern, *Hitler*, p. 41.
19. Rauschning, *Hitler m'a dit*, p. 252.
20. See the decree of 27 November 1936, reproduced by Wulf, *Die bildenden Künste im Dritten Reich*, pp. 127–29. See also Chap. 4, this volume.
21. Elvira Bauer, *Trau keinem Fuchs auf grüner Heid und keinem Jud bei seinem Heid: Ein Bilderbuch für Gross und Klein* (Don't trust a fox in a green meadow or the word of a Jew) (Nuremberg: Stürmer Verlag, 1936); cited by Peter Aley, "Das Bilderbuch im Dritten Reich," in *Das Bilderbuch: Geschichte und Entwicklung des bilderbuchs in Deutschland von den Anfängen bis zur Gegenwart*, eds. K. Doderer and H. Müller (Weinheim/Basel: Beltz, 1973), p. 330. I am grateful to Joseph Walch for having drawn my attention to this text.
22. See Norman Cohn, *Histoire d'un mythe: La "conspiration" juive et les protocoles des sages de Sion*, trans. L. Poliakov (Paris: Gallimard, 1967).

23. Werner Beumelburg, *Deutschland erwacht* (Bielefeld and Leipzig: Velhagen & Klasing, 1941), p. 56.

24. Baynes, vol. 1, pp. 59–60.

25. *Mein Kampf,* E 60, D 70. Emphasis added.

26. Ibid., E 163, D 196.

27. Ibid., E 348, D 317–18.

28. Nicephorus, *Discours contre les iconoclastes,* translated, edited, and with notes by M.-J. Mondzain-Baudinet (Paris: Klincksieck, 1989), pp. 86, sec. 244D; 9. When the German armies occupied Greece, Hitler was not surprised to learn that "the monks of Mount Athos, on whose morality he preferred not to comment, [had] proclaimed him successor to the emperor of Byzantium. . . . That is a document worth keeping," he said. Remarks made on 29 June 1942, midday. See Picker, *Hitler, cet inconnu,* pp. 473–74.

29. Baynes, vol. 1, p. 573.

30. *Mein Kampf,* E 31, D 66.

31. Ibid., E 278, D 336.

32. Ibid., E 294, D 355.

33. Oskar Schmitz cited in *Mythus,* pp. 460–61 (p. 286 in English translation).

34. *Der Jude,* special issue: "Antisemitismus und jüdisches Volkstum," 1926; Oskar Schmitz's contribution bore the unequivocal title "Wünschenswerte und nicht wünschenswerte Juden" (pp. 17–33).

35. *Mythus,* pp. 234, 273, 394.

36. *Mein Kampf,* E 452, D 557.

37. On the relationship between art and work in National Socialism, see Chapters 4 and 5 of this volume.

38. Ibid., E 265, 356; D 319–22, 432–33 for this quotation and those that follow.

39. See Goebbels, "Der Sturm bricht los" (originally published 9 July 1932), in *Signale der neuen Zeit,* p. 88; Serge Tchakotine, *Le Viol des foules par la propagande politique* (Paris: Gallimard, 1992; originally published 1932), p. 160; Pascal Ory, *La France allemand* (Paris: Gallimard/Julliard, 1977), p. 124.

40. Ernst Bloch, "Sur l'histoire originale du Troisième Reich" (originally published 1937), *Héritage de ce temps,* p. 121.

41. Cited by Krockow, *Les Allemands du XXe siècle,* p. 40. Stefan George, who claimed to support only a spiritual and artistic Reich, rejected its Nazi realization, unlike many other members of his group. One good example is provided by Claus Schenk von Stauffenberg, who at first enthusiastically regarded Hitler as the very embodiment of George's visions. Stauffenberg's slow rejection of such views gradually led him to oppose the regime and eventually to take part in the assassination attempt of 20 July 1944.

42. Included in the collection *Liederbuch des Nationalsozialistischen Deutschen Arbeiterpartei,* 50th ed. (Munich, 1941), p. 30.

43. Goebbels, *Tagebücher*, vol. 2, p. 678.

44. Billy F. Price, *Adolf Hitler: The Unknown Artist* (Houston: Billy F. Price, 1984), p. 203, cat. no. 496 (private collection, Stuttgart).

45. *Liederbuch des Nationalsozialisitischen Deutschen Arbeiterpartei*, pp. 12–13.

46. Goebbels, *Tagebücher*, vol. 2, pp. 767, 772. "Germany has awoken!" he noted on the following day (p. 773).

47. Vernon L. Lidtke, "Songs and Nazis: Political Music and Social Change in Twentieth-Century Germany," *Essays on Culture and Society in Modern Germany*, eds. G. D. Stark and B. K. Lackner (Arlington: Texas A & M University Press, 1982), p. 185; a remarkable essay on which I have drawn here.

48. See Volker Losemann, *Nazionalsozialismus und Antike* (Hamburg: Hoffmann & Campe, 1977); and Alain Schnapp, "Archéologie, archéologues et nazisme," in *Le Racisme: Mythes et Sciences*, ed. M. L. Poliakov (Brussels: Complexe, 1981).

49. The Ancestral Heritage was the name of an association founded by Himmler in July 1935. It was part of the SS and included a large archaeological section that incorporated a considerable number of distinguished universities. It devoted its efforts to showing that Germanic culture was the true heir to the Greek and Roman cultures. See Michael H. Kater, *Das Ahnenerbe der S. S., 1933–1945* (Stuttgart: DVA, 1974).

50. *Mythus*, p. 701 (p. 443 in English translation).

51. Kantorowicz, *Frederick the Second*, p. 607.

52. Hermann Goering, cited by Ayçoberry, *La Question nazie*, p. 128.

53. W. Hartmann, "Die Einheit deutscher Kunst," *Nazionalsozialistische Monatshefte*, July 1938, no. 100, pp. 611–27 (in particular 615–16).

54. Pierre Francastel, *L'Histoire de l'art: instrument de la propagande germanique* (completed in April 1940) (Paris: Librairie de Médicis, 1945), pp. 130–31. See, for example, L. Courajod, *Leçons professées à l'Ecole du Louvre (1887–1896)*, vol. 3 (Paris: Picard, 1903), pp. 127 ("Résistances de l'art national"), 241: "Les dangers du *Cosmopolitisme* en littérature et en art ont été très bien entrevus par Mme de Stael. La première, elle a compris comment l'Allemagne était parvenue à se relever par la culture du sentiment national, par le réveil du sentiment ethnique." ("The dangers of *Cosmopolitanism* in literature and art were very well understood by Mme de Stael. She was the first to see how Germany managed to rise again by cultivating national feeling and reawakening a sense of ethnicity.")

55. Charles Dempsey, "National Expression in Italian Sixteenth-Century Art: Problems of the Past and Present," in Erlin, *Nationalism in the Visual Arts*, pp. 15–24.

56. David Rousset, *L'Univers concentrationnaire* (Paris: Editions du Pavois, 1946), p. 114.

57. See *Devant l'histoire*, in particular pp. 56, 160.

58. *Mythus*, pp. 678–79 (pp. 428–29 in English translation).

59. *Mein Kampf*, E 191–95, D 229–34.

60. *Mythus*, pp. 455–56 (pp. 282–83 in English translation), italics in original.

61. Ibid., p. 689.

62. *Mythus*, p. 679 (p. 429 in English translation).

63. Baldur von Schirach, "Kunst und Wirklichkeit," in *Koralle: Wochenschrift für Unterhaltung, Wissen, Lebensfreude*, 9 November 1941, no. 45, p. 1086–88.

64. *L'Art et la Réalité, L'Art et l'Etat* (Paris: Institut international de coopération intellectuelle and League of Nations, 1935), pp. 30, 61, 71, 295.

65. See Paul Nizan, "Pour un réalisme socialiste par Aragon," *L'Humanité*, 12 August 1935; reprinted in Nizan, *Pour une nouvelle culture* (Paris: Grasset, 1971), p. 178; *La Querelle du réalisme* (Paris: Cercle d'Art, 1987; originally published 1936), p. 52.

66. André Breton, "Situation surréaliste de l'objet" (originally published 1935), *Oeuvres complètes*, vol. 2, ed. M. Bonnet (Paris: Gallimard, 1992), p. 496; Piet Mondrian, "La morphoplastique et la néoplastique," speech given 15 April, 1930, published in *Circle et Carré*, no. 2 (Paris: Belfond, 1971), p. 73.

67. Hans-Jürgen Syberberg, "Hitler artiste de l'Etat ou l'avant-garde méphistophélique du XXe siècle," *Les Réalismes 1919–1939*, ed. G. Régnier, exhibition catalogue (Paris: Centre Georges Pompidou, 1980), p. 378.

68. Jean-Claude Schmitt, "L'Occident, Nicée II et les images du VIIIe au XIIIe siècle," in *Nicée II, 787–1987: Douze siècles d'images religieuses*, eds. E. Boespflug and N. Losky (Paris: Cerf, 1987), p. 300.

69. Richard Wagner, "Das Kunstwerk der Zufunft," *G. S.*, vol. 10, p. 79.

70. Müller-Mehlis, *Die Kunst im dritten Reich*, 1938; cited by Adam, *Art of the Third Reich*, p. 130. Wagner wrote: "The work of art is living religion represented; but it is not the artist who invents the religions; they come only from the *people*" (*G. S.*, vol. 10, p. 70).

71. *Mythus*, p. 443: *Das Kunstwerk is die lebendig dargestellte Religion.* Wagner's statement also served as an epigraph to part 2 of *Mythus*, devoted to German art, p. 275 (pp. 271–72, 167 in English translation).

72. Gert Theunissen, "Der Mensch der Technik," *Der Deutsche Baumeister*, no. 2, Munich, 1942. Cited in an appendix to Speer, *L'Immoralité du pouvoir*, pp. 181–83.

73. K. J. Fischer, "Das Haus der deutschen Kunst in München," *Deutsche Kunst und Dekoration*, Sept. 1933, p. 369.

74. "Nachklang zum Fest der Deutschen Kunst," *Die Kunst*, December 1933, vol. 69, notebook 3, pp. 79–83.

75. *Mythus*, p. 700 (p. 442 in English translation).

76. Hans Schemm, "Dem deutschen Künstler zum Gruss! Die Totalität des künstlerischen und politischen Genius," *Völkischer Beobachter*, 15 October 1933.

77. See M. A. von Lüttichau,"Deutsche Kunst" und "Entartete Kunst," in *Die Münchner Ausstellung 1937, Die "Kunststadt" München 1937, Nationalsozialismus und "Entartete Kunst"* ed. P. K. Schuster (Munich: Prestel, 1987), pp. 83–118.

78. E. Schindler, "Gedanken zur deutschen bildenden Kunst in Vergangenheit und Gegenwart," *Das Bild,* September 1936, no. 9; cited in Klaus Wolbert, "Programmatische Malerei," *Kunst im 3. Reich: Dokumente der Unterwerfung,* p. 140.

79. Speech of 1 May 1936, at Chamber of Culture of the Reich.

80. Martin Heidegger, *Poetry, Language, Thought,* trans. A. Hofstadter (New York: Harper and Row, 1975), pp. 77–78.

81. Ayçoberry, *La Question nazie,* pp. 138–39, 159. The British political analyst cited and summarized by Ayçoberry is Harold J. Laski, author of "The Meaning of Fascism" and "The Threat of Counter-Revolution," in *Reflections on the Revolution of our Time* (London: Allen & Unwin, 1943).

82. Louis Aragon, Speech at the last Paris session of the Second International Congress of Writers, *Commune,* August 1937, pp. 1416, 1420–21, italics in original.

83. Louis Aragon, "Réalisme socialiste et réalisme français," *Europe,* March 1938; cited by Patrick Weiser, "L'Exposition internationale, L'Etat et les Beaux-Arts," *Paris 1937–1957,* exhibition catalogue (Paris: Centre Georges Pompidou, 1981), p. 58.

84. Hans Weigert, *Geschichte der deutschen Kunst* (Berlin: Propyläen Verlag, 1942), Preface; cited by Bettina Preiss, "Eine Wissenschaft wird zur Dienstleistung: Kunstgeschichte im Nationalsozialismus," in Brock and Preiss, *Kunst auf Befehl?,* p. 55.

85. "Le Trocadéro, nouveau Palais de Chaillot," *Le Livre d'or officiel de l'Exposition internationale des arts et techniques dans la vie moderne* (Paris, SPEC, 1937), p. 53.

86. Ibid., p. 58; and Speer, *Inside the Third Reich,* p. 81.

87. See K. Arndt, "Das 'Haus der Deutschen Kunst'," in *Die "Kunststadt München" 1937, Nationalsozialismus und "Entartete Kunst,"* ed. P. K. Schuster, pp. 73–75.

88. Mann, *Diaries 1918–1939,* pp. 170–71.

89. Anatole de Monzie, Preface to the catalogue *L'Affiche en couleurs: de Chéret à nos jours* (Paris: Conservatoire national des arts et métiers, 1939).

90. Otto Rank, *Art and Artist: Creative Urge and Personality Development,* translated by C. F. Atkinson (New York/London: Norton, 1989), pp. 19–20.

91. Schultze-Naumburg, *Kulturarbeiten,* vol. 1, *Hausbau,* Preface (no pagination).

92. Heinrich Wölfflin, *Principes fondamentaux de l'histoire de l'art: Le problème de l'évolution du style dans l'art moderne,* trans. C. and M. Raymond (Paris: Gallimard, 1966; originally published 1915), pp. 11, 13, 268, 270, 277.

93. The Union Fighting for German Culture was an offshoot of the National Socialist Society for German Culture, the statutes of which declared its goal to be "to enlighten the German people on the links between race, art, science, and moral and military values" (see Brenner, *La Politique artistique du national-socialisme,* pp. 18–20).

94. Wölfflin, *Principes fondamentaux de l'histoire de l'art,* p. 268.

95. Wilhelm Worringer, *Form in Gothic* (London: Putnam's, 1927), p. 180. Worringer explained, "We must not understand race in the narrow sense of racial purity: here the

word *race* must include all the peoples in the composition of which the Germans have played a decisive part. And that applies to the greater part of Europe. Wherever Germanic elements are strongly present, a racial connection in the widest sense is observable, which, *in spite of* racial differences in the ordinary sense, is unmistakenly operative" (ibid., p. 180).

96. Hagen, *Deutsches Sehen*, p. 126.

97. Jean-Claude Lebensztejn, *L'Art de la tache: Introduction à la nouvelle méthode d'Alexander Cozens* (Valence: Editions du Limon, 1990), p. 326.

98. Paul Schultze-Naumburg, "Hermann Urban: Der Meister der heroischen Landschaft," *Die Kunst im deutschen Reich* (Art in the German Reich), July 1941, pp. 196–203 (in particular p. 197).

99. In this case, however, the painting did not anticipate an ideal world but was quite simply lying, for it was not ordinary workers who were employed in these quarries of the Reich but prisoners from the camps.

100. See Herf, *Reactionary Modernism*, in particular chap. 4: "Ernst Jünger's Magical Realism," pp. 70–108.

101. Jünger, *Le Travailleur*, chaps. 59–62, pp. 253–56.

102. Wilhelm Rüdiger, *Kunst und Technik* (Munich: House of German Technique, 1941), pp. vi, viii. Leonardo da Vinci was one of the great artist figures constantly claimed by German-Nordic culture because of his "obviously" Aryan origins.

103. Ibid., p. xxiii and xv.

104. *Mein Kampf,* E 344, D 416.

105. Ibid., E 362, D 416.

106. On the internal NSDAP ideological conflicts during this period, see Brenner, *La Politique artistique du national-socialisme*, chap. 4: "L'art dans la bataille politique, 1933–1934," pp. 101–33.

107. Hitler, 5 September 1934, in *Der Kongress zu Nürnberg vom 5, bis 10, September 1934*, pp. 103–4.

108. Speer, *Journal de Spandau*, 16 January 1951, p. 204.

109. Fernand Léger, "Couleur dans le monde," in *Fonctions de la peinture* (Paris: Gonthier, 1965), p. 89; originally published in *Europe*, 1938.

110. Hitler, *Die deutsche Kunst als stolzeste Verteidigung des deutschen Volkes*, p. 13; *Principes d'action*, p. 71.

111. *Mein Kampf,* E 264, D 318.

4. REPRODUCING THE GENIUS

1. Fest, *Hitler*, book 6, chap. 2.

2. *Mein Kampf,* E 360–62, D 436–39.

3. Ibid., E 365–67, D 445–50 (Hitler's italics).

4. Ibid., E 27, D 29, italics in original.

5. Alexis Carrel, *Man, the Unknown* (New York/London: Harper, 1935), pp. 298, 299, 274, 273, 319.

6. Ibid., pp. 274–75. On Carrel, see Lucien Bonnafé and Patrick Tort, *L'Homme, cet inconnu? Alexis Carrel, Jean-Marie Le Pen et les chambres à gaz* (Paris: Syllepse, 1992).

7. Proctor, *Racial Hygiene*, chap. 4: "The Sterilization Law," pp. 95–117.

8. See Wulf, *Die bildenden Künste im dritten Reich*, pp. 388–89.

9. Brenner, *La Politique artistique du national-socialisme*, p. 266, document 7.

10. Brenner, ibid., p. 51, which provides a summary of the lecture given by Schultze-Naumburg in January 1935 at the NSDAP Egensdorf School, originally published in the *Allgemeine Thüringische Landeszeitung*, January 1935.

11. Hans F. K. Günther, *Rassenkunde des deutschen Volkes* (Munich: J. F. Lehmanns, 1923); Günther, *Rasse und Stil* (Munich: J. F. Lehmanns, 1926).

12. Ludwig Ferdinand Clauss, *Die nordische Seele* (Munich: J. F. Lehmanns, 1923); Clauss, *Rasse und Seele* (Munich: J. F. Lehmanns, 1926).

13. Cited by Bracher, *La Dictature allemande*, p. 343.

14. Schultze-Naumburg, *Kampf um die Kunst* (München: Eher, 1932), p. 43.

15. Schultze-Naumburg, *Kunst und Rasse*, pp. 5, 9.

16. Ibid., pp. 17–20.

17. Leonardo da Vinci, cited by Schultze-Naumburg, *Kunst und Rasse*, pp. 21–22. It is worth noting that Schultze-Naumburg translated "the true manner of painting" as *die wahre Art und Weise*.

18. Ibid., pp. 22–23.

19. Hitler, *Die deutsche Kunst als stolzeste Verteidigung des deutschen Volkes*, pp. 8, 11; Hitler, *Principes d'action*, pp. 65, 68.

20. *Mythus*, p. 303.

21. Jokisch, *Das dynamische Gestaltungsprinzip der deutschen Kunst*, p. 7.

22. Schmitt, *Staat, Bewegung, Volk*, p. 42. *Artgleichheit* translates as "racial similarity." The Nazis generally treated the words *Art* (species) and *Rasse* (race) as synonyms, as can be seen from what immediately follows the cited passage: "When the idea of race [*der Gedanke der Rasse*] was repeatedly treated as central in the Congress of German National Socialist Leipzig jurists in 1933—in the Führer's magnificent closing speech, in the rousing address of the leader of the *Deutsche Reichsfront*, Dr. Hans Frank; and in the remarkable reports of specialists, in particular that of H. Nicolai—it was by no means a postulate of theoretical imagination. Without the principle of *Artgleichheit*, the National Socialist State could not exist and its juridical life would be unthinkable; it would immediately be once again delivered up to its liberal and Marxist enemies, who would now condescendingly criticize it, now cravenly assimilate themselves with it."

23. Just as all non-Aryans were excluded from the *Volksgemeinschaft* because they could not "understand" a *Führung* who was not *artgleich* to them, so too did the Reich's

Chamber of Culture exclude all non-Aryan artists, thereby preventing them from exercising their profession. They were sent a circular letter that in itself set out the political and artistic program:

> By the will of the Führer and Chancellor of the Reich, the management of the German cultural legacy can be entrusted only to co-citizens [*Volksgenossen*] who are qualified and reliable in the sense of paragraph 10 of the first decree introducing the fundamental law of the Chamber of Culture of the Reich. In view of the loftiness of thought needed by the intellectual activity that creates culture, and in consideration of the existence and future development of the German people, the only people truly qualified to exercise such activity in Germany are those who not only belong to the German people as citizens but also are tied to it by the deep bond of race and blood. Only a man who feels linked to his people and under obligation to it by reason of his racial community is qualified to try to exert influence on the intimate life of the nation by producing works of a kind to bear fruit and be strongly constructed on these principles, as is required by all intellectual and cultural creation. Through your quality as a non-Aryan, you are not capable of feeling and understanding that obligation. . . .

From letter sent in February 1935 by the president of the Chamber of Literature of the Reich, cited by E. Wernert, *L'Art dans le III Reich: Une tentative d'esthétique dirigée* (Paris: Paul Hartmann, 1936), 130–31.

24. Schultze-Naumburg, *Kunst und Rasse*, pp. 74–77; italics in original.

25. Paul Westheim, "Rassebiologische Ästhetik," *Zeitschrift für freie deutsche Forschung*, 1938, vol. 1, no. 2, pp. 113–23; reprinted in Westheim, *Kunstkritik aus dem Exil*, pp. 18–19, 26.

26. Baynes, vol. 1, p. 574.

27. Gotthold Ephraim Lessing, *Laocoon*, trans. E. A. McCormick (Baltimore/London: Johns Hopkins University Press, 1962), pp. 13–14.

28. Ibid., p. 13, note g.

29. Louis Leroy, *Le Charivari*, 16 April 1877; cited by Michel Hoog, *L'Univers de Cézanne* (Paris: Crespel, 1971), p. 10.

30. Ambroise Paré, *Des monstres et prodiges* (Geneva: J. Céard, 1971), chap. 9, pp. 35–36.

31. Heliodorus, *The Ethiopica (Theagenes and Chariclea)*, book 4, chap. 8 (par. 3–5); book 10, chap. 14 (par. 7).

32. St. Augustine, *Against Julian*, trans. M. A. Schumacher (New York: Fathers of the Church, 1957), p. 292.

33. See Daniel P. Walker, *Spiritual and Demonic Magic: From Ficino to Campanella* (London: Warburg Institute, University of London, 1958), pp. 33, 160, 162, 179.

34. Claude Quillet, *La Callipédie ou manière de faire de beaux enfants*, trans. C.-P. de M. d'Egly (Paris: Durand, Pissot, 1749), p. 110; cited by Pierre Darmon, *Le Mythe de la procréation à l'âge baroque* (Paris: Le Seuil, 1981), pp. 167–68.

35. Giulio Mancini, *Considerazioni sulla pittura* (Rome: A. Marucchi, 1956), vol. 1, p. 143; cited by David Freedberg, *The Power of Images: Studies in the History and Theory of Response* (Chicago/London: University of London Press, 1989), p. 3.

36. Benn, "Expressionisme," in *Un poète et le monde*, p. 188.

37. Tommaso Campanella, *La Cité du soleil*, trans. A. Tripet (Geneva: Droz, 1972), pp. 37, 20, 49.

38. Johann Joachim Winckelmann, *Reflections on the Painting and Sculpture of the Greeks*, trans. H. Fusseli (London: Menston, 1972; originally published 1765), lines 180–84, 210–12.

39. Ibid., lines 319–20, 327–40.

40. Charles Baudelaire, "Le peintre de la vie moderne," in *Curiosités esthétiques: L'Art romantique*, ed. H. Lemaître, (Paris: Garnier, 1962), pp. 454–55.

41. Hyppolyte Taine, *De l'Idéal dans l'art* (Paris: G. Baillière, 1867), pp. 81, 126.

42. Oscar Wilde, "The Decay of Lying," in *The Complete Works* (Glasgow: Harper-Collins, 1994), pp. 1082–83. Readers curious about the avatars of this myth may also consult the first pages of Milan Kundera's *Life Is Elsewhere* (Glasgow: HarperCollins, 1974).

43. Speech of 22 May 1936, addressed to the Hitler Youth organization; see Himmler, *Discours secrets*, pp. 60–62.

44. Darré, *La Race*, pp. 35–36.

45. Ibid., p. 168.

46. Ibid., pp. 176–78.

47. Ibid., pp. 181, 183, 188.

48. Ibid., p. 227. The "desire for a type" (*Typensehnsucht*) had already been affirmed by Rosenberg in 1929, "Gestalt und Seele," *Mitteilungen des Kampfbundes für deutsche Kultur*, vol. 1, no. 1, p. 11 (CDJC CXLVI-1).

49. Darré, *La Race*, p. 238.

50. Ibid., p. 251.

51. Hans F. K. Günther, *Der nordische Gedanke unter den Deutschen* (Munich: Lehmanns, 1927); cited in Darré, ibid., p. 283.

52. W. Scheidt, cited by Benoit Massin, "Anthropologie raciale et national-socialisme: Heurs et malheurs du paradigme de la 'race'," in Olff-Nathan, *La Science sous le Troisième Reich*, p. 233.

53. Fritz Lenz, cited in Erwin Baur, Eugen Fischer, and F. Lenz, *Menschliche Erblichkeitlehre und Rassenhygiene*, vol. 2: *Menschliche Auslese und Rassenhygiene* (Munich: Lehmann, 1923), p. 334; cited in Massin, "Anthropologie raciale et national-socialisme," p. 246; see also p. 249 for parallel citations from Lenz and Hitler.

54. See Armand Zaloszyc, *Le Sacrifice au Dieu Obscur: Ténèbres et pureté dans la communauté*, (Nice: Z Editions, 1994), pp. 47–48.

55. Houston S. Chamberlain, *La Genèse du XIXe siècle* (Neuchâtel, Switzerland:

Delachaux et Niestlé, 1913; originally published 1899), p. 362; cited by Murard and Zylberman, *Le Soldat du travail,* p. 527, which rightly emphasizes this "racial state axiom": "race will come."

56. Erwin Panofsky, *Idea: A Concept in Art Theory,* trans. J. J. S. Peake (New York/London: Harper & Row, 1968), pp. 105–11, 155–57 (Appendix II).

57. Sir Joshua Reynolds, *Discourses on Art* (New Haven/London: Yale University Press, 1975), Discourse 3, p. 41.

58. Jean-Claude Lebensztejn, "De l'Imitation dans les beaux-arts," *Critique,* January 1982, no. 416, pp. 12–13. *Essay on Nature: The End and the Means of Imitation in the Fine Arts* was originally published in 1823.

59. Wilde, *The Decay of Lying,* p. 1083.

60. *Der Kongress zu Nürnberg, vom 5, bis 9, September 1934,* p. 99.

61. Kurt Engelbrecht, a pastor who was a lover of the arts, loudly proclaimed this in 1933: "The time for materialism in the natural sciences is over. We no longer regard race as something purely physiological, something materially natural. We know that the spirit and the *Gestalt,* the souls and the form, are deeply anchored in each other and mutually linked. We know that it is not matter that by chance constructs a spirit and a soul for itself, but rather the spirit and the soul create the *Gestalt* and form that suit them, in accordance with a plan." Kurt Engelbrecht, *Deutsche Kunst im totalen Staat* (Lahr in Baden: Keutel, 1933), pp. 18–19; cited in Wulf, *Literatur und Dichtung im dritten Reich,* pp. 439–40.

62. Jan Patočka, *L'Art et le temps,* trans. E. Abrams (Paris: P. O. L., 1990), p. 359.

63. "Rede Hitlers bei der Eröffnung der 'Ersten Grossen Deutschen Kunstausstellung' 1937," Hinz, p. 165–66.

64. "Rede Hitlers bei der Eröffnung der 'Zweiten Grossen Deutschen Kunstausstellung' 1938," Hinz, pp. 176–77.

65. *Mein Kampf,* E 238, D 287.

66. See Paul Schultze-Naumburg, "Unsere Sehnsucht und das griechische Menschenbild," *Die Sonne,* 1929, vol. 6, p. 416.

67. *Mein Kampf,* E 344, D 416, for this and the following quotation.

68. Proctor, *Racial Hygiene,* pp. 112–14.

69. A mistake recently made again by Stephanie Barron, "1937: Modern Art and Politics in Prewar Germany," in "Degenerate Art," p. 12.

70. Schultze-Naumburg, *Kunst und Rasse,* p. 89.

71. Ibid., pp. 100–101.

72. Joseph Goebbels, "Nationalsozialistische Kunstpolitik: Rede zur Jahrestagung der Reichskammer der bildenden Künste in München," speech given 15 July 1939, published in *Die Zeit ohne Beispiel,* pp. 206–7.

73. "Rede Hitlers auf der Kulturtagung des Reichs parteitages in Nürnberg 1935,"

Hinz, p. 147; Baynes, vol. 1, pp. 577, 578. In his lecture "The Origin of the Work of Art," Heidegger is emphatic: "A genuine beginning [*Anfang*], however, has nothing of the neophyte character of the primitive. The primitive, because it lacks the bestowing, grounding leap and head start, is always futureless. It is not capable of releasing anything more from itself because it contains nothing more than that in which it is caught." *Poetry, Language, Thought*, trans. A. Hofstadter (New York: Harper & Row, 1975), p. 76.

74. L. von Denger, *Blick in der Zeit* (Berlin, 26 April 1935), p. 14; cited by Wulf, *Die bildenden Künste im dritten Reich*, pp. 302–3.

75. Letter to Edouard Manet, 11 May 1865, in Charles Baudelaire, *Correspondance*, eds. C. Pichois and J. Ziegler (Paris: Gallimard, 1973), vol. 2, pp. 496–97.

76. In this respect, the same treatment was once again meted out to the Jew—or to any "enemy of the community"—and to Judeo-Bolshevik art. This treatment involved exhibitions, ostensibly for pedagogic purposes, such as "The Eternal Jew" (*Der ewige Jude*), which opened in Munich in 1937, soon after the other two exhibitions; expulsions from institutions and public places; locking up and exploitation (in camps and factories); exploitation of marketable valuables; and general destruction. It was clearly only at the last stage (of destruction) that the fantasy of total, pure Aryan visibility began to be realized.

77. Melita Maschmann, *Ma Jeunesse au service du nazisme (Fazit: Mein Weg in der Hitler-Jugend)* (Paris: Plon, 1964), pp. 253, 270.

78. Schmitt, *Staat, Bewungen, Volk*, p. 46.

79. Ibid., pp. 45, 46.

80. "Wir sind geboren, für Deutschland zu sterben"; cited by Peter D. Stachura, "Das Dritte Reich und die Jugenderziehung: Die Rolle der Hitler-Jugend 1933–1939," in Bracher, Funke, and Jacobsen, *Nationalsozialistische Diktatur 1933–1945*, p. 234, n. 46.

81. Arendt, *The Origins of Totalitarianism*, p. 470.

82. Ibid., p. 466.

83. Cited by Mann, *Dix Millions d'enfants nazis*, p. 127.

84. On the many *Judgment of Paris* paintings produced under the Third Reich, see Hinz, pp. 88–93.

85. Speech given 22 June 1936, published in *Discours secrets*, p. 54.

86. Hitler, "Rede vor der -NS-Frauenschaft," in *Der Kongress zu Nürnberg vom 5. bis 10. September 1934*, p. 170.

87. Cited by Koonz, *Les Mères-Patrie du III Reich*, p. 201.

88. Himmler, *Discours secrets*, pp. 54–55.

89. Baudelaire, "Les martyrs ridicules par Léon Cladel," *Oeuvres complètes*, vol. 2, ed. C. Pichois (Paris: Gallimard, 1976), p. 183.

90. *Informationsdienst*, 20 June 1938; cited by Proctor, *Racial Hygiene*, p. 290.

91. Speech of 18 February 1937 to the SS generals; Himmler, *Discours secrets*, pp. 84–85.

92. Cited by Arendt, *The Origins of Totalitarianism*, pp. 322–33.

93. On Gertrud Scholtz-Klink, see Koonz, *Les Mères-Patrie du III Reich*.

94. Speech given by G. Scholtz-Klink, published as "Die Tagung der deutschen Frauenschaft," *Der Parteitag der Ehre, vom 8, bis 14, September 1936*, p. 162.

95. Rita Thalmann, "Zwischen Mutterkreuz und Rüstungsbetrieb: Zur Rolle der Frau im Dritten Reich," in Bracher, Funke, and Jacobsen, *Nationalsozialistische Diktatur 1933–1945*, p. 205.

96. All of these faces and bodies may today appear quite unattractive. That does not, however, justify applying to them such terms as "Beauty without sensuality," as an ethnologist who has strayed among African women with plates in their lips might do (George L. Mosse, "Beauty Without Sensuality: The Exhibition *Entartete Kunst*," in Barron, *"Degenerate Art,"* pp. 25–31). The error is even more surprising coming from such a knowledgeable expert on Nazism.

97. Cited by Hillel and Henry, *Au nom de la race*, p. 37.

98. Cited by William L. Shirer, *The Rise and Fall of the Third Reich* (New York: Simon and Schuster, 1981), p. 254.

99. Cited by Hillel and Henry, *Au nom de la race*, p. 38.

100. Minutes of 11 January 1941, cited by Hillel and Henry, ibid., p. 61. We may assume that these were the works reproduced in 1936 in a Lebensborn brochure, the photographs of which were later published by Stefanie Poley, "Eine Mutter wie die Jungfrau Maria," in *Rollenbilder im Nationalsozialismus: Umgang mit dem Erbe*, p. 129 (illustrations 38–39).

101. Schirach, "Über die Bauten der Jugend," speech given 17 October 1937, published in *Revolution der Erziehung*, p. 85: "Ich glaube an die alles bestimmende Macht des Vorbildes."

102. Willrich, *Die Säuberung des Kunsttempels.*

103. Ibid., p. 151.

104. Ibid., p. 145.

105. Ibid., pp. 147–48.

106. Ibid., pp. 150–51, 153.

107. Letter from Willrich to Himmler, 2 November 1938; cited in Wulf, *Die bildenden Künste im Dritten Reich*, p. 394.

108. Cited by Ayçoberry, *La Question nazie*, pp. 45–46.

109. Adolf Hitler, "Rede Hitlers auf der Kulturagung des Reichsparteitages in Nürnberg 1935," Hinz, p. 139; Hitler, *Principes d'action*, p. 78.

110. This section owes much to an as yet unpublished essay on Gottfried Benn by Werner Hamacher, "Politisch Blau." It constitutes both a distant echo and a response to that essay.

111. See Wulf, *Die bildenden Künste im Dritten Reich*, pp. 136–44.

112. Benn, "Expressionisme," *Un poète et le monde*, pp. 178–82, 186, 188, originally published 1933; italics added.

113. Wilhelm Rüdiger, "Grundlagen deutscher Kunst," *Naitionalsozialistische Monatshefte*, October 1933, no. 43, p. 469 (which is entirely devoted to "the new Germany and art").

114. Benn, "Le monde dorien: Recherche sur les rapports de l'art et de la puissance," in *Un poète et le monde*, p. 215; originally published 1934.

115. Benn, "Problèmes de la création poétique," in *Un poète et le monde*, p. 88; originally published 1930.

116. Edgar Allen Poe, "Eureka" (chap. 4), *The Works of Edgar Allan Poe*, vol. 16 (New York:, AMS Press, 1965).

117. Benn, "La structure de la personnalité," in *Un poète et le monde*, p. 103; originally published 1930.

118. Benn, "Goethe et les sciences naturelles," in *Un poète et le monde*, p. 161; originally published 1932.

119. Benn, "L'Etat nouveau et les intellectuels," in *Un poète et le monde*, p. 168; originally published 1933.

120. Benn, "Ombres du passé," in *Double vie*, pp. 84–85.

121. Benn, "Vie provoquée," in *Un poète et le monde*, pp. 245, 247, 255, 254; originally published 1943.

122. Benn, "Ombres du passé," in *Double vie*, p. 87; italics added.

123. Benn, "Expressionisme," in *Un poète et le monde*, pp. 182, 187; originally published 1933.

124. Benn, "Le monde dorien," in *Un poète et le monde*, p. 216; originally published 1933.

125. Benn, "Problèmes de la création poétique," in *Un poète et le monde*, p. 170; originally published 1930.

126. Benn, "L'Etat nouveau et les intellectuels," *Un poète et le monde*, p. 170; originally published 1933.

127. Ibid., p. 169.

128. Benn, "Goethe et les sciences naturelles," in *Un poète et le monde*, p. 162; originally published 1932.

129. Hans Friedrich Blunck, *Völkischer Beobachter*, 22 September 1934, translated and cited by Richard, *Le Nazisme et la culture*, p. 200.

130. Schultze-Naumburg, *Kulturarbeiten*, Preface (not paginated).

131. Klemperer, *LTI*.

132. M. Simon, "Der Führer," *Das Inner Reich*, December 1938, p. 970; cited by Wulf, *Literatur und Dichtung im Dritten Reich*, p. 419.

133. Cited by Günter Kaufmann, *Das kommende Deutschland: Die Erziehung der Ju-*

gend im Reich Adolf Hitlers (Berlin: Junker und Dünnhaupt, 1943), p. 301; cited in Gamm, *Führung und Verfürung*, p. 358.

134. Hamacher, "Politisch Blau," pp. 17–18.

135. Speech given 18 February 1937, published in Himmler, *Discours secrets*, p. 81.

136. Alfred Bäumler, *Männerbund und Wissenschaft* (Berlin: Junker und Dünnhaupt, 1937), p. 127; cited by Wulf, *Literatur und Dichtung im Dritten Reich*, p. 403.

137. Jacques Lacan, "Hamlet: VII—Phallophanie," *Ornicar?*, 1983, nos. 26–27, p. 32. I am grateful to Werner Hamacher for drawing my attention to this text.

138. Leon Battista Alberti, *On Painting and On Sculpture*, trans. C. Grayson (London: Phaidon Press, 1972), p. 61, section 25.

139. Hitler cited by Baldur von Schirach, "Kunst und Wirklichkeit," *Koralle: Wochenschrift für Unterhaltung, Wissen, Lebensfreude*, 9 November 1941, no. 45, p. 1088.

140. *Mein Kampf,* E 263, 486; D 318, 598.

141. Benn, "Le monde dorien," in *Un poète et le monde*, originally published 1933.

142. Jünger, *Le Travailleur*, chap. 60, p. 259.

143. Ibid.

144. *Anordnung des Reichsminister für Volksaufklärung und Propaganda über Kunstkritik*, November 11, 1936, cited by Wulf, *Die bildenden Künste im Dritten Reich*, pp. 127–28.

145. *Mein Kampf,* E 427, D 526.

146. Emil Dovifat, *Zeitungslehre*, 1937, vol. 2, pp. 66–69; cited in Wulf, *Die bildenden Künste im Dritten Reich*, pp. 135–36. Goebbels, for his part, was more direct: "Who are the people to criticize? Party members? No. The rest of the Germans? They should consider themselves lucky to be still alive. It would be too much of a good thing altogether if those who live at our mercy should be allowed to criticize." Cited in Arendt, *The Origins of Totalitarianism*, p. 360, n. 52.

147. Rauschning, *Hitler m'a dit*, p. 252.

148. "Rede Hitlers auf der Kulturtagung des Reichsparteitages in Nürnberg 1935," Hinz, p. 151; Baynes, vol. 1, p. 583.

149. Speech given night of 1 December 1941; cited in Picker, *Hitler, cet inconnu*, p. 166.

150. Rauschning, *Hitler m'a dit*, p. 254.

151. H. von Hofmannstahl, cited by Stern, *Rêves et illusions*, p. 212.

152. François Guizot, "Philosophie politique: de la souveraineté," in *Histoire de la civilisation en Europe*, ed. P. Rosanvallon (Paris: Hachette, 1985), p. 320.

153. Thomas Carlyle, *History of Frederick II of Prussia, Called Frederick the Great* (London: Chapman & Hall, 1941); cited by Wagner in his introduction to volumes 3 and 4 of *Oeuvres en prose*, trans. J.-G. Prod'homme and F. Holl (Paris: Delagrave, 1928), p. 1.

154. Hitler cited in Wulf, *Martin Bormann*, p. 46.

155. Speech given evening of 31 March 1942; cited in Picker, *Hitler cet inconnu*, p. 257.

156. Robert Ley, "Deutschland wird so sein, wie wir es bauen!" speech given March 1937, published in *Soldaten der Arbeit*, pp. 141–55.

157. Ley, "Organisieren heisst: Wachen lassen!" *Soldaten der Arbeit*, p. 183.

158. Thomas Hobbes, *Leviathan* (London: J. M. Dent/Vermont; and Vermont: Charles E. Tuttle, 1994), chap. 43. "The laws of God are thus nothing but the laws of nature, the chief of which is that one must not violate one's faith."

159. Cited by Joachim Fest, *Les Maîtres du Troisième Reich* (Paris: Grasset, 1965), p. 25.

160. Cited by Shirer, *The Rise and Fall of the Third Reich*, vol. 1, p. 268; and Arendt, *Eichmann in Jerusalem*, chap. 8.

161. Arendt, *The Human Condition*, p. 252.

5. IMAGES OF NAZI TIME: ACCELERATIONS AND IMMOBILIZATIONS

1. Bultmann, *Histoire et Eschatologie*; Bultmann, "L'étrange de la foi chrétienne," in *Foi et Compréhension*, vol. 2: *Eschatologie et Démythologisation*, trans. A. Malet (Paris: Le Seuil, 1969), pp. 229–46.

2. Bultmann, *Histoire et Eschatologie*, pp. 55–75.

3. Ibid. p. 75. Bultmann gives two references: 2 Tim. 1:10 and Ign. Phil. d. 9:2.

4. See Jean-Michel Spieser, "Portes, limites et hiérarchisation de l'espace dans les églises paléochrétiennes," *Klio*, 1995, vol. 77, no. 1.

5. Pierre Prigent, *Le Judaisme et l'image*, Texte und Studien zum Studien zum Antiken Judentum, no. 24, eds. M. Hengel and P. Schäfer (Tübingen: Mohr, 1990), pp. 123–42.

6. Andre Grabar, *Les Voies de la création en iconographie chrétienne* (Paris: Flammarion, 1994), pp. 272–75.

7. For other examples of anticipation of the future through Byzantine images, see Herbert L. Kessler, "Gazing at the Future: The *Parousia* Miniature in Vatican Cod. gr. 699," in *Spiritual Seeing: Picturing God's Invisibility in Medieval Art* (Philadelphia: University of Pennsylvania Press, 2000), pp. 88–103; Jean-Michel Spieser, "De la vie des formes à leur fonction sociale et à leur fonctionnement anthropologique," in J. Hamesse, *Actes du premier Congrès européen d'études médiévales* (Spoleto, 27–29 May 1993; Louvain-la-Neuve: FIDEM, 1995).

8. St. Augustine, *City of God*, trans. H. Bettenson (Harmondsworth, Middlesex: Penguin Classics, 1972), book 12, chap. 30.

9. Imagery also seemed to resolve the double constraint that Christianity had thrust upon the faithful, namely the obligation to imitate God as the Son but not as the Father.

10. See Norman Cohn, *Les Fanatiques de l'Apocalypse*, trans. S. Clémendot (Paris: Julliard, 1983).

11. Cited by Reinhart Kosselleck, "La sémantique des concepts de mouvement dans la modernité," in *Le Futur passé: Contribution à la sémantique des temps historiques*, trans.

J. Hoock and M.-C. Hoock (Paris: Ecole des hautes études en sciences sociales, 1990), p. 283.

12. Cited by Francois Hartog, "Time, History and the Writing of History: The Order of Time," in *History-Making*, eds. R. Torstendahl and I. Veit-Brause *Konferenser*, 1996, pp. 95–113.

13. Reinhart Koselleck, "Point de vue, perspective et temporalité," *Le Futur passé*, pp. 178–81. See also Koselleck's article "Geschichte" in *Geschichtliche Grundbegriffe: Historisches Lexicon zur politisch-sozialen Sprache in Deutschland*, vol. 2, eds. O. Brunner, W. Conze, and R. Koselleck (Stuttgart: Klett, 1975), pp. 597.

14. On this point, see the following works by Zeev Sternhell: *La Droite révolutionnaire: Les origines françaises du fascisme, 1885–1914* (Paris: Le Seuil), 1978; *Ni droite, ni gauche: L'idéologie fasciste en France* (Paris: Le Seuil, 1983); *Naissance de l'idéologie fasciste*, (in collaboration with M. Sznajder and M. Ashéri) (Paris: Fayard, 1989). See also Robert A. Nye, "The Two Paths to a Psychology of Social Action: Gustave Le Bon and Georges Sorel," *Journal of Modern History*, September 1973, vol. 45, no. 3, pp. 411–38.

15. Le Bon, *The Crowd*, pp. 39, 68.

16. Ibid., p. 38.

17. Sorel, *Reflections on Violence*, pp. 122–23.

18. Ibid., p. 127.

19. Henri Bergson, *Matter and Memory*, trans. N. M. Paul and W. Scott Palmer (London: Allen & Unwin, 1962), p. 197. In the 1890s, both Bergson and Sorel studied "psychophysics" and its laws, a subject that also intrigued artists such as Georges Seurat and Paul Signac. As for Nietzsche, he defined art as "suggestion, a means of encouraging participation, and the domain of the invention of *psychomotivating induction*" ("A Physiology of Art," *The Will to Power*, no. 355, trans. W, Kaugmann and R. J. Hollingdale [London: Weidenfeld & Nicolson, 1968]).

20. Sorel, *Reflections on Violence*, p. 35.

21. Ibid., p. 126.

22. Ibid., p. 35.

23. Mussolini cited by Schmitt, *Parlementarisme et démocratie*, p. 94.

24. Schmitt, *Parlementarisme et démocratie*, pp. 93–95.

25. Rosenberg cited by Rauschning, *La Révolution du nihilisme*, p. 102; *Die Revolution der Nihilismus*, p. 77.

26. Rauschning, *Hitler m'a dit*, chap. 37, p. 254.

27. Fest, *Hitler*, book 6, chap. 2, p. 535.

28. Speech given evening of 27 March 1942; cited in Picker, *Hitler, cet inconnu*, p. 242.

29. Speech, evening of 11 Novemeber, 1941; cited in ibid., p. 164.

30. Speech, evening of 30 March 1942; cited in ibid., p. 254.

31. Le Bon, *The Crowd*, p. 40.

32. *Mein Kampf,* E 426, D 526.

33. Cited by Josef Greiner, *Das Ende des Hitler-Mythos* (Zurich: Amalthea, 1947), pp. 40–42; Fest, *Hitler,* vol. 1, book 1, chap. 3; John Toland, *Adolf Hitler* (Garden City, N.Y.: Doubleday, 1976), pp. 46–47.

34. See Billy F. Price, *Adolf Hitler: The Unknown Artist* (Houston: Eichler, 1984), p. 121, cat. no. 320.

35. Schoenbaum, *Hitler's Social Revolution,* p. 95.

36. Jünger, *Le Travailleur,* chap. 8, p. 65.

37. Ibid., chap. 57, p. 249.

38. Ibid., chap. 19, pp. 98–101; chap. 43, pp. 193–94; chap. 50, p. 222. On the notion of work developed by National Socialism, Jünger, and Heidegger, see Werner Hamacher, "Working Through Working," *Modernism/Modernity,* 1996, vol. 3, no. 1, pp. 1–33.

39. Benn, "L'Autonomie de l'art" (radio talk on 1 May 1933), *Un poète et le monde,* p. 173.

40. Gottfried Feder, *Das Programm des NSDAP und seine weltanschaulichen Grundgedanken* (Munich: Eher, 1933), p. 20: *"Erste Pflicht jedes Staatsbürgers muss sein, geistig oder körperlich zu schaffen";* italics added.

41. Speech of 1 May 1933, Baynes, vol. 1, p. 838 (partially translated); *Dokumente der deutschen Politik,* vol. 1 (Berlin: Hochschule für Politik, 1935), pp. 151.

42. Cited by Hofer, *Der Nationalsozialismus,* p. 87.

43. *Mein Kampf,* E 452, D 557.

44. Rauschning, *Hitler m'a dit,* p. 265.

45. Ferdinand Hoffmann, *Sittliche Entartung und Geburtenschwund* (Politische Biologie, no. 4) (Munich/Berlin: Lehmanns, 1939), p. 79.

46. Robert Ley, "Unsere Gemeinschaft muss klar, sauber und übersichtlich sein!" in *Soldaten der Arbeit,* p. 60.

47. Goebbels, "Das Kulturleben im Kriege," speech given 27 November 1939, published in *Die Zeit ohne Beispiel,* pp. 222–23.

48. Hans Kiener, "Dem Tag der Deutschen Kunst entgegen," *Münchener Neueste Nachrichten,* 1933; reprinted in *Kunstbetrachtungen* (Munich: Neuer Filser-Verlag, 1937), p. 327; cited in Karl Arndt, "Das 'Haus der Deutschen Kunst,'" in Schuster, *Die "Kunststadt" München 1937,* p. 63.

49. Jünger, *Le Travailleur,* chap. 28, p. 124.

50. Rittich, *Deutsche Kunst der Gegenwart,* vol. 2, p. 15.

51. Peter Schirmbeck, "Darstellung der Arbeit," a most remarkable contribution to the catalogue for *Kunst im 3. Reich: Dokumente der Unterwerfung,* p. 164.

52. *Kunst und Volk* (Art and the people), January 1937, vol. 5, p. 30; cited by Schirmbeck, "Darstellung der Arbeit," p. 164.

53. Kammerer, *Fritz Koelle* (Berlin: Rembrandt-Verlag, 1939), p. 13.

54. Ibid., p. 5.

55. Ibid.

56. Jünger, *Le Travailleur*, chap. 43, pp. 194–95; *sans phrase* is in French in the text.

57. See Anson G. Rabinbach, "L'Esthétique de la production sous le III Reich," *Journal of Contemporary History*, 1976, vol. 11; trans. P. Giuliani, in Murard and Zylberman, *Le Soldat du travail*, pp. 137–71. The information and quotations that follow come from this work unless indicated otherwise. See also Chup Friemert, *Produktionsästhetik im Faschismus: Das Amt 'Schönheit der Arbeit' von 1933 bis 1939* (Munich: Damnitz, 1980); Reichel, *La Fascination du nazisme*, pp. 221–29.

58. Hübbenet, *Das Taschenbuch Schönheit der Arbeit*, p. 17.

59. Ibid., p. 74.

60. Ibid., p. 238.

61. Ibid., p. 199.

62. Sorel, *Reflections on Violence*, p. 24.

63. On this point, see Schoenbaum, *Hitler's Social Revolution*, chap. 3: "The Third Reich and Labor."

64. Ley, "Das Volk gesund erhalten," speeach given 18 August 1937, published in *Soldaten der Arbeit*, p. 139.

65. Opening speech for the Automobile Exhibition of 1933, *Völkischer Beobachter*, 12–13 February 1933; cited in André Gunthert, "La voiture du peuple des seigneurs: Naissance de la Volkswagen," *Vingtième Siècle*, July–September 1987, no. 15, pp. 29–42 (in particular, p. 30, which provides an excellent analysis of the myth of the "beetle" under the Third Reich).

66. See *Die Welt*, 2 May 1981; Price, *Adolf Hitler*, p. 223, cat. no. 601.

67. Conversation with Anne O'Hare McCormick, *New York Times*, 10 July 1933; Baynes, vol. 1, p. 866.

68. In *Deutsche Allgemeine Zeitung*, 3 March 1933; Baynes, I, p. 829–30.

69. *Frankfurter Zeitung*, 25 September 1933, 15 February 1935, 19 February 1938; *Baynes*, vol. 1, pp. 871, 906, 949–50.

70. Hitler addressing the Hitler Youth members gathered in Nuremberg in 1935; Baynes, vol. 1, p. 542.

71. Filippo Tommaso Marinetti, "Manifeste du Futurisme," *Le Figaro*, 20 February 1909; in *Futurisme, Manifestes, Documents, Proclamations* (Lausanne: L'Age d'Homme, 1973), p. 87.

72. Karl Arnhold, *Die Technik ruft (nach einem Vortrag: "Jugend! Die Technik ruft!" auf dem Parteitag des Gaues Ostpreussen 1938)* (Berlin: DAF, 1939), p. 33.

73. *Mein Kampf*, E 264, D 318.

74. Hitler at the NSDAP Congress, 5 September 1934; *Der Kongress zu Nürnberg vom 5, bis 10, September 1934*, p. 28.

75. "Rede Hitlers auf der Kulturtagung des Reichsparteitages in Nürnberg 1935," Hinz, pp. 142–43; *Principes d'action*, p. 84.

76. "Die Grundsätze nationalsozialistischen Kunstschaffens," cited by Wulf, *Die bildenden Künste im Dritten Reich*, p. 239.

77. Walter Benjamin, *Das Kunstwerk im Zeitalter seiner technischen Reproduzierbarkeit* (Frankfurt: Suhrkamp, 1977; originally published 1936), p. 44; Benjamin, "The Work of Art in the Age of Mechanical Reproduction," in *Illuminations: Essays and Reflections*, eds. H. Arendt, trans. H. Zohn (New York: Schoken, 1989; originally published 1968), p. 242.

78. A. Moeller van den Bruck, *Das dritte Reich*, p. 317.

79. St. Augustine, *The City of God*, book 19, chap. 12.

80. Speech given night of 25–26 January 1942; cited in Picker, *Hitler, cet inconnu*, p. 183.

81. *Die Reden Hitlers am Reichsparteitag 1933*, p. 30, italics in original.

82. Hinz, p. 144; Hitler, *Principes d'action*, p. 86.

83. Hinz, p. 142; Hitler, *Principes d'action*, p. 83.

84. Théophile Gautier, "L'Art," *Emaux et Camées, Poésies nouvelles* (Paris: Charpentier, 1866; art originally published 1857), p. 142.

85. Preface to *Emaux et Camées*, p. 1.

86. Gautier, "L'Art," p. 143.

87. Schrade, *Bauten des Dritten Reiches*, pp. 19–20.

88. Georg W. F. Hegel, *Lectures on the Philosophy of Religion*, vol. 2, no. 2, trans. R. F. Brown and others (Berkeley/Los Angeles/London: University of California Press, 1987), p. 134.

89. Speer, *Inside the Third Reich*, p. 56.

90. Friedrich Tamms, "Die Kriegerehrenmäler von Wilhlem Kreis," *Die Kunst im Deutschen Reich* (Art in the German Reich), March 1943, pp. 50–57; see also Brenner, *La Politique artistique du national-socialisme*, pp. 196–97.

91. Hitler at the 1935 Nuremberg Congress, *Principes d'Action*, pp. 109–10.

92. Cited by Brenner, *La politique artistique du national-socialisme*, p. 195.

93. "Mein Führer, Du allein bist Weg und Ziel!" cited by Wulf, *Literatur und Dichtung im Dritten Reich*, p. 412.

94. Telegramme from Hadamovsky to Hitler, 23 March 1935; cited by Wulf, *Presse und Funk im Dritten Reich*, pp. 327–28.

95. "Aufruf des Reichsverbandes Deutscher Rundfunkteilnehmer," in *Mitteilungen der Reichsrundfunk-Gesellschaft*, 27 September 1935; cited by Wulf, ibid., pp. 328–29.

96. Cited by Brenner, *La Politique artistique du national-socialisme*, p. 78.

97. Archives of the Centre de documentation juive contemporaine, no. CXLV-588.

98. Archives of the Centre de documentation juive contemporaine, no. CXLV-642; cited by Brenner, *La Politique artistique du national-socialisme*, p. 309.

99. Josef Strzygowski, *Das indogermanische Ahnenerbe des deutschen Volkes*, pp. 65–81.

100. J. W. Harnisch, "Deutsche Schrift," *Berliner lokal-Anzeiger*, 21 June 1933; cited in Wulf, *Literatur und Dichtung im Dritten Reich*, p. 379.

101. Rudolf Koch, "Die deutsche Schrift," *Die Neue Literatur*, 1937, p. 538; cited in Wulf, *Literatur und Dichtung im Dritten Reich*, p. 380; italics added.

102. *Die Schrift als deutsche Kunst*, catalogue for the Germanisches Nationalmuseum, Nuremberg, 1940.

103. Cited in Lehmann-Haupt, *Art Under a Dictatorship*, p. 172, to which I am endebted for a number of items of information. See also Wulf, *Literatur und Dichtung im Dritten Reich*, pp. 379–83; Wulf, *Martin Bormann, l'ombre de Hitler*, pp. 128–29; Thomae, *Die Propaganda-Maschinerie*, pp. 183–85; Archives of the Centre de documentation juive contemporaine, no. CXLIII-374 (notes and reports on the "Jewish origins" of Gothic writing).

104. Speech given on the night of 28 January 1942, in the train; cited in Picker, *Hitler, cet inconnu*, pp. 188–89.

105. Speech on the night of 9 April 1942, ibid., pp. 295–97.

106. See Fest, *Hitler*, book 6, chap. 2.

107. Canetti, "Hitler, d'après Speer," in *La Conscience des mots*, p. 209.

108. Julius Petersen, *Die Sehnsucht nach dem Dritten Reich in deutscher Sage und Dichtung* (Stuttgart: Metzler, 1934), pp. 1, 61; cited by J. Hermand, *Der alte Traum vom neuen Reich*, p. 205.

109. Berning, *Vom "Abstammungsnachweis" zum "Zuchwart,"* pp. 55–58.

110. "*Erst wenn einmal eine Zeit nicht mehr von den Schatten des eigenen Schuldbewusstseins umgeistert ist, erhält sie mit der inneren Ruhe auch die äussere Kraft, brutal und rücksichtlos die wilden Schösslinge herauszuschneiden, das Unkraut auszujäten*" (*Mein Kampf*, D 30).

Glossary of Nazi Terms

Arbeitsgemeinschaft: Community of work. Qualifies the people's community (*Volks-gemeinschaft*) as a working community; sometimes also called *Leistungsgemein-schaft*: a community of performance, a productive community, a community of realization.

Art: species. Used by National Socialism generally as a synonym for race. The term also means "manner of being." See note 22, page 240.

Artfremd: racially alien, foreign species. Applied to all that was not recognized to be "Aryan" or "German-Nordic."

Entscheidung: decision. Used constantly by Hitler to indicate his "implacable will" in all domains. Jurist Carl Schmitt used it to denote an act of sovereign govern-ment that creates law, as opposed to the "discussion" of parliamentary democracy (*Political Theology*, 1922).

Erlebnis: Lived (affective, authentic, and sincere) experience. Nazi language transposed the term "from the sphere of subjectivity and poetry to that of public life" (Stern, *Hitler*).

Kultur: imperfectly translated as "culture." According to the thought of German conservatives, *Kultur* constituted a unique and organic whole that was opposed to *Zivilisation*, which was perceived as essentially universalist and mechanistic. Nazi language identified *Kultur* with all the positive aspects of tradition, and *Zivilisation* with all the evils of rationalist modernity that stemmed from the Enlightenment and the French Revolution in 1789.

Leistung: performance, work achieved, productivity. Just as there was a Führer principle (*Führerprinzip*), there was also a performance principle (*Leistungsprinzip*), which constituted one of the bases of "practical" National Socialism.

Völkisch: national and racial, or nationalist and racist. As used by the Nazis, the term covered both notions and designated that which belonged to "the people as a community of blood and race" (*Volk als einer Bluts-und Artsgemeinschaft*).

Volksgeist: the spirit of the people. For Johann Gottfried Herder, the *Volksgeist* was at once the soul, the spirit, and the genius or *daimon* of the *Volk*—that is to say, the people—but sometimes also the nation, as defined by the German language, customs, taste, physiognomy, and genes. Under National Socialism, through contamination with *völkisch*, it became the spirit of the people, seen as a community of blood and race (*Bluts und Artsgemeinschaft*).See note 43, page 226.

Volksgemeinschaft: the popular racial community. Ferdinand Tönnies (*Gemeinschaft und Gesellschaft*, 1887) opposed the natural and organic character of the community (*Gemeinschaft*) to the rational and historical character of the society or collectivity (*Gesellschaft*). National Socialism used the term to oppose the society divided into classes to the unity of a "community of destiny" founded on "the blood and the soil."

Volkskörper: the people as a body. A biological metaphor frequently used by Nazism to intimate the sacred nature of the racial unity of the community.

Weltanschauung: worldview. This term, which was forged in the nineteenth century and calls to mind the visions of mystics, replaced the word *philosophy* in the Nazi language. Hitler liked to describe National Socialism as first and foremost "a worldview."

Bibliography

The bibliography does not mention articles or works that have already been fully refer-enced in the notes.

Adam, Peter. *Art of the Third Reich.* New York: Harry N. Abrams, 1992.

Arendt, Hannah. *The Human Condition.* Chicago: University of Chicago Press, 1958.

Arendt, Hannah. *Between Past and Future, 1954–1968.* London: Faber and Faber, 1971.

Arendt, Hannah. *The Origins of Totalitarianism.* New York: Harcourt Brace Jovanovich, 1973.

Arendt, Hannah. *Eichmann in Jerusalem: A Report on the Banality of Evil.* London: Faber and Faber, 1963.

Ayçoberry, Pierre. *La question nazie: Essai sur les interprétations du national-socialisme (1922–1972)* (The Nazi question: An essay on the interpretations of National Social-ism, 1922–1972). Paris: Le Seuil, 1979.

Baynes, Norman H. *The Speeches of Adolf Hitler,* 2 vol. London/New York/Toronto: Ox-ford University Press, 1942.

Barron, Stephanie (ed.). *"Degenerate Art": The Fate of the Avant-Garde in Nazi Germany.* Los Angeles: Los Angeles County Museum of Art, 1991.

Benn, Gottfried. *Un poète et le monde* (A poet and the world), translated and Preface by R. Rovini. Paris: Gallimard, 1965. (*Gesammelte Werke.* Wiesbaden: Limes, 1958–1959; originally published 1936.)

Benn, Gottfried. *Double Vie* (Double life), translated by A. Vialatte, Preface by J.-M. Palmier. Paris: Minuit, 1981. (*Gesammelte Werke.* Wiesbaden: Limes, 1958–1959.)

Berning, Cornelia. *Vom "Abstammungsnachweis" zum "Zuchtwart": Vokabular des National-sozialismus.* Foreword by W. Abetz. Berlin: Walter de Gruyter, 1964.

Bloch, Ernst. *Héritage de ce temps,* translated by J. Lacoste. Paris: Payot, 1978. (*Erbschaft dieser Zeit.* Franfurt am Main: Suhrkamp, 1962.)

Bracher, Karl Dietrich. *La Dictature allemande: Naissance, structure et conséquences du National-Socialisme* (German dictatorship: The origins, structure, and effects of na-tional socialism). Preface by A. Grosser. Toulouse: Privat, 1986. (*Die deutsche Dik-*

tatur: Entstehung Struktur Fogen des Nationalsozialismus. Cologne: Kiepenheuer & Witsch, 1969/1980.)

Bracher, Karl D., Manfred Funke and Hans-Adolf Jacobsen (eds.). *Deutschland 1933–1945: Neue Studien zur nationalsozialistischen Herrschaft.* Düsseldorf: Droste, 1992.

Brenner, Hildegard. *La politique artistique du national-socialisme,* translated by Lucien Steinberg. Paris: Maspéro, 1980. (*Die Kunstpolitik des Nationalsozialismus.* Reinbeck bei Hamburg: Rowohlt, 1963.)

Brock, Bazon, and Achim Preiss. *Kunst auf Befehl? Dreiunddreissig bis Fünfundvierzig.* Munich: Klinkhard & Biermann, 1990.

Broszat, Martin. *L'Etat hitlérien: L'origine et l'évolution des structures du troisième Reich* (The Hitler state: The foundation and development of the internal structure of the Third Reich), translated by P. Moreau. Paris: Fayard, 1985. (*Der Staat Hitlers.* Munich: D. T. V., 1970.)

Bultmann, Rudolf. *Histoire et eschatologie* (History and eschatology), translated by R. Brandt. Neuchâtel, Switzerland: Delachaux et Niestlé, 1959. (*Geschichte und Eschatologie.* Tübingen: J.C.B. Mohr, 1958.)

Canetti, Elias. *La Conscience des mots* (The conscience of words), translated by R. Lewinter. Paris: Albin Michel, 1984. (*Das Gewissen der Worte.* Munich: Carl Hanser, 1976.)

Clauss, Ludwig Ferdinand. *Rasse und Seele: Eine Einführung in den Sinn der lieblichen Gestalt.* Munich/Berlin: J. F. Lehmanns, 1940.

Darré, Walther. *La Race: Nouvelle noblesse du sang et du sol* (Race: The new nobility of the blood and the soil), translated by P. Mélon and A. Pfannstiel. Paris: Fernand Sorlot, 1939. (*Neuadel aus Blut und Boden.* Munich: J. F. Lehmanns, 1930.)

Delage, Christian. *La Vision nazie de l'histoire: Le cinéma documentaire du Troisième Reich,* preface by Marc Ferro. Lausanne: L'Age d'Homme, 1989.

Denzler, Georg, and Volker Fabricius, eds. *Christen und National-sozialisten: Darstellung und Dokumente (mit einem Exkurs: Kirche im Sozialismus).* Frankfurt: Fischer, 1993. (Originally published 1984.)

Der Parteitag der Ehre, vom 8, bis 14, September 1936. Munich: Franz Eher, 1936.

Devant l'histoire: Les documents de la controverse sur la singularité de l'extermination des Juifs par le régime nazi, Preface by L. Ferry, Introduction by J. Rovan. Paris: Cerf, 1988. (*Historikerstreit.* Munich: Piper, 1987.)

Etlin, Richard A. (ed.). *Nationalism in the Visual Arts,* Studies in the History of Art, 29, Symposium Papers 13. Hanover/London: National Gallery of Art, Washington, Center for the Advanced Study in the Visual Arts, 1991. Distributed by the University Press of New England.

Fest, Joachim. *Hitler: A Biography,* translated by R. and C. Winston. London: Wiedenfeld & Nicolson, 1973. (*Hitler: Eine Biographie.* Frankfurt am Main/Berlin/Wien: Ullstein, 1973.)

Gamm, Hans-Jochen. *Der braune Kult.* Hamburg: Rütten & Loening, 1962.

Gamm, Hans-Jochen. *Führung und Verführung: Pädagogik des National-sozialismus.* Munich: Paul List, 1990.

Goebbels, Joseph. *Tagebücher*, 5 vols. (1924–1945), ed. Ralf Georg Reuth. Munich: Piper, 1992.

Goebbels, Joseph. *Michael: Ein deutsches Schicksal in Tagebuchblättern.* Munich: Franz Eher, 1934.

Goebbels, Joseph. *Signale der neuen Zeit.* Munich: Franz Eher, 1934.

Goebbels, Joseph. *Die Zeit ohne Beispiel: Reden und Aufätze aus den Jahren 1939/40/41.* Munich: Franz Eher, 1941.

Hagen, Oskar. *Deutsches Sehen: Gestaltungsfragen der deutschen Kunst.* Munich: R. Piper, 1933.

Herf, Jeffrey. *Reactionary Modernism: Technology, Culture, and Politics in Weimar and the Third Reich.* Cambridge/New York/Port Chester/Melbourne/Sydney: Cambridge University Press, 1984.

Hermand, Jost. *Der alte Traum vom neuen Reich: Völkische Utopien und Nationalsozialismus* (Old dreams of a new Reich: Völkish Utopia and national socialism). Frankfurt: Athenäum, 1988.

Hillel, Marc (with Clarissa Henry). *Au nom de la race.* Paris: Fayard, 1975.

Himmler, Heinrich. *Discours secrets*, eds. B. F. Smith and A. F. Peterson, Introduction by J. Fest, translated by M.-M. Husson. Paris: Gallimard, 1978. (*Geheimreden 1933 bis 1945 und andere Ansprachen.* Frankfurt am Main/Berlin/Vienna: Ullstein, 1974.)

Hinz, Berthold. *Die Malerei im deutschen Faschismus: Kunst und Revolution.* Munich: Carl Hanser, 1974.

(Pos)Hitler, Adolf. *Die Reden Hitlers am Reichsparteitag 1933.* Munich: Franz Eher, 1934.

Hitler, Adolf. *Mein Kampf* (My struggle), translated by R. Manheim (London: Hutchinson, 1969). (*Mein Kampf.* Munich: Franz Eher, 1940; originally published 1925 and 1927 in 2 vols.)

Hitler, Adolf. *Die deutsche Kunst als stolzeste Vertiedigung des deustschen Volkes (Rede, gehalten auf der Kulturtagung des Parteitages 1933).* Munich: Franz Eher, 1934.

Hitler, Adolf. *L'expansion du III Reich*, translated by F. Brière. Paris: Plon, 1962. (*Hitlers Zweites Buch*, ed. R. L. Weinberg. Stuttgart: Deutsche Verlags-Anstalt, 1961.)

Hitler, Adolf. *Principes d'action*, translated by A. S. Pfannstiel. Paris: Grasset, 1936.

Hitler, Adolf. *Libres propos sur la guerre et la paix*, collected by order of Martin Bormann (French version translated by Françoise Genoud), 2 vol. Paris: Flammarion, 1952.

Hofer, Walther. *Der Nationalsozialismus Dokumente, 1933–1945*, ed. W. Hofer. Frankfurt: Fischer, 1993. (Originally published 1957.)

Hübbenet, Anatol von. *Das Taschenbuch Schönheit der Arbeit*, introduction by Albert Speer. Berlin: Verlag der deutschen Arbeitsfront, 1938.

Jäckel, Eberhard. *Hitler idéologue*, translated by J. Chavy. Paris: Calmann-Lévy, 1973. (*Hitlers Weltanschauung*. Tübingen: Hermann Leins, 1969.)

Jaspers, Karl. *La culpabilité allemande* (The question of German guilt). Translated by Jeanne Hersch. Paris: Minuit, 1948. (*Die Schuldfrage*. Heidelberg: L. Schneider, 1946.)

Jokisch, Gotthold. *Das dynamische Gestaltungsprinzip der deutschen Kunst*. Leipzig: Jordan & Gramberg, 1941.

Jünger, Ernst. *Le Travailleur*, ed. J. Hervier. Paris: Christian Bourgeois, 1989. (*Der Arbeiter*, Stuttgart: Ernst Klett, 1981; originally published 1932.)

Kafka, Franz. "Méditations sur le péché, la souffrance, l'espoir et le vrai chemin," *Préparatifs de noce à la campagne*, translated by M. Robert. Paris: Gallimard, 1985, p. 47.

Kantorowicz, Ernst. *Frederick the Second*, translated by E. O. Lorimer. London: Constable, 1957.

Kantorowicz, Ernst. *The King's Two Bodies*. Princeton: Princeton University Press, 1957.

Kershaw, Ian, *The "Hitler Myth": Image and Reality in the Third Reich*. Oxford/New York: Oxford University Press, 1989. (Originally published 1987.)

Kershaw, Ian. *Hitler*. London/New York: Longman Group UK, 1991.

Kershaw, Ian. *The Nazi Dictatorship: Problems and Perspectives of Interpretation*. London: Edward Arnold, 1989. (*Qu'est-ce que le nazisme? Problèmes et perspectives d'interprétation*, translated by J. Carnaud, with additional previously unpublished material in French. Paris: Gallimard, 1992.)

Keyserling, Hermann von. *Sur l'art de la vie*. Paris: Stock, 1936.

Klemperer, Victor. *LTI: Notizbuch eines Philologen*. Leipzig: Reclam, 1993. (Originally published 1947.)

Koonz, Claudia. *Les mères-patrie du IIIe Reich: Les femmes et le nazisme*, trans. M.-L. Colson and L. Gentil. Paris: Lieu Commun, 1989. (*Mothers in the Fatherland: Women, the Family, and Nazi Politics*. New York: St. Martin's Press, 1986.)

Krockow, Christian von. *Les Allemands du XXe siècle: Histoire d'une identité*, translated by A. Collas, P. Hervieux, and M. Hourst; preface by R. Fauroux. Paris: Hachette, 1990. (*Die Deutschen in ihren Jahrhundert*, Reinbeck bei Hamburg: Rowohlt, 1990.)

Der Kongress zu Nürnberg, vom 5, bis 10, September 1934. Munich: Franz Eher, 1934.

Kunst im 3. Reich: Dokumente der Unterwerfung. Frankfurt: Frankfurter Kunstverein, 1975.

Lacoue-Labarthe, Philippe, and Jean-Luc Nancy. *Le mythe nazi*. La Tour d'Aigues: Editions de l'Aube, 1991.

Le Bon, Gustave. *The Crowd: A Study of the Popular Mind*. Harmondsworth, Middlesex: Viking Press, 1977. (*Psychologie des foules*. Paris, Félix Alcan, 1909; originally published 1895.)

Lehmann-Haupt, Hellmut. *Art Under a Dictatorship*. New York: Oxford University Press, 1954.

Ley, Robert. *Soldaten der Arbeit.* Munich: Eher, 1938.

Ludwig, Emil. *Talks with Mussolini.* Translated by Eden and Cedar Paul. London: Allen & Unwin, 1932.

Mann, Erika. *Dix millions d'enfants nazis,* translated by E. Wintzen, R. Wintzen, and D. Luquet; Preface by A. Grosser. Paris: Tallandier, 1988. (*Zehn Millionen Kinder: Die Erziehung der Jugend im Dritten Reich.* Munich: Heinrich Ellermann, 1986; *School for Barbarians: Education Under the Nazis.* New York: Modern Age Books, 1938.)

Mann, Heinrich. *La Haine: Histoire contemporaine d'Allemagne.* Paris: Gallimard, 1933.

Mann, Thomas. *Reflections of a Nonpolitical Man,* translated by W. D. Morris. New York: Ungar, 1983. (*Betrachtungen eines Unpolitischen.* Berlin: Fischer, 1918.)

Mann, Thomas. *Diaries, 1918–1921, 1933–1939,* translated by R. and G. Winston. London: André Deutsch, 1983. (*Tagebücher, 1918–1921/1933–1934/1935–1936/1937–1939.* Frankfurt am Main: Fischer, 1977–79.)

Mann, Thomas. *Les exigences du jour,* translated by L. Servicen and J. Naujac. Paris: Grasset, 1976.

Moeller van den Bruck, Arthur. *Das dritte Reich.* Hamburg: Hanseatische Anstaltverlag, 1931. (Originally published 1923.)

Müller-Mehlis, Reinhard. *Die Kunst im Dritten Reich.* Munich: Wilhelm Heyne, 1976.

Murard, Lion, and Patrick Zylberman (eds.). *Le soldat du travail: Guerre, fascisme et taylorisme-Recherches,* special issue of *Revue Recherches,* September 1978, no. 32/33.

Neumann, Franz. *Béhémoth: Structure et pratique du national-socialisme* (Behemoth: The structure and practice of national socialism). London: Oxford University Press, 1942.

Olff-Nathan, Josiane (ed.). *La science sous le Troisième Reich.* Paris: Le Seuil, 1993.

Picker, Henry. *Hitler, cet inconnu,* Introduction by Percy Ernst Schramm. Paris: Presses de la Cité, 1969. (*Hitlers Tischgespräge im Führerhauptquartier.* Stuttgart: Seewald, 1983.)

Poley, Stefanie (ed.). *Rollenbilder im Nationalsozialismus: Umgang dem Erbe,* exhibition catalogue for Kunsthistorisches Institut der Rheinischen Friedrich-Wilhelms-Universität, Bonn. Bad Honnef: Karl Heinrich Bock, 1991.

Proctor, Robert N. *Racial Hygiene: Medicine Under the Nazis.* Cambridge, Mass./London: Harvard University Press, 1988.

Rauschning, Hermann. *La révolution du nihilisme,* translated by P. Ravoux and M. Stora, Preface by Golo Mann. Paris: Gallimard, 1980. (*Die Revolution des Nihilismus: Kulisse und Wirklichkeit im dritten Reich.* Zurich: Europa, 1964; originally published 1938.)

Rauschning, Hermann. *Hitler m'a dit,* translated by A. Lehman, Foreword by M. Ray. Paris: Coopération, 1939 (*Gespräche mit Hitler.* Zurich: Europa, 1940.)

Reichel, Peter. *La fascination du nazisme,* translated by O. Mannoni. Paris: Odile Jacob, 1993. (*Das schöne Schein des Dritten Reiches.* Munich: Carl Hanser, 1991.)

Richard, Lionel. *D'une apocalypse à l'autre: Sur l'Allemagne et ses productions intellectuelles de Guillaume II aux années vingt.* Paris: U. G. E., 18 October 1976.

Richard, Lionel. *Le nazisme et la culture.* Paris: Maspéro, 1978.

Rittich, Werner. *Architektur und Bauplastik der Gegenwart.* Berlin: Rembrandt, 1938.

Rittich, Werner. *Deutsche Kunst der Gegenwart 2. Band: Malerei und Graphik.* Breslau: Hirt, 1943.

Rosenberg, Alfred. *The Myth of the Twentieth Century.* Translated by Vivian Bird. Torrance, Calif.: Noontide Press, 1982; (*Der Mythus des XX. Jahrhunderts.* Munich: Hoheneichen, 1941; originally published 1930.)

Rüdiger, Wilhelm. *Kunst und Technik.* Munich: Verlag der deutschen Technik, 1941.

Schirach, Baldur von. *Revolution der Erziehung: Reden aus den Jahren des Aufbaus.* Munich: Franz Eher, 1938.

Schmitt, Carl. *Political Theology: Four Chapters on the Concept of Sovereignty,* translated by G. Schwab. Cambridge, Mass./London: MIT Press, 1985. (*Politische Theologie: Vier Kapital zur Lehre von der Souveränität.* Munich/Leipzig: Dunker & Humblot, 1922; *Politische Theologie, vol. 2: Die Legende von der Erledigung jeder politischen Theologie.* Berlin: Dunker & Humblot, 1970.)

Schmitt, Carl. *Staat, Bewegung, Volk: Die Dreigliederung der politischen Einheit* (State, movement, people: The triadic structure of the political unity). Hamburg: Hanseatische Verlagsantstalt, 1933.

Schmitt, Carl. *The Concept of the Political,* translated by G. Schwab. (New Brunswick, N.J.: Rutgers University Press, 1976. (*Der Begriffe des Politischen,* Berlin: Dunker & Humblot, 1928, 1932.)

Schmitt, Carl. *Parlementarisme et démocratie,* translated by J.-L. Schlegel. Paris: Le Seuil, 1988. (*Die geistesgeschichtliche Lage des heutigen Parliamentarismus.* Berlin: Dunker & Humblot, 1923, 1926.)

Schoenbaum, David. *Hitler's Social Revolution: Class and Status in Nazi Germany 1933–1939.* Garden City, N.Y.: Doubleday, 1966).

Schrade, Hubert. *Bauten des Dritten Reiches.* Leipzig: Bibliographisches Institut, 1939.

Schultze-Naumburg, Paul. *Kunst und Rasse* (Art and race), Munich: Lehmanns, 1928.

Schultze-Naumburg, Paul. *Kulturarbeiten, Band 1: Hausbau.* Munich: Callwey, 1912.

Schuster, Peter-Klaus (ed.). *Nationalsozialismus und "Entartete Kunst": Die "Kunststadt" München 1937.* Munich: Prestel, 1987.

Sorel, Georges. *Reflections on Violence.* Translated by T. E. Hulme. London: Collier-Macmillan, 1969. (*Réflexions sur la violence.* Paris/Geneva: Slatkine, 1981; originally published 1907.)

Speer, Albert. *Inside the Third Reich,* translated by Richard and Clara Winston. New York: Macmillan, 1970. (*Erinnerungen.* Frankfurt am Main: Ullstein, 1969.)

Speer, Albert. *L'Immoralité du pouvoir* (conversations with A. Reif), translated by J.-M. Vigilens. Paris: La table ronde, 1981. (*Technik und Macht.* Esslingen am Neckar: Bechtle, 1979.)

Speer, Albert. *Journal de Spandau,* translated by D. Auclères and M. Brottier. Paris: Robert Laffont, 1975. (*Spandauer Tagebücher.* Frankfurt am Main: Ullstein, 1975.)

Stern, Fritz. *The Politics of Cultural Despair: A Study in the Rise of the Germanic Ideology.* Berkeley: University of California Press, 1961. (*Politique et désespoir,* translated by C. Malamoud. Paris: Armand Colin, 1990.)

Stern, Fritz. *Dreams and Illusions.* London: Weidenfeld & Nicolson, 1987. (*Rêves et illusions,* translated by J. Etoré. Paris: Albin Michel, 1989.)

Stern, Joseph P. *Hitler: The Führer and the People.* London: Fontana, 1990. (Originally published 1975.)

Strzygowski, Josef. *Das indogermanische Ahnenerbe des deutschen Volkes und die Kunstgeschichte der Zukunft: Die Forschung über Bildende Kunst als Erzieher—Eine Kampfschrift.* Vienna: Deutscher Verlag für Jugend und Volk, 1941.

Thomae, Otto. *Die Propaganda-Maschinerie: Bildende Kunst und Offentlichheitsarbeit im Dritten Reich.* Berlin: Gebrüder Mann, 1978.

Troost, Gerdy (ed.). *Das Bauen im neuen Reich.* Bayreuth: Gauverlag Bayerische Ostmark, 1939.

Vermeil, Edmond. *Doctrinaires de la révolution allemande, 1918–1938.* Paris: Nouvelles Editions Latines, 1948.

Viereck, Peter. *Metapolitics: From the Romantics to Hitler.* New York: Knopf, 1941.

Voegelin, Eric. *Les religions politiques* (Political religions), translated by J. Schmutz. Paris: Cerf, 1994. (*Die politischen Religionen.* Stockholm: Bermann-Fischer, 1939.)

Vondung, Klaus. *Magie und Manipulation: Ideologischer Kult und politische Religion des Nationalsozialismus.* Göttingen: Vandenhoeck & Ruprecht, 1971.

Wagner, Richard. *Gesammelte Schriften,* fourteen books in 4 vols., ed. Julius Kapp. Leipzig, Germany: Hesse & Becker, n.d.

Westheim, Paul. *Kunstkritik aus dem Exil,* ed. Tanja Frank. Hanau/Main: Müller & Kiepenheuer, 1985.

Willrich, Wolfgang. *Die Säuberung des Kunsttempels.* Munich/Berlin: Lehmanns, 1937.

Wulf, Joseph. *Martin Bormann: L'ombre de Hitler,* translated by J. Tardy-Marcus. Paris: Gallimard, 1963. (*Martin Bormann: Hitlers Schatten.* Gütersloh: Sigbert Mohm, 1962.)

Wulf, Joseph. *Die bildenden Künste im Dritten Reich: Eine Dokumentation.* Frankfurt am Main/Berlin/Vienna: Ullstein, 1983. (Originally published 1966.)

Wulf, Joseph. *Literatur und Dichtung im Dritten Reich: Eine Dokumentation.* Frankfurt am Main/Berlin/Vienna: Ullstein, 1983. (Originally published 1966.)

Wulf, Joseph. *Theater und Film im Dritten Reich: Eine Dokumentation.* Frankfurt am Main/Berlin/Vienna: Ullstein, 1983. (Originally published in 1966.)

Wulf, Joseph. *Presse und Funk im Dritten Reich: Eine Dokumentation.* Frankfurt am Mein/Berlin/Vienna: Ullstein, 1983. (Originally published 1966.)

Index of Names of Persons

Cultural Memory | *in the Present*

Bernard Faure, *Double Exposure: Cutting Across Buddhist and Western Discourses*

Alessia Ricciardi, *The Ends Of Mourning: Psychoanalysis, Literature, Film*

Alain Badiou, *Saint Paul: The Foundation of Universalism*

Gil Anidjar, *The Jew, the Arab: A History of the Enemy*

Jonathan Culler and Kevin Lamb, eds., *Just Being Difficult? Academic Writing in the Public Arena*

Jean-Luc Nancy, *A Finite Thinking*, edited by Simon Sparks

Theodor W. Adorno, *Can One Live after Auschwitz? A Philosophical Reader*, edited by Rolf Tiedemann

Patricia Pisters, *The Matrix of Visual Culture: Working with Deleuze in Film Theory*

Andreas Huyssen, *Present Pasts: Urban Palimpsests and the Politics of Memory*

Talal Asad, *Formations of the Secular: Christianity, Islam, Modernity*

Dorothea von Mücke, *The Rise of the Fantastic Tale*

Marc Redfield, *The Politics of Aesthetics: Nationalism, Gender, Romanticism*

Emmanuel Levinas, *On Escape*

Dan Zahavi, *Husserl's Phenomenology*

Rodolphe Gasché, *The Idea of Form: Rethinking Kant's Aesthetics*

Michael Naas, *Taking on the Tradition: Jacques Derrida and the Legacies of Deconstruction*

Herlinde Pauer-Studer, ed., *Constructions of Practical Reason: Interviews on Moral and Political Philosophy*

Jean-Luc Marion, *Being Given That: Toward a Phenomenology of Givenness*

Theodor W. Adorno and Max Horkheimer, *Dialectic of Enlightenment*

Ian Balfour, *The Rhetoric of Romantic Prophecy*

Martin Stokhof, *World and Life as One: Ethics and Ontology in Wittgenstein's Early Thought*

Gianni Vattimo, *Nietzsche: An Introduction*

Jacques Derrida, *Negotiations: Interventions and Interviews, 1971–1998*, ed. Elizabeth Rottenberg

Brett Levinson, *The Ends of Literature: The Latin American 'Boom' in the Neoliberal Marketplace*

Timothy J. Reiss, *Against Autonomy: Cultural Instruments, Mutualities, and the Fictive Imagination*

Hent de Vries and Samuel Weber, eds., *Religion and Media*

Niklas Luhmann, *Theories of Distinction: Re-Describing the Descriptions of Modernity*, ed. and introd. William Rasch

Johannes Fabian, *Anthropology with an Attitude: Critical Essays*

Michel Henry, *I am the Truth: Toward a Philosophy of Christianity*

Gil Anidjar, *"Our Place in Al-Andalus": Kabbalah, Philosophy, Literature in Arab-Jewish Letters*

Hélène Cixous and Jacques Derrida, *Veils*

F. R. Ankersmit, *Historical Representation*

F. R. Ankersmit, *Political Representation*

Elissa Marder, *Dead Time: Temporal Disorders in the Wake of Modernity (Baudelaire and Flaubert)*

Reinhart Koselleck, *The Practice of Conceptual History: Timing History, Spacing Concepts*

Niklas Luhmann, *The Reality of the Mass Media*

Hubert Damisch, *A Childhood Memory by Piero della Francesca*

Hubert Damisch, *A Theory of /Cloud/: Toward a History of Painting*

Jean-Luc Nancy, *The Speculative Remark: (One of Hegel's bon mots)*

Jean-François Lyotard, *Soundproof Room: Malraux's Anti-Aesthetics*

Jan Patočka, *Plato and Europe*

Hubert Damisch, *Skyline: The Narcissistic City*

Isabel Hoving, *In Praise of New Travelers: Reading Caribbean Migrant Women Writers*

Richard Rand, ed., *Futures: Of Jacques Derrida*

William Rasch, *Niklas Luhmann's Modernity: The Paradoxes of Differentiation*

Jacques Derrida and Anne Dufourmantelle, *Of Hospitality*

Jean-François Lyotard, *The Confession of Augustine*

Kaja Silverman, *World Spectators*

Samuel Weber, *Institution and Interpretation: Expanded Edition*

Jeffrey S. Librett, *The Rhetoric of Cultural Dialogue: Jews and Germans in the Epoch of Emancipation*

Ulrich Baer, *Remnants of Song: Trauma and the Experience of Modernity in Charles Baudelaire and Paul Celan*

Samuel C. Wheeler III, *Deconstruction as Analytic Philosophy*

David S. Ferris, *Silent Urns: Romanticism, Hellenism, Modernity*

The authorized representative in the EU for product safety and compliance is:
Mare Nostrum Group
B.V Doelen 72
4831 GR Breda
The Netherlands